1994

Edmund's

NEW CAR
PRICES

Publisher: Peter Steinlauf

NEW CAR PRICES

TABLE OF CONTENTS

FEBRUARY 1994

VOL N2703 - 9402

Published by:
Edmund Publications Corp.
300 N Sepulveda   Suite 2050
Los Angeles, CA 90245

SBN: 87759-430-9
ISSN: 1047-0751
Library of Congress Catalog No:
71-80100

Editor:
William Badnow

*Creative
/Design Director:*
Julie Finger

Production:
Rachel Abrash
Kevin McMillan
John Ward

Advertising Manager:
Barbara Abramson

Printed in the United States

Understanding the Language
  of Auto Buying....................4
Abbreviations 5
Buying your
  next New Car......................6
Specifications....................201
Manufacturer's Rebates 220
Step-By-Step
  Costing Forms.................222

BUICK
Century 7
LeSabre...............................10
Park Avenue/Ultra.................12
Regal...................................15
Roadmaster..........................18
Skylark.................................22
National One-Price Models ...25

CADILLAC 27

CHEVROLET
Astro Passenger Van 32
Beretta 36
Camaro 39
Caprice Classic.....................41
Cavalier................................44
Corsica.................................47
Corvette 49
Lumina.................................51
Lumina Minivan....................53

CHRYSLER
Concorde..............................56
LeBaron Convertible 58
LeBaron Sedan.....................59
LHS 61

New Yorker 62
Town & Country....................63

DODGE
Caravan FWD 65
Grand Caravan FWD 68
Grand Caravan AWD 71
Colt (1993) 73
Intrepid................................76
Shadow................................78
Spirit 81
Stealth (1993) 83
Viper (1993) 85

EAGLE
Summit Cpe/Sdn 86
Summit Wagon.....................88
Talon...................................90
Vision 92

FORD
Aerostar Wagon....................94
Crown Victoria......................97
Escort...................................99
Probe 101
Taurus................................104
Tempo................................107
Thunderbird........................109

GEO
Metro 111
Prizm 112
Tracker 115

LINCOLN
Continental.........................117
Mark VIII............................119

Town Car............................120

MERCURY
Capri 122
Cougar 124
Grand Marquis...................126
Sable................................128
Topaz...............................131
Tracer 133
Villager (1993)...................135

OLDSMOBILE
Achieva S Cpe/Sdn 137
Achieva SC Cpe/SL Sdn 139
Bravada............................140
Cutlass Ciera S Sedan 142

Cutlass Cruiser S Wagon 144
Cutlass Supreme Conv 145
Cutlass Supreme
 S Cpe/Sdn 147
88 Royale Sedan 149
88 Royale LS Sedan 150
98 Regency Sedan 152
98 Regency Elite Sedan......154
Silhouette.........................155
Special One-Price Models...157

PLYMOUTH
Acclaim 162
Colt (1993) 163
Laser (1993)......................166
Sundance/Duster................168

Voyager FWD.....................170
Grand Voyager FWD 173
Grand Voyager AWD 176

PONTIAC
Bonneville SE 179
Bonneville SSE 181
Firebird 183
Grand Am 186
Grand Prix Coupe 189
Grand Prix Sedan...............191
Sunbird 194
Trans Sport 196

SATURN 199

NOTE: All information and prices published herein are gathered from sources which, in the editor's opinion, are considered reliable, but under no circumstances is the reader to assume that this information is official or final. All prices are represented as approximations only, and are rounded to the highest whole dollar amount over 50 cents. Unless otherwise noted, all prices are effective as of 10/1/93 but are subject to change without notice. The publisher does not assume responsibility for errors of omission or interpretation. ■ The computerized consumer pricing services advertised herein are not operated by nor are they the responsibility of the publisher. The publisher assumes no responsibility for claims made by advertisers regarding their products or services.

Understanding the Language of Auto Buying

Buying a new vehicle is an expensive, confusing and sometimes frustrating experience. If you feel confused, you are not alone! The problem is that the language and terms used by dealers and manufacturers are often unclear. To assist you, here are some helpful definitions:

Dealer Invoice The amount that dealers are initially billed for a car and/or its optional accessories. The dealer, however, actually ends up paying less. Here's why. On every vehicle purchased, the manufacturer withholds 2-3% of the suggested list. This "holdback allowance" is then credited to the dealer's account on a scheduled basis, usually quarterly. Consequently, the dealer can make a "small profit" selling to you at their dealer invoice.

Suggested List Price The manufacturer's recommended selling price.

Destination Charge The amount charged to cover the cost of delivery from the Port of Entry or manufacturer to the dealer. This charge is passed on to the buyer without any mark-up.

Advertising Fee The amount you are charged to cover the cost of national and local advertising. This fee should be no more than 1-1½% of the suggested list price.

Dealer Charges These are highly profitable "extras" that dealers try to sell in addition to the vehicle. Items such as rustproofing, undercoating and extended warranties fall into this category. Most consumer experts do not recommend purchasing these "extras".

Manufacturer's Rebates/Dealer Incentives Programs offered by the manufacturers to increase the sales of low-selling models or to reduce excess inventories. While manufacturer's rebates are passed directly on to the buyer, dealer incentives are passed on only to the dealer —who may or may not elect to pass the savings on to the customer.

Note: Occasionally there will appear in the "Dealer Invoice" and "Sgst'd List" columns, prices enclosed in brackets. —Example: (90). This indicates a credit or refunded amount is involved.

ABS	—Anti-lock Braking System	
ADJ	—Adjustable or Adjuster	
AC	—Air Conditioning	
AH	—Ampere Hours	
ALT	—Alternator	
ALUM	—Aluminum	
AMP	—Amperes	
ANT	—Antenna	
APP	—Appearance	
AT	—Automatic Transmission	
AUTO	—Automatic	
AUX	—Auxiliary	
AVAIL	—Available	
AWD	—All Wheel Drive	
BLK	—Black	
BSW or BW (tires)		
	—Black Sidewall	
CAP	—Capacity	
CASS	—Cassette	
CD	—Compact Disc	
CID	—Cubic Inch Displacement	
COL	—Column	
COMP	—Compartment	
CONV	—Convertible	
CPE	—Coupe	
CTRL	—Control	
CUST	—Custom	
CU IN	—Cubic Inches	
CYL	—Cylinder	
DFRS	—Dual Facing Rear Seats	
DIAM	—Diameter	
DK	—Dark	
DLX	—Deluxe	
DOHC	—Dual Overhead Camshaft	
DR	—Door	
DRW	—Dual Rear Wheels	
EFI	—Electronic Fuel Injection	
ELEC	—Electronic or Electronically	
ENG	—Engine	
EQUAL	—Equalizer	
EQUIP	—Equipment	
ETR	—Electronically Tuned Radio	
EX	—Except	
EXT	—Exterior	
EXTD	—Extended	
F (tires)	—Fiberglass	
F & R	—Front & Rear	
FB	—Fastback	
FI	—Fuel Injection	
FRT	—Front	
FWD	—Front Wheel Drive	
GAL	—Gallon	
GRP	—Group	
HB	—Hatchback	
HD	—Heavy Duty	
HO	—High Output	

HP	—Horsepower	
HSC	—High Swirl Combustion	
HT	—Hardtop	
HUD	—Head Up Display	
HVY	—Heavy	
ILLUM	—Illuminated or Illumination	
INCLS	—Includes	
INCLD	—Included	
INJ	—Injection	
INT	—Interior	
L (eng)	—Liter	
L & R	—Left & Right	
LB	—Liftback or Long Bed	
LBS	—Pounds	
LD	—Light Duty	
LH	—Left Hand	
LT	—Light	
LTD	—Limited	
LUX	—Luxury	
LWB	—Long Wheelbase	
LWR	—Lower	
MAN	—Manual	
MAX	—Maximum	
MDLS	—Models	
MED	—Medium	
MH	—Must Have	
MIN	—Minimum	
MLDGS	—Moldings	
MPI or		
MPFI	—Multi Port Fuel Injection	
MPG	—Miles Per Gallon	
MSR	—Minimum Size Required	
MT	—Manual Transmission	
NA or		
N/A	—Not Available	
NB	—Notchback	
NC	—No Charge	
NL	—Not Listed	
OD	—Overdrive	
OHC	—Overhead Camshaft	
OHV	—Overhead Valves	
OPT	—Optional	
OS	—Outside	
OWL		
(tires)	—Outline White Letter	
OZ	—Ounce	
PASS	—Passenger	
PEG	—Preferred Equipment Group	
PEP	—Preferred Equipment Package	
PERF	—Performance	
PGM FI	—Programmed Fuel Injection	
PKG	—Package	
PR	—Pair	
PREM	—Premium	
PU	—Pickup	
PWR	—Power	

QTR	—Quarter	
QTS	—Quarts	
RBL		
(tires)	—Raised Black Letters	
RDSTR	—Roadster	
REQ	—Requires	
REV	—Reverse	
RH	—Right Hand	
R or RR	—Rear	
RPM	—Revolution Per Minute	
RWD	—Rear Wheel Drive	
RWL		
(tires)	—Raised White Letters	
SB	—Short Bed	
SBR (tires)		
	—Steel Belted Radial	
SDN	—Sedan	
SEFI or		
SFI	—Sequential Electronic Fuel Injection	
SRS	—Supplemental Restraint System	
SOHC	—Single Overhead Camshaft	
SP or		
SPD	—Speed	
SPFI	—Sequential Port Fuel Injection	
SPKRS	—Speakers	
SPT	—Sport	
S/R	—Sunroof	
SRW	—Single Rear Wheels	
STD	—Standard	
SWB	—Short Wheelbase	
SYNC	—Synchromesh or Synchronized	
TACH	—Tachometer	
TBI	—Throttle Body Injection	
TEMP	—Temperature	
TPI	—Tuned Port Injection	
TRANS	—Transmission	
TRU	—Truck	
TW or		
T/W	—Together With	
VOL	—Volume	
W/	—With	
WB	—Wheelbase	
WGN	—Wagon	
W/O	—Without	
WSW or WW		
(tires)	—White Side Wall	
W/T	—Work Truck	
2WD	—Two Wheel Drive	
4WD	—Four Wheel Drive	
4WS	—Four Wheel Steering	
3A/4A	—3-Speed Automatic /4-Speed Automatic	
4M/5M	—4-Speed Manual /5-Speed Manual.	

Buying your next New Car

Every new car buyer has but one thought in mind — to save money by getting a "good deal". Your goal should be to pay 2-3% over the dealer invoice, not the 10-12% the dealer wants you to pay. Use the following guide to help you plan your new car purchases:

Step 1 Choose the make, model and accessories you want.

Step 2 Visit a local dealership to test drive the model you intend to buy. Pay special attention to all-around visibility, convenience of controls, seating comfort, steering response, handling, acceleration and braking.

Step 3 Once you've decided on a particular model, check with your insurance company to make sure the cost of insuring the vehicle falls within your budget.

Step 4 Contact your bank or credit union to obtain loan-rate information. Later on, you can compare their arrangement with the dealer's financing plan.

Step 5 Use the information in this book to determine the dealer's actual cost. To do this:

—total the Dealer Invoice column costs for the model and accessories you want

—add the destination charge and advertising fee to this amount

—add to the dealer's cost what you think is a reasonable dealer profit. (On most American cars, a reasonable amount is $200-$500 – this excludes "hot selling models" which will command a higher dealer profit) *This sum represents the dealer's cost. Remember the dealer also makes an additional profit because of the "holdback allowance".*

Step 6 Bargain for the best price – visit several dealerships. The dealer who comes closest to your "target price" should get your business. Be sure that the dealer's price quote will be your final cost. Beware of dealer charges! When you buy a car, you should be buying the car – not the extras. Don't be coerced into buying items such as rustproofing, undercoating, extended warranties, etc., unless you really want them.

Step 7 Deduct any manufacturer's rebates/dealer incentives from your final cost.

Step 8 If your present car will be used as a "trade-in" now is the time to deduct the dealer's appraised value. (It's often better to sell your "trade-in" privately. You'll get a better price than the wholesale price a dealer will offer you).

Step 9 Add applicable state and/or local taxes.

CODE	DESCRIPTION	DEALER	LIST

BUICK

CENTURY

CENTURY SPECIAL 4 CYL
G69	4-Dr Sedan	13868	15495
G35	4-Dr 2 Seat Wagon	14629	16345

CENTURY CUSTOM 4 CYL
H69	4-Dr Sedan	14608	16695
	Destination Charge:	525	525

Standard Equipment

CENTURY—SPECIAL: Driver side air bag, air conditioning, fixed mast antenna, front seat armrest, Delco Freedom II Plus battery, anti-lock power front disc/rear drum brakes, front and rear bumper guards, load floor carpet (Wagon), front and rear carpeting, engine and transmission cooling, front and side window defogger outlets, power door locks with automatic lock/unlock and relock feature, front wheel drive, electronic warning tone (ignition key, seat belts and "headlamps-on"), 2.2 liter 4 cylinder MFI engine, tinted glass, lockable glove compartment, halogen headlamps, adjustable front seat head restraints, inside hood lock release, dual horns, instrument gauges (speedometer, fuel gauge, voltage, temperature and trip odometer), rear compartment light (Wagon), lights (ashtray, instrument panel, courtesy, dome, glove box, trunk and engine compartment and map), deluxe black outside mirrors (left remote, right manual), moldings (belt reveal, roof drip, black door and window frame), black bodyside moldings (bodycolor on Sedan), clearcoat paint with anti-chip lower protection, ETR AM/FM stereo radio with seek/scan and clock, driver and passenger power seatback recliners, 55/45 seats armrest, split folding rear seatback (Wagon), automatic front safety system seatbelts, dual speakers (standard-range front, extended-range rear), power rack and pinion steering, tilt wheel adjustable steering column, deluxe steering wheel, lockable floor storage compartment (Wagon), gas cylinder hood strut supports, Dynaride suspension (Sedans), front independent MacPherson strut suspension, electric remote tailgate release (Wagon), compact spare tire, P185/75R14 steel belted radial ply all-season BW tires, 3-speed automatic transmission, 14" deluxe wheel covers (Special Sedan), 14" styled wheel covers (Wagon), 2-speed wipers with low speed delay.

CUSTOM (in addition to or instead of Special equipment): Front seat armrest with storage and dual cup holders, driver and passenger non-lighted covered visor vanity mirrors, bright wheel opening moldings, 55/45 seats with storage armrest, P185/75R14 steel belted radial ply all-season whitewalls.

CODE	DESCRIPTION	DEALER	LIST

Accessories

CODE	DESCRIPTION	DEALER	LIST
SA	**Century Base Pkg**	NC	NC
	incls vehicle plus standard equipment		
SD	**Century Special Sedan Luxury Pkg**	501	582
	incls elec rear window defogger, front carpet savers, rear carpet savers, front seat storage armrest, P185/74R14 WW tires, cruise control, covered visor vanity mirrors, cass player		
SE	**Century Special Sedan Prestige Pkg**	1070	1244
	incls SE Century Special Sedan luxury pkg equip plus cass player, remote trunk release, pwr windows, front seat reading lights, trunk convenience net, elec o/s rear view mirrors		
SD	**Century Special Wagon Luxury Pkg**	634	737
	incls air deflector, front carpet savers, rear carpet savers, elec rear window defogger, roof rack luggage carrier, P185/75R14 WW tires, storage armrest, elec cruise control, covered visor mirrors		
SE	**Century Special Wagon Prestige Pkg**	1370	1593
	incls SD Century Special Wagon luxury pkg equip plus cargo area security cover, cass tape player, front reading lights, pwr windows, third seat & swing-out vent window, elect o/s rear view mirrors		
SD	**Century Custom Sedan Luxury Pkg**	1078	1254
	incls elec cruise control, elec rear window defogger, cass tape player, front carpet savers, rear carpet savers, accent stripes, pwr windows, P195/75R14 W/S tires, auto pwr antenna, elec trunk release, trunk convenience net, dual elec remote mirrors, reading lights on mirror		
SE	**Century Custom Sedan Prestige Pkg**	1596	1856
	incls SD Century Custom Sedan luxury pkg equip plus lighted visor vanity mirrors, 6-way pwr drivers seat, remote keyless entry, prem spkr system		
—	**Engines**		
LN2	2.2 liter PFI L4	STD	STD
L82	3.1 liter SFI V6	525	610
—	**Transmissions**		
MX1	automatic (req'd w/LN2)	STD	STD
MX0	automatic w/overdrive (req'd w/L82)	172	200
BF9	**Carpet Savers Delete** (from pkgs) - all ex SA	(39)	(45)
C47	**Delete Rear Defogger** (from pkgs) - Special ex SA	(146)	(170)
—	**California/New York State Emissions** — w/L82	86	100
	w/LN2	NC	NC
AU0	**Keyless Entry, Remote**	116	135
V08	**Cooling, Heavy Duty Engine & Transmission** — all w/V6	34	40
V58/5	**Luggage Rack, Deck Lid** — Sedan, Wagon	99	115
B93	**Door Edge Guards** — Sedan, Wagon	22	25
DC4	**Reading Lights On ISRV Mirror** — Special & SE	5	6
DH6	**Mirrors** — lighted visor vanity - Special & SE	79	92
—	**Radio Equipment**		
UM6	cassette player w/auto reverse - Special & SA/SD	120	140
U1C	compact disc player - Special & SD	356	414
	Special & SE	236	274
	Custom & SD/SE	236	274
U62	speakers, premium - Sedans	60	70
U79	speakers, premium - Wagon	30	35
U75	power antenna (incl'd in some pkgs) - Special	73	85

BUICK

CODE	DESCRIPTION	DEALER	LIST
WG1	**6-Way Power Driver's Seat Adjuster** - Special & SD/SE	262	305
	Custom & SD	262	305
—A	**Stripes - Body Side** (order color) - Special	39	45
—	**Tires** (steel belted radial ply)		
QFF	P185/75R14 WW - Special & SA	58	68
	Custom	STD	STD
QFE	P185/75R14 BW - Special & SD/E, Custom	(58)	(68)
	Special & SA	STD	STD
QMW	P195/75R14 BW - Special & SA	34	40
	Special & SD/E	(24)	(28)
	Custom & SD/E	(58)	(68)
QMX	P195/75R14 WW - Special & SA	93	108
	Special & SD/E	34	40
—	**Interior Trim**		
	Custom		
AM6	cloth 55/45 w/storage armrest - Sedan	STD	STD
AM6	leather & vinyl 55/45 w/storage armrest - Sedan	430	500
	Special		
AM6	cloth 55/45 w/armrest - Sedan	STD	STD
	Wagon	STD	STD
A90	**Remote Trunk Release** — Sedan	52	60
—	**Wheels & Wheel Covers**		
N91	locking wire wheel covers	206	240
PC7	styled steel wheels (4) - Special	99	115
PG4	aluminum wheels (4)	254	295
BX3	**Woodgrain Body Side Applique** — Wagon & SD/E	301	350
A31	**Power Windows** — Special & SD	284	330
C25	**Windshield Wiper** — rear window (Wagon) - Special & SD/E	73	85

LE SABRE

LE SABRE CUSTOM 6 CYL
P69   4-Dr Sedan 18253   20860

LE SABRE LIMITED 6 CYL
R69   4-Dr Sedan 21368   24420

Destination Charge: 575   575

Standard Equipment

LE SABRE: Driver-side and front passenger-side air bag, air conditioning, fixed-mast antenna, front-seat armrest, Delco Freedom II Plus battery, push to set and release parking brake, anti-lock power front disc/rear drum brakes, front bumper guards, front and rear carpeting, front and side window defogger outlets, power door locks, front-wheel drive, electronic warning tone includes seat belts, ignition key, headlamps on, parking brake on; 3800 V6 engine with tuned-port injection, stainless steel exhaust system, Soft-Ray tinted glass, wraparound composite tungsten-halogen headlamps, adjustable front-seat head restraints, inside hood lock release, instrumentation includes backlit analog gauge cluster with trip odometer, center high-mounted stop lamp, lights (front ashtray, front and rear door operated dome, trunk, engine compartment, glove box, instrument panel courtesy), deluxe bodycolor outside mirrors (left remote, right manual), black bodyside moldings, moldings (wheel opening, belt reveal, roof drip), multi-function control lever (turn signal, headlamp high/low beam, windshield wiper/washer controls), basecoat/clearcoat paint with anti-chip lower protection, AM/FM ETR stereo radio with seek and scan and clock, driver and passenger manual seatback recliners, 55/45 cloth seats, rear-door child security locks, speakers (dual front and extended-range rear), power rack and pinion steering, tilt-wheel adjustable steering column, deluxe steering wheel, extendable and supplemental sunshades, DynaRide suspension, front independent MacPherson strut suspension, independent rear suspension, PASS-Key II theft-deterrent system, P205/70R15 steel-belted radial ply all-season BW tires, electronically controlled 4-speed automatic transmission with overdrive, full trunk trim, deluxe wheel covers, power windows with driver's express down and passenger lockout feature, 2-speed wipers with low-speed delay.

LIMITED (in addition to or instead of Le Sabre equipment): Power antenna, front seat storage armrest with dual cup holders, front and rear carpet savers, electronic cruise control, electric rear window defogger, front and rear door courtesy lights, lights (front and rear door operated dome, front header courtesy and reading, instrument panel courtesy, ashtray, glove box, trunk, engine compartment, rear roof rail courtesy/reading), deluxe bodycolor outside mirrors (left remote, right manual), lighted visor vanity passenger mirror, ETR AM/FM stereo radio with seek and scan, cassette, and clock; remote keyless entry, 6-way power driver's seat, variable effort power rack and pinion steering, P205/70R15 steel-belted radial ply all-season WW tires, trunk convenience net, electric remote trunk lock release, 15" aluminum wheels.

Accessories

CODE	DESCRIPTION	DEALER	LIST
SA	**Le Sabre Base Pkg**...	NC	NC
	incls vehicle plus standard equipment		
SD	**Le Sabre Custom Sedan Luxury Pkg**................................	951	1106
	incls frnt seat storage armrest, frnt carpet savers, rear carpet savers, trunk convenience net, elec cruise control, elec rear window defogger, cass tape player, body side stripe, P205/70R15 WW tires, 15" alum wheels (4)		
SE	**Le Sabre Custom Sedan Prestige Pkg**..............................	1593	1852
	incls SD Le Sabre Custom Sdn luxury pkg equip + door edge guards, remote keyless entry sys, pass lighted vanity mirror, elec remote rear view mirrors, auto pwr antenna, 6-way driver's pwr seat, elec remote trunk release		
SE	**Le Sabre Limited Sedan Prestige Pkg**..............................	576	670
	incls dual comfortemp climate control, rear seat comfortemp, cornering lamps, AM stereo w/music search, 6-way pass pwr seat		
L27	**Engine** — 3.8 litre 3800 (231 CID) SFI V6	STD	STD
MX0	**Transmission** — auto w/overdrive	STD	STD
YF5	**California Emissions**	NC	NC
NG1	**New York State Emissions**	NC	NC
UB3	**Instrumentation** — Limited..	140	163
	incls tach, gauges, oil monitors, low fuel indic		
DG7	**Mirrors** — elec remote o/s rearview - Custom & SD............	67	78
WG1	**Power Seat, 6-Way Driver** — Custom & SD........................	262	305
—	**Radio Equipment**		
U1L	cass tape w/music search, seek/scan, AM stereo, concert sound II spkrs -		
	Custom & SE..	103	120
	Limited & SD..	103	120
UM3	compact disc player, AM stereo, concert sound II spkrs -		
	Custom & SE..	313	364
	Limited & SD..	313	364
	Limited & SE..	210	244
—	**Tires** (steel belted radial ply)		
QGY	P205/70R15 BW - Custom & SD/SE...................................	(65)	(76)
	Limited	(65)	(76)
QGZ	P205/70R15 WW - Custom & SA..	65	76
NW9	**Traction Control System** — Limited	151	175
V92	**Trailer Towing Pkg** — w/o Y56..	280	325
	w/Y56..	129	150
	incls engine & trans oil coolers & auto level control suspension		
—	**Trims**		
	Custom		
AM6	cloth 55/45 - Custom..	STD	STD
	Limited		

CODE	DESCRIPTION	DEALER	LIST
AM6	cloth 55/45 & storage armrest - Limited	STD	STD
AM6	leather/vinyl 55/45 seat - Limited	430	500
—	**Wheels & Wheel Covers**		
PH3	styled aluminum wheels (4) 15" - Custom & SA............................	280	325
N91	locking wire wheel covers - Custom & SD & SE	NC	NC
	Limited	NC	NC
Y56	**Gran Touring Pkg** — Custom & SE..	343	399
	Limited	343	399
	incls gran touring suspension, 16" alum whls (4), & P215/60R16 BW touring tires, 3:06 axle ratio, leather wrapped steering whl, & auto level control		

PARK AVENUE/ULTRA

PARK AVENUE 6 CYL

W69	4-Dr Sedan...	23354	26999

PARK AVENUE ULTRA 6 CYL

U69	4-Dr Sedan...	27420	31699
	Destination Charge:..	625	625

Standard Equipment

PARK AVENUE: Driver and front passenger air bags, air conditioning, fixed-mast antenna, front seat storage armrest with dual cup holders, rear seat armrests, three-passenger assist handles, Delco Freedom II Plus battery, push-to-set/release parking brake, anti-lock front disc power brakes, rear drum brakes, front bumper guards, front and rear carpet savers, overhead console (front seat reading lights, garage door opener storage), electronic cruise control, electric rear window defogger, front and side window defogger outlets, power door locks, front-wheel drive, electronic warning tone (seat belts, ignition key, headlamps on, parking brake on), 3800 SFI V6 engine with tuned-port injection, stainless steel exhaust system, electric remote fuel filler door release, solar-control Solar-Ray glass, wraparound composite tungsten-halogen headlamps, adjustable front seat head restraints, inside release hood lock, stand-up hood ornament, dual horns, backlit analog gauge cluster instrumentation with trip odometer, center high-mounted stop lamp, lights (front ashtray, trunk, engine compartment, glove box, instrument panel courtesy), front and rear door courtesy/warning lights, front and rear seat reading and courtesy lights, passenger lighted visor vanity mirror, deluxe body color outside electric rearview mirrors (left and right remote), black bodyside wheel opening/belt reveal moldings, multi-function control lever (turn signal, headlamp high/low beam, windshield wiper/washer controls, cruise control), basecoat/clearcoat paint with anti-chip lower protection, ETR AM/FM stereo radio with seek and scan, cassette, 4-speaker system and clock; driver and passenger manual seatback recliners, 6-way power driver's seat, 55/45 cloth seats with front-seat storage armrest, rear-door child security locks, extended range speakers, variable effort power rack and pinion steering, tilt wheel adjustable steering column, deluxe steering wheel, supplemental extendable sunshades, automatic level control suspension, DynaRide suspension, front and rear independent suspension, Pass-Key II theft deterrent system, P205/70R15 SBR all-season BW tires, electronically controlled 4-speed automatic transmission with overdrive, electric remote trunk lock release with security switch, full trunk trim, specific 15" aluminum wheels, power windows with driver's express down and pass lockout feature, 2-speed windshield wiper with low speed delay feature.

ULTRA (in addition to or instead of Park Avenue equipment): Automatic dual ComforTemp climate control air conditioning, rear seat ComforTemp air conditioning, power antenna, heavy-duty Delco Freedom II Plus battery, body color door edge guards, automatic programmable door locks, 3800 supercharged V6 engine, twilight sentinel headlamp control, rear-seat head restraints, four-note horn, analog gauge cluster instrumentation (tachometer, coolant temperature, oil pressure, voltage, low-fuel indicator, oil level indicator, oil life monitor, trip odometer), front and rear lamp monitor, cornering lamps, automatic dimming inside rearview mirror, driver lighted visor vanity mirror, rear-seat passenger lighted vanity mirrors, moldings (belt reveal, wheel opening, wide bodyside, lower panel, door edge guard), specific lower accent moldings, driver and passenger electric seatback recliners, reminder package (low washer fluid indicator, low coolant level, door ajar, trunk ajar), remote keyless entry, retained accessory power (illuminated door locks, light control), driver and passenger 6-way power seat, 55/45 leather/vinyl seats with front-seat storage armrest, Concert Sound II speakers, leather-wrapped steering wheel, theft-deterrent system with starter interrupt, P215/70R15 SBR all-season BW tires, trunk convenience net, electric trunk pull-down.

Accessories

CODE	DESCRIPTION	DEALER	LIST
SA	**Park Avenue/Ultra Base Pkg**	NC	NC
	incls vehicle plus standard equipment		
SD	**Park Avenue Sedan Luxury Pkg**	1566	1821
	incls illum entry & accessory pwr retention, twilight sentinel, door edge guards, pwr antenna, analog gauge cluster, pwr pass seat, remote keyless entry, reminder pkg, trunk net, four note horn, lamp monitors, concert sound II, driver vanity mirror, auto inside rear view mirror, dual comfortemp, auto programmable door locks, pwr pass seat recliner, theft deterrent sys, pwr trunk pull-down, cornering lamps, P205/70R15 WW tires		
SE	**Park Avenue Sedan Prestige Pkg**	2147	2496
	incls SD Park Avenue Sedan luxury pkg equip plus sealant tires, heated o/s mirrors w/left auto dim, rear comfortemp, AM stereo w/music search, redundant steering wheel controls, trunk mat, memory seat & mirrors		
SD	**Ultra Luxury Pkg**	628	730
	incls AM stereo w/music search, redundant steering wheel controls, auto ride control, traction control		
SE	**Ultra Prestige Pkg**	1071	1245
	incls SD Ultra Luxury Pkg equip plus sealant tires, heated o/s mirrors w/left auto dim, trunk mat, memory seat & mirrors, heated driver seat		
—	**Engines**		
L27	3.8 liter 3800 (231 CID) SFI V6 - Park	STD	STD
L67	supercharged 3800 (231 CID) SFI V6 - Ultra.................................	STD	STD

BUICK

CODE	DESCRIPTION	DEALER	LIST
MX0	**Transmission** — auto w/overdrive	STD	STD
YF5	**California Emissions**	NC	NC
NG1	**New York State Emissions**	NC	NC
D83	**Monotone Paint** — Ultra	NC	NC
CF5	**Astroroof** — electric sliding - Park SE	789	918
	Ultra SD/SE	690	802
—	**Stripes** — Accent - Park	STD	STD
	Ultra	STD	STD
FX3	**Suspension** — auto adjustable - Park & SE	327	380
KA1	**Seat** — elec heated driver side -Park & SE	90	105
	Ultra & SD	52	60
	incls driver & pass pwr recliners		
—	**Tires** (steel belted radials)		
QGY	P205/70R15 BW - Park & SA	STD	STD
	Park & SD	(65)	(76)
	Park & SE	(194)	(226)
QGZ	P205/70R15 WW - Park & SA	65	76
QPN	P215/70R15 WW - Ultra	STD	STD
QPK	P215/70R15 BW - Ultra & SA/SD	(69)	(80)
P42	self sealing tires - Park & SA	129	150
	Park & Ultra w/o SE	NA	NA
NW9	**TractionControl System** - Park & SD/SE	151	175
—	**Trims**		
	Park Avenue (55/45 split frt)		
AM6	cloth w/storage armrest - Park	STD	STD
AM6	leather/vinyl w/storage armrest - Park	430	500
	Ultra (55/45 split frt)		
AQ7	ultra soft leather w/storage armrest - Ultra	STD	STD
N91	**Wheel Covers, Locking Wire** — Park	NC	NC
V92	**Trailering Pkg** — Park w/Y56	106	123
	Park less Y56	129	150
	Ultra w/Y56	106	123
	Ultra less Y56	(198)	(230)
—	*incls auxiliary trans oil & eng cooling, gran touring susp'n & 3.06 axle ratio* **Radio Equipment**		
U1L	radio - Park & SD	43	50
	Ultra & SC	43	50
	incls std cass w/auto reverse, music search, AM stereo & concert sound		
UT0	radio - Ultra & SC	622	723
	Ultra & SD/SE	579	673
	incls Bose music system (w/AM stereo)		
UM3	radio - Park & SA	313	364
	Park SD/Ultra SC	253	294
	Park SE/Ultra SD & SE	210	244
	incls compact disc player w/AM stereo & concert sound spkrs		
Y56	**Gran Touring Pkg** — Park	193	224
	Ultra	(253)	(294)
	incls gran touring susp'n, P215/60R16 touring tires, 3.06 axle ratio, 16" *aluminum wheels, leather wrapped steering wheel on Park (std Ultra)*		

EDMUND'S NEW CAR PRICES

BUICK

REGAL

REGAL CUSTOM 6 CYL
Code	Description	Dealer	List
B19	4-Dr Sedan	16012	18299
B57	2-Dr Coupe	15749	17999

REGAL LIMITED 6 CYL
Code	Description	Dealer	List
D19	4-Dr Sedan	17324	19799

REGAL GRAN SPORT 6 CYL
Code	Description	Dealer	List
F19	4-Dr Sedan	17762	20299
F57	2-Dr Coupe	17499	19999
	Destination Charge:	525	525

Standard Equipment

REGAL: Driver side air bag, air conditioning, fixed-mast antenna, front seat storage armrest with cup holders, rear seat or two door armrest ashtrays, Delco Freedom II Plus battery, 2-sided galvanized body panels, push-to-set/release parking brake, 4-wheel disc anti-lock power brakes, front bumper guards (Custom Sedan only), front and rear bumper guards, front and side window defogger outlets, black door handles (Coupes), body color door handles (Sedans), automatic power door locks with relock feature, front-wheel drive, electronic warning tone (seat belt, ignition key, turn signal on, headlamps on), 3.1 liter 3100 SFI V6 engine, stainless steel exhaust system, flash-to-pass signal lever, Soft-Ray tinted glass, chrome grille, composite tungsten halogen headlamps, adjustable front seat head restraints, rear-seat heat ducts, inside floor-mounted hood lock release, illuminated driver door lock (Coupe only), interior illumination with theatre dimming, analog gauge cluster instrumentation (tachometer, voltage, temperature, oil pressure, fuel gauges, trip odometer), center high-mounted stop lamp, amber park/turn lens lamps (Sedan), Crystalline park/turn lens lamps (Coupe), door-operated dome light, lights (front ashtray, instrument panel courtesy, trunk and engine compartment, glove box), deluxe black outside mirrors (left remote, right manual), driver and passenger dual covered non-lighted visor vanity mirrors, moldings (black windshield, black window frame, black side window, belt reveal—Coupe), moldings (black windshield, black window frame, bright rear quarter window, belt reveal—Sedan), front and rear wheel opening black and chrome moldings (Sedan), protective bodyside black moldings (Custom Coupe), protective bodyside body color moldings (NA on Custom Coupe), multi-function control lever (turn signal, headlamp high/low beam, flash-to-pass, windshield wiper/washer controls), basecoat/clearcoat paint with anti-chip lower protection, ETR AM/FM stereo radio with seek/scan and clock, driver and passenger manual seatback recliners, driver and passenger 2-way manual seat adjusters, 55/45 cloth reclining seats with storage armrest, speakers (front dual standard range, four rear extended range), power steering, tilt wheel adjustable steering column, deluxe steering wheel, slide out extension sunshades, independent front and rear suspension, DynaRide suspension, PassKey II theft-deterrent system, P205/70R15 SBR all-season BW tires, electronically controlled 4-speed automatic transmission with overdrive, trunk trim, 15" deluxe wheel covers, 2-speed wipers with low-speed delay, power windows with driver's express down and passenger lockout feature.

LIMITED (in addition to or instead of Regal equipment): 3.8 liter 3800 SFI V6 engine with tuned-port injection, stand-up hood ornament, integrated dome and reading lights, overhead console courtesy lights with integral reading lights, front seatback map pocket, aero panel molding, body color front and rear wheel opening moldings, wide bright protective bodyside moldings, 4-way manual driver's seat adjuster.

GRAN SPORT (in addition to or instead of Limited equipment): Front air dam (Coupe), full-length operating console with storage armrest and integrated cup holder, body color grille, fog lamps (Coupe), sail panel reading lights (Coupe), argent protective bodyside gray moldings (Sedan), two-tone Slate Gray metallic lower accent paint (Sedan), cloth bucket seats with console, leather-wrapped steering wheel, Gran Touring suspension (requires 3800 V6 engine), P225/60R16 SBR Eagle GA touring BW tires, four 16" aluminum wheels.

Accessories

CODE	DESCRIPTION	DEALER	LIST
SA	**Regal Base Pkg**	NC	NC
	incls vehicle standard equipment		
SD	**Regal Custom Sedan Luxury Pkg**	729	848
	incls frt carpet savers, rear carpet savers, elec cruise control, elec rear window defogger, dual comfortemp climate control, elec remote control mirrors, auto pwr antenna, cass tape player, remote trunk lid release		
SE	**Regal Custom Sedan Prestige Pkg**	1241	1443
	incls SD Regal Custom Sedan luxury pkg equip plus frt courtesy/reading lamps, rear reading/courtesy lights, trunk convenience net, 6-way driver's pwr seat, concert sound spkrs, remote keyless entry		
SD	**Regal Custom Coupe Luxury Pkg**	729	848
	incls frt carpet savers, rear carpet savers, elec cruise control, elec rear window defogger, dual comfortemp climate control, elec remote control mirrors, auto pwr antenna, cass tape player, remote trunk lid release		
SE	**Regal Custom Coupe Prestige Pkg**	1232	1432
	incls SD Regal Custom Coupe luxury pkg equip plus frt courtesy/reading lamps, sail panel courtesy lamps, trunk convenience net, 6-way driver's power seat, concert sound spkrs, remote keyless entry		
SD	**Regal Limited Sedan Luxury Pkg**	789	918
	incls frt carpet savers, rear carpet savers, elec cruise control, elec rear window defogger, dual comfortemp climate control, elec remote control mirrors, auto pwr antenna, cass tape player, remote trunk lid release, concert sound spkrs		
SE	**Regal Limited Sedan Prestige Pkg**	1410	1640
	incls SD Regal Limited Sedan luxury pkg equip plus door courtesy lights, trunk convenience net, 6-way driver's pwr seat, dual lighted vanity mirrors, remote keyless entry, steering wheel radio controls		
SD	**Regal Gran Sport Sedan Luxury Pkg**	789	918
	incls frt carpet savers, rear carpet savers, elec cruise control, elec rear window defogger, dual comfortemp climate control, elec remote control mirrors, auto pwr antenna, cass tape player, remote trunk lid release, concert sound spkrs		

BUICK

CODE	DESCRIPTION	DEALER	LIST
SE	**Regal Gran Sport Sedan Prestige Pkg**	1410	1640
	incls SD Regal Gran Sport Sedan luxury pkg equip plus driver's 6-way pwr seat, dual lighted vanity mirrors, remote keyless entry, steering radio controls, trunk convenience net, door courtesy lights		
SD	**Regal Gran Sport Coupe Luxury Pkg**	789	918
	incls frt carpet savers, rear carpet savers, elec cruise control, elec rear window defogger, dual comfortemp climate control, elec remote control mirrors, auto pwr antenna, cass tape player, remote trunk lid release, concert sound spkrs		
SE	**Regal Gran Sport Coupe Prestige Pkg**	1350	1570
	incls SD Regal Gran Sport luxury pkg equip plus driver's 6-way pwr seat, dual lighted vanity mirrors, remote keyless entry, steering wheel radio controls, trunk convenience net		
—	**Engines**		
L82	3.1 liter (191 CID) V6 w/SFI - Custom	STD	STD
L27	3.8 liter 3800 (231 CID) V6 w/MFI - Custom.....................................	340	395
	Limited/Gran Sport..	STD	STD
MX0	**Transmission** — auto w/overdrive	STD	STD
V08	**Cooling, HD** — w/eng oil cooler - all w/L27	129	150
BF9	**Carpet Savers Delete** — (from pkgs) - all ex SA.........................	(39)	(45)
C47	**Defogger Delete** — (from pkgs)	(146)	(170)
	all where applicable		
B93	**Door Edge Guards** — Limited & SE	22	25
BX4	**Chrome Body Side/Fascia Pkg** — Custom Coupe & SE	129	150
YF5	**California Emissions**...	NC	NC
NG1	**New York State Emissions**	NC	NC
K05	**Engine Block Heater**	15	18
AU0	**Keyless Entry, Remote** — Limited & GS w/SD	116	135
VK3	**License Holder**	NC	NC
V56	**Luggage Rack** — deck lid (blk) - GS Coupe.............................	99	115
V58	**Luggage Rack** — deck lid (bright) - Sedans...........................	99	115
DH6	**Mirrors, Lighted Visor Vanity** — Custom & SE	79	92
WG1	**Power Seat 6-Way** — driver - Custom & SD	262	305
	Limited & GS w/SD	232	270
WG5	**Dual Power Seats, 6-Way** — Limited & GS w/SE.........................	262	305
—	**Radio Equipment**		
UX1	graphic equalizer, AM stereo, & search/repeat for cass - Custom & SD/SE...	129	150
	Limited & GS/SD & SE..	129	150
U1C	compact disc player - Custom & SD/SE..................................	236	274
	Limited & GS/SD & SE..	236	274
UK3	steering wheel mounted radio controls - Custom & SD/SE	108	125
UW6	concert sound II- Custom & SD	60	70
U75	antenna power auto - Custom & SA	73	85
C75	**Sunroof** - elec, glass...	598	695
—	**Tires**		
QGY	P205/70R15 BW - Custom, Limited.......................................	STD	STD
QGZ	P205/70R15 WW - Custom, Limited......................................	65	76
—	**Trims**		
	Custom		
AM6	cloth 55/45 w/storage armrest - Custom.................................	STD	STD

BUICK

CODE	DESCRIPTION	DEALER	LIST
AR9	cloth buckets & console - Custom	NC	NC
	Limited		
AM6	cloth 55/45 w/storage armrest - Limited	STD	STD
AM6	leather/vinyl 55/45 - Limited	430	500
AR9	leather/vinyl buckets - Limited	430	500
	Gran Sport		
AR9	cloth buckets - Gran Sport	STD	STD
AR9	leather/vinyl buckets - Gran Sport	430	500
—	**Wheels & Wheelcovers**		
N91	locking wire wheelcovers - Custom & Limited	206	240
PH6	15" aluminum wheels - Custom & Limited	280	325
Y56	**Gran Touring Pkg** — Custom & Limited	581	675
	incls gran touring susp'n, 16" alum wheels & P225/60R16 tires, leather wrapped steering wheel		

ROADMASTER

ROADMASTER 8 CYL
N69	4-Dr Sedan	20999	23999

ROADMASTER LIMITED 8 CYL
T69	4-Dr Sedan	23099	26399

ESTATE WAGON 8 CYL
R35	4-Dr 3 Seat Wagon	22399	25599
	Destination Charge:	575	575

Standard Equipment

ROADMASTER SEDAN: Driver and front passenger air bag, air conditioning, fixed-mast antenna, front seat storage armrests, rear-seat armrests, front and rear assist straps, heavy-duty battery, mechanical parking brake, anti-lock power front brakes, disc/rear drum brakes, front snap down and rear carpet savers, electronic cruise control, electric rear window defogger, front and side window defogger outlets, door edge guards, power door locks, electronic warning tone (seat belts, ignition key, turn signal on, headlamps on), 5.7 liter SFI V8 engine, stainless steel dual exhaust system, Soft-Ray tinted glass, composite tungsten halogen headlamps, 4-note horn, delayed entry system illumination, indicators (low windshield washer fluid, oil, coolant level, volts, fuel), analog gauge cluster instrumentation (coolant temperature, trip odometer, oil level, fuel level), center high-mounted stop lamp, indirect lighting for controls and switches, lights (front and rear door operated dome, front ashtray, glove box, engine compartment, instrument panel, trunk), front seat reading lights (integral with rearview mirror), rear roof rail lights with integral reading lights, inside day/night mirror with integral reading lights, driver and passenger cloth covered visor vanity mirrors, deluxe outside body color rearview mirrors (left remote, right manual), moldings (deluxe wide bodyside, front wheel opening, hood and deck lid), multi-function control lever (turn signal, headlamp high/low beam, windshield wiper/washer controls), oil life monitor, basecoat/clearcoat paint with anti-chip lower protection, ETR AM/FM stereo radio with seek/scan and clock, driver and passenger manual seatback recliners, 55/45 cloth seats with storage armrest, rear door child security locks, dual standard range front speakers, dual extended range rear speakers, power steering, tilt wheel adjustable steering column, deluxe steering wheel, front and rear door built-in lower storage compartments, front seatback storage pockets, DynaRide suspension, Pass-Key II theft-deterrent system with starter interrupt, compact spare tire, P235/70R15 SBR all-season WW tires, electronically controlled 4-speed automatic transmission with overdrive, trunk convenience net, remote trunk release, deluxe trunk trim, 15" deluxe wheel covers, power windows with driver's express down and passenger lockout feature, 2-speed wipers with low-speed delay.

LIMITED (in addition to or instead of Roadmaster Sedan equipment): Electronic touch climate control air conditioning, automatic power antenna, rear seat storage armrest, automatic door locks with relock feature, 6-way front head restraints, electroluminescent coach lamps, door courtesy and warning lights, power lumbar, automatic dimming rearview mirror with integral reading lights, electric outside heated left and right rearview mirrors, driver and passenger lighted visor vanity mirrors, ETR AM/FM stereo radio with seek/scan, cassette and clock; driver and passenger electric seatback recliners, remote keyless entry, illuminated entry, driver and passenger 6-way power seats, cloth up-level split-frame design seats with front and rear storage armrest, premium dual fit coaxial speakers, extended range rear speakers, variable effort steering with steering dampener.

ROADMASTER ESTATE WAGON: Driver and front passenger air bag, air conditioning, fixed-mast antenna, third seat assist handles, front and rear assist straps, heavy-duty battery, mechanical parking brake, front disc/rear drum anti-lock power brakes, front bumper guards, front/rear and load area carpeting, electric rear window defogger, front and side window defogger outlets, door edge guards, power door locks, electronic warning tone (seat belts, ignition key, turn signal on, headlamps on), 5.7 liter SFI V8 engine, stainless steel dual exhaust system, Soft-Ray tinted glass, Solar-Ray solar-control windshield glass, lockable glove box, composite tungsten halogen headlamps, stand-up hood ornament, dual horn, delayed entry system illumination, tailgate ajar indicator, indicators (low windshield washer fluid, oil, low coolant level, volts, fuel), analog gauge cluster instrumentation (coolant temperature, trip odometer, oil level, fuel level), center high-mounted stop lamp, indirect lighting for controls and switches, lights (front and rear door operated dome, front ashtray, glove box, engine compartment, instrument panel, load compartment), front-seat reading lights (integral with rearview mirror), rear roof rail with integral reading lights, integral luggage rack with vista roof, inside day/night mirror with integral reading lights, driver and passenger cloth covered visor vanity mirrors, deluxe body color outside mirrors (left remote, right manual), narrow rocker panel molding, deluxe wide bodyside moldings, multi-function control lever (turn signal, headlamp high/low beam, windshield wiper/washer controls), oil life monitor, basecoat/clearcoat paint with anti-chip lower protection, ETR AM/FM stereo radio with seek/scan and clock, driver and passenger manual seatback recliners, 55/45 cloth seats with armrest, seats (2nd—fold-down seatback, 3rd—rear-facing vinyl), rear door child security locks, four dual standard range

CODE	DESCRIPTION	DEALER	LIST

front speakers, dual extended range rear speakers, power steering, variable effort steering with steering dampener, tilt-wheel adjustable steering column, deluxe steering wheel, front and rear door lower built-in storage compartments, lockable hidden storage compartments, front seatback storage pockets, instrument panel pull-out storage tray, heavy-duty suspension, two-way manual tailgate, remote tailgate lock release, Pass Key II theft-deterrent system with starter interrupt, compact spare tire, P225/75R15 SBR all-season WW tires, electronically controlled 4-speed automatic transmission with overdrive, dual-function trunk convenience net, vista roof with tinted glass, 15" aluminum wheels, power windows with driver's express down and passenger lockout feature, 2-speed wipers with low speed delay feature, rear-window wipers with washer, light Colonial Oak woodgrain vinyl applique.

Accessories

CODE	DESCRIPTION	DEALER	LIST
SA	**Roadmaster Base Pkg**	NC	NC
	incls vehicle plus standard equipment		
SD	**Roadmaster Sedan Luxury Pkg**	738	858
	incls elec climate control, elec o/s heated mirrors, auto pwr antenna, 6-way driver's pwr seat, cass tape player, concert sound spkrs		
SE	**Roadmaster Sedan Prestige Pkg**	1346	1565
	incls SD Roadmaster Sedan luxury pkg equip plus auto programmable door locks, remote keyless entry, door courtesy & warning lamps, auto rear view mirror, pass lighted vanity mirror, driver lighted vanity mirror, 6-way pass pwr seat		
SE	**Roadmaster Limited Sedan Prestige Pkg**	301	350
	incls elec trunk pull-down, self sealing WW tires, twilight sentinel, cornering lamps		
SD	**Roadmaster Estate Wagon Luxury Pkg**	1262	1467
	incls elec climate control, storage armrest, F & R carpet savers, elect cruise control, door courtesy & warning lamps, auto rear view mirror, elec o/s heated mirrors, auto pwr antenna, 6-way driver pwr seat, cass tape player, rear storage security cover, vista shade		
SE	**Roadmaster Estate Wagon Prestige Pkg**	1844	2144
	incls SD Roadmaster Estate Wagon luxury pkg equip plus cornering lamps, auto programmable door locks, remote keyless entry, pass lighted vanity mirror, driver lighted vanity mirror, 6-way pass pwr seat, twilight sentinel		
LT1	**Engine** — 5.7 liter (350 CID) SFI V8	STD	STD
MX0	**Transmission** — auto w/overdrive	STD	STD
G80	**Limited Slip Differential**	86	100
V03	**Cooling** — HD - Wagon	129	150
V03	**Cooling** — HD - Sedan SD & SE	172	200
	Limited	172	200
	incls solar control windshield		
AU4	**Door Locks Automatic Programmable** — Wagon & SD	22	25
	Sedan & SD	22	25
	req's remote keyless entry		
YF5	**California Emissions**	86	100
NG1	**New York State Emissions**	86	100
D84	**Paint** — lower accent - Sedans SD & SE	129	150
AU0	**Remote Keyless Entry** — Wagon & SD	116	135
	Sedan & SD	116	135
	req's auto programmable door locks		
G67	**Suspension** — auto level control - SD & SE	151	175
6Y2	**Third Seat - Delete** - Wagon & SA/SD	(185)	(215)

CODE	DESCRIPTION	DEALER	LIST
P42	**Tires** — self sealing P225/75R15 - Wagon..	129	150
QUK	**Tires** — self sealing P235/70R15 - Sedan/Limited SD	129	150
—	**Radio Equipment**		
U1A	radio - Wagon & SD/SE...	369	429
	Base Sedan & SD/SE...	339	394
	Limited Sedan..	339	394
	incls compact disc, graphic equalizer & AM stereo radio & premium spkrs (premium spkrs std on Limited, & incl'd in Sedan SD/SE pkgs)		
UX1	radio - Wagon & SD/SE...	159	185
	Base Sedan & SD/SE...	129	150
	Limited Sedan..	129	150
	incls graphic equalizer, auto reverse cass w/search/repeat ETR AM stereo, FM stereo radio w/seek & scan, premium spkrs & clock		
N81	**Tires** — full size spare & steel wheel - Sedans w/o PA3............................	56	65
N81	**Tires** — full size spare & aluminum wheels - Sedans w/PA3......................	99	115
C04	**Top** — vinyl landau - Sedans & SD/SE	598	695
V92	**Trailer Towing Pkg** — Wagon	280	325
	consists of 2.93 axle ratio, HD eng & trans cooling, auto level control, & eng oil cooler		
V92	**Trailer Towing Pkg** — Base Sedan	323	375
	Limited & SD..	323	375
	Limited & SE	194	225
	consists of 2.93 axle ratio, HD eng & trans cooling, auto level control, eng oil cooler, FE2 susp'n, solar control windshield		
—	**Trim**		
	Estate		
	cloth 55/45 w/armrest - Wagon	STD	STD
	leather/vinyl 55/45 - Wagon...	464	540
	Sedan		
	cloth 55/45 & storage armrest - Sedan	STD	STD
	leather/vinyl 55/45 - Sedan..	654	760
	Limited Sedan		
	cloth 55/45 & storage armrest - Limited	STD	STD
	leather/vinyl 55/45 - Limited	654	760
N91	**Wheel Covers** — custom locking wire - Wagon	NC	NC
	Sedans	206	240
PA3	**Wheels** — 15" aluminum (std Wagons) - Sedans....................................	280	325
WB4	**Woodgrain Delete** — Wagon..	NC	NC

SKYLARK

SKYLARK CUSTOM 4 CYL
		DEALER	LIST
V69	4-Dr Sedan	12715	13599
V37	2-Dr Coupe	12715	13599

SKYLARK LIMITED 4 CYL
I69	4-Dr Sedan	14660	16199

SKYLARK GRAN SPORT 6 CYL
M69	4-Dr Sedan	16561	18299
M37	2-Dr Coupe	16561	18299
	Destination Charge:	485	485

Standard Equipment

SKYLARK: Driver-side air bag, front air dam, fixed mast black antenna, Delco Freedom II battery (Rundown protection system), power disc anti-lock front brakes, rear drum brakes, front and rear carpeting, column shift with split bench seat, front overhead storage console with integral courtesy lights, front and side window defogger outlets, door map pockets and pull straps, power door locks with automatic relock, front wheel drive, electric warning tone (seat belts, ignition key, turn signal on, headlamps on), 2.3 liter Quad OHC engine, stainless steel exhaust system, flash to pass lever, remote fuel filler door release, Soft-Ray tinted glass, lockable glove box, bright grille, composite tungsten-halogen headlamps, base headliner (dual sunshades, front and rear courtesy lights), rear-seat head restraints, instrumentation (backlit analog gauge cluster with speedometer, temperature, fuel gauge, trip odometer, oil level telltale), high-mounted stop lamp, lights (ashtray, glove box, engine compartment, instrument panel courtesy, trunk compartment, front courtesy, rear-rail reading and courtesy), theatre dimming lights, deluxe black outside mirrors (left remote, right manual), body color bodyside moldings with bright insert, basecoat/clearcoat paint, ETR AM/FM stereo radio with seek and scan and clock, driver and passenger seatback recliner 55/45 cloth split bench seats, rear-door child security locks (Sedans), dual extended-range front/rear speakers, power rack and pinion steering, tilt-wheel adjustable steering column, deluxe steering wheel, front independent MacPherson strut suspension, DynaRide suspension, compact spare tire, P185/75R14 SBR Michelin all-season BW tires, 3-speed automatic transmission, remote trunk lock release, 14" bright wheel covers.

LIMITED (in addition to or instead of Skylark equipment): Air conditioning, electronic cruise control, custom headliner (dual covered visor vanity mirrors, map strap), front and rear courtesy lights, backlit analog gauge cluster instrumentation with speedometer, tachometer, voltmeter, oil pressure, oil temperature, fuel gauge, trip odometer, oil level telltale; driver's 4-way manual seat adjuster, power windows, 2-speed wipers with low-speed delay.

GRAN SPORT (in addition to or instead of Limited equipment): Full-length operating console, 3.1 liter 3100 SFI V6 engine, body color grille, bodyside moldings with black inserts, two-tone lower accent paint, reclining leather/cloth bucket seats, split folding rear seatback with inertia lock, leather-wrapped shift handle, leather-wrapped steering wheel, Gran Touring suspension, P205/55R16 SBR Eagle GA Touring BW tires, electronically controlled 4-speed automatic transmission with overdrive, trunk convenience net, 16" aluminum wheels.

Accessories

CODE	DESCRIPTION	DEALER	LIST
SA	**Skylark Base Pkg**..	NC	NC
	incls vehicle plus standard equipment		
SD	**Skylark Custom Sedan Luxury Pkg**...	1396	1623
	incls air conditioner, elec rear defogger, tilt steering column, F & R carpet savers, elec cruise control, delay feature windshield wipers, frt seat center armrest, 4-way manual seat adjuster		
SE	**Skylark Custom Sedan Prestige Pkg**	1851	2152
	incls SD Skylark Custom Sedan luxury pkg equip plus pwr windows, covered visor mirrors, cass tape player		
SD	**Skylark Custom Coupe Luxury Pkg**...	1396	1623
	incls air conditioner, elec rear defogger, tilt steering column, F & R carpet savers, elec cruise control, delay feature windshield wipers, frt seat center armrest, 4-way manual seat adjuster		
SE	**Skylark Custom Coupe Prestige Pkg**	1795	2087
	incls SD Skylark Coupe luxury pkg equip plus pwr windows, covered visor mirrors, cass tape player		
SE	**Skylark Limited Sedan Prestige Pkg**......................................	871	1013
	incls elec rear defogger, concert snd spkrs, carpet savers, cass tape player, auto pwr antenna, pwr driver's seat, dual elec remote mirrors, trunk convenience net, dlx headliner (lighted visor vanity mirrors, reading lights)		
SE	**Skylark Gran Sport Coupe & Sedan Prestige Pkg**	931	1083
	incls elec rear defogger, dlx headliner (lighted visor vanity mirrors, reading lights), cass tape player, remote keyless entry system, dual elec remote mirrors, auto pwr antenna, 6-way pwr driver's seat, concert sound spkrs		
—	**Engines**		
L40	2.3 liter quad OHC MFI L4 - Custom, Limited	STD	STD
L82	3.1 liter SFI V6 (std Gran Sport) - Custom, Limited	353	410
—	**Transmissions**		
MX1	automatic (3-spd) - Custom, Limited...	STD	STD
MX0	automatic (4-spd) - Custom, Limited...	172	200
C60	**Air Conditioner** — Custom SA...	714	830
BF9	**Delete Carpet Savers** — (from pkgs)	(39)	(45)
C47	**Delete Defogger** — (from pkgs)...	(146)	(170)
—	**California/New York State Emissions** — w/L40	86	100
	w/L82	NC	NC
K05	**Heater** — engine block	15	18
AP9	**Net, Trunk Convenience** — Custom, Limited...............................	17	20
AX3	**Keyless Entry Remote** — Limited & SE......................................	116	135

CODE	DESCRIPTION	DEALER	LIST
D84	**Paint** — lower accent - Custom, Limited..	168	195
—	**Radio Equipment**		
UM6	cassette tape player - SA/SD	142	165
UP3	compact disc player, auto reverse, seek/scan & graphic equalizer -		
	Limited & SE..	339	394
	Gran Sport & SE..	339	394
UW6	concert sound speakers - where applicable	39	45
AM9	**Seat, Rear Folding/Split** — Limited SE..	129	150
—	**Tires** — (steel belted radials)		
QFF	P185/75R14 WW - Custom/Limited..	58	68
QPD	P195/65R15 touring BW - Custom/Limited.................................	113	131
	PG1 wheelcovers req'd		
QMS	P205/55R16 touring BW - Limited, incl'd w/PG0		
WG1	**6-Way Power Driver's Seat** — Custom & SD/SE.........................	232	270
	Limited & Gran Sport SD	232	270
—	**Trims**		
	Skylark Custom		
AM8	split bench w/recliners - Coupe, Sedan	STD	STD
AR9	buckets & full console - SE	138	160
	Skylark Limited		
AM8	split bench w/storage armrest & recliners	STD	STD
AR9	buckets w/full console - SE...	138	160
	Gran Sport		
	leather/cloth bucket seats w/full lgth operating console - Coupe, Sedan	STD	STD
FE2	**Gran Touring Suspension** — Limited SE	23	27
—	**Wheels & Wheelcovers**		
PG1	styled wheel covers 15" (QPD tires req'd) - Custom, Limited........................	24	28
PG0	16" aluminum wheels w/ P205/55R16 touring BW tires - Limited & SE........	495	575
PC4	styled polycast wheels 14" - Custom, Limited............................	99	115
DG7	**Dual Electric Remote Mirrors** — Custom SD & SE	67	78
	Limited/GS & SD	67	78
U75	**Automatic Power Antenna** — (where applicable)	73	85
UB3	**Analog Gauge Cluster** — Custom SD & SE	108	126

BUICK NATIONAL MARKETING VEHICLES

Listed below are the "national marketing" vehicles that Buick will be selling in 1994. These cars are value priced with no-haggle window stickers. Buick's goal is to give customers bottom-line prices up front. These "national marketing" models are each equipped with a designated package of popular accessories and carry a lower manufacturer's suggested retail price than the traditional models from which they are derived.

CENTURY NATIONAL MARKETING VEHICLES

Code	Description	Dealer	List
G69	**Special 4-Dr Sedan**	13689	14470
	incls Century Special Sedan standard equipment plus speed control, power windows, rear window defroster, carpeted front and rear floor mats, armrest with storage compartment, dual visor vanity mirrors, P185/75R14 all-season whitewall tires, power trunk release		
G35	**Special 4-Dr Wagon**	14666	15470
	incls Century Special Wagon standard equip plus speed control, power windows, rear window defroster, carpeted front/rear floor mats, armrest w/storage compartment, dual visor vanity mirrors, P185/75R14 all-season whitewall tires, third rear seat, luggage rack, cargo cover, air deflector		
	Destination Charge:	525	525

Accessories for Century National Marketing Vehicles

Code	Description	Dealer	List
QFE	**P185/75R14 BW Tires**	NC	NC
UM6	**Cassette Tape Player**	120	140
WG1	**Power Driver Seat**	262	305
VK3	**Front License Plate Mounting Pkg**	NC	NC

REGAL NATIONAL MARKETING VEHICLES

Code	Description	Dealer	List
B19	**Custom 4-Dr Sedan**	17018	17970
	incls Regal standard equipment plus air cond, speed control, dual power mirrors, concert sound II speakers, AM/FM ETR stereo radio with cassette, front and rear floor mats, power driver's seat with 6-way adjuster, rear window defroster, reading lights, keyless remote control entry system, power trunk release, convenience net, reclining bucket seats, alum wheels		
B57	**Custom 2-Dr Coupe**	16122	16970
	incls Regal standard equipment plus air conditioning, speed control, dual power mirrors, concert sound II speakers, AM/FM ETR stereo radio with cassette, front and rear floor mats, power driver's seat with 6-way adjuster, rear window defroster, reading lights, keyless remote entry system, power trunk release, convenience net		
F57	**Gran Sport 2-Dr Coupe**	17602	18470
	incls Regal Gran Sport standard equipment plus air conditioning, speed control, dual power mirrors, concert sound II speakers, AM/FM ETR stereo radio with cassette, front and rear floor mats, power driver's seat with 6-way adjuster, rear window defroster, reading lights, keyless remote control entry sys, power trunk release, convenience net, dual illum vanity mirrors		
	Destination Charge:	525	525

Accessories for Regal National Marketing Vehicles

Code	Description	Dealer	List
VK3	**Front License Plate Mounting Pkg**	NC	NC

BUICK ONE-PRICE MODELS

CODE	DESCRIPTION	DEALER	LIST
VO8	**Heavy Duty Cooling**..	129	150
Y56	**Gran Touring Pkg — Sedan**	301	350
AR9	**Leather Bucket Seats & Console**	430	500
L27	**3800 V6 Engine** — Custom Coupe...............................	340	395
BX4	**Chrome Bodyside Molding** — Custom Coupe.................	129	150
N91	**Locking Wire Wheel Covers** — Custom Coupe	206	240
PH6	**Aluminum Wheels (15")** — Custom Coupe....................	280	325
QGZ	**P205/70R15 WW Tires** — Custom Coupe......................	65	76
UX1	**Graphic Equalizer** — Coupes.....................................	129	150
U1C	**Compact Disc Player** — Coupes..................................	236	274
AR9	**Bucket Seats w/Console** — Custom Coupe....................	NC	NC
CF5	**Electric Sliding Astroroof** — Gran Sport Coupe	598	695
UK3	**Steering Wheel Controls** — Gran Sport Coupe..............	108	125
V56	**Luggage Rack Deck Lid (Black)** — Gran Sport Coupe......	99	115

SKYLARK NATIONAL MARKETING VEHICLES

V69	**Custom 4-Dr Sedan** (4 cyl)	12888	13510
	incls Skylark standard equipment plus air conditioning, speed control, tilt steering wheel, armrest with storage compartment, rear window defroster, windshield washer/wiper with delay feature, 4-way manual driver's seat adjuster		
V37	**Custom 2-Dr Coupe** (4 cyl)	12888	13510
	incls Skylark standard equipment plus air conditioning, speed control, tilt steering wheel, armrest with storage compartment, rear window defroster, windshield washer/wiper with delay feature, 4-way manual driver's seat adjuster		
	Destination Charge:	485	485

Accessories for Skylark National Marketing Vehicles

A31	**Power Windows** — Sedan	292	340
	Coupe..	237	275
VK3	**Front License Plate Mounting Pkg**	NC	NC
UM6	**Cassette Tape Player**	142	165
DG7	**Electric Mirrors** — NA w/o WG1	67	78
U75	**Power Antenna** — NA w/o WG1	73	85
WG1	**Power Driver Seat** — DG7 & U75 req'd........................	232	270
MXO	**4-Speed Overdrive Transmission**	172	200

CADILLAC

CADILLAC 8 CYL

CODE	DESCRIPTION	DEALER	LIST
6KD69	B De Ville Sedan	NA	NA
6KF69	P De Ville Concours	NA	NA
6DW69	L Fleetwood	NA	NA
6EL57	H Eldorado	32256	37290
6ET57	T Eldorado Touring Coupe	35110	40590
6KS69	M Seville Luxury Sedan	35456	40990
6KY69	G Seville Touring Sedan	38830	44890
	Destination Charge:	625	625

Standard Equipment

CONCOURS: Driver and front passenger air bags, power antenna, anti-lock braking system, ignition anti-lock-out feature, front and rear seat center armrests, audible reminders, body-frame integral construction, power four-wheel disc brakes, brake/transmission shift interlock, center high-mounted stop lamp, electronic climate control, digital display clock, on-board computer diagnostics, controlled cycle wiper system, cornering lights, cruise control, front side window defoggers, electric rear window defogger, automatic door locks, rear door child security locks, electrically powered door locks, driver information center, electronic level control, 4.6 liter 270 HP DOHC V8 Northstar engine, engine oil life indicator, dual exhaust outlets, flash-to-pass, stainless steel exhaust, front/rear carpeted floor mats, front-wheel drive, fuel data center, remote release fuel filler door, digital fuel gauge, Gold Key delivery system, tungsten halogen composite headlamps, digital instrumentation cluster, leather seating areas, low fuel warning indicator, low windshield washer fluid level indicator, carpeted luggage compartment, automatic day/night electrochromic inside rearview mirror, automatic day/night electrochromic outside driver-side mirror, driver and passenger illuminated visor vanity mirrors, electrically powered/heated right and left outside rearview mirrors, multi-function turn signal lever, outside temperature digital display, clearcoat paint, automatic parking brake release, Pass-Key II anti-theft system, platinum tipped spark plugs, radio (AM/FM stereo, signal seeking and scanner with digital display, ETR cassette player), driver and front passenger power recliners, remote keyless entry system, retained accessory power, road-sensing suspension, driver and front passenger 6-way power seat adjuster, dual comfort front seats, short/long arm rear suspension, solar-ray tinted glass, compact spare tire, speed-sensitive

CADILLAC

steering, power steering, tilt steering wheel, leather- trimmed steering wheel rim, sunshade extensions, independent four-wheel suspension, all-season mud and snow SBR BW tires, traction control, automatic transmission, trip odometer, trunk convenience net, power trunk lid release, power trunk lid pull-down, trunk lockout, trunk mat and sill plate, twilight sentinel, cast aluminum wheels, electrically powered windows, rear window child lockout system, driver's window express-down feature.

SEDAN DE VILLE: Driver and front passenger air bags, power antenna, anti-lock braking system, ignition anti-lock-out feature, front and rear seat center armrests, audible reminders, body-frame integral construction, power four-wheel disc brakes, brake/transmission shift interlock, center high-mounted stop lamp, electronic climate control, digital display clock, on-board computer diagnostics, controlled cycle wiper system, cornering lights, cruise control, front side window defoggers, electric rear window defogger, automatic electrically-powered door locks, rear door child security locks, driver information center, electronic level control, 4.9 liter SPFI V8 engine, engine oil life indicator, stainless steel exhaust, flash-to-pass, front and rear carpeted floor mats, front-wheel drive, fuel data center, remote release fuel filler door, digital fuel gauge, Gold Key delivery system, tungsten halogen composite headlamps, digital instrument cluster, low fuel warning indicator, low windshield washer fluid level indicator, carpeted luggage compartment, automatic day/night electrochromic inside rearview mirror, electrically powered and heated right/left outside rearview mirrors, multi-function turn signal lever, outside temperature digital display, clearcoat paint, automatic parking brake release, Pass-Key II anti-theft system, platinum tipped spark plugs, radio (AM/FM stereo, signal seeking and scanner with digital display, ETR cassette player), driver and front passenger manual recliners, remote keyless entry system, retained accessory power, driver and front passenger 6-way power seat adjuster, dual comfort front seats, short/long arm rear suspension, solar-ray tinted glass, compact spare tire, speed-sensitive steering, speed-sensitive suspension, power steering, tilt steering wheel, leather- trimmed steering wheel rim, sunshade extensions, independent four-wheel suspension, all-season mud and snow SBR WW tires, automatic transmission, trip odometer, power trunk lid release, trunk lockout, trunk sill plate, twilight sentinel, cast aluminum wheels, electrically powered windows, rear window child lockout system, driver's window express-down feature.

ELDORADO COUPE: Driver and front passenger air bags, power antenna, anti-lock braking system, ignition anti-lockout feature, front and rear seat center armrests, audible reminders, body-frame integral construction, power four-wheel disc brakes, brake/transmission shift interlock, center high-mounted stop lamp, electronic climate control, digital display clock, on-board computer diagnostics, controlled cycle wiper system, cornering lights, cruise control, front side window defoggers, electric rear window defogger, electrically powered automatic door locks, driver information center, electronic level control, 4.6 liter DOHC 270 HP Northstar V8 engine, engine oil life indicator, dual exhaust outlets, stainless steel exhaust, flash-to-pass, front and rear carpeted floor mats, front-wheel drive, fuel data center, remote release fuel filler door, digital fuel gauge, Gold Key delivery system, tungsten halogen composite headlamps, digital instrument cluster, low fuel warning indicator, low windshield washer fluid level indicator, carpeted luggage compartment, automatic day/night inside rearview electrochromic mirror, driver and passenger illuminated visor vanity mirrors, electrically powered and heated right/left outside rearview mirrors, multi-function turn signal lever, outside temperature digital display, clearcoat paint, automatic parking brake release, Pass-Key II anti-theft system, platinum tipped spark plugs, radio (AM/FM stereo, signal seeking and scanner with digital display, ETR cassette player), driver and front passenger power seat recliners, remote keyless entry system, retained accessory power, road-sensing suspension, driver and front passenger 6-way power seat adjuster, front bucket seats, short/long arm rear suspension, solar-ray tinted glass, compact spare tire, speed-sensitive steering, power steering, tilt steering wheel, leather-trimmed steering wheel rim, sunshade extensions, independent four-wheel suspension, all-season mud and snow SBR BW tires, traction control, auto transmission, trip odometer, trunk convenience net, power trunk lid release, power trunk lid pull-down, trunk mat, trunk sill plate, twilight sentinel, cast alum wheels, elec powered windows, driver's window express-down feature.

ELDORADO TOURING COUPE: Driver and front passenger air bags, power antenna, anti-lock braking system, ignition anti-lock-out feature, front and rear seat center armrests, audible reminders, body-frame integral construction, power four-wheel disc brakes, brake/transmission shift interlock, center high-mounted stop lamp, electronic climate control, digital display clock, on-board computer diagnostics, controlled cycle wiper system, cornering lights, cruise control, front side window defoggers, electric rear window defogger, automatic electrically-powered door locks, driver information center, electronic level control, 4.6 liter DOHC 295 HP Northstar V8 engine, engine oil life indicator, dual exhaust outlets, stainless steel exhaust, flash-to-pass, front and rear carpeted floor mats, fog lamps, front-wheel drive, fuel data center, remote release fuel filler door, Gold Key delivery system, tungsten halogen composite headlamps, leather seating areas, low fuel warning indicator, low windshield washer fluid level indicator, carpeted luggage compartment, automatic day/night inside electrochromic rearview mirror, automatic day/night outside electrochromic driver-side mirror, driver and passenger illuminated visor vanity mirrors, electrically powered and heated right/left outside rearview mirrors, multi-function turn signal lever, outside temperature digital display, clearcoat paint, automatic parking brake release, Pass-Key II anti-theft system, platinum tipped spark plugs, AM/FM stereo radio with signal seeking and scanner/digital display/ETR cassette player; driver and front passenger power recliners, remote keyless entry system, retained accessory power, road-sensing suspension, driver and front passenger 6-way power seat adjuster, front bucket seats, short/long arm rear suspension, solar-ray tinted glass, compact spare tire, speed-sensitive steering, power steering, tilt steering wheel, leather-trimmed steering wheel rim, sunshade extensions, independent four-wheel suspension, theft deterrent system, all-season mud and snow SBR BW tires, traction control, automatic transmission, trip odometer, trunk convenience net, power trunk lid release, power trunk lid pull-down, trunk mat, trunk sill plate, twilight sentinel, cast aluminum wheels, electrically powered windows, driver's window express-down feature.

FLEETWOOD SEDAN: Driver and front passenger air bags, power antenna, anti-lock braking system, front and rear seat center armrests, audible reminders, power front disc/rear drum brakes, brake/transmission shift interlock, center high-mounted stop lamp, electronic climate control, digital display clock, on-board computer diagnostics, controlled cycle wiper system, cornering lights, cruise control, front side window defoggers, electric rear window defogger, electrically-powered door locks, rear door child security locks, electronic level control, 5.7 liter SPFI V8 engine, engine oil life indicator, dual exhaust outlets, stainless steel exhaust, flash-to-pass, front and rear carpeted floor mats, digital fuel gauge, Gold Key delivery system, tungsten halogen composite headlamps, digital instrument cluster, low fuel warning indicator, low windshield washer fluid level indicator, carpeted luggage compartment, driver and passenger illuminated visor vanity mirrors, electrically powered and heated right/left outside rearview mirrors, multi-function turn signal lever, outside temperature digital display, clearcoat paint, automatic parking brake release, Pass-Key II anti-theft system, platinum tipped spark plugs, radio (AM/FM stereo, signal seeking and scanner with digital display, ETR cassette player), driver and front passenger power recliners, retained accessory power, driver and front passenger 6-way power seat adjuster, dual comfort front seats, Solar-Ray tinted glass, compact spare tire, variable-assist steering, power steering, tilt steering wheel, leather-trimmed steering wheel rim, all-season mud and snow SBR WW tires, traction control, automatic transmission, trip odometer, trunk convenience net, power trunk lid release, power trunk lid pull-down, trunk mat, twilight sentinel, cast aluminum wheels, electrically powered windows, rear window child lockout system, driver's window express-down feature.

SEVILLE LUXURY SEDAN: Driver and front passenger air bags, power antenna, anti-lock braking system, ignition anti-lock feature, front/rear seat center armrests, audible reminders, body-frame integral construction, power four-wheel disc brakes, brake/transmission shift interlock, center high-mounted

CADILLAC

stop lamp, electronic climate control, digital display clock, on-board computer diagnostics, controlled cycle wiper system, cornering lights, cruise control, front side window defoggers, electric rear window defogger, automatic electrically powered door locks, rear door child security locks, driver information center, electronic level control, 4.6 liter DOHC 270 HP Northstar V8 engine, engine oil life indicator, dual exhaust outlets, stainless steel exhaust, flash-to-pass, front and rear carpeted floor mats, front-wheel drive, fuel data center, remote-release fuel filler door, digital fuel gauge, Gold Key delivery system, tungsten halogen composite headlamps, digital instrument cluster, low fuel warning indicator, low windshield washer fluid level indicator, carpeted luggage compartment, automatic day/night inside electrochromic rearview mirror, driver and passenger illuminated visor vanity mirrors, electrically powered and heated right/left outside rearview mirrors, multi-function turn signal lever, outside temperature digital display, clearcoat paint, automatic parking brake release, Pass-Key II anti-theft system, platinum tipped spark plugs, radio (AM/FM stereo, signal seeking and scanner with digital display and ETR cassette player), driver and front passenger power reclining seats, remote keyless entry system, retained accessory power, road-sensing suspension, driver and front passenger 6-way power seat adjuster, front bucket seats, short/long arm rear suspension, Solar-Ray tinted glass, compact spare tire, speed-sensitive steering, power steering, tilt steering wheel, leather-trimmed steering wheel rim, sunshade extensions, independent four-wheel suspension, all-season mud and snow SBR BW tires, traction control, automatic transmission, trip odometer, trunk convenience net, power trunk lid release, power trunk lid pull-down, trunk mat, trunk sill plate, twilight sentinel, cast aluminum wheels, electrically powered windows, driver's window express-down feature.

SEVILLE TOURING SEDAN: Driver and front passenger air bags, power antenna, anti-lock braking system, ignition anti-lockout feature, front and rear seat center armrests, audible reminders, body-frame integral construction, power four-wheel disc brakes, brake/transmission shift interlock, center high-mounted stop lamp, electronic climate control, digital display clock, on-board computer diagnostics, controlled cycle wiper system, cornering lights, cruise control, front side window defoggers, electric rear window defogger, electrically powered automatic door locks, rear door child security locks, driver information center, electronic level control, 4.6 liter DOHC 295 HP Northstar V8 engine, engine oil life indicator, dual exhaust outlets, stainless steel exhaust, flash-to-pass, front and rear carpeted floor mats, fog lamps, front-wheel drive, fuel data center, remote release fuel filler door, Gold Key delivery system, tungsten halogen composite headlamps, leather seating areas, low fuel warning indicator, low windshield washer fluid level indicator, carpeted luggage compartment, automatic day/night inside electrochromic rearview mirror, automatic day/night outside electrochromic driver side mirror, driver and passenger illuminated visor vanity mirrors, electrically powered and heated right/left outside rearview mirrors, multi-function turn signal lever, outside temperature digital display, clearcoat paint, automatic parking brake release, Pass-Key II anti-theft system, platinum tipped spark plugs, radio (AM/FM stereo, signal seeking and scanner with digital display, ETR cassette player), driver and front passenger power reclining seats, remote keyless entry system, retained accessory power, road-sensing suspension, driver and front passenger 6-way power seat adjuster, front bucket seats, short/long arm rear suspension, solar-ray tinted glass, compact spare tire, speed-sensitive steering, power steering, tilt steering wheel, leather-trimmed steering wheel rim, sunshade extensions, independent four-wheel suspension, theft-deterrent system, all-season mud and snow SBR BW tires, traction control, auto trans, trip odometer, trunk convenience net, power trunk lid release, power trunk lid pull-down, trunk mat, trunk sill plate, twilight sentinel, cast alum wheels, elec powered windows, driver's window express-down feature.

Accessories

CODE	DESCRIPTION	DEALER	LIST
1SB	**De Ville Option Pkg B — B**.. *incls auto day/night electrochromic driver o/s rearview mirror, driver &* *pass illuminated vanity mirrors, trumpet horn, trunk convenience net, pwr*	364	428

CODE	DESCRIPTION	DEALER	LIST
	trunk lid pull down, trunk mat		
V4R	**Fleetwood Security Pkg** — L..	463	545
	incls auto door locks, remote keyless entry system, remote release fuel filler door, theft deterrent system		
V4C	**Eldorado Sport Appearance Pkg** — H.............................	124	146
	incls analog instrument cluster, floor console w/leather-wrapped trans shift lever, cast aluminum Eldorado Touring Coupe wheels w/BW tires		
UY9	**Seville Sport Interior** — M...	124	146
	incls analog instrument cluster, flr cnsl w/leather-wrapped trans shift lever		
D98	**Accent Striping** — B, P, H, M...	64	75
CF5	**Astroroof** — B, P, L, H, T, M, G.......................................	1318	1550
GW9	**Axle Performance (2.93:1)** — L (incl in V4S & V92).........	NC	NC
V4U	**Coachbuilder Limousine Pkg** — L..................................	NA	NA
FE9	**Federal Emissions** — B, P, L, H, T, M, G........................	NC	NC
YF5	**California Emissions** — B, P, L, H, T, M, G.....................	85	100
NG1	**New York Emissions** — B, P, L, H, T, M, G.....................	85	100
V4S	**Fleetwood Brougham (Cloth)** — L..................................	1428	1680
V4S	**Fleetwood Brougham (Leather)** — L...............................	1913	2250
KA1	**Heated Front Seats** — P, H, T, M, G...............................	102	120
	B (incls pwr recliners)..	264	310
C50	**Heated Windshield System** — B, P, H, T, M, G...............	263	309
R1P	**Heavy Duty Livery Pkg** — L (NA w/B9Q, V4U, V92).........	128	150
YL1	**Leather Seating Area** — L (w/o V4S).............................	485	570
	B (std on P)..	667	785
	H, M (std on G, T)...	553	650
VK3	**License Plate Front Mounting Provision** — B, P, L, H, T, M, G..	NC	NC
AQ9	**Lumbar Support** — power H, M (std on P, G, T)...............	248	292
—	**Mirrors** — automatic day/night, electrochromic		
DD8	inside - L (std on P, B, H, T, M, G)................................	94	110
DD0	outside driver side - H, M (std on P, G, T 1SB on B)........	74	87
V1F	**Paint** — white diamond - B, P, H, T, M, G (w/93U)...........	425	500
—	**Radios**		
	all radios (including base UW7/UX1/U1L) are AM/FM stereo, electronically tuned, digital display w/signal seeking & scanner, cass tape player		
U1H	w/compact disc - L..	337	396
	Radios		
	incls 11 spkr active audio system		
U1L	cassette only - B (std on P)...	233	274
U1R	cass & compact disc - B...	570	670
	P..	337	396
U1G	w/Delco Bose sound system, CD & cassette - H, T, M, G.....	826	972
CB5	**Full Padded Vinyl Roof** — L (incl w/V4S).......................	786	925
CA2	**Vinyl Roof Delete** — L..	NC	NC
UY9	**Sport Interior** — M...	124	146
UA6	**Theft Deterrent System** — B, P, H, M (std on T, G, V4R on L)..	251	295
N81	**Tire** — full size spare - L (incl w/B9Q & V4U)...............	81	95
QPY	**Tires** — WW P225/60R16 - H.......................................	65	76
NW9	**Traction Control** — B (std on P, L, H, T, M, G)...............	149	175
V92	**Trailer Towing Pkg** — L..	60	70
PH6	**Cast Aluminum Wheels** — B..	NC	NC

CADILLAC

CODE	DESCRIPTION	DEALER	LIST
N83	Chrome Wheels — L (NA w/B9Q & V4U)	523	1195
N98	Chrome Wheels — B	523	1195
PH2	Chrome Wheels — M	523	1195
P05	Chrome Wheels — H, T, G	523	1195
QB9	Chrome Wheels — P	523	1195
A23	Windshield Sunshade — L	43	50

ASTRO PASSENGER VAN

ASTRO M10 REAR WHEEL DRIVE 6 CYL

CM10906	ZW9 Astro	14732	16278
CM11006	ZW9 Extended Astro	15005	16580

ASTRO L10 ALL WHEEL DRIVE 6 CYL

CL10906	ZW9 Astro	16839	18607
CL11006	ZW9 Extended Astro	17112	18909
	Destination Charge:	545	545

Standard Equipment

ASTRO VAN: Four-speed electronically controlled automatic transmission with overdrive, 100 amp alternator, power-assisted front disc/rear drum 4-wheel anti-lock brakes, brake/transmission shift interlock, front and rear lower body color painted bumpers (includes front bumper guards), doors (driver and passenger front side, sliding RH side, RH and LH rear-load), solar-ray tinted glass, swing-out glass on sliding side door, molded plastic black grille, halogen headlamps, screw-operated scissor-type jack with ratchet handle, extension and 2-wheel blocks; front license plate bracket, RH and LH painted mirrors with pivoting arm and adjustable heads, winch-type mounted spare tire carrier under the floor at the rear, compact spare tire/wheel mounted under floor, four all-season SBR tires, underbody corrosion protection, bright metal hub caps with black trim, four 15" x 6" steel painted argent wheels, black painted window pillars, intermittent windshield wipers, driver's facial air bag, RH/LH armrests, front and rear passenger-side assist handles, cigarette lighter with ashtray light, two LH and one RH coat hook, two dome lamps with front door actuated switches, color-keyed carpeting on wheel housing and entire load floor, gauges (coolant temperature, fuel level, odometer, oil pressure, speedometer, trip odometer and voltmeter), beverage holders on top of engine cover extension, headlamp warning, full-length color-keyed foam-backed cloth headliner, deluxe heater with side window defogger, electronically tuned AM radio with fixed-mast antenna, Scotchgard fabric protector optional cloth trims and carpeting, highback adjustable front bucket seats with vinyl trim, removable adjustable 3-passenger center bench seat (seat adjuster included on all 2nd and 3rd seats), 4-spoke black steering wheel with anti-theft locking feature, molded color-keyed storage compartment in LH rear 2nd seat area, LH/RH color-keyed cloth sunshades with RH visor mirror, color-keyed vinyl door trim panels with front door map pockets, black plastic door sill plates, swing-out glass on sliding side door.

CL (in addition to or instead of Astro equipment): Air dam with fog lamps, front and rear painted lower body color bumpers with matching color-keyed end caps, black rub strips and rear combination top step surface; molded black plastic grille with argent paint on feature surfaces, black bodyside moldings with bright inserts and wheel opening moldings, 15" x 6.5" color-keyed steel rally wheels, color-keyed expanded vinyl door trim panels with carpet inserts, insulation and front door map pockets; color-keyed floor mats for all seating positions, lamps (stepwell, storage compartment, two dome with front, rear, and sliding door-actuated switches, door jamb defeat switch), molded color-keyed plastic storage compartment in LH rear quarter area, LH/RH color-keyed cloth sunshades with lighted RH visor mirror, swing-out glass on sliding side door, left front quarter panel and rear doors.

Accessories

CODE	DESCRIPTION	DEALER	LIST
ASA1	**Passenger Preferred Equipment Group 1**	NC	NC
ASA2	**Passenger Preferred Equipment Group 2 — w/YC6**	299	348
	w/o YC6	434	505
ASA3	**Passenger Preferred Equipment Group 3 — w/o YC6**	1284	1493
	w/YC6	884	1028
ASA4	**Passenger Preferred Equipment Group 4 — CM10906 - w/YC6**	2322	2700
	w/YC7	2391	2780
	CM11006, CL10906 or CL11006 - w/YC6	2315	2692
	w/YC7	2384	2772
ASA5	**Passenger Preferred Equipment Group 5 — CM10906 - w/o YC7**	3203	3724
	w/YC6	2992	3479
	w/YC7	2768	3219
	CM11006, CL10906 or CL11006 - w/o YC7	3195	3716
	w/YC6	2985	3471
	w/YC7	2761	3211
—	**Radio Equipment**		
UM7	radio - w/PEG ASA1	130	151
	w/PEG ASA2 or ASA3	NC	NC
	incls elec tuned AM/FM stereo radio with seek and scan and digital clock		
UM6	radio - w/PEG ASA1	235	273
	w/PEG ASA2 or ASA3	105	122
	w/PEG ASA4 or ASA5	NC	NC
	incls electronically tuned AM/FM stereo radio with seek and scan, stereo cassette tape and digital clock		
UX1	radio - w/PEG ASA1	364	423
	w/PEG ASA3	234	272
	w/PEG ASA4 or ASA5	129	150
	incls electronically tuned AM stereo/FM stereo with seek and scan, stereo cassette tape with search and repeat, graphic equalizer and digital clock		
U1C	radio - w/PEG ASA1	479	557
	w/PEG ASA2 or ASA3	349	406

CODE	DESCRIPTION	DEALER	LIST
	w/PEG ASA4 or ASA5	244	284
	incls electronically tuned AM/FM stereo radio with seek and scan, compact disc player and digital clock		
UL5	radio delete	(82)	(95)
—	**Air Conditioning**		
C60	front - w/PEG ASA1	727	845
	w/PEG ASA2, ASA3, ASA4 or ASA5	NC	NC
C69	front and rear - w/PEG ASA1	1176	1368
	w/PEG ASA2, ASA3, ASA4 or ASA5	450	523
—	**Axles, Rear**		
GU5	3.23 ratio	NC	NC
GU6	3.42 ratio	NC	NC
GT4	3.73 ratio	NC	NC
G80	locking differential	217	252
—	**Body**		
ZW9	standard body	NC	NC
E54	dutch doors	313	364
VE5	**Bumper Equipment —**		
	bumpers, deluxe front and rear - w/o YC6 or YC7 or ZL7	110	128
	w/YC6 or YC7 or ZL7	65	76
V54	**Carrier, Luggage** — black - w/PEG ASA1, ASA2, ASA3 or ASA4	108	126
	w/PEG ASA5	NC	NC
V10	**Cold Climate Package**	40	46
DK6	**Console, Roof** — w/o YC6 or YC7	71	83
	w/YC6 or YC7	43	50
	w/PEG ASA5	NC	NC
—	**Convenience Groups**		
ZQ2	w/PEG ASA1, ASA2 or ASA3	373	434
ZQ2	w/PEG ASA4 or ASA5	NC	NC
ZQ3	w/PEG ASA1 or ASA2	329	383
ZQ3	w/PEG ASA3, ASA4 or ASA5	NC	NC
VO8	**Cooling System** — w/Z82	NC	NC
	heavy duty	170	198
ZL7	**CS Value Package** — w/PEG ASA3	NC	NC
	w/PEG ASA1 or ASA2	400	465
—	**Decor**		
YC6	**CL: custom luxury** - w/PEG ASA4 or ASA5	NC	NC
	w/o ZL7	934	1086
YC7	**LT: luxury touring** - w/PEG ASA4 or ASA5	1551	1804
	w/o ZL7	2491	2896
C49	**Defogger** — electric rear window	132	154
AU3	**Door Lock System, Power** — all doors - w/o ZQ2	192	223
	w/ZQ2	NC	NC
FE9	**Federal Emission Requirements**	NC	NC
YF5	**California Emission Requirements**	86	100
NG1	**New York State Emission Requirements** — CL1100	NC	NC
	CL1090	86	100
—	**Engines**		

CODE	DESCRIPTION	DEALER	LIST
	gasoline		
LB4	4.3 liter (262 cu. in.) EFI V6	NC	NC
L35	4.3 liter (262 cu. in.) CPI V6 - CL10906 or CL11006	NC	NC
	CM10906 or CM11006	430	500
ZW6	**Glass Arrangement** — complete body - w/PEG ASA1	135	157
	w/PEG ASA2, ASA3, ASA4, ASA5 or YC7	NC	NC
AJ1	**Glass, Deep Tinted** — w/o YC7 or ZW6	138	161
	w/ZW6	249	290
	w/YC7	NC	NC
C36	**Heater** — rear	176	205
U52	**Instrumentation, Electronic**	168	195
TR9	**Lighting, Auxiliary** — w/o DK6 console, YC6 or YC7	109	127
	w/DK6 console	81	94
	w/YC6 or YC7	NC	NC
—	**Mirrors** — below eye line		
D44	exterior, black - w/PEG ASA1	45	52
	w/PEG ASA2 or ASA3	NC	NC
D48	exterior, electric remote, black - w/PEG ASA1	129	150
	w/PEG ASA2 or ASA3	84	98
	w/PEG ASA4 or ASA5	NC	NC
—	**Paints, Exterior**		
ZY1	solid	NC	NC
ZY2	custom two-tone - w/o YC6, YC7 or ZL7	283	329
	w/YC6, YC7 or ZL7	89	104
ZY3	special two-tone	148	172
ZY4	deluxe two-tone - w/o YC6 or ZL7	409	476
	w/YC6 or ZL7	216	251
—	**Seating Arrangements**		
ZP5	five passenger seating	NC	NC
ZP7	seven passenger seating - w/PEG ASA1 or ASA2 w/o YC6 or YC7	897	1043
	w/YC6	821	955
	w/YC7	733	852
	w/PEG ASA3 or ASA4 w/o YC6 or YC7	369	429
	w/PEG ASA3 or ASA4 and YC6	271	315
	w/PEG ASA3 or ASA4 and YC7	(22)	(25)
	w/PEG ASA5	NC	NC
ZP8	eight passenger seating - w/o YC7	340	395
	w/YC7	754	877
	w/PEG ASA3 or ASA4	NC	NC
	w/PEG ASA5 w/o YC6 or YC7	(369)	(429)
	w/PEG ASA5 and YC6	(271)	(315)
	w/PEG ASA5 and YC7	22	25
A78	**Seat Back Recliner & Dual Armrests**		
	w/PEG ASA1 or ASA2 w/o ZP7 or YC7	211	245
	w/PEG ASA3, ASA4 or ASA5 or w/ZP7 or YC7	NC	NC
AC3	**Seat, Power** — driver's side only, electric, 6-way control -		
	w/PEG ASA1, ASA2, ASA3 or ASA4	206	240
	w/PEG ASA5	NC	NC

CODE	DESCRIPTION	DEALER	LIST
—	**Seat Trim**		
X4	custom vinyl high back bucket	NC	NC
K4	custom cloth high back bucket	NC	NC
L6	velour cloth reclining bucket	NC	NC
BA8	**Stowage Compartment** — w/PEG ASA1, ASA2 or ASA3	26	30
	w/PEG ASA4 or ASA5	NC	NC
—	**Tires** — tubeless		
QCE	P205/75R15 blackwall	NC	NC
QCF	P205/75R15 white lettered - w/PEG ASA1, ASA2 or ASA3	83	96
	w/PEG ASA4 or ASA5	NC	NC
QCG	P205/75R15 white stripe	62	72
QCU	P215/75R15 blackwall	NC	NC
QCV	P215/75R15 white stripe	52	60
QCM	P215/75R15 white lettered - w/PEG ASA1, ASA2 or ASA3	76	88
	w/PEG ASA4 or ASA5	NC	NC
—	P235/65R15 white outlined letter	NA	NA
Z82	**Trailering Special Equipment** — heavy duty - w/LB4	436	507
	w/L35	266	309
MXO	**Transmission** — 4-speed automatic w/overdrive	NC	NC
—	**Wheels**		
PF3	aluminum - w/PEG ASA1, ASA2, ASA3 or ASA4 w/o YC6 or YC7	292	340
	w/YC6 or YC7 or ZL7 or FE2	213	248
	w/PEG ASA5	NC	NC
ZJ7	rally - w/o YC6 or YC7 or ZL7 or FE2	79	92
	w/YC6 or YC7 or ZL7 or FE2	NC	NC

BERETTA

BERETTA 4 CYL

1LV37	2-Dr Coupe	11236	12415
1LW37/Z04	Z26 2-Dr Coupe	13856	15310
Destination Charge:		485	485

CODE	DESCRIPTION	DEALER	LIST

CHEVROLET

Standard Equipment

BERETTA: Four-wheel anti-lock brake system, power front disc/rear drum brakes, brake/transmission shift interlock (auto trans only), 5-mph bumpers, 2.2 liter MFI L4 engine, stainless steel exhaust, tinted glass, composite halogen headlamps, underhood insulator blanket, black dual remote mirrors, color-keyed bodyside moldings and fascia rub strips, gloss black door and quarter window moldings, basecoat/clearcoat paint, power rack and pinion steering, Level I soft-ride suspension, P185/75R14 BW tires, 5-speed manual transmission, full trunk trim, 14" steel wheels with bolt-on full wheel covers, driver side air bag, air conditioning, center shift console (integral armrest covered storage, lighter, cupholder, ashtray), retractable cupholder in instrument panel, automatic door locks with relock and unlock feature, Scotchgard fabric protector (seats, door trim, floor covering included), rear seat heat ducts, courtesy lamps (dome, under dash, trunk), low oil level light, front door map pockets, radio (electrically tuned AM/FM stereo radio with seek-scan, digital clock, extended range front/rear speakers), headlamps-on reminder, comfort guide rear safety belts, passive front seat belt system, seats (cloth reclining bucket with adjustable head restraints and driver's side 4-way manual seat adjuster), sport steering wheel, LH/RH visors with map straps and passenger side vanity mirror.

Accessories

Code	Description	DEALER	LIST
—	**Beretta Base Equipment Group**	NC	NC
UM6	w/UM6 radio, add	120	140
U1C	w/U1C radio, add	341	396
	incl'd w/model		
—	**Beretta Preferred Equipment Group 1**	142	165
UM6	w/UM6 radio, add	120	140
U1C	w/U1C radio, add	341	396
	incls covered LH & RH visor mirrors, luggage area convenience net, intermittent windshield wiper system, F & R color-keyed carpeted mats w/Scotchgard, day/night rearview mirror w/reading lamps		
—	**Beretta Preferred Equipment Group 2**	641	745
UM6	w/UM6 radio, add	120	140
U1C	w/U1C radio, add	341	396
	incls covered LH & RH visor mirrors, luggage area convenience net, split folding rear seat w/armrest, pwr trunk opener, elect speed control w/resume speed, tilt wheel adjustable steering column, intermittent windshield wiper system, F & R color-keyed carpeted mats w/Scotchgard, day/night rearview mirror w/reading lamps		
—	**Beretta Z26 Base Equipment Group**	NC	NC
U1C	w/U1C radio, add	220	256
	incl'd w/model		
—	**Beretta Z26 Preferred Equipment Group 1**	398	463
U1C	w/U1C radio, add	220	256
	incls tilt wheel adjustable steering column, elect speed control w/resume speed, pwr trunk opener, F & R color-keyed carpeted mats w/Scotchgard		
—	**Interior Trim**		
C2	cloth bucket seats	NC	NC
L2	custom cloth sport bucket seats	NC	NC
—	**Exterior Color** — paint, solid	NC	NC
—	**Engines**		
LN2	2.2 liter MFI L4	NC	NC
L82	3.1 liter SFI V6 (reqs MX0 trans) - w/Coupe	1097	1275
	w/Z26	452	525

CODE	DESCRIPTION	DEALER	LIST
LG0	2.3 liter Quad 4 (H.O.) MFI (reqs MM5 trans)	NC	NC
VK3	**Bracket, Front License Plate**	NC	NC
C49	**Defogger, Rear Window** — electric	146	170
R9W	**Defogger, Rear Window, Delete**	NC	NC
YF5	**California Emissions**	86	100
FE9	**Federal Emissions**	NC	NC
NG1	**New York Emissions**	86	100
K05	**Heater, Engine Block**	17	20
—	**Radio Equipment** — see preferred equip pkgs		
UM6	electronically tuned AM/FM stereo radio w/seek-scan, digital clock, & stereo cass tape, *incls extended range spkrs*		
U1C	electronically tuned AM stereo/FM stereo radio w/seek-scan, digital clock, compact disc player, & Delco Loc II, *incls coaxial front & extended range rear spkrs*		
D52	**Spoiler, Rear** — incl'd w/Z26	95	100
AD3	**Sun Roof** — manual, removable	301	350
—	**Tires**		
QME	P195/70R14 BW	80	93
QIM	P205/60R15 BW (reqs PG1 wheels) (std on Z26)...	151	175
QMS	P205/55R16 BW (reqs PF4 wheels)..	320	372
—	**Transmissions**		
MM5	5-speed manual standard	NC	NC
MX1	3-speed automatic..	477	555
MX0	4-speed automatic (reqs L82 eng)	NC	NC
—	**Wheels**		
PG1	15" steel bolt-on wheel covers .... *(reqs QIM tires) (std on Z26)*	NC	NC
PF4	16" styled aluminum wheels w/locks.. *reqs QMS tires)*	NC	NC
A31	**Windows, Power** — w/driver's express down	237	275
UB3	**Gauge Pkg**... *incls tachometer, trip odometer, voltmeter, oil pressure and temp gauges (std on Z26)*	95	111

CAMARO

CAMARO 6 CYL
Code	Description	Dealer	List
1FP87	2-Dr Coupe	12260	13399

CAMARO 8 CYL
Code	Description	Dealer	List
1FP87/Z28	Z28 2-Dr Coupe	15353	16779
	Destination Charge:	490	490

Standard Equipment

CAMARO: Single serpentine belt accessory drive, 4-wheel anti-lock brake system, brake-transmission shift interlock (auto trans only), front disc/rear drum power brakes (Base only), energy-absorbing front and rear 5-mph bumpers with body color fascias, side window defoggers, stainless steel exhaust system, solar-ray tinted glass, miniquad halogen headlamps, black LH remote/RH manual dual sport mirrors, 2 component clearcoat paint, gas charged front and rear monotube shocks, integral rear spoiler, front and rear stabilizer bars, power rack and pinion steering, firm ride and handling suspension (Base only), 4-wheel coil spring suspension system with computer-selected springs, front short/long arm suspension system (SLA), Pass-Key II theft deterrent system, high pressure compact spare tire, P215/60R16 BW tires (Base only), 5-speed manual transmission (Base only), 16" steel wheels with bolt-on wheel covers (Base only), intermittent wipers, driver and passenger air bag system, full carpeting including cargo area, closeout panel for cargo compartment area, center console with cup holder and lighted storage compartment, Scotchgard fabric protector (includes seat, door trim, floor mats, floor carpeting), front carpeted floor mats, gauge package with tachometer, low oil level indicator system, dome lamp, day/night rearview mirror with dual reclining/courtesy lamps, electrically tuned AM/FM stereo with seek-scan, digital clock, stereo cassette tape, search, repeat, extended range speakers; headlamps-on reminder, driver's side 4-way manual seat adjuster, full folding back rear seat, cloth reclining bucket seats with integral head restraints.

Accessories

Code	Description	Dealer	List
—	**Camaro Coupe Base Equipment Group**	NC	NC
UU8	w/UU8 radio, add	237	275
U1T	w/U1T radio, add	457	531
	incld w/model		

CODE	DESCRIPTION	DEALER	LIST
—	**Camaro Coupe Preferred Equipment Group 1**	1066	1240
UU8	w/UU8 radio, add	237	275
U1T	w/U1T radio, add	457	531
	incls air conditioning, electronic speed control w/resume speed, remote hatch release, fog lamps		
—	**Camaro Coupe Preferred Equipment Group 2**	1751	2036
UU8	w/UU8 radio, add	237	275
U1T	w/U1T radio, add	457	531
	incls air conditioning, electronic speed control w/resume speed, remote hatch release, fog lamps, power windows with driver side express down, power door lock system, sport twin remote electric mirrors, leather-wrapped steering wheel, leather-wrapped transmission shifter and parking brake handle, remote keyless entry with illuminated interior feature		
—	**Z28 Coupe Base Equipment Group**	NC	NC
UU8	w/UU8 radio, add	237	275
U1T	w/U1T radio, add	457	531
	incld w/model		
—	**Z28 Coupe Preferred Equipment Group 1** — w/MN6	1161	1350
	w/MX0	1066	1240
UU8	w/UU8 radio, add	237	275
U1T	w/U1T radio, add	457	531
	incls air conditioning, electronic speed control w/resume feature, remote hatch release, engine oil cooler (w/MN6 only), fog lamps		
—	**Z28 Coupe Preferred Equipment Group 2** — w/MN6	1846	2146
	w/MX0	1751	2036
UU8	w/UU8 radio, add	237	275
U1T	w/U1T radio, add	457	531
	incls air conditioning, electronic speed control with resume speed, remote hatch release, engine oil cooler (w/MN6 only), fog lamps		
—	**Radio Equipment** — see pkgs		
UU8	Delco/Bose music system		
	incls electronically tuned AM/FM stereo radio with seek-scan, stereo cassette tape and digital clock		
U1T	Delco/Bose music system		
	incls electronically tuned AM/FM stereo radio with seek-scan, compact disc player, digital clock and Delco LOC II		
—	**Interior Trim**		
C2	cloth bucket seats	NC	NC
—	**Exterior Color** — paint, solid	NC	NC
—	**Engines**		
L32	3.4 liter SFI V6 - std on Camaro Coupe	NC	NC
LT1	5.7 liter SFI V8 - std on Z28 Coupe	NC	NC
C60	**Air Conditioning**	770	895
GU5	**Axle, Optional** — incls engine oil cooler	95	110
VK3	**Bracket, Front License Plate**	NC	NC
C49	**Defogger** — rear window, electric	146	170
R9W	**Defogger** — rear window, delete	NC	NC
AU3	**Door Lock System, Power** — electric	189	220
YF5	**California Emission Requirements**	86	100
FE9	**Federal Emission Requirements**	NC	NC
NG1	**New York State Emission Requirements**	NC	NC

CODE	DESCRIPTION	DEALER	LIST
B84	**Moldings, Bodyside**	52	60
1LE	**Performance Package**	267	310
	incls engine oil cooler and special handling suspension system		
CC1	**Roof Panels** — removable glass - incls locks	770	895
AC3	**Seat, Power** — driver side only	232	270
—	**Tires**		
QPE	P215/60R16 SBR ply BW - std on Camaro Coupe	NC	NC
QMT	P235/55R16 SBR ply BW - std on Z28 Coupe................................	114	132
QLC	P245/50ZR16 SBR ply BW	124	144
—	**Transmissions**		
MN6	6-speed manual - std on Z28 Coupe......................................	NC	NC
MM5	5-speed manual - std on Camaro Coupe...................................	NC	NC
MXO	4-speed automatic w/overdrive..	512	595
—	**Wheel Trim**		
N96	wheels, aluminum cast 16" - std on Z28 Coupe, incls wheel locks	237	275
QB3	wheels, steel cast 16" - std on Camaro Coupe, incls bolt-on wheel covers ..	NC	NC

CAPRICE CLASSIC

CAPRICE CLASSIC 8 CYL

1BL19	4-Dr Sedan..	16621	18995
1BN19	LS 4-Dr Sedan	18756	21435
1BL35	4-Dr Wagon	18248	20855
Destination Charge:..		575	575

Standard Equipment

CAPRICE: Full wheel covers, stainless steel exhaust system, tinted glass, LH remote/RH manual outside mirrors, wide bodyside moldings, basecoat/clearcoat paint, P215/75R15 BW tires, intermittent windshield wipers, driver and passenger air bag system, air conditioning, cup holders, 4-wheel anti-lock brake system, brake/transmission shift interlock (auto trans only), child security rear door locks, color-keyed front/rear carpeted floor mats, voltmeter and oil pressure gauges, RH covered visor mirror, oil change monitor, trip odometer Pass-Key theft deterrent system, door map pockets, electronically tuned

CODE	DESCRIPTION	DEALER	LIST

AM/FM stereo radio with seek-scan, digital clock, dual front and rear speakers; standard cloth bench seats with center front armrest and adjustable head restraints, Scotchgard fabric protector includes seats, door trim and floor covering; adjustable tilt-wheel steering column, 4-speed automatic transmission, low oil level warning light.

LS SEDAN (in addition to or instead of Caprice equipment): Gold accent (grille, pinstriping), cornering lamps, twin remote electric mirrors, aluminum wheels with locks, luggage area cargo net, power door locks, covered LH visor mirror, illuminated RH visor mirror, power trunk opener, electrically tuned AM/FM stereo radio with seek-scan, stereo cassette tape with auto reverse, digital clock with coaxial front and extended range rear speakers; front and rear compartment courtesy reading lamps, driver's side power seat, standard custom cloth 55/45 seat with center front and rear armrests, adjustable head restraints, driver and passenger seat recliners and seatback pockets; electronic speed control, low fluid warning lights, driver's side power windows with express down.

Accessories

CODE	DESCRIPTION	DEALER	LIST
—	**Caprice Classic Sedan Base Equipment Group**	NC	NC
UM6	w/UM6 radio, add	151	175
U1C	w/U1C radio, add	371	431
	incl w/model		
—	**Caprice Classic Sedan Preferred Equipment Group 1**	820	953
UM6	w/UM6 radio, add	151	175
U1C	w/U1C radio, add	371	431
	incls elect speed control w/resume speed, pwr windows w/driver's express down, elec twin remote mirrors, pwr door lock system, pwr trunk opener		
—	**Caprice Classic Sedan Preferred Equipment Group 2**	1382	1607
U1C	w/U1C radio, add	220	256
	incls pwr windows w/driver's express down, pwr door lock system, elect speed control w/resume speed, elec twin remote mirrors, pwr trunk opener, electronically tuned AM/FM stereo radio w/seek-scan, stereo cass tape w/auto reverse & digital clock, coaxial front & extended range spkrs, 6-way driver's pwr seat, pwr antenna, dual reading lamps in rearview mirror, rear compartment reading lamps, illum RH covered visor mirror		
—	**Caprice Classic LS Sedan Base Equipment Group**	NC	NC
U1C	w/U1C radio, add	220	256
	incl w/model		
—	**Caprice Classic LS Sedan Preferred Equipment Group**	740	860
U1C	w/U1C radio, add	220	256
	incls pwr antenna, auto day/night rearview mirror, pass side 6-way pwr seat, rear window defogger, heated o/s rearview mirrors, remote keyless entry w/trunk release, twilight sentinel headlamp system		
—	**Caprice Classic Wagon Base Equipment Group**	NC	NC
U1C	w/U1C radio, add	220	256
	incl w/model		
—	**Caprice Classic Wagon Preferred Equipment Group 1**	1095	1273
U1C	w/U1C radio, add	220	256
	incls elect speed control w/resume speed, pwr door lock system, tailgate lock, elec twin remote mirrors, driver's side 6-way pwr seat, pwr windows w/driver's express down		
—	**Caprice Classic Wagon Preferred Equipment Group 2**	1846	2146
U1C	w/U1C radio, add	220	256
	incls pwr windows w/express down, pwr door lock system including tailgate, driver's 6-way pwr seat, elect speed control w/resume speed, elec twin remote mirrors, deluxe rear compartment decor, rear window		

	defogger, heated o/s mirrors, pass side 6-way pwr seat, security rear compartment cover, rear compartment reading lamps, pwr antenna, automatic day/night rearview mirror w/dual reading lamps, illuminated RH covered visor mirror		
—	**Interior Trim**		
C1	cloth bench seat	NC	NC
C5	cloth 55/45 seat	192	223
A5	leather 55/45 seat	555	645
F5	custom cloth 55/45 seat (std on Classic LS)	294	342
—	**Exterior Color Paint**		
—	solid	NC	NC
D84	custom two-tone	121	141
	incls lower body accent & door handle inserts		
—	**Engines**		
L99	4.3 liter SFI V8 std	NC	NC
LT1	5.7 liter SFI V8	280	325
—	**Axle, Rear** — limited slip differential		
G80	Sedans	215	250
G80	Wagon	86	100
VK3	**Bracket, Front License Plate**	NC	NC
AP9	**Cargo Convenience Net**	26	30
—	**Defogger, Rear Window** — electric		
X49	w/heated outside mirrors	176	205
C49	w/o heated outside mirrors	146	170
R9W	**Defogger, Rear Window Delete**	NC	NC
AU3	**Door Lock System, Power** — electric		
	Sedans (std on Classic LS)	215	250
	Wagon, incls tailgate lock	280	325
YF5	**California Emissions**	86	100
FE9	**Federal Emissions**	NC	NC
NG1	**New York Emissions**	NC	NC
D90	**Pinstriping** — body side & rear (std on LS)	52	61
—	**Radio Equipment** — see preferred equip pkgs		
UM6	elec tuned AM/FM stereo radio w/seek-scan, stereo cass tape w/auto reverse & digital clock, incls coaxial front/ext range rear spkrs		
U1C	elec tuned AM/FM stereo radio w/seek-scan compact disc player, digital clock & Delco-Loc II, incls coaxial front/ext range rear spkrs		
K34	**Speed Control, Electronic w/Resume Speed**		
—	**Suspension Equipment**		
G67	auto leveling suspension (Classic Wagon only)	151	175
B4U	sport suspension	437	508
F41	ride/handling suspension	42	49
	incls increased cap F & R shock absorbers, F & R springs, rear stabilizer & large front stabilizer bar		
V92	trailering pkg (incls HD cooling)	18	21
N81	**Spare Tire, Full Size** — Classic LS incls aluminum wheel w/QCU or QMU tires		
	Classic Sedan, Classic LS w/N91	52	60
	Classic LS w/o N91	95	110

CHEVROLET

CODE	DESCRIPTION	DEALER	LIST
	w/QCV, QEU, QMV or QNP tires		
	Classic Sedan, Classic LS w/N91, Wagon	56	65
	Classic LS w/o N91	99	115
—	**Tires**		
QCU	P215/75R15 all seasons SBR BW	NC	NC
QCV	P215/75R15 all seasons SBR white stripe	59	80
QNP	P225/70R15 all seasons SBR white stripe	151	176
QEU	P225/75R15 all seasons SBR white stripe (std on Wagon)	NC	NC
QMU	P235/70R15 all seasons SBR BW	NA	NA
QMV	P235/70R15 all seasons SBR white stripe	77	90
N91	**Wheel Covers w/Locks, Wire**		
	Classic LS	(52)	(61)
	Classic Sedan & Wagon only	185	215
PB1	**Deluxe Wheel Covers** — Classic Sedan & Wagon only	60	70
BX3	**Woodgrain Exterior**	512	595

CAVALIER

CAVALIER 4 CYL

CODE	DESCRIPTION	DEALER	LIST
1JC37/WV9	VL 2-Dr Coupe	8359	8845
1JC69/WV9	VL 4-Dr Sedan	8500	8995
1JC35	4-Dr Wagon	10720	11465
1JC37	RS 2-Dr Coupe	10019	10715
1JC69	RS 4-Dr Sedan	10580	11315
1JC67	RS 2-Dr Convertible	15890	16995
CAVALIER 6 CYL			
1JF37	Z24 2-Dr Coupe	12665	13995
1JF67	Z24 2-Dr Convertible	18095	19995
	Destination Charge:	475	475

Standard Equipment

CAVALIER: Brake-transmission shift interlock (auto trans only), 4-wheel anti-lock brake system, 5-mph

CODE	DESCRIPTION	DEALER	LIST

bumpers, 14" bolt-on wheel covers, 2.2 liter MFI L4 engine, composite halogen headlamps, engine compartment hood insulator pad, LH remote/RH manual sport mirror, basecoat/clearcoat paint, power rack and pinion steering, P185/75R14 BW tires, 5-speed transmission, passenger floor and trunk carpeting (Conv, Coupe and Sedan), load floor carpeting (Wagon), cloth reclining front bucket seats with integral head restraints, console with integral armrest, courtesy lamps (glove box, trunk, overhead, rear compartment [Wagon only]), side window defoggers, power door locks with automatic locking/unlocking feature, stainless steel exhaust system, tinted glass, headlamp-on reminder, cupholder, day/night inside rearview mirror, rear seat child safety belt comfort guide, self-aligning steering wheel.

RS COUPE & SEDAN (in addition to or instead of Cavalier equipment): Color-keyed bodyside moldings, body color striping, 3-speed automatic transmission (Coupe), air conditioning, dome/reading lamps, floor mats, dual covered visor mirrors with map straps, mechanical trunk opener, elec tuned AM/FM stereo radio with seek-scan, digital clock and ext range front and rear speakers; passenger seat easy entry (Coupe), sport cloth reclining front bucket seats with integral head restraints, intermittent wipers.

Accessories

Code	Description	Dealer	List
—	**Cavalier VL Base Equipment Group** — 1JC69-1JC37, WV9 only	NC	NC
UM7	w/UM7 radio, add	286	332
UM6	w/UM6 radio, add	406	472
U1C	w/U1C radio, add	626	728
	incld w/model		
—	**Cavalier VL Preferred Equipment Group 1** — 1JC69-1JC37, WV9 only	149	173
UM7	w/UM7 radio, add	286	332
UM6	w/UM6 radio, add	406	472
U1C	w/U1C radio, add	626	728
	incls mechanical trunk opener, intermittent windshield wiper system, dual covered visor mirrors with map straps, bodyside moldings, color-keyed front and rear carpeted floor mats		
—	**Cavalier VL Preferred Equipment Group 2** — 1JC69-1JC37, WV9 only	467	543
UM7	w/UM7 radio, add	286	332
UM6	w/UM6 radio, add	406	472
U1C	w/U1C radio, add	626	728
	incls tilt adjustable steering column, electronic speed control with resume speed, intermittent windshield wiper system, mechanical trunk opener, dual covered visor mirrors with map straps, bodyside molding, color-keyed front and rear carpeted floor mats		
—	**Cavalier Wagon Base Equipment Group** — 1JC35	NC	NC
UM6	w/UM6 radio, add	120	140
U1C	w/U1C radio, add	341	396
	incld w/model		
—	**Cavalier Wagon Preferred Equipment Group 1** — 1JC35	374	435
UM6	w/UM6 radio, add	120	140
U1C	w/U1C radio, add	341	396
	incls tilt adjustable steering column, electronic speed control with resume speed, intermittent windshield wiper system		
—	**Cavalier RS Base Equipment Group 1** — 1JC37-1JC69 only	NC	NC
UM6	w/UM6 radio, add	120	140
U1C	w/U1C radio, add	341	396
	incld w/model		
—	**Cavalier RS Preferred Equipment Group 1** — 1JC37-1JC69 only	318	370
UM6	w/UM6 radio, add	120	140
U1C	w/U1C radio, add	341	396

CODE	DESCRIPTION	DEALER	LIST
	incls electronic speed control with resume speed, adjustable steering column tilt wheel		
—	**Cavalier RS Convertible Base Equipment Group** — 1JC67	NC	NC
UM6	w/UM6 radio, add	120	140
U1C	w/U1C radio, add	341	396
	incld w/model		
—	**Cavalier RS Convertible Preferred Equipment Group 1** — 1JC67	318	370
UM6	w/UM6 radio, add	120	140
U1C	w/U1C radio, add	341	396
	incls adjustable steering column tilt wheel, electronic speed control with resume speed		
—	**Cavalier Z24 Coupe Base Equipment Group** — 1JF37	NC	NC
U1C	w/U1C radio, add	220	256
	incld w/model		
—	**Cavalier Z24 Coupe Preferred Equipment Group 1** — 1JF37	576	670
U1C	w/U1C radio, add	220	256
	incls power windows with express down driver's side, split folding rear seat, luggage area cargo retaining net, electronic speed control with resume speed		
—	**Cavalier Z24 Convertible Base Equipment Group** — 1JF67 only	NC	NC
U1C	w/U1C radio, add	220	256
	incld w/model		
—	**Radio Equipment** — see pkgs		
UM7	radio - see pkgs		
	incls electronically tuned AM/FM stereo radio with seek and scan and digital clock, extended range front and rear speakers		
UM6	radio - see pkgs		
	incls electronically tuned AM/FM stereo radio w/seek-scan, stereo cassette tape and digital clock, extended range front/rear speakers		
U1C	radio - see pkgs		
	incls electronically tuned AM/FM stereo radio w/seek-scan, compact disc player, Delco-Loc II, and digital clock, ext range front and rear speakers		
UL5	radio delete (std on VL models)		
—	**Interior Trim**		
C2	cloth bucket seats (std on VL models)	NC	NC
J2	sport cloth bucket seats (std on Z24, RS and Wagon models only)	NC	NC
V2	vinyl bucket seats - Convertibles only	65	75
—	**Exterior Color** — paint, solid	NC	NC
—	**Engines**		
LN2	2.2 liter MFI L4 (std on all models except Z24 Coupe & Z24 Convertible)	NC	NC
LHO	3.1 liter MFI V6 (std w/Z24 Coupe & Z24 Convertible)	717	834
C60	**Air Conditioning**	675	785
VK3	**Bracket, Front License Plate**	NC	NC
V54	**Carrier** — roof	99	115
C49	**Defogger** — rear window, electric	146	170
K05	**Heater, Engine Block**	17	20
YF5	**California Emission Requirements** — w/LN2 Eng	NC	NC
	w/LHO Eng	86	100
FE9	**Federal Emission Requirements**	NC	NC
NG1	**New York State Emission Requirements** — w/LN2 Eng	NC	NC
	w/LHO Eng	86	100
AM9	**Seat, Rear, Split Folding** — incls cargo area net	155	180

CHEVROLET

CODE	DESCRIPTION	DEALER	LIST
T43	**Spoiler, Rear** — std on Z24 models...	95	110
AD3	**Sunroof** — removable - Z24 Coupe only	301	350
—	**Tires**		
QME	P195/70R14 all-season SBR ply BW	NC	NC
	incld w/LHO Engine on RS and Wagon models only		
QIM	P205/60R15 SBR ply BW	NC	NC
	std on Z24 Coupe & Z24 Convertible		
QIQ	P205/60R15 SBR ply white outline lettered	84	98
—	**Transmissions** — floor-mounted control		
MX1	automatic (std on Wagon and RS Sedan & RS Convertible models)...............	426	495
MM5	5-speed manual (std on VL, RS Coupe & Z24 models).................................	NC	NC
A31	**Windows, Power** — Coupes only	228	265
	Sedans and Wagons	284	330

CORSICA

CORSICA 4 CYL

1LD69 4-Dr Sedan	11896	13145
Destination Charge:..	485	485

Standard Equipment

CORSICA: Four-wheel anti-lock brake system, power front disc/rear drum brakes, brake/transmission shift interlock (auto trans only), 5-mph bumpers, 2.2 liter MFI L4 engine, stainless steel exhaust, tinted glass, black grille, composite halogen headlamps, under hood insulator blanket, dual remote body color outside rearview mirrors, black bodyside moldings and fascia rub strips with narrow black insert, door and window reveal moldings, basecoat/clearcoat paint, smart battery rundown protection, power rack and pinion steering, Level I soft ride suspension, P185/75R14 BW tires, 3-speed automatic transmission, full trunk trim, full bolt-on wheel covers, driver side air bag system, air conditioning, center shift console with integral armrest, covered storage, lighter, cupholder and ashtray; retractable cupholder in instrument panel, automatic door locks with relock and unlock feature, Scotchgard fabric protector (seats, door trim, floor covering), rear seat heat ducts, courtesy lamps (dome, under dash, trunk), delayed entry/exit lighting with theatre dimming, low coolant level light (V6 only), low oil level light, front

CODE	DESCRIPTION	DEALER	LIST

door map pockets, electronically tuned AM/FM stereo radio with seek-scan, digital clock and extended range speakers; headlamps-on reminder, rear comfort guide safety belt, passive front seat belt system, cloth reclining bucket seats with adjustable head restraints and driver's side 4-way manual seat adjuster, LH/RH visors with map straps and passenger side vanity mirror.

Accessories

CODE	DESCRIPTION	DEALER	LIST
—	**Corsica Base Equip Group**	NC	NC
UM6	w/UM6 radio, add	120	140
U1C	w/U1C radio, add	341	396
—	**Corsica Preferred Equipment Group 1**	142	165
UM6	w/UM6 radio, add	120	140
U1C	w/U1C radio, add	341	396
	incls day/night rearview mirror w/reading lamps, covered LH & RH visor mirrors, luggage area convenience net, intermittent windshield wipers, F & R color-keyed carpeted mats w/Scotchgard		
—	**Corsica Preferred Equipment Group 2**	641	745
UM6	w/UM6 radio, add	120	140
U1C	w/U1C radio, add	341	396
	incls elect speed control w/resume speed, day/night rearview mirror w/reading lamps, covered LH & RH visor mirrors, luggage area convenience net, tilt wheel adjustable steering column, split folding rear seat w/armrest, intermittent windshield wipers, pwr trunk opener, F & R color-keyed carpeted mats w/Scotchgard		
C2	**Interior Trim** — cloth bucket seats	NC	NC
—	**Exterior Color** — paint, solid	NC	NC
—	**Engines**		
LN2	2.2 liter MFI L4	NC	NC
L82	3.1 liter SFI V6 (reqs MX0 trans)	619	720
VK3	**Bracket, Front License Plate**	NC	NC
C49	**Defogger, Rear Window** — electric	146	170
R9W	**Defogger, Rear Window, Delete**	NC	NC
YF5	**California Emissions**	NC	NC
FE9	**Federal Emissions**	NC	NC
NG1	**New York Emissions**	86	100
K05	**Heater, Engine Block**	17	20
—	**Radio Equipment** — see preferred equip pkgs		
UM6	elec tuned AM/FM stereo radio w/seek-scan, digital clock & stereo cass tape, incls extended range spkrs		
U1C	elec tuned AM/FM stereo radio w/seek-scan, digital clock, compact disc player, & Delco Loc II, incls coaxial front/ext range spkrs		
QFF	**Tires** — P185/75R14 all-seasons SBR white stripe	58	68
—	**Transmissions**		
MX1	3-speed automatic	NC	NC
MX0	4-speed automatic (reqs L82 eng)	NC	NC
PC4	**Wheels** — 14" styled steel	48	56
A31	**Windows, Power** — w/driver's express down	292	340

CORVETTE

CORVETTE 8 CYL

Code	Description	Dealer	List
1YY07	Coupe	30938	36185
1YY67	Convertible	36731	42960
	Destination Charge:	550	550

Standard Equipment

CORVETTE: Acceleration slip regulation (ASR), Pass-Key II anti-theft system, uniframe design body structure with corrosion-resistant coating, 4-wheel anti-lock brake system, power front/rear disc brake system, brake-transmission shift interlock (auto trans only), 5-mph bumpers, side and rear window defoggers, 5.7 liter SFI V8 engine with aluminum heads, composite valve rocker covers, sequential-port fuel injection, aluminum intake manifold and roller valve lifters, passive keyless entry with remote hatch release, clamshell-opening front-end assembly for easy engine access, solar-ray glass, full-glass rear hatch with two remote releases and roller-shade cargo cover (Coupe), power operated retractable halogen headlamps, distributorless opti-spark ignition system, outside air induction system, acoustic insulation package, halogen fog lamps, front cornering lamps, underhood courtesy lamps, outside dual electrically adjustable heated rearview mirrors, basecoat/clearcoat paint, one-piece removable fiberglass roof panel (Coupe), full-folding roof (Convertible), Bilstein Digressive Valving Monotube shock absorbers, power rack and pinion steering, independent front and rear suspension with transverse fiberglass leaf springs and forged aluminum A-arms, P255/45ZR17 front tires, P285/40ZR17 rear tires, 17 x 8" aluminum front wheels, 17 x 9" aluminum rear wheels, intermittent wipers.

Accessories

Code	Description	Dealer	List
—	**Corvette Coupe Preferred Equipment Group**	1120	1333
U1F	w/U1F radio, add	333	396
	incls elect air conditioning, Delco/Bose music system, electronically tuned AM/FM stereo radio w/seek-scan, stereo cass tape & digital clock, special tone & balance control & 4 spkrs, 6-way pwr driver's seat		
—	**Corvette Convertible Preferred Equipment Group**	1120	1333
U1F	w/U1F radio, add	333	396
	incls elect air conditioning, Delco/Bose music system, electronically tuned AM/FM stereo radio w/seek & scan, stereo cass tape & digital clock, special tone & balance control & 4 spkrs		

CHEVROLET

CODE	DESCRIPTION	DEALER	LIST
—	**Interior Trim**		
A2	leather bucket seats	NC	NC
A8	leather adjustable sport bucket seats	525	625
—	**Exterior Color** — paint solid	NC	NC
LT1	**Engine** — 5.7 liter SFI V8	NC	NC
G92	**Axle, Performance Ratio**	42	50
YF5	**California Emissions**	84	100
FE9	**Federal Emissions**	NC	NC
NG1	**New York Emissions**	84	100
Z07	**Adjustable Handling Pkg**	1718	2045
	incls HD brakes Bilstein adjustable ride control system w/perf oriented calibration, stiffer springs, shocks, stabilizer bars & bushings		
FX3	**Selective Ride & Handling** — electronic	1424	1695
UJ6	**Low Tire Pressure Warning Indicator**	273	325
—	**Radio Equipment** — see preferred equip pkgs		
	incls Delco/Bose music system, electronically tuned AM/FM stereo radio w/seek-scan, stereo cass tape, compact disc player, digital clock, Delco Loc II, special tone & balance control & 4 spkrs		
—	**Roof Panels** — removable		
24S	blue tint, transparent	546	650
64S	bronze tint, transparent	546	650
C2L	dual	798	950
	incls body color-keyed roof panel & 24S or 64S		
CC2	hard top, removable	1676	1995
—	**Seats, Power** — 6-way		
AC3	driver side only	256	305
AC1	passenger side only	256	305
ZR1	**Special Performance Pkg**	26257	31258
	incls 5.7 liter MPFI DOHC 32 valve V8 eng, P315/35ZR-17 tires (rear), 17" x 9.5" front & 17" x 11" rear styled aluminum wheels, HD brake system, side body panels, selective ride & handling pkg, leather adjustable sport seats, 6-way pass & driver pwr seats, elect air conditioning, low tire pressure warning, Delco/Bose gold series music system w/CD & cass player & Solar-Ray glass		
WY5	**Tires, Extended Mobility**	59	70
	P255/45ZR17 BW (front), P285/40ZR17 BW (rear) *reqs UJ6 low tire pressure warning*		
—	**Transmissions**		
MX0	automatic w/overdrive (std)	NC	NC
MN6	6-speed manual	NC	NC

CODE	DESCRIPTION	DEALER	LIST

LUMINA

LUMINA 6 CYL

1WL69	4-Dr Sedan	13392	15305
1WN27/ZV8	Euro 2-Dr Coupe	14766	16875
1WN69/ZV8	Euro 4-Dr Sedan	14451	16515
1WP27/Z34	Z34 2-Dr Coupe	16896	19310
	Destination Charge:	525	525

Standard Equipment

LUMINA: Four-wheel power disc brakes, 5-mph bumpers, deluxe 14" wheel covers, deluxe trunk decor, stainless steel exhaust system, soft body color fascias, tinted glass, body colored grille, composite halogen headlamps, dual horns, dual black sport mirrors (LH remote), bodyside moldings, basecoat/clearcoat paint, Scotchgard fabric protector (seats, door trim, floor covering), lubed-for-life suspension components, independent 4-wheel tuned suspension, P195/75R14 BW tires, 4-speed automatic electronic transmission, intermittent windshield wipers, air conditioning, power door locks with automatic locking feature, panel lamp with delay illumination, auxiliary lighting, color-keyed front/rear floor carpeted mats, RH/LH covered visor mirrors, day/night rearview mirror with integral reading lamps, electronically tuned AM/FM stereo radio with seek-scan, digital clock and extended range front and rear speakers; 60/40 standard cloth seats with center armrest, reclining seatbacks, adjustable head restraints and 4-way manual driver seat adjuster; power steering, self-aligning steering wheel, tilt-wheel adjustable steering column.

EURO COUPE & SEDAN (in addition to or instead of Lumina equipment): Four-wheel anti-lock brake system, rear spoiler, ride and handling suspension, P205/70R15 BW radial tires, 15" aluminum wheels, electronically tuned AM/FM stereo radio with seek-scan, digital clock, stereo cassette tape and extended range front and rear speakers; standard custom cloth 60/40 seat with center storage armrest, reclining seatbacks, adjustable head restraints and 4-way manual driver seat; power windows (Coupe).

Accessories

—	Lumina Base Equipment Group	NC	NC
UM6	w/UM6 radio, add	120	140
UU8	w/UU8 radio, add	409	475

CODE	DESCRIPTION	DEALER	LIST
U1C	w/U1C radio, add	341	396
	incl w/model		
—	**Lumina Preferred Equipment Group 1**	679	790
	w/o deck-lid carrier (Sedan)	581	675
	w/UM6 radio, add	120	140
	w/UU8 radio, add	409	475
	w/U1C radio, add	341	396
	incls pwr windows, comfortilt steering wheel, pwr trunk opener, luggage area cargo retaining net, blk deck-lid carrier, twin remote sport mirrors		
—	**Lumina Euro Base Equipment Group**	NC	NC
UU8	w/UU8 radio, add	288	335
U1C	w/U1C radio, add	220	256
	incl w/model		
—	**Lumina Euro Preferred Equipment Group 1** — Coupe	383	445
	Sedan	667	775
UU8	w/UU8 radio, add	288	335
U1C	w/U1C radio, add	220	256
	incls pwr windows (std on Coupe), elect speed control w/resume speed, pwr trunk opener, gauge pkg w/tachometer, twin remote sport mirrors, luggage area cargo retaining net		
—	**Lumina Euro 3.4 Preferred Equipment Group 1**	667	775
UU8	w/UU8 radio, add	288	335
U1C	w/U1C radio, add	220	256
	incls gauge pkg w/tachometer, pwr windows, elect speed control w/resume speed, pwr trunk opener, twin remote sport mirrors, luggage area cargo retaining net		
—	**Lumina Z34 Base Equipment Group**	NC	NC
UU8	w/UU8 radio, add	288	335
U1C	w/U1C radio, add	220	256
—	**Interior Trim**		
C3	cloth 60/40 seat	NC	NC
F2	custom cloth bucket seat w/console	43	50
F3	custom cloth 60/40 seat w/ctr storage armrest	77	90
L2	custom cloth bucket seat w/console - Z34 Coupe & 3.4 Euro Sedan only	NC	NC
—	**Exterior Color** — paint, solid	NC	NC
—	**Engines**		
LH0	3.1 liter MFI V6	NC	NC
LQ1	3.4 liter MFI V6 - Z34 Coupe & 3.4 Euro Sedan only	NC	NC
BYP	**3.4 Euro Sedan Pkg**	1183	1376
VK3	**Bracket, Front License Plate**	NC	NC
JL9	**Brakes, Four Wheel Anti-Lock**	387	450
V56	**Carrier, Deck Lid** — black	99	115
UV8	**Cellular Telephone Provision**	39	45
C49	**Defogger, Rear Window** — electric	146	170
R9W	**Defogger, Rear Window Delete**	NC	NC
YF5	**California Emissions**	86	100
FE9	**Federal Emissions**	NC	NC
NG1	**New York Emissions**	NC	NC
—	**Radio Equipment** — see preferred equip pkgs		
UM6	elec tuned AM/FM stereo radio w/seek-scan, stereo cass tape &		

CODE	DESCRIPTION	DEALER	LIST
	digital clock, incls ext range F & R spkrs		
UU8	Delco/Bose sound system, elec tuned AM/FM stereo radio w/seek-scan, stereo cass tape & digital clock		
UIC	elec tuned AM/FM stereo radio w/seek-scan, compact disc player & digital, *incls extended range F & R spkrs & Delco-Loc II*		
WG1	**Seat, Power** — 6-way control - driver's side only	232	270
K34	**Speed Control, Electronic w/Resume Speed**	194	225
D58	**Spoiler, Rear Delete**	(110)	(128)
—	**Tires**		
QMX	P195/75R14 all-seasons SBR white stripe	62	72
QPE	P215/60R16 all-seasons SBR BW	96	112
—	**Transmissions** — automatic w/overdrive	NC	NC
NW0	**Wheels** — 16" aluminum - Euro only	NC	NC
P03	**Wheel Covers, Sport** — 14"	NC	NC

LUMINA MINIVAN

LUMINA MINIVAN 6 CYL

1UM06	Minivan	15218	16815
Destination Charge:		530	530

Standard Equipment

LUMINA MINIVAN: 3.1 liter EFI V6 engine, 3-speed automatic transmission, integrated roof antenna, power front disc/rear drum brakes, 4-wheel anti-lock brake system, accent color front/rear/rocker moldings (body color - LS trim), sliding side door, stainless steel exhaust system, tinted glass, solar-ray windshield, liftgate handle, composite halogen headlamps, one-piece rear liftgate, LH remote/RH manual black painted fold-away mirrors, basecoat/clearcoat paint, body color pillars, roof and windshield; compact spare tire with underbody spare tire carrier, power rack and pinion steering, independent front suspension with MacPherson struts, P205/70R15 BW tires, bolt-on wheel covers, rear wiper/washer, intermittent windshield wipers, driver side air bag system, forward instrument panel carpeting, full floor carpeting, lockable center storage console with permanently mounted cup holders, front and rear color-keyed carpeted floor mats, lamps (glove box, ashtray, front and rear reading, footwell, sliding door, tailgate), auxiliary lighting, rear auxiliary power outlet, electronically tuned AM/FM stereo radio with seek feature, digital clock, coaxial front and extended range rear speakers; Scotchgard fabric protector (seats, door trim, floor covering), cloth highback reclining bucket seats with adjustable head restraints and driver's side 4-way manual seat adjuster.

Accessories

Code	Description	Dealer	List
—	**Lumina Minivan Base Equipment Group**	NC	NC
UM6	w/UM6 radio, add	120	140
U1C	w/U1C radio, add	341	396
	incld w/model		
—	**Lumina Minivan Preferred Equipment Group 1**	669	778
UM6	w/UM6 radio, add	120	140
U1C	w/U1C radio, add	341	396
	incls air conditioning, electric twin remote fold-away mirrors, power door/tailgate locks with side door delay, electronic speed control with resume speed, adjustable steering column tilt wheel		
—	**Lumina Minivan Preferred Equipment Group 2**	1998	2323
U1C	w/U1C radio, add	220	256
	incls air conditioning, electronically tuned AM/FM stereo with seek feature, digital clock, stereo cassette tape, coaxial front and extended range rear speakers; luggage area cargo convenience net, power windows with driver's express down, power door/tailgate locks with side door delay, electronic speed control with resume speed, adjustable steering column tilt wheel, electric fold-away twin remote mirrors, electric rear window defogger, deep tinted glass, remote keyless entry, 7-passenger seating		
—	**Lumina Minivan Preferred Equipment Group 3**	2445	2843
U1C	w/U1C radio, add	220	256
	incls electronically tuned AM/FM stereo with seek feature, digital clock, stereo cassette tape, coaxial front and extended range rear speakers, power windows with driver's express down, power door/tailgate locks with side door delay, luggage area cargo convenience net, electronic speed control with resume speed, electric fold-away twin remote mirrors, air conditioning, adjustable steering column tilt wheel, electric rear window defogger, deep tinted glass, remote keyless entry, 7-passenger seating, LS trim package, driver side power seat with 6-way adjuster		
—	**Radio Equipment** — see pkgs		
UM6	radio	NA	NA
	incls elec tuned AM/FM stereo radio w/seek feature, digital clock, stereo cassette tape, coaxial front and extended range rear speakers		
U1C	radio	220	256
	incls elec tuned AM/FM stereo radio w/seek-scan, digital clock, compact disc player, Delco-Loc II, coaxial front and ext range rear speakers		
—	**Interior Trim**		
C2	cloth bucket seat - std	NC	NC
F2	custom cloth bucket seats	NC	NC
—	**Exterior Color** — paint, solid	NC	NC
D84	custom two-tone	127	148
—	**Engines**		
LG6	3.1 liter EFI V6	NC	NC
L27	3.8 liter SFI V6	532	619
C67	**Air Conditioning**	714	830

CODE	DESCRIPTION	DEALER	LIST
C34	**Air Conditioning** — front & rear, w/PEG WPA2 or WPA3	387	450
VK3	**Bracket, Front License Plate**	NC	NC
V54	**Carrier, Roof**	125	145
C49	**Defogger** — rear window, electric	146	170
E58	**Door, Power Sliding**	254	295
YF5	**California Emission Requirements**	NC	NC
FE9	**Federal Emission Requirements**	NC	NC
NG1	**New York State Emission Requirements**	NC	NC
AUO	**Entry, Keyless, Remote**	108	125
AJ1	**Glass, Deep Tinted**	211	245
KO5	**Heater, Engine Block**	17	20
AB5	**Locks, Power** — door & tailgate	258	300
AP9	**Lug0gage Area, Cargo Convenience Net**	26	30
DD9	**Mirrors, Twin Remote Fold-Away, Electric**	67	78
AG9	**Seat, Power** — driver's side only, electric 6-way control	232	270
AD9	**Seats, Child** — integral	194	225
—	**Seating Arrangements**		
ZP5	five-passenger seating	NC	NC
	incls two front bucket seats & three pasgr bench seat - also incls seat belts		
ZP7	seven-passenger seating	568	660
	incls two front bucket seats & five modular rear seats - also incls seat belts		
K34	**Speed Control, Electronic w/Resume Speed**	194	225
C54	**Sunroof, Manual, Non-Removable**	258	300
G67	**Suspension, Load Leveling**	146	170
N33	**Tilt-Wheel, Adjustable Steering Column**	125	145
—	**Tires**		
XIN	P205/70R15 touring radial BW	30	35
P42	self-sealing option (req's XIN tires)	129	150
NW9	**Traction Control**	301	350
V92	**Trailering Package**	275	320
—	**Transmissions**		
MX1	3-speed automatic	NC	NC
MXO	4-speed automatic	172	200
PH3	**Wheels** — aluminum cast, w/locks 15"	237	275
A31	**Windows, Power w/Driver's Express Down**	237	275

CONCORDE

CONCORDE 6 CYL

LP414-Dr Sedan..	17053	19457
Destination Charge:	525	525

Standard Equipment

CONCORDE: Manual air conditioning w/non CFC refrigerant, floor console (cupholder, rear heat/AC ducts, armrest, covered storage), power decklid release, rear child protection door locks, stainless steel exhaust system with aluminized coating, two-tone fascias wit bright insert, front and rear floor mats, three folding grab handles, bright grille, woodgrain instrument panel accents, interior lamps (front reading/courtesy, rear courtesy, four door with fade-off and time out), luggage compartment cargo net, message center (warning lamps - door ajar, trunk ajar, low washer fluid, two traction control [when equipped], ABS), dual covered visor mirrors, dual power foldaway heated outside mirrors, full bodyside cladding with bright insert, AM/FM cassette ETR stereo radio with six speakers, electric rear window defroster, bucket front seats with manual driver lumbar support and seatback map pockets, contoured rear seat with center armrest, Premium cloth seat trim, speed control, tilt steering column, compact spare tire, ride-biased tires and touring suspension, four "Prototec" wheel covers, speed-sensitive intermittent windshield wipers/washers with fluidic high-volume washer nozzles, 3.3 liter SMPI V6 engine, 4-speed automatic transmission, power assisted rack and pinion steering, power 4-wheel anti-lock disc brakes.

Accessories

B	**Pkg B**	507	596
	incls power door locks, illuminated dual visor vanity mirrors, power windows with one-touch-down feature		
C	**Pkg C**	1042	1226
	incls Pkg B contents plus air conditioning with auto temp control, 8-way power driver's seat, remote/illuminated entry group		
D	**Pkg D**	1998	2350
	incls power door locks, power windows with one-touch-down feature, air conditioning with auto temp control, 8-way power driver's seat, remote/illuminated entry group, full overhead console, mirror (rearview		

CODE	DESCRIPTION	DEALER	LIST
	with auto day/night feature), Chrysler Infinity radio with spatial imaging cassette sound system, security alarm, speed sensitive steering with variable power assist		
EGE	**Engine** — 3.5L 24V OHC V6 - w/Pkg C or D	616	725
CFK	**Child Seat** — integrated	85	100
NAE	**California Emissions**	87	102
NBY	**New York Emissions**	87	102
NHK	**Engine Block Heater** — available in Alaska only	17	20
GWA	**Power Moonroof** — w/Pkg C	930	1094
	w/Pkg D	609	716
	incls mini overhead console and auto day/night mirror		
—	**Radio Equipment**		
ARA	Chrysler Infinity spatial imaging cassette sound system - w/Pkg C	602	708
	incls AM/FM ETR radio with seek-scan, cassette player, 5-band graphic equalizer, 120 watt 8 channel amplifier, 11 Infinity speakers, instructional tape, rear mounted power antenna		
ARB	Chrysler Infinity spatial imaging compact disc sound system		
	w/Pkg C	745	877
	w/Pkg D	144	169
	incls AM/FM ETR radio with seek-scan, compact disc player, 5-band graphic equalizer, 120 watt 8 channel amplifier, 11 Infinity speakers, instructional CD, rear mounted power antenna		
AJF	**Remote/Illuminated Entry Group** — w/Pkg B	188	221
JPV	**Seat** — 8-way power driver side - w/Pkg B	320	377
JPR	**Seats** — 8-way power driver & passenger - w/Pkg B	641	754
	w/Pkg C or D	320	377
LSA	**Security Alarm** — w/Pkg C	127	149
TRR	**Tire** — conventional spare	81	95
BNM	**Traction Control** — w/Pkg C or D	149	175
AGC	**16" Wheel & Handling Group** — w/Pkg B or C	534	628
	w/Pkg D	445	524
	incls 16" touring tires, 16" "Spiralcast" aluminum wheels		
CUN	**Full Overhead Console** — w/Pkg C	321	378
	incls compass/temp/trip computer, garage door opener and sunglass storage compartment, dual illuminated visor vanity mirrors (NA w/GWA)		
—	**Paint** — special color or metallic	82	97
—	**Seats** — cloth front buckets, rear bench	STD	STD
—	**Seats** — cloth front 50/50 split bench, rear bench .... NA w/Pkg D	NC	NC
—	**Seats** — leather front buckets, rear bench - w/Pkg D	909	1069
	incls 8-way power seats, leather steering wheel and shift knob (NA w/Pkg B or CFK)		

LE BARON GTC CONVERTIBLE

LE BARON GTC CONVERTIBLE 6 CYL

CH27	GTC 2-Dr Convertible		15939	16999
Destination Charge:			530	530

Standard Equipment

LE BARON CONVERTIBLE: Air conditioning, soft fascia bumpers with 5-mph protection, chimes (seat belt warning, key-in-ignition, headlights-on, turn signal cancel), center console (transmission selector, ash receiver with light, hand brake, covered storage, convertible top switch, armrest), power convertible top, electric rear window defroster, stainless steel exhaust system, dual exhaust tips, GTC exterior decor (body color grille, fascias, bodyside moldings with accent color inserts, GTC graphics, body color door handles, gloss black decklid and taillight applique, accent color "Triad" wheel covers), tinted glass, exposed aero-style headlights with time delay, lamps (door courtesy with time out feature, ignition with time delay, trunk, glove box, rear floor courtesy, two rear view mirror reading/courtesy), message center (low washer fluid, deck lid ajar, door ajar), radio (AM/FM stereo cassette with digital clock, seek, Dolby, four speakers), lowback reclining cloth bucket front seats, cloth fixed-bench rear seat, road touring suspension, four accent color "Triad" wheel covers, power door and quarter windows, deluxe windshield wipers/washers with intermittent wipe, power rack and pinion steering, power assisted front disc/rear drum brakes, 3.0 liter SMPI V6 engine, 4-speed automatic transmission.

Accessories

Code	Description	Dealer	List
T	**Pkg T**	850	1000
	incls deluxe convenience group, power convenience group, remote decklid release, 6-way pwr driver seat, F & R floor mats		
W	**Pkg W**	1700	2000
	incls pkg T contents plus leather seating, leather-wrapped steering wheel, light group & 15" cast aluminum "Cathedral" design wheels		
BR1	**Brakes** — anti-lock	594	699
AJK	**Deluxe Convenience Group**	316	372
	incls elect speed control & tilt steering wheel		
AJW	**Power Convenience Group**	287	338
	incls auto pwr door locks, body color pwr heated o/s mirrors		
ASW	**Bright "LX" Decor Group** — NA w/AY4	43	50
	incls bright grille, bright pentastar medallion & nameplates, body color bodyside molding w/bright insert, 15" "Conclave" design wheel covers		

CHRYSLER

CODE	DESCRIPTION	DEALER	LIST
NAE	**California Emissions**	87	102
NBY	**New York Emissions**	87	102
ADA	**Light Group** — w/pkg T		
	>incls illuminated entry & illuminated visor vanity mirrors		
LET	**Mini-Trip Computer** — w/pkg T or W....................................	79	93
RAY	**Radio** — w/pkg T or W...	445	524
	incls AM/FM stereo w/cassette, equalizer, clock & 6 Infinity spkrs		
RBC	**Radio** — w/pkg T or W...	590	694
	incls AM/FM stereo w/CD player, equalizer, clock & 6 Infinity spkrs		
LSA	**Security Alarm** — w/pkg T or W..	127	149
AY4	**16" Aluminum Wheel/Performance Group** - w/pkg T	439	516
	w/pkg W	160	188
	incls performance handling susp'n, P205/55R16 all season performance LBL SBR tires, 16" cast aluminum "spiralcast" design wheels [NA w/ASW]		
WJE	**Wheels** — 15" cast aluminum "Cathedral" design - w/pkg T.....	279	328
—	**Paint** — special color or metallic	82	97
—	**Seats** — NA w/pkg W	STD	STD
	incls cloth frt buckets, rear bench		
—	**Seats** — w/pkg T...	87	102
	incls vinyl frt buckets, rear bench		
—	**Seats** — w/pkg T...	568	668
	incls leather frt buckets w/6-way pwr driver seat & rear bench		
—	**Seats** — w/pkg T...	928	1092
	w/pkg W	360	424
	incls prem leather frt bucket seats w/12-way pwr driver seat, rear bench		

LE BARON SEDAN

LE BARON SEDAN 4 CYL
CM41/22P LE 4-Dr Sedan 13625 15121
incls 2.5 liter 4 cylinder engine, 3-speed automatic transmission

LE BARON SEDAN 6 CYL
CM41/26U LE 4-Dr Sedan 14869 16551
incls 3.0 liter V6 engine, 3-speed auto trans, air cond, remote decklid
release, power door locks, heated dual outside power remote mirrors

CM41/28U LE 4-Dr Sedan 15016 16724
incls 3.0 liter V6 engine, 4-speed auto trans, air cond, remote decklid
release, power door locks, heated dual outside power remote mirrors

CM41/28X LE 4-Dr Sedan 15560 17363
incls 3.0 liter V6 engine, 4-speed automatic transmission, air conditioning,
remote decklid release, power door locks, heated dual outside power
remote mirrors, radio (AM/FM stereo with cassette and clock), handling
suspension, P205/60R15 BSW SBR tires, 15" cast aluminum wheels

CP41 Landau 4-Dr Sedan.. 16072 17933
incls 3.0 liter V6 engine and 4-speed automatic transmission

Destination Charge: 505 505

Standard Equipment

LE BARON—LE SEDAN: Air conditioning, soft fascia bumpers with integral nerf and 5-mph protection,
warning chimes (headlights on, seat belt, key in ignition), electric rear window defroster, power door

CODE	DESCRIPTION	DEALER	LIST

locks, stainless steel exhaust system, front/rear carpeted floor mats, tinted glass, locking glove box, bright grille, single halogen aero style headlights, counter balanced inside hood release, dual electric horn, premium sound insulation, lamps (ash receiver, glove box, trunk, dome, map, underhood, cigarette lighter, ignition key with time delay), message center (low washer fluid, door ajar, deck ajar, headlight out, taillight out, stoplight out), dual visor mirrors, dual power heated bright outside mirrors, moldings (bright wheel lip and lower bodyside, narrow body color bodyside, grooved molded quartz lower bodyside cladding), radio (AM/FM stereo ETR with digital clock, seek and four speakers), 50/50 split bench front seats with dual recliners and folding armrests, 55/45 split-back folding rear seats, "Sexton" cloth seat trim, electronic speed control, tilt steering column, remote trunk release, four "Preceptor" wheel covers, power windows, deluxe windshield wipers/washers with intermittent wipe, 3.0 liter SMPI V6 engine, 3-speed auto trans, power rack and pinion steering, power front disc/rear drum brakes.

LE BARON—LANDAU SEDAN (in addition to or instead of LE Sedan equipment): Landau vinyl roof, mounted courtesy door lamps, AM/FM stereo ETR radio with cassette, digital clock, seek, Dolby and four speakers; seatback map pockets and adjustable driver lumbar support, fixed rear bench seat with folding center armrest, "Kimberly" cloth seat trim, four white sidewall tires, 4-speed auto transmission.

Accessories

CODE	DESCRIPTION	DEALER	LIST
L	**Pkg L** — Landau..	646	760
	incls overhead console, interior illumination group, leather-wrapped		
	steering wheel, wire wheel covers		
BR1	**Brakes** — 4-wheel anti-lock disc..	594	699
	NA on LE CM41/26U model		
JPS	**Driver Seat** — power...	260	306
	NA on LE CM41/22P model		
ADM	**Electronic Display Group** — Landau.....................................	269	317
	incls electronic instrument cluster, mini trip computer		
NAE	**California Emissions**	87	102
NBY	**New York Emissions**	87	102
AJN	**Interior Illumination Group**	166	195
	incls illuminated entry, dual illuminated visor vanity mirrors		
RAS	**Radio** — LE	145	170
	incls AM/FM stereo w/cassette and clock		
RAY	**Radio** — LE 26U & 28U models	442	520
	LE 28X model	298	350
	Landau	298	350
TBB	**Tire** — conventional spare - LE 26U & 28U models	81	95
	Landau	81	95
TKJ	**Tires** — LE 26U & 28U models..	62	73
	incls P195/70R14 all-season WSW SBR		
W4L	**Wire Wheel Covers** — Landau	204	240
—	**Paint** — special or metallic	82	97
—	**Seats** — LE...	STD	STD
	incls cloth front buckets, rear folding split bench seat		
—	**Seats** — LE...	NC	NC
	incls cloth frt 50/50 bench, rear split flg bench (NA on LE CM41/22P mdl)		
—	**Seats** — Landau	STD	STD
	incls cloth front 50/50 bench, rear bench		
—	**Seats** — Landau	828	974
	incls leather front 50/50 bench, rear bench, 6-way power driver's seat and		
	leather steering wheel		

LHS

LHS 6 CYL
CP41 4-Dr Sedan 26491   30283
Destination Charge: 585   585

Standard Equipment

LHS: Air conditioning with automatic temperature control, passenger and driver air bags, 4-wheel disc brakes with anti-lock brake system, traction control, floor console, mini overhead console with compass, temp, 5-function trip computer, power decklid release, power door locks, door trim with leather bolsters, map pockets, stainless steel exhaust system with dual chrome outlets, front and rear floor mats, "projector" style fog lamps, driver's left foot rest, folding grab handles, body color grille, illuminated entry system, instrument cluster (speedometer, tachometer, fuel gauge, temp gauge, odometer, trip odometer), leather steering wheel and shift knob, luggage compartment cargo net, dual illuminated visor mirrors, heated foldaway dual power outside mirrors, bodyside molding with bright insert, Chrysler/Infinity radio with spatial imaging cassette sound system, power antenna, electric rear window defroster, remote keyless entry system, premium leather bucket seats with manually adjustable driver lumbar support, contoured leather rear seat with center armrest, 8-way power passenger's and driver's seat with power recliner, tinted glass, premium sound insulation, speed control, tilt steering column, power sunroof, dual sunvisors with sliding extension, conventional spare tire, full trunk dress-up, 16" aluminum "spiralcast" wheels (4), speed sensitive intermittent windshield wipers with high volume washers, 3.5 liter V6 EFI SOHC 24-valve engine, 4-speed overdrive automatic transmission, front wheel drive, P225/60R16 SBR touring BW tires.

Accessories

NAE	**California Emissions**	87	102
NBY	**New York Emissions**	87	102
P	**Paint** — extra cost	82	97
FZ	**Seats** — premium cloth front buckets	NC	NC
RBC	**Radio**	144	169
	incls Chrysler/Infinity spatial imaging sound system, AM/FM ETR stereo radio with compact disc player, 11 Infinity speakers, 5-band graphic equalizer, rear-mounted power antenna		
NHK	**Engine Block Heater** — available in Alaska only	17	20

CHRYSLER

NEW YORKER

NEW YORKER 6 CYL

	DEALER	LIST
CH41 4-Dr Sedan	21310	24294
Destination Charge:	585	585

Standard Equipment:

NEW YORKER: Manual air conditioning, passenger and driver air bags, 4-wheel disc brakes with anti-lock brake system, power door locks, two-tone door trim, map pockets, stainless steel exhaust system with dual outlets, front and rear floor mats, driver's left foot rest, folding grab handles, bright grille, rear heater ducts, instrument cluster (speedometer, tachometer, fuel gauge, temperature gauge, odometer, trip meter), luggage compartment cargo net, dual illuminated visor mirrors, heated foldaway dual power outside mirrors, full length bodyside molding with bright insert, AM/FM ET stereo radio with cassette and 6 speakers, electric rear window defroster, premium cloth 50/50 split bench seats with dual arm rests and manually adjustable driver lumbar support, contoured rear seat with center armrest, 8-way power driver's seat, tinted glass, premium sound insulation, speed control, tilt steering column, dual sunvisors with sliding extension, full trunk dress-up, power trunk lid release, 15" "Prototec" wheelcovers (4), speed sensitive intermittent windshield wipers with high volume washers, 3.5 liter V6 EFI SOHC 24-valve engine, power assisted rack and pinion steering, P205/70R15 SBR all season BSW tires, T135/80D15 compact spare tire, front wheel drive.

Accessories

CODE	DESCRIPTION	DEALER	LIST
NAE	**California Emissions**	87	102
NBY	**New York Emissions**	87	102
TBB	**Conventional Spare Tire**	81	95
P	**Paint** — extra cost	82	97
BNM	**Traction Control**	149	175
JP	**Seats**	914	1075
	incls 50/50 split front bench seat, 8-way pwr driver and passenger, leather-faced rear bench seat, leather-wrapped steering wheel [req 26B or 26C quick order pkg]		
RBC	**Radio**	144	169

CHRYSLER

CODE	DESCRIPTION	DEALER	LIST
	incls Chrysler/Infinity spatial imaging system, AM/FM stereo radio, compact disc player, 11 Infinity speakers, 5-band graphic equalizer, rear mounted pwr antenna [req 26B or 26C quick order pkg]		
26B	**Quick Order Pkg 26B**	932	1097
	incls automatic air conditioning, mini overhead console, illuminated keyless remote control entry system, AM/FM ETR stereo w/cassette, graphic equalizer, pwr antenna and 11 speakers		
26C	**Quick Order Pkg 26C**.........................	1893	2227
	incls quick order pkg 26B + leather seat trim, leather-wrapped strng whl, traction control, conventional spare tire and dual 8-way pwr seat adjusters		
AGC	**Wheel & Handling Group**........................	445	524
	incls 16" spiralcast aluminum wheels, P225/60R16 SBR touring BW tires, touring suspension [req 26B or 26C quick order pkg]		

TOWN & COUNTRY

TOWN & COUNTRY 6 CYL

YP53	FWD Wagon..	24612	27184
CP53	AWD Wagon..	26456	29280
	Destination Charge:.....................................	560	560

Standard Equipment

TOWN & COUNTRY: Front and rear air conditioning, lower bodyside and sill body color applique with bright nerf, headlamps on/seat belt/key in ignition chimes, forward storage console with coin holder, overhead console with compass, outside temperature, 4-function trip computer, front and rear reading lamps; cup holders, rear window electric defroster, power door locks, front and rear body color fascias with bright nerf, floor mats, fog lights, sunscreen glass (side, quarter, rear window), tinted glass (front doors, windshield), locking glove box, rear heater, inside hood release, dual horns, illuminated entry system, padded instrument panel with wood tone bezels, deluxe body sound insulation, remote keyless entry, power liftgate release, automatic time delay headlights, lamps (front door courtesy and rear dome

CHRYSLER

with time out feature, ignition switch with time delay, headlight switch, ash receiver, liftgate, underhood, glove box), roof-mounted luggage rack, heated dual power remote control body color outside mirrors, right and left illuminated visor mirrors, AM/FM stereo ETR radio with cassette, graphic equalizer, seek and scan, clock and four Infinity amplified speakers; front reclining bucket seats with adjustable head rests, leather and cloth trim seats, power 6-way driver seat, Quad command reclining buckets (2) with tilting right seat and 3-passenger quick release rear bench, electronic speed control, tilt steering column, leather-wrapped steering wheel, storage compartments, conventional spare tire (underslung with cable winch), four cast aluminum "Spiralcast" wheels, front door and rear quarter vent power windows, side and sliding door vented windows, windshield and rear window wiper/washer with intermittent wipe, woodgrain bodyside and liftgate moldings, 3.8 liter SMPI V6 engine, 4-speed automatic transmission, power assisted rack and pinion steering, power front disc/rear drum brakes.

Accessories

CODE	DESCRIPTION	DEALER	LIST
Y	**Woodgrain Delete Pkg Y** .... *incls gold stripe & gold painted aluminum wheels*	NC	NC
NAE	**California Emissions**	87	102
NBY	**New York Emissions**	87	102
GAC	**Tinted Glass**	NC	NC
NHK	**Engine Block Heater** - avail in Alaska only - FWD Wagon	29	34
CYK	**Seating Group** — 7-pass w/integrated child seat	NC	NC
RBC	**Radio** .... *incls AM/FM stereo w/CD player, graphic equalizer, clock & 6 Infinity spkrs*	145	170
TPC	**Tires** — P205/70R15 WSW SBR	59	69
AHT	**HD Trailer Tow Group** .... *incls 120 amp alternator, 685 amp battery, HD brakes, flasher, radiator, susp'n trailer tow wiring harness*	230	270
WJ6	**Wheels** — cast aluminum, gold - w/o pkg Y	NC	NC
WJ7	**Wheels** — cast aluminum, white - w/pkg Y	NC	NC
—	**Seats** — cloth/leather low back buckets (NA w/CYK).................................	STD	STD
—	**Seats** — leather low back buckets..	NC	NC
—	**Paint** — special color or metallic	82	97

CARAVAN FWD

CARAVAN FWD 4 CYL
KL52   Base 13541   14819

CARAVAN FWD 6 CYL
KH52   SE 16374   18039
KP52   LE 19739   21863
KP52   ES 20187   22372

Destination Charge: 560   560

Standard Equipment

CARAVAN FWD - BASE: Chimes (headlights on, seat belt, key in ignition), cupholders, child protection side door locks, stainless steel exhaust system, front and rear body color fascias with accent nerf, tinted glass, inside hood release, single horn, body sound insulation, front/rear dome lamps, fold away exterior aero manual mirrors, non-illuminated visor mirrors, AM/FM stereo ETR radio with digital clock, seek and four speakers; five-passenger seating, quick release intermediate and rear seats, driver and passenger highback reclining bucket seats, molded deluxe cloth seat trim, underbody spare tire carrier with cable winch, electronic speed control, storage compartments, compact spare tire, four "Virgo" wheel covers, vented side/quarter/sliding door windows, liftgate window wipers/washers with fixed intermittent wipe, 2-speed windshield wipers with variable intermittent wipe.

SE (in addition to or instead of Base equipment): Dual horn, power liftgate release, power fold away exterior aero black mirrors, bodyside accent color (2 colors) moldings, AM/FM stereo ETR radio with cassette, seek, Dolby and four speakers, seven-passenger seating, tilt steering column, four "Triad" wheel covers.

LE (in addition to or instead of SE equipment): Front air conditioning, front storage console with coin holder, overhead console (compass, outside temperature, 4-function trip computer, front and rear reading lights), electric rear window defroster, power front and side door locks, front and rear body color fascias, floor mats, automatic time delay headlights, deluxe body sound insulation, remote keyless entry, front dome lamp deleted, map and liftgate lamps, light group (ash receiver, front map/reading [header mounted], glove box, ignition switch [time delayed], rear cargo dome, underhood, illuminated entry system, liftgate-mounted dual floodlights), roof luggage rack, heated power foldaway exterior aero black mirrors, illuminated visor mirrors, driver and passenger reclining bucket seats, luxury cloth molded seat trim, power quarter vent windows, lower bodyside and sill accent color cladding.

DODGE

CODE	DESCRIPTION	DEALER	LIST

Accessories

Code	Description	Dealer	List
T	**Base Family Value Pkg T**	181	213
	incls air conditioning, dual horns, accent color bodyside molding, under front passenger seat storage drawer, power liftgate release, map and cargo lighting enhancements		
B	**SE Family Value Pkg B**..	181	213
	incls air cond, map and cargo lighting enhancements, rear window defroster		
D	**SE Family Value Pkg D**..	985	1159
	incls air conditioning, map and cargo lighting enhancements, rear window defroster, forward and overhead consoles, power door locks, floor mats, gauges (oil pressure, voltage and tachometer), deluxe insulation, light group, power rear quarter vent windows		
K	**Two Tone Pkg K — LE**	260	306
	incls power driver seat, power windows, radio (AM/FM with cassette, equalizer and six Infinity speakers), sunscreen glass		
M	**"ES" Pkg M — ES**	366	431
	incls power driver's seat, power windows, radio (AM/FM with cassette, equalizer and six Infinity speakers), sunscreen glass, sport handling group, "ES" decor group		
HAA	**Climate Group I — Base**	728	857
	incls air conditioning		
AAA	**Climate Group II — w/family value pkg**.....................................	352	414
	incls air conditioning and sunscreen glass [NA w/ASK]		
AJK	**Convenience Group I — Base w/Pkg T**	316	372
	incls speed control and tilt		
AAC	**Convenience Group II — Base w/Pkg T**	590	694
	SE w/Pkg B	225	265
	incls speed control and tilt, power mirrors and power door locks		
AAD	**Convenience Group III — SE w/Pkg B**.......................................	572	673
	SE w/Pkg D..	347	408
	incls speed control and tilt, power mirrors, power door locks, power windows and keyless remote entry		
CYE	**Seating Group I — 7-passenger seating - Base**	294	346
CYK	**Seating Group II — 7-passenger seating w/integrated child seat - Base**	485	570
	SE, LE, ES	191	225
CYS	**Seating Group III — 7-passenger quad command - SE, LE, ES**	507	597
CYT	**Seating Group IV — 7-passenger convert-a-bed - SE, LE, ES**	470	553
TBB	**Loading & Towing Group I**..	93	109
	incls conventional spare		
AAE	**Loading & Towing Group II — Base w/Pkg T**.............................	151	178
	SE, LE...	151	178
	w/AAG (SE w/Pkg B or D, LE w/Pkg K, ES).................................	124	146
	incls conventional spare tire and firm ride heavy load suspension		
AAF	**Loading & Towing Group III — SE w/Pkg B or D**	473	556
	w/ASH (SE w/Pkg B or D)	376	442
	LE w/Pkg K	376	442
	w/AAG or ASK (SE w/Pkg B or D, LE w/Pkg K, ES)	349	410
	incls conven'l spare tire, firm ride heavy load suspension & trailer tow grp		
WJV	**Wheels I — 15" aluminum wheels - LE w/Pkg K**.........................	309	363
AAG	**Sport Handling Group — SE w/Pkg B or D (NA w/ASK)**	203	239

CODE	DESCRIPTION	DEALER	LIST
	LE w/Pkg K (incls WJV)	415	488
—	**Radio Equipment**		
RAS	radio - Base	145	170
	incls AM/FM stereo with cassette, clock & four speakers		
RCE	Infinity speaker system - SE	172	202
RBC	radio - SE w/Pkg D	426	501
	incls AM/FM stereo with CD player, equalizer, clock and six Infinity speakers		
BRL	**Brakes** — anti-lock - SE w/Pkg B or D	584	687
	w/AAF, AAG, ASH, ASK or WJV (SE w/Pkg B or D)	509	599
	LE, ES	509	599
ASH	**Gold Special Edition Decor Group** — SE w/Pkg B or D	213	250
	incls gold badging, 15" front disc/rear drum brakes, gold day light opening accent stripe, bodyside body color molding, P205/70R15 BSW SBR tires, 15" cast aluminum "Lace" wheels with gold accents		
ASK	**Sport Wagon Decor Group** — SE w/Pkg B or D	638	750
	incls accent color fascias with black rub strips, fog lights, leather-wrapped steering wheel, sunscreen glass, sport handling group, 15" cast aluminum 5-spoke wheels		
—	**Paint** — special color or metallic	82	97
—	**Seats** — leather lowback buckets - LE	735	865
	ES	735	865
GFA	**Rear Window Defroster** — SE	143	168
JPB	**Power Door Locks** — Base w/Pkg T	225	265
NAE	**California Emissions**	87	102
NBY	**New York Emissions**	87	102
NHK	**Engine Block Heater** — available in Alaska only	29	34
MWG	**Luggage Rack**	122	143
TLB	**Tires** — Base w/Pkg T, SE w/Pkg B or D	122	143
	incls P205/70R14 WSW SBR tires (NA w/AAF, AAG, BRL, ASH or ASK)		
TPC	**Tires** — SE w/Pkg B or D, LE w/Pkg K	59	69
	incls P205/70R15 WSW SBR tires (req's BRL or AAF on SE models; NA w/AAG, ASH or ASK)		
EDM	**Engine** — 2.5L EFI 4 cylinder - Base	STD	STD
EFA	**Engine** — 3.0L MPI V6 - SE, LE, ES	STD	STD
EGA	**Engine** — 3.3L MPI V6 - SE, LE, ES	87	102
DDM	**Transmission** — 5-speed manual - Base	STD	STD
DGA	**Transmission** — 3-speed automatic - Base	511	601
	SE, LE	STD	STD
DGB	**Transmission** — 4-speed automatic - Base	679	799
	SE, LE	168	198
	ES	STD	STD

DODGE

CODE	DESCRIPTION	DEALER	LIST

GRAND CARAVAN FWD

GRAND CARAVAN FWD 6 CYL

Code	Description	Dealer	List
KL53	Base	16434	18078
KH53	SE	17425	19204
KP53	LE	20574	22783
KP53	ES	21022	23292
	Destination Charge:	560	560

Standard Equipment

GRAND CARAVAN FWD - BASE: Chimes (headlights on, seat belt, key in ignition), cupholders, child protection side door locks, stainless steel exhaust system, front and rear body color fascias with accent nerf, tinted glass, single horn, body sound insulation, front/rear dome lamps, fold away exterior aero manual mirrors, non-illuminated visor mirrors, AM/FM ETR stereo radio with digital clock, seek and four speakers; seven-passenger seating, quick release intermediate and rear seats, driver and passenger highback reclining bucket seats, deluxe cloth molded seat trim, underbody spare tire carrier with cable winch, electronic speed control, compact spare tire, four "Triad" wheel covers, vented side/quarter/sliding door windows, liftgate window wipers/washers with fixed intermittent wipe, 2-speed wipers with variable intermittent wipe.

SE (in addition to or instead of BASE equipment): Dual horn, power liftgate release, power fold away exterior aero black mirrors, bodyside accent color (2 colors) moldings, AM/FM ETR stereo radio with cassette, seek, Dolby, four speakers; tilt steering column, storage compartments.

LE (in addition to or instead of SE equipment): Front air conditioning, lower bodyside and sill accent color cladding, front storage console with coin holder, overhead console (compass, outside temperature, 4-function trip computer, front and rear reading lights), electric rear window defroster, power front and side door locks, front and rear body color fascias, floor mats, automatic time delay headlights, deluxe body sound insulation, remote keyless entry, front dome lamps deleted, map and liftgate lamps, light group (ash receiver, front map/reading [header mounted], glove box, ignition switch [time delayed], rear cargo dome, underhood, illum entry system, liftgate-mounted dual floodlights), roof luggage rack, heated power fold away exterior aero black mirrors, illum visor mirrors, bodyside accent color moldings deleted, driver and passenger reclining bucket seats, molded luxury cloth seat trim, power quarter vent windows.

CODE	DESCRIPTION	DEALER	LIST

Accessories

CODE	DESCRIPTION	DEALER	LIST
T	**Base Family Value Pkg T**	181	213
	incls air conditioning, dual horns, bodyside accent color molding, under front passenger seat storage drawer, power liftgate release, map and cargo lighting enhancements		
B	**SE Family Value Pkg B**	181	213
	incls air cond, map, cargo lighting enhancements, rear window defroster		
D	**SE Family Value Pkg D**	985	1159
	incls air conditioning, map and cargo lighting enhancements, rear window defroster, forward and overhead consoles, power door locks, floor mats, gauges (oil pressure, voltage, tachometer), deluxe insulation, light group, illuminated visor vanity mirror, power rear quarter vent windows		
K	**Two-Tone Pkg K** — LE	260	306
	incls power driver seat, power windows, radio (AM/FM w/cassette, equalizer and six Infinity speakers), sunscreen glass		
L	**Woodgrain Pkg L** — LE	818	962
	incls power driver seat, power windows, radio (AM/FM w/cassette, equalizer and six Infinity speakers), sunscreen glass, woodgrain group		
M	**"ES" Pkg M** — ES	366	431
	incls power driver seat, power windows, radio (AM/FM w/cassette, equalizer and six Infinity speakers), sunscreen glass, sport handling group, "ES" decor group		
HAA	**Climate Group I** — Base	728	857
	incls air conditioning		
AAA	**Climate Group II** — w/family value pkg	352	414
	incls air conditioning and sunscreen glass [NA w/ASK]		
AAB	**Climate Group III** — Base w/Pkg T	840	988
	SE w/Pkg B	840	988
	SE w/Pkg D	748	880
	w/ASK (SE w/Pkg B)	488	574
	w/ASK (SE w/Pkg D)	396	466
	w/AAF (SE w/Pkg B)	786	925
	w/AAF (SE w/Pkg D)	695	818
	w/ASK & AAF (SE w/Pkg B)	434	511
	w/ASK & AAF (SE w/Pkg D)	343	404
	LE w/Pkg K or L, ES	396	466
	w/AAF (LE w/Pkg K or L, ES)	343	404
	incls air cond, sunscreen glass, rear heat/air conditioning		
AJK	**Convenience Group I** — Base w/Pkg T	316	372
	incls speed control and tilt		
AAC	**Convenience Group II** — Base w/Pkg T	590	694
	SE w/Pkg B	225	265
	incls speed control and tilt, power mirrors/power door locks		
AAD	**Convenience Group III** — SE w/Pkg B	572	673
	SE w/Pkg D	347	408
	incls speed control and tilt, power mirrors, power locks, power windows and keyless entry		
CYK	**Seating Group I** — 7-passenger seating w/integrated child seat - Base	191	225
CYS	**Seating Group II** — 7-passenger quad command - SE, LE, ES	507	597
CYT	**Seating Group IV** — 7-passenger convert-a-bed - SE, LE, ES	470	553
TBB	**Loading & Towing Group I**	93	109

DODGE

CODE	DESCRIPTION	DEALER	LIST
	incls conventional spare		
AAE	**Loading & Towing Group II** — Base w/Pkg T	151	178
	SE, LE	151	178
	w/AAG (SE w/Pkg B or D, LE w/Pkg K or L, ES)	124	146
	incls conventional spare tire and firm ride heavy load suspension		
AAF	**Load & Towing Group III** — SE w/Pkg B or D	376	442
	LE w/Pkg K or L	376	442
	w/AAG or ASK (SE w/Pkg B or D, LE w/Pkg K or L, ES)	349	410
	incls conventional spare tire, firm ride heavy load suspension and trailer tow group		
WJV	**Wheels I** — 15" aluminum wheels - LE w/Pkg K	309	363
AAG	**Sport Handling Group** — SE w/Pkg B or D (NA w/ASK)	106	125
	LE w/Pkg L (NA w/ASK)	106	125
	LE w/Pkg K (incls WJV)	415	488
—	**Radio Equipment**		
RAS	radio - Base	145	170
RCE	Infinity speaker system - SE w/Pkg B or D	172	202
RBC	radio - SE w/Pkg D	426	501
	LE w/Pkg K or L, ES	145	170
	incls AM/FM stereo w/CD player, equalizer, clock and 6 Infinity spkrs		
BRL	**Brakes** — anti-lock - SE w/Pkg B or D	509	599
	LE, ES	509	599
ASH	**Gold Special Edition Decor Group** — SE w/Pkg B or D	213	250
	incls gold badging, gold day light opening accent stripe, bodyside body color molding, 15" cast aluminum "Lace" wheel with gold accents		
ASK	**Sport Wagon Decor Group** — SE w/Pkg B or D	638	750
	incls accent color fascias with black rub strips, fog lights, leather-wrapped steering wheel, sunscreen glass, sport handling group, 15" cast aluminum 5-spoke wheels		
GFA	**Rear Window Defroster** — Base, SE	143	168
JPB	**Power Door Locks** — Base w/Pkg T	225	265
NAE	**California Emissions**	87	102
NBY	**New York Emissions**	87	102
NHK	**Engine Block Heater** — available in Alaska only	29	34
MWG	**Luggage Rack**	122	143
TPC	**Tires** — Base w/Pkg T	59	69
	SE w/Pkg B or D	59	69
	LE w/Pkg K or L	59	69
	incls P205/70R15 WSW SBR tires (NA w/AAG, ASH or ASK)		
—	**Paint** — special color or metallic	82	97
—	**Seats** — cloth highback buckets - Base, SE	STD	STD
—	**Seats** — cloth lowback buckets - LE, ES	STD	STD
—	**Seats** — leather lowback buckets (NA w/CYK) - LE, ES	735	865
EFA	**Engine** — 3.0L MPI V6 - Base	STD	STD
EGA	**Engine** — 3.3L MPI V6 - SE, LE, ES	STD	STD
EGH	**Engine** — 3.8L MPI V6 - LE, ES	257	302
DGA	**Transmission** — 3-speed automatic - Base	STD	STD
DGB	**Transmission** — 4-speed automatic - Base	168	198
	SE, LE, ES	STD	STD

DODGE

GRAND CARAVAN AWD

GRAND CARAVAN AWD 6 CYL

CODE	DESCRIPTION	DEALER	LIST
DH53	SE	19781	21882
DP53	LE	22930	25460
DP53	ES	23378	25969
	Destination Charge:	560	560

Standard Equipment

GRAND CARAVAN AWD - SE: Chimes (headlights on, seat belt, key in ignition), cupholders, child protection side door locks, stainless steel exhaust system, front and rear body color fascias with accent nerf, tinted glass, dual horn, body sound insulation, power liftgate release, front/rear dome lamps, power fold away exterior aero black mirrors, non-illuminated visor mirrors, accent color (2 colors) bodyside moldings, AM/FM ETR stereo radio with cassette, seek, Dolby and four speakers; seven-passenger seating, quick release intermediate and rear seats, driver and passenger highback reclining bucket seats, deluxe cloth molded seat trim, underbody spare tire carrier with cable winch, electronic speed control, tilt steering column, storage compartments, compact spare tire, four "Triad" wheel covers, vented side/quarter/sliding door windows, liftgate window wipers and washers with fixed intermittent wipe, 2-speed wipers with variable intermittent wipe.

LE (in addition to or instead of SE equipment): Front air conditioning, lower bodyside and sill accent color cladding, front storage console with coin holder, overhead console (compass, outside temperature, 4-function trip computer, front and rear reading lights), electric rear window defroster, power front and side door locks, front and rear body color fascias, floor mats, automatic time delay headlights, deluxe body sound insulation, remote keyless entry, front dome lamps deleted, map and liftgate lamps, light group (ash receiver, front map/reading [header mounted], glove box, ignition switch [time delayed], rear cargo dome, underhood, illuminated entry system, liftgate-mounted dual floodlights), roof luggage rack, heated power fold away exterior aero black mirrors, illum visor mirrors, accent color bodyside moldings deleted, driver and passenger reclining bucket seats, molded luxury cloth seat trim, power quarter vent windows.

Accessories

B	**SE Family Value Pkg B**	985	1159
	incls air cond, map/cargo lighting enhancements, rear window defroster		

DODGE

CODE	DESCRIPTION	DEALER	LIST
D	**SE Family Value Pkg D**...	985	1159
	incls air conditioning, map and cargo lighting enhancements, rear window defroster, forward and overhead consoles, deluxe insulation, floor mats, gauges (oil pressure, voltage and tachometer), illuminated visor vanity mirrors, light group, power door locks, power rear quarter vent windows		
K	**Two-Tone Pkg K** — LE..	260	306
	incls power driver's seat, power windows, radio (AM/FM stereo w/cassette, equalizer, clock and 6 speakers), sunscreen glass		
L	**Woodgrain Pkg L** — LE...	818	962
	incls power windows, power driver's seat, radio (AM/FM stereo w/cassette, equalizer, clock and 6 speakers), sunscreen glass, woodgrain group		
M	**"ES" Pkg M** — ES..	260	306
	incls power driver's seat, power windows, radio (AM/FM stereo w/cassette, equalizer, clock and 6 speakers), "ES" decor group		
AAC	**Convenience Group I** — SE w/Pkg B..	225	265
	incls power mirrors and power locks		
AAD	**Convenience Group II** — SE w/Pkg B......................................	572	673
	SE w/Pkg D..	347	408
	incls power mirrors, power locks, power windows/keyless remote entry		
AAA	**Climate Group I** — SE w/Pkg B or D.......................................	352	414
	incls sunscreen glass		
AAB	**Climate Group II** — SE w/Pkg B	840	988
	SE w/Pkg D..	748	880
	w/ASK (SE w/Pkg B)...	488	574
	w/ASK (SE w/Pkg D)...	396	466
	w/AAF (SE w/Pkg B)...	786	925
	w/AAF (SE w/Pkg D)...	695	818
	w/ASK & AAF (SE w/Pkg B)..	434	511
	incls sunscreen glass and rear heater/air conditioning		
CYK	**Seating Group II** — 7-passenger seating w/integrated child seat	191	225
CYS	**Seating Group III** — 7-passenger quad command	507	597
CYT	**Seating Group IV** — 7-passenger convert-a-bed........................	470	553
TBB	**Loading & Towing Group I**...	93	109
	incls conventional spare tire		
AAF	**Loading & Towing Group II** — SE w/Pkg B or D	317	373
	LE w/Pkg K or L, ES..	317	373
	incls conventional spare tire and heavy duty trailer tow group		
—	**Radio Equipment**		
RCE	Infinity speaker system - SE w/Pkg B or D	172	202
RBC	radio - SE w/Pkg D	426	501
	LE w/Pkg K or L, ES..	145	170
	incls AM/FM stereo w/CD player, graphic equalizer, clock/6 Infinity spkrs		
ASH	**Gold Special Edition Decor Group** — SE w/Pkg B or D	213	250
	incls gold badging, gold day light opening accent stripe, bodyside body color moldings, 15" cast aluminum "Lace" wheels with gold accents [NA w/ASK]		
ASK	**Sport Wagon Decor Group** — SE w/Pkg B or D.........................	638	750
	incls accent color fascias with black rub strip, fog lights, leather-wrapped steering wheel, sunscreen glass, P205/70R15 all-season touring LBL SBR tires, 15" cast aluminum 5-spoke wheels		
GFA	**Rear Window Defroster** — SE	143	168

CODE	DESCRIPTION	DEALER	LIST
NAE	**California Emissions**	87	102
NBY	**New York Emissions**	87	102
NHK	**Engine Block Heater** — available in Alaska only	29	34
MWG	**Luggage Rack**	122	143
TPC	**Tires** — SE w/Pkg B or D	59	69
	LE w/Pkg K or L 59	69	
	incls P205/70R15 WSW SBR (NA w/ASH or ASK)		
WJV	**Wheels** — 15" cast aluminum - LE w/Pkg K	309	363
EGA	**Engine** — 3.3L MPI V6	STD	STD
EGH	**Engine** — 3.8L MPI V6 - LE w/Pkg K or L, ES	257	302
—	**Seats** — cloth highback buckets - SE	STD	STD
—	**Seats** — cloth lowback buckets - LE, ES	STD	STD
—	**Seats** — leather lowback buckets - LE, ES	735	865
	NA w/CYK		
—	**Paint** — special color or metallic	82	97

1993 COLT
NOTE:Information for the 1994 Colt models was unavailable at time of publication.

1993 COLT 4 CYL

DE21	Base 2-Dr Sedan	7705	8039
DL21	GL 2-Dr Sedan	8343	8741
DL41	Base 4-Dr Sedan	9140	9597
DH41	GL 4-Dr Sedan	9992	10580
	Destination Charge:	430	430

Standard Equipment

COLT - 2 DR: 75 amp alternator, front armrests, power assisted front disc/rear drum brakes, 5-mph bumper system, passenger compartment carpeting, center floor console with armrest and storage, side window demisters, stainless steel exhaust system, gauges include: temperature / fuel / speedometer/odometer; flush aero-style halogen headlights, molded cloth headliner, inside hood release, single note horn, lights include: dome/variable intensity panel; warning lights include: oil pressure/brakes/seat belts/door ajar/parking brake/check engine/alternator/automatic transmission indicator; 1.5 liter 4-cylinder engine, 5-speed manual transmission, black side window opening moldings, manual rack and pinion type steering, 2-spoke steering wheel, strut-type independent front suspension with coil springs, multi-link rear suspension with coil springs, vinyl mat trunk trim, 2-speed windshield wipers, gray bumpers, black outside door handles, vinyl door/quarter trim, floor instrument cluster illumination, outside left manual mirror, high-back vinyl bucket reclining front seats, low-back vinyl rear bench seat, four argent styled steel wheels, four bright center cap wheel covers.

GL 2 DR (in addition to or instead of BASE 2 DR equipment): One assist grip, color-keyed bumpers, cigarette lighter, dual sliding instrument panel cupholder, color-keyed door handles, cloth and vinyl door/quarter trim with map pockets, trip odometer gauge with push button reset, back lighting instrument cluster illumination, remote dual manual outside mirrors, passenger side visor mirror (uncovered), bodyside color-keyed moldings, reclining cloth-face bucket front seats with adjustable head restraints, low-back cloth-face rear bench seat, split-folding rear seat, rear seat passenger side easy entry, full wheel covers.

COLT - 4 DR: 75 amp alternator, front and rear armrests, three assist grips, power-assisted front disc/rear drum brakes, 5-mph color-keyed bumper system, passenger compartment carpeting, center floor console with armrest storage, dual sliding instrument panel cupholder, side window demisters, child protection door locks, cloth and vinyl door/quarter trim with map pockets, stainless steel exhaust system, gauges include: temperature/fuel/speedometer/odometer/trip odometer with push-button reset; rear seat heater ducts, flush aero-style halogen headlights, molded cloth headliner, inside hood release, back lighting instrument cluster illum, lights include: dome/variable intensity panel; warning for: oil pressure/brakes/seat belts/door ajar/parking brake/check engine/alternator/automatic trans indicator; 5-speed manual transmission, black side window opening moldings, manual rack and pinion type steering, strut-type independent front suspension w/coil springs, multi-link rear suspension w/coil springs, carpeted mat trunk trim, 2-speed windshield wipers, black outside door handles, single note horn, outside left manual mirror, 1.5 liter 4-cylinder engine, reclining cloth-face front bucket seats w/adjust\-able head restraints, low-back cloth-face rear bench seat, 2-spoke steering wheel, half wheel covers.

GL 4 DR (in addition to or instead of BASE 4 DR equipment): Lower sill and bumper accent, cigarette lighter, color-keyed door handles, remote fuel-filler door release, tachometer gauge (manual trans. only), dual note horn, low fuel/trunk warning light; remote outside dual manual mirrors, covered driver side visor mirror, uncovered passenger side visor mirror, 1.8 liter 4-cylinder engine, color-keyed bodyside moldings, reclining full-cloth front bucket seats with adjustable head restraints, split-folding full-cloth rear bench seat with center armrest, driver's seat tilt/height control, 3-spoke luxury soft-feel steering wheel, semi-sport suspension with front sway bar and gas-pressure shocks, remote trunk release with over-ride feature, side trunk trim, full wheel covers, fixed-time intermittent windshield wipers.

Accessories

—	**Value Pkgs** — Base 2-Dr		
B	**Pkg B** — Base 2-Dr	57	66
	incls rear window defroster		
C	**Pkg C** — Base 2-Dr	344	400
	incls rear window defroster, tinted glass, AM/FM radio w/clock & 4 speakers		
—	**Value Pkgs** — Base 4-Dr		
B	**Pkg B** — Base 4-Dr	57	66
	incls rear window defroster		
C	**Pkg C** — Base 4-Dr	738	858
	incls rear window defroster, 4-door convenience group 1, floor mats, tinted		

DODGE

CODE	DESCRIPTION	DEALER	LIST
	glass, bodyside moldings, AM/FM stereo radio w/clock & 4 speakers, power steering		
D	**Pkg D** — Base 4-Dr	501	582
	incls rear window defroster, 4-door convenience group 1, floor mats, tinted glass, black bodyside moldings, AM/FM radio w/clock & 4 speakers, full wheel covers		
—	**Value Pkgs** — GL 2-Dr		
G	**Pkg G** — GL 2-Dr	NC	NC
	incls rear window defroster, tinted glass, AM/FM radio w/clock & 4 spkrs		
H	**Pkg H** — GL 2-Dr	1099	1278
	incls rear window defroster, tinted glass, 2-door convenience group, air conditioning, AM/FM radio w/cassette, clock & 4 speakers; power steering		
K	**Pkg K** — 2-Dr	1570	1826
	incls rear window defroster, tinted glass, 2-door convenience group, air conditioning, AM/FM radio w/cassette, clock & 4 speakers; power steering, sport appearance pkg		
—	**Value Pkgs** — GL 4-Dr		
G	**Pkg G** — GL 4-Dr	1242	1444
	incls air conditioning, rear window defroster, 4-door convenience group 2, floor mats, tinted glass, AM/FM radio w/cassette, clock & 4 speakers; power steering		
H	**Pkg H** — GL 4-Dr	1570	1826
	incls air conditioning, rear window defroster, 4-door convenience group 2, floor mats, tinted glass, AM/FM radio w/cassette, clock & 4 speakers; power steering, power locks, power windows		
K	**Pkg K** — GL 4-Dr	1576	1832
	incls air conditioning, rear window defroster, 4-door convenience group 2, floor mats, tinted glass, AM/FM radio w/cassette, clock & 4 speakers; power steering, sport appearance group		
L	**Pkg L** — GL 4-Dr	1990	2314
	incls air cond, rear window defroster, 4-door convenience group 2, floor mats, tinted glass, AM/FM radio w/cass, clock & 4 speakers; power steering, power door locks, power windows, sport appearance group		
HAA	**Air Conditioning** — std on GL 4-Dr	679	790
MJC	**Moldings** — bodyside, gray - Base 2-Dr	46	54
NAE	**California Emissions**	NC	NC
RAT	**Radio** — AM/FM w/clock & 4 speakers - Base	233	271
RAW	**Radio** — AM/FM w/cassette, clock & 4 speakers - Base 4-Dr, GL 2-Dr	156	181
AJB	**Brakes** — 4-wheel anti-lock - GL 4-Dr	829	964
EJA	**Engine** — 1.8L 4-cylinder MPI - Base 4-Dr	324	377
DGA	**Transmission** — 3-speed automatic - GL 2-Dr	445	518
DGB	**Transmission** — 4-speed automatic - Base 4-Dr	603	701
	GL 4-Dr	551	641

DODGE

INTREPID

INTREPID 6 CYL

DH41	Base 4-Dr Sedan	15163	17251
DP41	ES 4-Dr Sedan	16812	19191
	Destination Charge:	525	525

Standard Equipment

INTREPID: Manual air conditioning, floor console (cupholders, rear seat heater/AC ducts, covered storage, armrest), rear child protection door locks, stainless steel exhaust system with aluminized coating, body color fascias, tinted glass side windows, solar control glass windshield and rear window, interior lamps (two front reading/courtesy, two rear courtesy, two with fade-off and time out), gloss black dual exterior manual remote mirrors, dual covered visor mirrors, functional bodyside protection moldings, AM/FM ETR stereo radio with seek and four speakers, electric rear window defroster, cloth front bucket seats, rear bench seats, tilt steering column, compact spare tire, all-season tires, touring suspension, four "Flying V" wheel covers, speed sensitive intermittent windshield wipers/washers, 3.3 liter SMPI V6 engine, 4-speed automatic transmission, power front disc/rear drum brakes, power assisted rack and pinion steering.

ES (in addition to or instead of Intrepid equipment): Unique two-tone or body color fascias, fog lights, front and rear floor mats, four door courtesy interior lamps, luggage compartment cargo net, warning lamps (door ajar, trunk ajar, low washer fluid, two traction control (when equipped), ABS (when equipped), ground effect bodyside cladding, AM/FM stereo radio with cassette player and six speakers, premium style and fabric front seats with manual lumbar adjustment and upgraded door trim, rear contoured bench seat with center armrest, speed control, power trunk lid release, four "Extender" aluminum wheels, touring tires, speed proportional power steering, power 4-wheel disc brakes.

Accessories

CODE	DESCRIPTION	DEALER	LIST
EGB	**Engine** — 3.3L MPI V6	STD	STD
EGE	**Engine** — 3.5L 24V OHC V6 - Base w/pkg D	616	725
	ES w/pkg L or M	616	725
DGB	**Transmission** — 4-spd auto	STD	STD

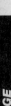

CODE	DESCRIPTION	DEALER	LIST
C	**Pkg C** — Base	757	891
	incls F & R floor mats, speed control, pwr door locks, radio (AM/FM stereo w/cass, clock & 6 spkrs), pwr windows w/one-touch-down feature		
	Pkg D — Base	1405	1653
	incls pkg C contents plus 4 wheel disc brakes, pwr remote decklid release, 8-way pwr driver's seat, message center, heated dual o/s pwr remote mirrors, illuminated dual visor vanity mirrors, 3 pass assist handles		
L	**Pkg L** — ES	1078	1268
	incls pwr door locks, 8-way pwr driver's seat, heated dual o/s pwr remote mirrors, illuminated dual visor vanity mirrors, 3 pass assist handles, remote/illuminated entry group, leather-wrapped steering wheel, pwr windows w/one-touch-down feature		
M	**Pkg M** — ES	2564	3016
	incls pkg L contents plus air conditioning w/auto temp control, anti-lock brakes, full overhead console, auto day/night rearview mirror, Chrysler Infinity spatial imaging cass sound system, security alarm, conventional spare tire		
HAB	**Air Conditioning w/Auto Temp Control** — ES w/pkg L	129	152
BRT	**Brakes** — anti-lock - Base, Base w/pkg C	530	624
	Base w/pkg D	509	599
	ES..	509	599
CFK	**Child Seat** — integrated	85	100
CUN	**Console** — full overhead - Base w/pkg D.......................	252	296
	ES w/pkg L	321	378
	GWA NA w/ES model		
JPC	**Power Decklid Release** — Base w/pkg C	52	61
AJP	**Convenience Group** — power - ES...............................	581	684
	incls pwr door locks, heated dual o/s pwr remote mirrors, pwr windows w/one-touch-down feature		
NAE	**California Emissions**	87	102
NBY	**New York Emissions**	87	102
NHK	**Engine Block Heater** — avail in Alaska only	17	20
GWA	**Power Moonroof** — Base w/pkg D...............................	860	1012
	ES w/pkg L (NA w/CUN)	930	1094
	ES w/pkg m	609	716
	incls mini overhead console		
AWT	**Performance Handling Group** — ES w/pkg L or M	184	217
	incls 16" performance tires & performance susp'n [reqs BRT, TBB & BNM]		
RAS	**Radio** — Base..	170	200
	incls AM/FM stereo w/cass, clock & 6 spkrs		
ARA	**Radio** — Base w/pkg D..	602	708
	ES w/pkg L	602	708
	incls AM/FM ETR stereo w/seek/scan, cass player w/fast forward, rewind & auto reverse, DNR, 5-band graphic equalizer, 120 watt 8 channel amplifier, 11 Infinity spkrs, clock, instructional tape, rear mounted pwr antenna		
ARP	**Radio** — Base w/pkg D..	745	877
	ES w/pkg L	745	877
	ES w/pkg M	144	169
	incls AM/FM ETR stereo radio w/seek/scan, integral compact disc player, 5-band graphic equalizer, 120 watt 8 channel amplifier, 11 Infinity speakers, clock, instructional CD, rear mounted pwr antenna		
JPR	**Seat** — 8-way power driver & pass - ES w/pkg L or M............	320	377

DODGE

CODE	DESCRIPTION	DEALER	LIST
LSA	**Security Alarm** — ES w/pkg L... *reqs HAB*	127	149
AJF	**Remote/Illuminated Entry Group** — Base w/pkg D	188	221
NHM	**Speed Control** — Base...	190	224
TBB	**Tire** — conventional spare	81	95
AGC	**16" Wheel & Handling Group** — Base w/pkg C or D................................ *incls 16" polycast "Polystar" wheels, 16" touring tires, variable assist spd* *proportional steering*	343	404
BNM	**Traction Control** — ES w/pkg L or M .... *reqs BRT*	149	175
—	**Seats** — Base.. *incls cloth frt buckets, rear bench*	STD	STD
—	**Seats** — Base.. *incls cloth frt 50/50 bench, rear bench*	NC	NC
—	**Seats** — ES .... *incls cloth frt buckets, rear bench w/center armrest*	STD	STD
—	**Seats** — ES w/pkg L or M... *incls leather faced frt buckets, rear bench w/center armrest (incls driver &* *pass 8-way pwr seats & leather shift knob) [NA w/CFK]*	858	1009
—	**Paint** — special color or metallic	82	97

SHADOW

SHADOW 4 CYL

DL24	Base 2-Dr	8263	8806
DL44	Base 4-Dr	8631	9206
DS24	ES 2-Dr..	9532	10252
DS44	ES 4-Dr..	9892	10652
	Destination Charge:	505	505

Standard Equipment

SHADOW: Black exterior door handles, black fascias, narrow black bodyside moldings, body color grille, 5-mph protection bumpers, warning buzzer (headlights on, seat belts, key in ignition), child protection

| CODE | DESCRIPTION | DEALER | LIST |

door locks (4-Door only), full stainless steel quiet tuned exhaust system, clear windshield and door glass, tinted quarter (2-Door only) and rear window glass, single rectangular halogen aero-style headlights, counter balanced hood with inside release, color-keyed passenger compartment carpeting, mini console with front/rear storage trays, cloth covered headliner, black instrument panel bezel (with quartz interior on ES), removable shelf panel, "Classic" upper cloth/lower vinyl door trim panels, lamps (dome, ignition key, cigar lighter), black outside left remote/right manual mirrors, cloth and vinyl reclining front bucket seats, cloth and vinyl bench rear seat with one-piece folding back, firm suspension, four "Mirage" styled steel wheels with black hub caps, 2.2 liter EFI 4-cylinder engine, 5-speed manual transmission, power rack and pinion steering, power front disc/rear drum brakes.

ES (in addition to or instead of Shadow equipment): Color-keyed lower bodyside appliques, body color door handles, unique color-keyed fascias, body color rear spoiler, bodyside accent stripes with "Shadow ES" decals, woodgrain instrument panel bezel with champagne interior, "Austin" cloth upper door trim panels with contrasting insert, carpeted lower door trim panels, black outside dual remote manual mirror, AM/FM ETR stereo radio with seek, clock and two speakers; sport suspension, four color-keyed "Triad" wheel covers, 2.5 liter EFI 4-cylinder engine.

Accessories

Code	Description	Dealer	List
Y	**Pkg Y** — Base	1313	1545
	incls air conditioning, rear window defroster, body color fascias, front and rear floor mats, color-keyed instrument panel bezels, light group, manual remote dual outside mirrors, dual visor vanity mirrors, color-keyed narrow bodyside moldings, AM/FM stereo radio with clock and four speakers, bodyside and decklid stripe, tinted glass, 14" "Centrifuge" wheel covers, deluxe windshield wipers		
H	**Pkg H** — ES	831	978
	incls air conditioning, console (incls cupholders, storage and armrest), rear window defroster, front and rear floor mats, fog lamps, dual note horn, remote liftgate release, light group, dual visor vanity mirrors, AM/FM stereo radio with clock and four speakers, tachometer, tinted glass, warning chimes, deluxe windshield wipers		
HAA	**Air Conditioning**	765	900
BR1	**Brakes** — anti-lock - NA w/5-speed manual trans.....................................	594	699
CUN	**Overhead Console** — ES w/Pkg H	225	265
	incls compass and temp (req's JPA, JPB, GTK; NA w/GWB)		
GFA	**Rear Window Defroster** — req'd in New York..	147	173
JPB	**Door Locks** — power - Base 2-Dr w/Pkg Y, ES 2-Dr................................	169	199
	Base 4-Dr w/Pkg Y, ES 4-Dr	204	240
JPS	**Driver Seat** — power - ES w/Pkg H	260	306
	req's JPA, JPB & GTK		
NAE	**California Emissions**	87	102
NBY	**New York Emissions**	87	102
CLE	**Floor Mats** — front & rear	39	46
NHK	**Engine Block Heater** — available in Alaska only	17	20
ADA	**Light Group**	65	77
JKE	**Liftgate Release** — remote - Base w/Pkg Y	20	24
GTE	**Mirrors** — dual outside manual remote - Base	59	69
GTK	**Mirrors** — dual outside power remote - ES w/Pkg H................................	48	57
	req's JPB		
RAL	**Radio** — Base...	241	284

DODGE

CODE	DESCRIPTION	DEALER	LIST
	incls AM/FM stereo w/clock & 2 speakers		
RAS	**Radio** — Base w/o Pkg Y	428	504
	Base w/Pkg Y	145	170
	ES	187	220
RAY	**Radio** — ES w/o Pkg H	442	520
	ES w/Pkg H (req's JPB & JHA)	255	300
	incls AM/FM stereo radio w/cass, graphic equalizer, clock & 4 Infinity spkrs		
RBC	**Radio** — ES w/o Pkg H	587	690
	ES w/Pkg H (req's JPB & JHA)	400	470
TBB	**Spare Tire** — conventional - Base	72	85
	w/steel wheel (ES)	72	85
	w/aluminum wheel WHK or WJP (ES)	181	213
NHM	**Speed Control** — req's SUA	190	224
GWB	**Sunroof** — Base	322	379
	ES (NA w/CUN)	322	379
SUA	**Tilt Steering Column** — req's JHA	126	148
TLN	**Tires** — P205/60R14 all-season BSW SBR - ES	(91)	(107)
WHK	**Wheels** — Base w/o Pkg Y	320	376
	Base w/Pkg Y	279	328
	ES (req's TLN)	279	328
	incls 14" cast aluminum "Teardrop" design		
WJP	**Wheels** — ES	279	328
	incls 15" cast aluminum "Eurocast II" design		
JPA	**Windows** — power - ES 2-Dr w/Pkg H	225	265
	ES 4-Dr w/Pkg H	281	331
	req's GTK & JPB on ES 2-Dr		
JHA	**Deluxe Windshield Wipers**	56	66
EDF	**Engine** — 2.2L EFI 4 cylinder - Base	STD	STD
EDM	**Engine** — 2.5L EFI 4 cylinder - Base	243	286
	ES	STD	STD
EFA	**Engine** — 3.0L MPI V6 - ES	590	694
DDM	**Transmission** — 5-speed manual	STD	STD
	NA on ES 6 cylinder models		
DDN	**Transmission** — heavy duty 5-speed manual		
	ES 6 cylinder models	STD	STD
DGA	**Transmission** — 3-speed automatic	473	557
DGB	**Transmission** — 4-speed automatic - ES	621	730
—	**Paint** — special color or metallic	82	97

CODE	DESCRIPTION	DEALER	LIST

SPIRIT

SPIRIT 4 CYL

DH41/21A 4-Dr Sedan.. 11339 12470
incls 2.5L 4 cylinder engine & 5-speed manual transmission

DH41/22D 4-Dr Sedan 12376 13949
*incls 2.5L 4 cylinder engine, 3-speed automatic transmission, air
conditioning, rear window defroster, floor mats, speed control, tilt steering
column*

DH41/24D 4-Dr Sedan 12376 13649
*incls 2.5L flex fuel 4 cylinder engine, 3-speed automatic transmission, air
conditioning, rear window defroster, floor mats, speed control, tilt steering
column*

DH41/24E 4-Dr Sedan.. 13127 14532
*incls 2.5L flex fuel 4 cylinder engine, 3-speed automatic transmission, air
conditioning, rear window defroster, floor mats, speed control, tilt steering
column, power door locks, remote mirrors, remote trunk release, power
windows, rear split folding bench seat*

SPIRIT 6 CYL

DH41/26D 4-Dr Sedan 12992 14374
*incls 3.0L V6 engine, 3-speed automatic transmission, P195/70R14 BSW
tires, air conditioning, rear window defroster, floor mats, speed control, tilt
steering wheel*

DH41/28E 4-Dr Sedan.. 13890 15430
*incls 3.0L V6 engine, 4-speed automatic transmission, P195/70R14 BSW
tires, air conditioning, rear window defroster, floor mats, speed control, tilt
steering wheel, power door locks, heated dual power remote mirrors,
remote trunk release, power windows, rear split folding bench seat*

Destination Charge: 505 505

Standard Equipment

SPIRIT: Air conditioning, soft fascia bumpers with integral nerf and 5-mph protection, warning chimes
(headlights on, seat belts, key in ignition), electric rear window defroster, full stainless steel exhaust
system, front and rear floor mats, tinted glass, locking glove box, body color grille, single halogen aero-
style headlights, counter balanced internal release hood, electric dual note horn, lamps (ash receiver,

dome, glove box, trunk), black outside dual remote control mirrors, dual visor mirrors, narrow bodyside moldings with bright stripe, AM/FM ETR stereo radio with digital clock, seek and four speakers; "Austin" cloth seat trim, 50/50 split bench dual reclining front seats with folding armrests, full fixed rear bench seat, electronic speed control, tilt steering column, four "Centrifuge" wheel covers, deluxe windshield wipers/washers with intermittent wipe, 2.5 liter EFI 4-cylinder engine, 3-speed automatic transmission, power rack and pinion steering, power front disc/rear drum brakes.

Accessories

CODE	DESCRIPTION	DEALER	LIST
BR1	**Brakes** — 4-wheel anti-lock disc - NA on 26D	594	699
ADS	**Argent Special Equipment Group** — 22D, 26D, 28E	170	200
	incls luggage rack, P196/70R14 all-season BSW SBR tires, 14" cast aluminum "Teardrop" road wheels		
ASH	**Gold Special Equipment Group** — 22D, 26D, 28E	170	200
	incls gold badging and molding inserts, luggage rack, P195/70R14 all-season BSW SBR tires, 14" cast aluminum "Teardrop" road wheels (NA w/TKJ or ADS)		
GFA	**Rear Window Defroster** — 21A	147	173
	req'd in New York		
JPS	**Driver Seat** — power - 24E, 28E	260	306
JPB	**Door Locks** — power - 22D, 24D, 26D	213	250
NAE	**California Emissions**	87	102
NBY	**New York Emissions**	87	102
LET	**Mini Trip Computer/Message Center** — 24D, 24E	79	93
RAS	**Radio** — 22D, 24D, 26D, 24E, 28E	145	170
	incls AM/FM stereo w/cassette, clock & 4 speakers		
TBB	**Tire** — conventional spare	81	95
TKJ	**Tires** — 22D, 24D, 24E	88	104
	26D, 28E	62	73
	incls P195/70R14 WSW SBR tires (NA w/ADS or ASH)		
—	**Seats** — 24E, 28E	NC	NC
	incls cloth front 50/50 bench, rear split folding		
—	**Paint** — special color or metallic	82	97

CODE	DESCRIPTION	DEALER	LIST

1993 STEALTH

NOTE:Information for the 1994 Stealth models was unavailable at time of publication.

1993 STEALTH 6 CYL

CODE	DESCRIPTION	DEALER	LIST
DL24	Base 2-Dr	16900	18506
DS24	ES 2-Dr	18498	20322
DP24	R/T 2-Dr	24697	27366
DX24	R/T Turbo AWD 2-Dr	29749	33107
	Destination Charge: Alaska	550	550
	Other States	430	430

Standard Equipment

STEALTH - BASE: Power front/rear disc brakes, floor console includes: ashtray/cigar lighter/coin holder/storage box with cupholder/padded armrest; electric rear defroster, remote fuel door release, pop-up halogen headlights with automatic off, instrument cluster includes: speedometer/tachometer/trip odometer/tamper resistant odometer/indicator lights; gauges for: oil pressure/fuel/temperature/voltage; remote liftgate release, lights include: license plate/back up/dome with delay timer/map/door courtesy/cargo area lamp/foot well/glove box/underhood illumination/ignition key/cigar lighter; dual exterior body color folding power mirror, visor mirrors, driver air bag, low-back bucket front seats with recliners, split-back folding type rear seats, front strut suspension with coil springs, gas-filled shocks and stabilizer bar, double wishbone-type rear suspension, power-assisted rack and pinion steering, tilt steering column, leather-wrapped steering wheel, intermittent wipers, 5-mph body color bumpers with black nerf, front wheel drive, bodyside moldings, sill with wheel extension moldings, 3.0 liter SOHC V6 engine, AM/FM stereo ETR radio with 4 speakers, manual driver's lumbar and height adjustment seat, four 15" x 6" "Sofera" wheels.

ES (in addition to or instead of Base equipment): Fog lamps, 3.0 liter DOHC V6 engine, four 16" x 8" aluminum sport wheels with center cap.

R/T (in addition to or instead of ES equipment): Automatic temperature control air conditioning, 4-wheel anti-lock brakes, body color bumpers, carpet protectors, console also contains: additional accessory outlet/power lumbar/side-wing switch; power door locks with illuminated switches, radio wave-type

CODE	DESCRIPTION	DEALER	LIST

remote keyless entry system, heated mirror, illuminated visor vanity mirrors, bodyside cladding molding, ultimate sound AM/FM stereo cassette radio with 6 speakers/6 AM-FM presets/seek-scan/auto reverse/7-band graphic equalizer/CD jack; driver's power seat with power lumbar/back wing/cushion height adjustment; security alarm system includes: door/hatch/hood sensors/visual and audible alarms; electronic speed control with steering wheel mounted switches, body color rear spoiler, electronic variable damping suspension with touring and sport settings, power windows with illuminated switches, rear wiper/washer.

R/T TURBO (in addition to or instead of ES equipment): All-wheel drive with viscous coupling and limited slip differential, instrument cluster includes turbo boost, 3.0 liter DOHC twin intercooled turbo V6 engine, 4-wheel hydraulic control steering, 17" x 8.5" aluminum ultimate wheels with center cap.

Accessories

CODE	DESCRIPTION	DEALER	LIST
DGB	**Transmission** — 4-speed automatic	742	863
	NA on R/T Turbo		
AJB	**Security Pkg** — Base w/o pkg B or C	1200	1395
	Base w/pkg B or C (power door incl in pkg B & C)	1075	1250
	ES (power door locks std)	1075	1250
	incls anti-lock brakes, security alarm, power door locks/keyless entry		
NAE	**California Emissions** —	NC	NC
REM	**Compact Disc Changer** — Base w/pkg C	466	542
	ES	466	542
WFC	**Chrome Wheels** — R/T Turbo	415	482
—	**Seats** — ES	725	843
	R/T, R/T Turbo	725	843
	incls leather front buckets w/recliners, rear split folding rear bench		
—	**Value Pkgs - Base Models**		
B	**Pkg B** — Base	1689	1964
	incls air conditioning, power door locks, floor mats, speed control, upper decklid rear spoiler, rear window wiper/washer, power windows, AM/FM stereo radio w/cassette, clock and 4 speakers		
C	**Pkg C** — Base	1943	2259
	incls air conditioning, power door locks, floor mats, speed control, upper decklid rear spoiler, rear window wiper/washer, AM/FM stereo radio w/cassette, graphic equalizer, clock and 6 speakers		
—	**Value Pkgs - ES**		
H	**Pkg H** — ES	1943	2259
	incls air conditioning, power door locks, floor mats, AM/FM stereo radio w/cassette, graphic equalizer, clock and 6 speakers; speed control, upper decklid rear spoiler, power windows, rear window wiper/washer		
K	**Pkg K** — ES	2253	2620
	incls air conditioning, power door locks, floor mats, AM/FM stereo radio w/cassette, graphic equalizer, clock and 6 speakers; speed control, upper decklid rear spoiler, power windows, rear window wiper/washer, sunroof		
—	**Value Pkgs - R/T & R/T Turbo**		
N	**Pkg N** — incls compact disc changer - R/T	466	542
P	**Pkg P** — incls compact disc changer & sunroof - R/T	777	903
W	**Pkg W** — incls compact disc changer - R/T Turbo	466	542
Y	**Pkg Y** — incls compact disc changer & sunroof - R/T Turbo	777	903

DODGE

CODE	DESCRIPTION	DEALER	LIST

1993 VIPER
NOTE:Information for the 1994 Viper was unavailable at time of publication.

1993 VIPER 10 CYL

DS27	2-Dr Sport Coupe	43625	50000
Destination Charge:		700	700
Gas Guzzler Tax:		2600	2600

Standard Equipment

VIPER: 50/120 amp alternator, 770 cold cranking amp battery, power-assisted front/rear disc brakes, soft fascia bumpers w/high density foam energy 5-mph absorbers, Euro-look short pile carpet, chimes include: door/key/seat belt/headlamp; console, 10-year anti-corrosion protection, clutch-type limited slip differential, 8.0 liter OHC V10 eng w/tuned intake and exhaust manifolds/alum block w/cast iron liners/ alum heads/bottom-feed sequential multi-port fuel injection; fog lamps w/covers, manual fuel filler door, tinted windshield glass, removable rear window glass, Aero-Polyellipsoid (low-beam) headlights, halogen high beam headlights, dual latch hood release w/single release located in grille opening, dual horn, direct distributorless ignition system, analog instrument cluster includes: speedometer/ tachometer; gauges for: oil pressure/voltage/coolant temperature/fuel level; air outlets, glove box, lamps include: license plates/back up/park and turn/side marker/center high-mounted stop/taillamps/front fog/ map; message center, inside 8" day/night mirrors w/integral map light, outside manual mirror, L/R breakaway mirrors, AM/FM/MX ETR radio w/cass (Chrysler/Alpine)/seek-scan/130 watt dual pwr amplifiers/digital time-frequency-function display/six speakers/compact disc compatible; 3-point unibelt passive restraint system, full width roof support, premium sport-style high back left/right bucket seats (includes leather seating surfaces with leather-grain vinyl facings, adjustable lumbar supports, continuously adjustable recliner for precise back adjustment); remote control security alarm system, power-assisted rack/pinion steering, tilt steering column, leather-wrapped steering wheel, snap-in Tonneau cover, removable folding soft top w/side curtains, six-speed manual trans (fully synchronized, alum housing w/1-4 skip shift).

Accessories

NAE	**California Emissions**	NC	NC
EWB	**Engine** — 8.0L V10 SFI	STD	STD
DEC	**Transmission** — 6-speed manual w/overdrive	STD	STD
—	**Tires** — P275/40ZR17 front & P335/35ZR17 rear high performance BSW...	STD	STD

SUMMIT COUPE/SEDAN

SUMMIT COUPE/SEDAN 4 CYL

Code	Description	Dealer	List
XE21	DL 2-Dr Coupe	8714	9120
XL21	ES 2-Dr Coupe	9571	10060
XL21	ESi 2-Dr Coupe	9571	10060
XL41	LX 4-Dr Sedan	10844	11428
XH41	ES 4-Dr Sedan	11472	12181
XH41	ESi 4-Dr Sedan	11472	12181
Destination Charge:		430	430

Standard Equipment

SUMMIT 2 DOOR - DL: Gray fascias, black side window opening moldings, black outside door handles, 5-mph bumper system, passenger compartment carpeting, instrument panel coin holder, center floor console with armrest and storage, side window demisters, vinyl door/quarter trim, stainless steel exhaust system, driver side foot rest, flush aero-style halogen headlights, single note horn, flood instrument cluster illumination, dome lamps, outside left manual mirror, vinyl seat trim with cloth insert, reclining highback front bucket seats, lowback rear bench seats, 4-spoke steering wheel, carpeted floor trunk trim, four argent styled steel wheels with bright center cap, 2-speed windshield wipers, 1.5 liter SMPI 4-cylinder engine, 5-speed man trans, man/rack/pinion steering, pwr front disc/rear drum brakes.

ES/ESi 2 DOOR (in addition to or instead of DL equipment): Body color fascias, body color bodyside moldings, outside body color door handles, rear spoiler, assist grip, cigarette lighter, dual sliding instrument panel cupholder, cloth and vinyl door/quarter trim with map pockets, back lighting instrument cluster illumination, outside dual manual remote mirrors, passenger-side covered visor mirror, cloth and vinyl seat trim, reclining bucket front seats with adjustable head restraint, rear seat easy entry (passenger side), four full-wheel covers.

SUMMIT 4 DOOR - LX: Body color fascias, black side window opening moldings, black outside door handles, rear armrests, three assist grips, 5-mph bumper system, passenger compartment carpeting, instrument panel coin holder, center floor console with armrest and storage, instrument panel dual sliding cupholders, side window demisters, child protection door locks, cloth and vinyl door/quarter trim with map pockets, stainless steel exhaust system, driver side foot rest, rear seat heater ducts, flush aero-style halogen headlights, single note horn, backlighting instrument cluster illumination, dome lamps, non-remote outside dual manual mirrors, cloth and vinyl seat trim, reclining front bucket seats with adjustable head restraint, lowback rear bench seat, 4-spoke steering wheel, carpeted floor trunk trim, four full-wheel covers, 2-speed windshield wipers, 1.8 liter SMPI 4-cylinder engine, 5-speed man trans, pwr assisted rack/pinion steering, pwr front disc/rear drum brakes.

CODE	DESCRIPTION	DEALER	LIST

ES/ESi 4 DOOR (in addition to or instead of LX equipment): Body color bodyside moldings, outside body color door handles, rear spoiler, cigarette lighter, remote fuel filler door release, dual note horn, trunk lamp, remote outside dual manual mirrors, driver/passenger side covered visor mirrors, full cloth seat trim, split folding rear bench seat with center armrest, driver's seat tilt/height control, remote trunk release with override feature, side trunk trim, fixed intermittent windshield wipers.

Accessories

CODE	DESCRIPTION	DEALER	LIST
C	**Coupe Pkg C** — DL Coupe	361	419
	incls rear window defroster, tinted glass, mirrors (black dual non-remote), radio (AM/FM stereo w/4 speakers and clock)		
D	**Coupe Pkg D** — DL Coupe	1057	1229
	incls Pkg C contents plus air conditioning		
G	**Coupe Pkg G** — ES Coupe	86	100
	incls rear window defroster, tinted glass, radio (AM/FM w/4 spkrs/clock)		
H	**Coupe Pkg H** — ES Coupe	1192	1386
	incls Pkg G contents plus air cond, Convenience Group A (split folding rear seat, fuel door/trunk release, trunk carpet and light, fixed speed inter-mittent wipers), radio (AM/FM cass w/4 speakers and clock), pwr steering		
K	**Coupe Pkg K** — ESi Coupe	1577	1834
	incls Pkg G contents plus ESi Pkg (14" alum wheels, P185/65R14 BSW tires, touring suspension, front vented disc brakes, dual chrome tip exhaust, tachometer [w/manual trans only])		
C	**Sedan Pkg C** — LX Sedan	499	580
	incls Convenience Group B (dual remote mirrors, fuel door and trunk release, trunk trim and light, passenger side vanity mirror, cigar lighter, fixed speed intermittent wipers), rear window defroster, floor mats, tinted glass, black bodyside moldings, radio (AM/FM stereo w/4 spkrs and clock)		
D	**Sedan Pkg D** — LX Sedan	1195	1390
	incls Sedan Pkg D contents plus air conditioning		
K	**Sedan Pkg K** — ES Sedan	1043	1213
	incls air cond, Convenience Group C (tilt steering wheel, color-keyed dual elec mirrors, variable speed intermittent wipers, speed control), rear win-dow defroster, floor mats, tinted glass, radio (AM/FM stereo cass w/4 spkrs and clock)		
L	**Sedan Pkg L** — ESi Sedan	1717	1996
	incls Sedan Pkg K contents plus pwr windows, pwr door locks and ESi Pkg (14" alum wheels)		
HAA	**Air Conditioning** — ES Coupe w/Pkg G	696	810
MJC	**Rear Window Defroster**	57	66
NAE	**California Emissions**	NC	NC
NBY	**New York Emissions**	NC	NC
MJC	**Bodyside Moldings** — gray - DL Coupe w/Pkg C or D	46	54
RAW	**Radio** — DL Coupe w/Pkg C or D	156	181
	ES Coupe w/Pkg G	156	181
	LX Sedan w/Pkg C or D	156	181
	incls AM/FM stereo cassette w/4 speakers and clock		
RAT	**Radio** — LX Sedan	233	271
	incls AM/FM stereo w/4 speakers and clock		
EJB	**Engine** — 1.5L MPI 4 cyl - Coupes except ESi	STD	STD
EJA	**Engine** — 1.8L MPI 4 cyl - Sedans	STD	STD
	ESi Coupe	STD	STD
DDR	**Transmission** — 5-speed manual	STD	STD
DGA	**Transmission** — 3-speed automatic - ES Coupe w/Pkg G or H	445	518
	req's 1.5L 4 cyl engine		

CODE	DESCRIPTION	DEALER	LIST
DGB	**Transmission** — 4-speed automatic - ESi Coupe	551	641
	LX Sedan w/Pkg C or D	603	701
	ES Sedan w/Pkg K	551	641
	ESi Sedan	551	641

SUMMIT WAGON

SUMMIT WAGON 4 CYL

XM52	DL Wagon	12036	12979
XH52	LX Wagon	13130	14194
FM52	AWD Wagon	13751	14884
	Destination Charge:	430	430

Standard Equipment

SUMMIT - DL WAGON: Body color fascias, black side window opening moldings, gray bodyside moldings, upper black tailgate applique, 5-mph bumpers, cigarette lighter, cupholders, side sliding door, child protection sliding door locks, full stainless steel exhaust system, remote release fuel filler door, aero halogen headlights, rear heat ducts, remote hood release, single horn, three assist grips, floor console, front full vinyl door trim, molded cloth covered headliner, driver's sunvisor with ticket holder, inner tailgate assist handle, dome and cargo area lamps, passenger side covered visor mirror, outside dual manual mirrors, front lowback reclining bucket seats with adjustable head rests, removable fold and tumble bench rear seat, full-face fabric seat trim, tilt steering column, flat cargo floor storage, two door map pockets, four argent styled steel wheels with bright center cap, side and rear quarter vented windows, 2-speed variable intermittent wipers/washers, 1.8 liter SMPI 16-valve 4-cylinder engine, 5-speed manual transmission, power assisted rack and pinion steering, power front disc/rear drum brakes.

LX WAGON (in addition to or instead of DL equipment): Upper red and black tailgate applique, two-tone paint with accent color fascias, bodyside moldings and tailgate lower applique; power door locks, tinted glass, dual horn, front door trim with cloth insert, driver foot rest, driver side covered visor mirror, outside dual power mirrors, front center armrest, reclining split back bench seat, Premium full-fabric seat trim (vinyl on back of front seats), passenger seat-back pocket storage, rear side left shelf storage, power lock/unlock tailgate, four 7-spoke full-wheel covers, fixed rear intermittent wipers/washers, 2.4 liter SMPI 16-valve 4-cylinder engine.

AWD WAGON (in addition to or instead of LX equipment): Body color fascias, lower gray tailgate applique, bodyside moldings and tailgate lower applique deleted, power door locks deleted, tinted glass deleted, single horn, full vinyl front door trim, driver foot rest deleted, front and rear mudguards, front center armrest deleted, rear bench seat, full-face fabric seat trim, passenger seat-back storage pocket deleted, left rear side storage shelf deleted, power lock/unlock tailgate deleted.

Accessories

CODE	DESCRIPTION	DEALER	LIST
C	**Pkg C** — DL Wagon	994	1156
	incls air cond, rear window defroster, tinted glass, dual power mirrors, radio (AM/FM stereo w/4 speakers and clock), power remote liftgate, lock and unlock, rear stabilizer bar, 9-spoke full wheel covers, rear window wiper/washer		
D	**Pkg D** — DL Wagon	1545	1796
	incls Pkg C contents plus power door locks, floor mats, radio (AM/FM stereo cassette w/4 speakers and clock), speed control		
K	**Pkg K** — LX Wagon	1384	1609
	incls air cond, cargo area cover, rear window defroster, floor mats, radio (AM/FM stereo cassette w/6 speakers and clock), speed control, keyless remote entry and power windows		
S	**Pkg S** — AWD Wagon	579	673
	incls Custom Group (low back cloth bucket seats w/headrest, passenger seat back pocket, front center armrest, split back and reclining rear bench seat, driver's side foot rest, fabric door trim insert w/two front map pockets, rear left-side storage, dual horns, power door locks, power tailgate lock/unlock, six speaker radio accommodation group), cargo area cover, rear window defroster, tinted glass, floor mats, keyless remote entry, radio (AM/FM stereo w/6 speakers and clock)		
W	**Pkg W** — AWD Wagon	1839	2138
	incls Pkg S contents plus air cond, radio (AM/FM stereo cass w/6 speakers and clock), speed control, tachometer, power windows		
HAA	**Air Conditioning** — AWD Wagon w/Pkg S	679	790
BGF	**Brakes** — anti-lock - DL Wagon	601	699
	LX Wagon w/Pkg K	601	699
GFA	**Rear Window Defroster**	57	66
CLA	**Floor Mats** — DL Wagon w/Pkg C	47	55
MWA	**Roof Rack** — DL Wagon w/Pkg C or D	130	151
	LX Wagon w/Pkg K	130	151
	AWD Wagon w/Pkg S or W	130	151
NAE	**California Emissions**	NC	NC
NBY	**New York Emissions**	NC	NC
APB	**Two-Tone Paint** — AWD Wagon	166	193
RAT	**Radio** — DL Wagon	248	288
	incls AM/FM stereo w/4 speakers and clock		
RAW	**Radio** — DL Wagon w/Pkg C	156	181
	AWD Wagon w/Pkg S	156	181
	incls AM/FM stereo w/6 speakers and clock		
EJA	**Engine** — 1.8L MPI 4 cyl - DL Wagon	STD	STD
EY7	**Engine** — 2.4L MPI 4 cyl - DL Wagon w/Pkg D	156	181
	LX Wagon	STD	STD
	AWD Wagon	STD	STD
DDR	**Transmission** — 5-speed manual	STD	STD
DGB	**Transmission** — 4-speed automatic overdrive - DL w/Pkg C or D	622	723
	LX Wagon	622	723
	AWD Wagon	622	723

TALON

TALON 4 CYL

CODE	DESCRIPTION	DEALER	LIST
XM24	DL 3-Dr Liftback	11083	11892
XH24	ES 3-Dr Liftback	13331	14362
XP24	TSi FWD 3-Dr Liftback	14717	15885
FP24	TSi AWD 3-Dr Liftback	16620	17978
	Destination Charge:	430	430

Standard Equipment

TALON - DL: Front/rear body color fascias, body color bodyside moldings, power front and rear disc brakes, 5-mph impact resistant bumpers, stainless steel exhaust system, full-tinted glass with windshield sun shade band, single horn, floor console with coin holder, molded door trim, driver's side foot rest, locking glove box, molded urethane shift knob, lamps (cargo, cigarette lighter, glove box, ignition, illumination delay interior, overhead dual map, dome, footwell), dual visor mirrors with covers, black exterior dual manual remote mirrors, AM/FM ETR stereo radio w/four speakers and digital clock, remote release fuel fill and liftgate, front highback bucket seats with recliner, 2-passenger split-folding rear seat, "Jasper" cloth seat trim, tilt steering column, sport suspension, headlights-on warning tone, four full-wheel covers, variable intermittent windshield wipers/washers, 1.8 liter SMPI 4-cylinder engine, 5-speed man trans, manual rack and pinion steering.

ES (in addition to or instead of DL equipment): Bodyside body color cladding, body color rear liftgate and quarter panel mounted spoiler, electric rear window defroster, sport tuned dual chrome tip exhaust system, lower fascia mounted front fog lights, dual horn, armrest and covered storage interior trim, padded vinyl door trim with cloth insert and lower carpet, front color-keyed carpeted floor mats, removable Tonneau cover, dual power remote body color exterior mirrors, AM/FM ETR stereo radio with cassette, six speakers and clock; driver's adjustable lumbar support seat, "Gemini/Bishop" cloth seat trim, performance suspension, four Polycast wheels, 2.0 liter SMPI 16-valve 4-cylinder engine, power assisted rack and pinion steering.

TALON - TSi FWD: Front and rear body color fascias, bodyside body color cladding, body color rear liftgate and quarter panel mounted spoiler, power front and rear disc brakes, 5-mph impact resistant bumpers, electric rear window defroster, stainless steel exhaust system, sport tuned dual chrome tip exhaust system, lower fascia mounted front fog lights, full-tinted glass with windshield sun shade band, dual horn, interior floor trim with armrest and covered storage, padded vinyl door trim with cloth insert and lower carpet, front color-keyed carpeted floor mats, driver side foot rest, locking glove box, leather-wrapped shift knob, leather-wrapped sport steering wheel, removable Tonneau cover, lamps (cargo, cigarette lighter, glove box, ignition, illumination delay interior, overhead dual map, dome, footwell), dual covered visor mirrors, exterior body color dual power remote mirrors, AM/FM ETR stereo radio with cassette, six speakers and clock; remote release fuel fill and liftgate, highback reclining front bucket seats, driver seat (back wing, lumbar, thigh and head rest adjustments), 2-passenger split-folding rear seat, "Malibu/Bishop" cloth, tilt steering column, performance suspension, headlights-on warning tone, four Polycast wheels, variable intermittent windshield wipers/washers, 2.0 liter SMPI 16-valve 4-cylinder turbo engine, 5-speed manual transmission, power assisted rack and pinion steering.

TSi AWD (in addition to or instead of TSi FWD): Enthusiast suspension, color-keyed "Five Spoke" cast aluminum wheels.

Accessories

CODE	DESCRIPTION	DEALER	LIST
T	**Pkg T** — DL..	934	1099
	incls air conditioning and power steering		
L	**Pkg L** — DL..	438	515
	incls pwr steering, cargo area cover, console w/cupholder, rear window defroster, front floor mats		
M	**Pkg M** — DL..	1494	1758
	incls Pkg L contents plus air cond, radio (AM/FM stereo cass w/6 spkrs), speed control		
B	**Pkg B** — ES..	888	1045
	incls air conditioning and speed control		
C	**Pkg C** — ES..	1399	1646
	incls Pkg B contents plus liftgate window wiper/washer, power windows and power door locks		
D	**Pkg D** — ES..	1839	2164
	incls Pkg C contents plus radio (AM/FM stereo cass w/6 speakers and graphic equalizer), 16" alloy wheels (4)		
G	**Pkg G** — TSi FWD..	1839	2164
	incls air cond, speed control, liftgate window wiper/washer, power windows, power door locks, radio (AM/FM stereo cass w/6 speakers and graphic equalizer), 16" alloy wheels (4)		
J	**Pkg J** — TSi AWD..	1583	1862
	incls same contents as Pkg G		
BRF	**Brakes** — anti-lock - ES..	594	699
	TSi FWD, TSi AWD..	594	699
NAE	**California Emissions**...	NC	NC
NBY	**New York Emissions**...	NC	NC
RAN	**Radio** — DL...	168	198
	incls AM/FM stereo cassette w/6 speakers		
RDP	**Radio** — ES w/Pkg D...	439	517
	TSi FWD w/Pkg G..	439	517
	TSi AWD w/Pkg J..	439	517
	incls AM/FM stereo cass, compact disc player w/graphic equalizer		
GFA	**Rear Window Defroster** — DL..	111	130
GWB	**Sunroof** — glass (removable) - DL w/Pkg L or M...................	317	373
	ES w/Pkg B, C or D...	317	373
	TSi FWD, TSi AWD..	317	373
DGB	**Transmission** — 4-speed automatic overdrive - DL w/Pkg T, L or M...........	608	716
	ES w/Pkg B, C or D...	609	716
	TSi FWD w/Pkg G..	728	857
	TSi AWD w/Pkg J..	728	857
—	**Seats** — TSi AWD..	377	444
	incls leather high back buckets w/split folding rear		

CODE	DESCRIPTION	DEALER	LIST

VISION

VISION 6 CYL

XP41	ESi 4-Dr Sports Sedan	16927	19308
XS41	TSi 4-Dr Sports Sedan	19908	22773
Destination Charge:		525	525

Standard Equipment

VISION - ESi: Manual control air conditioning with non-CFC refrigerant, floor console (cupholders, rear seat heat/AC ducts, armrest, covered storage), power door locks, child protection rear door locks, stainless steel exhaust system with aluminized coating, two-tone fascias, front and rear floor mats, glass (solar control, windshield and rear window; tinted side windows), three folding grab handles, interior lamps (front reading/courtesy, rear courtesy with fade-off and time out, door courtesy), message center (door ajar, trunk ajar, low washer fluid), dual covered visor mirrors, foldaway heated dual power mirrors, bodyside protection moldings, full bodyside cladding, AM/FM ETR stereo radio with cassette, seek, Dolby and six speakers; electric rear window defroster, front bucket seats with premium style and fabric, manual lumbar adjustment and upgraded door trim; contoured rear bench seat with center armrest, speed control, tilt steering column, compact spare tire, power trunk lid release, touring tires and touring suspension, four "Six Spoke" wheel covers, power windows with driver override and one-touch down, speed-sensitive intermittent wipers/washers with high volume fluidic washers, 3.3 liter SMPI V6 engine, 4-speed auto transmission, power 4-wheel anti-lock brakes, variable assist rack and pinion steering.

TSi (in addition to or instead of ESi equipment): Air conditioning with automatic temperature control, full overhead console (compass, thermometer, trip computer, storage, courtesy/reading lamps), fog lights, illuminated entry, remote keyless entry, leather shift knob, luggage compartment cargo net, dual illuminated visor mirrors, 8-way power driver's seat, leather-wrapped steering wheel, dual sunvisors with sliding extensions and secondary visors, four "Caisson" aluminum wheels, touring tires, touring suspension and speed, 3.5 liter SMPI V6 engine.

Accessories

B	**Pkg B** — ESi	NC	NC
	incls model with standard equipment		

CODE	DESCRIPTION	DEALER	LIST
C	**Pkg C** — ESi	511	601
	incls dual illuminated vanity mirrors, 8-way power driver's seat, remote/illuminated entry group		
D	**Pkg D** — ESi	1502	1767
	incls Pkg C contents plus air conditioning with auto temp control, full overhead console with compass, temperature and trip; auto day/night mirror, Chrysler/Infinity spatial imaging cassette radio, security alarm		
K	**Pkg K** — TSi	NC	NC
	incls model with standard equipment		
L	**Pkg L** — TSi	833	980
	incls 8-way power driver and passenger seats (incls power recliners), auto day/night mirror, Chrysler/Infinity spatial imaging cassette radio		
M	**Pkg M** — TSi	1450	1706
	incls Pkg L contents + leather seats, security alarm, conventional spare tire		
EGB	**Engine** — 3.3 liter V6 MPI - ESi	STD	STD
EGE	**Engine** — 3.5 liter V6 MPI 24-valve HO - TSi	STD	STD
DGB	**Transmission** — 4-speed automatic overdrive	STD	STD
BRT	**Brakes** — anti-lock - ESi	509	599
CFK	**Child Seat** — integrated	85	100
	NA with leather trim on TSi		
NHK	**Engine Block Heater** — avail Alaska only	17	20
JPV	**Driver's Seat** — 8-way power - ESi	320	377
	incls power recliner		
JPR	**Driver's Seat** — 8-way power - TSi	320	377
	incls power recliner		
TL	**Leather Seats** — NA w/CFK - TSi	527	620
TBB	**Tire** — conventional spare	81	95
BNM	**Traction Control** — TSi	149	175
LSA	**Security Alarm** — TSi	127	149
NAE	**California Emissions**	87	102
NBY	**New York Emissions**	87	102
—	**Paint** — special color or metallic	82	97
AGC	**16" Polycast Wheels & 16" Touring Tires** — ESi	318	374
AWT	**Performance Handling Group** — TSi	184	217
	incls performance suspension, P225/60R16 RBL all-season performance tires (req's conventional spare and traction control)		
ARA	**Radio** — Chrysler/Infinity spatial imaging	602	708
	incls AM/FM ET stereo radio, cassette player, graphic equalizer, 11 Infinity speakers, rear-mounted power antenna, clock		
ARB	**Radio** — Chrysler/Infinity spatial imaging	144	169
	incls AM/FM ET stereo radio, integral compact disc player, 11 Infinity speakers, rear-mounted power antenna, clock		

CODE	DESCRIPTION	DEALER	LIST

AEROSTAR WAGON

AEROSTAR WAGON 6 CYL

CODE	DESCRIPTION	DEALER	LIST
A11	XL Regular Length 2WD	13342	14980
A31	XL Extended Length 2WD	14614	16425
A21	XL Regular Length 4WD	16397	18450
A41	XL Extended Length 4WD	17183	19345
A11	XL Plus Regular Length 2WD	14693	16515
A31	XL Plus Extended Length 2WD	15609	17555
A21	XL Plus Regular Length 4WD	17342	19525
A41	XL Plus Extended Length 4WD	18068	20350
A11	XLT Regular Length 2WD	18130	20420
A31	XLT Extended Length 2WD	18552	20900
A21	XLT Regular Length 4WD	19498	21975
A41	XLT Extended Length 4WD	20259	22840
A11	Eddie Bauer Regular Length 2WD	20664	23300
A31	Eddie Bauer Extended Length 2WD	21368	24100
A21	Eddie Bauer Regular Length 4WD	22345	25210
A41	Eddie Bauer Extended Length 4WD	23146	26120
	Destination Charge:	535	535

Standard Equipment

AEROSTAR - XL: Color-coordinated front and rear bumpers with bright moldings, tinted glass, aero headlights, black aero fold-away LH and RH mirrors, bodyside moldings, underbody spare tire carrier (except Regular Length 4WD), black aero front spoiler, full face wheel cover, rear washer/wiper, RH/LH bodyside sliding and liftgate windows, front interval windshield wipers, driver air bag, color-keyed carpeting, front cigarette lighter, coat hooks, convenience group (includes courtesy lamp switches and cargo lamp, carpet-covered engine cover, inside fuel filler release, headlamps-on warning, four-gauge mechanical instrument cluster, front dome lights, rearview 10" day/night mirror, electronic AM/FM stereo radio with digital clock, color-coordinated scuff plates, color-keyed dual front high-back bucket seats, one three-passenger rear bench seat with folding seat back, bodyside storage bins with fishnet covers, RH and LH color-keyed sunvisors with sunglass strap and vanity mirror.

XLT (in addition to or instead of XL equipment): Dual-note horn, lower two-tone paint, premium wheel covers, front air conditioning, carpet-covered lower door trim with map pocket and vinyl accent stripe, liftgate convenience net, light group, carpet-covered lower quarter trim panels and vinyl accent color stripe, dual captain's chairs with recliners, inboard fold-down armrests and power lumbar support, one two-passenger and one three-passenger bench seat with folding seat back, color-keyed deluxe leather-wrapped tilt steering wheel, speed control.

EDDIE BAUER (in addition to or instead of XLT equipment): Luggage rack, Eddie Bauer two-tone paint with tape stripe, forged aluminum wheels, rear air conditioning with auxiliary heater, electric rear window defroster, electronics group (includes autolamp, electrochromic day/night mirror, electronic instrument cluster and super sound system), mini floor consolette, carpeted front and rear floor mats, electronic cluster including trip computer, power equipment group (includes power windows, power door locks, electric remote mirrors), unique Eddie Bauer cloth seat trim.

Accessories

CODE	DESCRIPTION	DEALER	LIST
—	**Preferred Equipment Pkgs** — prices include pkg discounts		
400A	**XL Base Pkg**	31	37
401A	**XL Plus Pkg**	624	734
401A	**XL Plus Regular Length 2WD Pkg** — double bonus discount	(808)	(950)
403A	**XLT Pkg**	267	315
403A	**XLT Extended Length 4WD Pkg**— bonus discount	(680)	(800)
405A	**Eddie Bauer Pkg**	287	338
99U	**Engine** — 3.0L EFI V6 - 2WD models	STD	STD
99X	**Engine** — 4.0L EFI V6 - 2WD models	255	300
	4WD models	STD	STD
44M	**Transmission** — 5-speed manual overdrive - 2WD models	STD	STD
44T	**Transmission** — automatic overdrive (std on 4WD models)	638	750
—	**Limited Slip Axle** — use w/o trailer towing pkg	215	252
	use w/trailer towing pkg	NC	NC
—	**Optional Axle Ratio**	32	38
422	**California Emissions System**	85	100
428	**High Altitude Emissions System**	NC	NC
—	**Tires**		
T85	P215/70R14SL steel radial BSW all-season	STD	STD
T8E	P215/70R14SL steel radial WSW all-season	72	84
T86	P215/75R14SL steel radial BSW all-season	NC	NC
—	**Optional Seating**		
214	5-passenger w/dual captain's chairs	547	644
21D	7-passenger w/dual captain's chairs & 2 & 3 passenger seat/bed - use w/Pkg 401 or 403	470	552
21B	7-passenger w/dual captain's chairs - use w/XL Base	886	1043
21E	7-passenger w/quad captain's chairs - use w/XLT	508	598
21F	7-passenger w/quad captain's chairs & 3-passenger seat/bed - use w/XLT	529	622
	use w/Eddie Bauer	NC	NC
21F	7-passenger w/quad captain's chairs & 3-passenger seat/bed (leather trim)	720	848
87C	**Child Safety Seat**	191	224
572	**Air Conditioning**	729	857

FORD

CODE	DESCRIPTION	DEALER	LIST
574	**Air Conditioning, High Capacity & Auxiliary Heater**	489	576
414	**Console, Floor**	148	174
—	**Console, Floor Delete**	(52)	(61)
57Q	**Defroster, Electric Rear Window**	143	168
151	**Electronics Group** — use w/Pkg 403	691	813
558	**Exterior Appearance Group** — use w/Pkg 400	489	576
	use w/Pkg 401	148	174
	use w/Pkg 403	80	94
	use w/XLT trim w/o Privacy Glass & Power Convenience Group	436	513
94A	**XL Plus Convenience Group** — use w/Pkg 401 only	703	827
94B	**XLT Convenience Group** — use w/Pkg 403 only -		
	use w/Exterior Appearance Group	721	849
	use w/o Exterior Appearance Group	766	901
924	**Glass, Privacy**	351	413
41H	**Heater, Engine Block**	28	33
153	**License Plate Bracket**	NC	NC
593	**Light Group**	135	159
615	**Luggage Rack**	121	143
542	**Mirrors, Swing Lock "A" Pillar** — use w/o 558 or 903	45	52
	use w/558 or 903	NC	NC
963	**Molding, Bodyside Protection**	54	63
853	**Paint Stripe, Deluxe**	36	43
—	**Paint Stripe, Deluxe Credit** — use w/XL Plus	(25)	(29)
903	**Power Convenience Group** — use w/Exterior Appearance Group	413	485
	use w/o Exterior Appearance Group	457	538
52N	**Speed Control/Tilt Steering Wheel**	315	371
552	**Sport Appearance Package**	623	733
534	**Trailer Towing Package**	239	282
434	**Underseat Stowage Bin** — front passenger side - use w/captain's chairs	NC	NC
	use w/o captain's chairs	31	37
646	**Wheels, Forged Aluminum**	309	363
589	**Radio** — electronic AM/FM stereo w/cassette & clock (incls headphones)...	166	195

FORD

CODE	DESCRIPTION	DEALER	LIST

CROWN VICTORIA

CROWN VICTORIA 8 CYL

P73	Crown Victoria 4-Dr Sedan	17743	19300
P74	LX 4-Dr Sedan	19096	20715
Destination Charge:		575	575

Standard Equipment

CROWN VICTORIA - BASE: Tinted glass, bright grille, low profile dual aero headlamps, color-keyed dual remote control power mirrors, black rocker panel moldings, wide bodyside moldings with bright insert, clearcoat paint, lower bodyside urethane protection, deluxe wheel covers, rear quarter windows, driver and front passenger air bags, rear seat center fold-down armrest, dual fold-down front seat, 16 oz. carpeting, cigarette lighter, electronic digital clock with dimming feature, courtesy lamps, dual ashtray mounted cupholders, side window demisters, color-keyed four-spoke steering wheel, illuminated lockable glove box, gauge cluster (volt, oil pressure, water temperature and fuel), two-way head restraints, dual instrument panel courtesy lamps, dome light, luggage compartment light, front door map pockets, day/night inside rearview mirror, electronic AM/FM stereo radio, cloth split bench seat with center fold-down armrests, driver/passenger manual 2-way seat back adjusters, tilt steering wheel, trip odometer, manual air conditioning, 95 amp alternator, 58 amp maintenance-free battery, coolant recovery system, power 4-wheel disc brakes, driver footrest, 4.6 liter OHC V8 SEFI engine, stainless steel exhaust system, front stabilizer bar, tinted glass, automatic headlamps with on/off delay, headlamps-on reminder chime, dual note horn, scissors jack, mini-spare tire, automatic parking brake release, speed sensitive variable assist power steering, rear stabilizer bar, luxury sound insulation package, P215/70R15 all-season BW tires, electronically controlled automatic overdrive transmission, power windows with express down driver's window, dual jet interval windshield wipers.

LX (in addition to or instead of Base equip): Deluxe 18 oz. carpeting, split bench seat w/fold-down armrests trimmed in luxury cloth, power driver's seat, carpeted spare tire cover, remote release fuel door.

Accessories

—	**Preferred Equipment Pkgs** — prices include pkg discounts		
111A	**STD Pkg 111A**	406	445

CODE	DESCRIPTION	DEALER	LIST
113A	**LX Pkg 113A**...	767	845
114A	**LX Pkg 114A**...	3060	3435
99W	**Engine** — 4.6L SEFI V8..	STD	STD
44P	**Transmission** — electronic automatic overdrive................	STD	STD
422	**California Emissions System**...	85	95
428	**High Altitude Emissions System**.....................................	NC	NC
—	**Tires**		
T37	P215/70R15 BSW...	STD	STD
T3P	P215/70R15 WSW...	71	80
508	conventional spare tire - w/41G Handling & Performance Pkg.....................	232	260
	all other..	71	80
—	**Seats**		
I	cloth split bench - Crown Victoria......................................	STD	STD
6	luxury cloth split bench - LX..	STD	STD
C	leather seating surfaces split bench - LX only -		
	w/21J Power Passenger Seat..	472	530
	all other..	557	625
68A	**Option Group 1** — w/Crown Victoria.................................	685	770
	w/LX...	596	670
65C	**Option Group 2** — LX only...	218	245
67A	**Option Group 3** — LX only...	432	485
65D	**Option Group 4** — LX only - w/Option Group 2	2274	2555
	all other..	2421	2720
553	**Anti-Lock Braking System/Electronic Traction Assist**....	592	665
516	**Cellular Telephone w/Storage Armrest** — LX only	663	745
12H	**Floor Mats, Front Color-Keyed Carpet**.............................	23	25
12Q	**Floor Mats, Rear Color-Keyed Carpet**..............................	18	20
41G	**Handling & Performance Package** — LX only - w/PEP 114A	365	410
	w/Group 4..	739	830
	w/Group 3..	1197	1345
	w/all other..	1571	1765
47J	**Illuminated Entry System**...	71	80
144	**Keyless Entry, Remote** — LX..	191	215
943	**Light/Decor Group**..	201	225
664	**Rear Air Suspension** — LX..	240	270
21A	**Seat, Driver 6-Way Power**...	258	290
21J	**Seats, Passenger 6-Way Power w/Dual Power Lumbar**		
	& Dual Power Recliner — LX...	427	480
524	**Steering Wheel, Leather-Wrapped** — LX...........................	80	90
535	**Trailer Towing Package, Heavy Duty** — w/Pkg 114A	352	395
	all other..	614	690
—	**Audio**		
58H	radio, electronic AM/FM stereo cassette............................	147	165
586	audio system, high level - w/Group 2 or Pkg 113A or 114A......................	280	315
	all other..	427	480
916	Ford JBL audio system - LX..	445	500
919	trunk-mounted compact disc changer................................	699	785
41H	**Heater, Engine Block Immersion**.....................................	23	25

EDMUND'S NEW CAR PRICES

CODE	DESCRIPTION	DEALER	LIST

ESCORT

ESCORT 4 CYL

P10	Escort 3-Dr	8322	9035
P11	LX 3-Dr	9100	9890
P12	GT 3-Dr	11293	12300
P13	LX 4-Dr	9701	10550
P15	LX Wagon	10000	10880
P14	LX 5-Dr	9496	10325
Destination Charge:		375	375

FORD

Standard Equipment

ESCORT - HATCHBACKS: Bodycolor door handles (LX, GT), flip-out quarter window (3 Dr), single rectangular halogen headlamps, black remote-control driver's side mirror (Base, LX), black dual electric remote-control mirrors (GT), bodycolor bodyside molding (LX), rear reflex applique (LX, GT), rocker panel cladding (GT), rear spoiler (GT), 13" x 5" semi-styled steel wheels with center cap (Base), 13" x 5" semi-styled steel wheels with full luxury wheel covers (LX), 15" x 5.5" styled aluminum wheels (GT), driver air bag, rear ashtrays (LX, GT), removable cargo area cover, cigarette lighter, center console with bin and cupholders, vinyl door trim (Base), cloth door trim (LX, GT), light group (GT), non-illuminated passenger visor mirrors (Base, LX), illuminated driver/passenger visor mirrors (GT), low-back cloth and vinyl reclining bucket seats (Base), upgraded low-back cloth with vinyl seat back, reclining bucket seats with luxury trim (LX), sport performance cloth reclining bucket seats (GT), full-fold bench type rear seat (Base), split/fold 60/40 rear seat (LX, GT), integral rear seat head restraints (GT), four-spoke steering wheel (Base, LX), leather sport black steering wheel (GT), heavy duty alternator, maintenance-free battery, power front disc/rear drum brakes (Base, LX), power 4-wheel disc brakes (GT), remote decklid release (GT), side window demisters, 1.9 liter 4 cylinder SEFI engine (Base, LX), 1.8 liter DOHC 16-valve 4 cylinder EFI engine (GT), engine fuel cutout light, engine malfunction indicator light, engine low coolant warning light, front wheel drive, remote fuel door release (GT), tinted glass, inside hood release, single note horn (dual note on GT), radio prep package (Base), electronic AM/FM stereo radio with digital clock (LX), electronic AM/FM stereo radio with cassette and digital clock (GT), rear seat heater ducts, front and rear stabilizer bars, manual rack and pinion steering (Base, LX), power rack and pinion steering (GT), four-wheel independent suspension, sport handling suspension (GT), tachometer (GT), temperature gauge, P175/70R13 BW all-season tires (Base, LX), P185/60R15 84H BW performance all-season tires (GT), mini-spare tire, trip odometer, 5-speed manual transmission, 2-speed interval windshield wipers.

FORD

ESCORT

CODE	DESCRIPTION	DEALER	LIST

ESCORT - SEDANS & WAGONS: Single rectangular headlamps, black remote-control driver's side mirror, bodycolor bodyside moldings, rear reflex applique (Sedan), 14" x 5" semi-styled steel wheels with full luxury wheel covers, driver air bag, rear ashtrays, color-keyed window shade type cargo area cover (Wagon), cigarette lighter, center console with bin and cupholders, cloth door trim, non-illuminated passenger visor mirror (Wagon), non-illuminated driver/passenger visor mirrors (Sedan), low-back cloth with vinyl seat back reclining bucket seats with luxury trim, split/fold 60/40 rear seat, integral rear seat head restraints (Sedan), four-spoke black steering wheel, heavy-duty alternator, maintenance-free battery, power front disc/rear drum brakes, side window demisters, 1.9 liter 4 cylinder SEFI engine, engine fuel cutout light, engine malfunction indicator light, engine low coolant warning light, front wheel drive, tinted glass, inside hood release, single note horn, electronic AM/FM stereo radio with digital clock, rear seat heater ducts, front and rear stabilizer bars, four-wheel independent suspension, tachometer (Sedan), temperature gauge, P175/65R14 BW all-season tires, mini-spare tire, trip odometer, 5-speed manual transmission, 2-speed interval windshield wipers.

Accessories

CODE	DESCRIPTION	DEALER	LIST
—	**Preferred Equipment Pkgs** — prices include pkg discounts		
321A	LX 3-Dr Pkg 321A Manual	1008	1130
321A	LX 5-Dr Pkg 321A Manual	621	695
321A	LX 4-Dr Pkg 321A Manual	420	470
321A	LX 4-Dr Wgn Pkg 321A Manual	126	140
322A	LX 3-Dr Pkg 322A Automatic	1711	1920
322A	LX 5-Dr Pkg 322A Automatic	1324	1485
322A	LX 4-Dr Pkg 322A Automatic	1123	1260
322A	LX 4-Dr Wgn Pkg 322A Automatic	829	930
320A	LX Pkg 320A	211	235
330A	GT Pkg 330A	472	530
99J	Engine — 1.9L SEFI - Escort & LX	STD	STD
998	Engine — 1.8L DOHC - GT	STD	STD
445	Transaxle — 5-speed manual	STD	STD
44T	Transaxle — 4-speed overdrive automatic	703	790
422	California Emissions System — NC w/PEP 321A or 322A	62	70
428	High Altitude Emissions System	NC	NC
—	Tires		
T15	P175/70R13 BSW - Escort	STD	STD
T39	P185/60R15 84H BSW performance - GT	STD	STD
T75	P175/65R14 BSW - LX	STD	STD
—	Seats		
Z	cloth & vinyl low-back bucket - Escort	STD	STD
1	upgraded cloth & vinyl low-back bucket - LX	STD	STD
X	cloth sport performance bucket - GT	STD	STD
572	Air Conditioning - LX, GT	646	725
552	Anti-Lock Braking System	503	565
59C	Comfort Group — Escort	712	800
57Q	Defroster, Rear Window	143	160
41H	Engine Block Immersion Heater	18	20
153	Front License Plate Bracket	NC	NC
60A	Light & Convenience Group - LX	268	300
68A	Light Group/Removable Cupholder Tray	98	110
54J	Dual Electric Remote Control Mirrors	85	95

FORD

CODE	DESCRIPTION	DEALER	LIST
68B	**Remote Fuel Door/Liftgate Releases**...	85	95
60B	**Luxury Convenience Group** — LX 4-Dr, GT	316	355
	LX 3-Dr/5-Dr/Wgn..	365	410
53A	**Power Equipment Group** —		
	LX 4-Dr, 5-Dr/Wgn w/Luxury Convenience Group.....................	463	520
	5-Dr/Wgn w/o Luxury Convenience Group................................	512	575
	3-Dr LX w/Luxury Convenience Group, GT...............................	410	460
	3-Dr LX w/o Luxury Convenience Group	459	515
13B	**Moonroof, Power** — LX, GT	468	525
—	**Paint, Clearcoat** — NC w/PEP 321A, 322A or Sport Appearance Group	76	85
434	**Sport Appearance Group** — 3-Dr LX	641	720
52H	**Steering, Power** — LX	223	250
60W	**Wagon Group**	213	240
—	**Audio**		
587	radio, electronic AM/FM stereo w/clock - Escort	267	300
589	radio, electronic AM/FM stereo w/clock & cassette - Escort	414	465
	LX	147	165
585	radio, electronic AM/FM stereo w/clock & compact disc player - Escort	658	740
	LX...	396	445
	GT	249	280
913	radio sound system, premium..	116	130
58Y	radio credit option - LX	(267)	(300)
	GT	(414)	(465)
415	**Sunrise Red Decor Group** — GT...	312	350
	incls clearcoat paint		

PROBE

PROBE 4 CYL			
T20	Base 3-Dr	12325	13685
PROBE 6 CYL			
T22	GT 3-Dr	14398	16015
Destination Charge:	....	350	350

CODE	DESCRIPTION	DEALER	LIST

Standard Equipment

PROBE - BASE: Fixed rear quarter antenna, concealed headlamps, LH remote RH direct activating sail mounted outside mirrors, tinted backlight and quarter window glass, driver and front passenger air bags, electronic digital clock, center console, side window demisters, locking glove box, instrument cluster (includes 120 mph speedometer, odometer, trip odometer, tachometer, fuel gauge, water temperature gauge, oil pressure gauge, voltmeter), flash-to-pass lights, day/night inside rearview mirror, electronic AM/FM stereo radio with four speakers, driver and passenger seat back recline with memory, front bucket seats with dual recliners and integral head restraints, 50/50 fold down rear seat, floor mounted shift, cloth covered sunvisors with LH stowage band and covered RH vanity mirror, warning light system, power front disc/rear drum brakes, 2.0 liter DOHC 4 cylinder engine, inside hood release, dual note horn, power rack and pinion steering, MacPherson strut front suspension, Quadralink rear suspension, front and rear stabilizer bars, P195/65R14 BSW all-season tires, 5-speed manual transmission, 2-speed windshield wipers.

GT (in addition to or instead of Base equipment): Lower bodyside cladding, GT exterior treatment (includes unique front and rear fascia with rectangular fog lamps and unique side badging), clear front combination lamp lens, 16" 5-spoke aluminum wheels, cargo net, full center console with folding armrest, driver side power lumbar support and seat back side bolsters/seat back stowage compartment, leather wrapped steering wheel, power four-wheel disc brakes, 2.5 liter DOHC V6 engine, fog lamps, P225/50VR16 BW tires.

Accessories

CODE	DESCRIPTION	DEALER	LIST
—	**Preferred Equipment Pkgs** — prices include pkg discounts		
251A	**Base Probe Pkg 251A**	329	370
253A	**Base Probe Pkg 253A**	2082	2340
261A	**GT Probe Pkg 261A**	1233	1385
263A	**GT Probe Pkg 263A**	2484	2790
99	**Engine** — 2.0L DOHC I4 - Base	STD	STD
99B	**Engine** — 2.5L DOHC V6 - GT	STD	STD
445	**Transaxle** — 5-spd manual	STD	STD
44T	**Transaxle** — 4-spd automatic overdrive	703	790
422	**California Emissions**	85	95
428	**High Altitude Emissions**	NC	NC
—	**Tires**		
T82	P195/65Rx14 BSW - Base	STD	STD
64V	wheels, 15" aluminum/P205/55Rx15 BSW tires - Base	383	430
T27	wheels, 16"aluminum/P225/50VRx16 BSW performance - GT	STD	STD
—	**Seats**		
9	cloth buckets - Base	STD	STD
8GT	cloth buckets multi-adjust seats w/console - GT	STD	STD
7	leather seating surfaces buckets (front buckets only) - GT	445	500
572	**Air Conditioning, Manual**	694	780
552	**Anti-Lock Braking System, 4-Wheel Disc Brakes & Spt Suspension** — Base	654	735
552	**Anti-Lock Braking System** — GT	503	565
18A	**Anti-Theft System**	169	190
153	**Bracket, Front License Plate**	NC	NC
184	**Console w/Storage Armrest w/Cupholder**	54	60

CODE	DESCRIPTION	DEALER	LIST
415	**Feature Car**..	191	215
12H	**Floor Mats, Front Color-Keyed**	27	30
50C	**Group 1**	232	260
	incls rear window defroster, dual elec remote control mirrors		
65B	**Group 2**	440	495
	incls tilt steering column, convenience group (tinted glass, interval windshield wipers, remote fuel door/liftgate releases, battery saver, headlamp warning chime, convenience lights)		
67A	**Group 3**	984	1105
	incls manual air conditioning, electronic AM/FM stereo radio w/clock/cassette/premium sound		
85A	**Group 4**	1019	1145
	incls color-keyed bodyside moldings, light group (illuminated entry system, dual illuminated visor vanity mirrors, fade-to-off dome lamp w/map lights, remote keyless entry), power group (power side windows/power door locks, speed control)		
97A	**Group 5**	658	740
	incls anti-lock braking system, rear wiper/washer & heated dual elec remote mirrors		
41H	**Heater, Engine Block**	18	20
943	**Light Group**	352	395
961	**Moldings, Color-Keyed Bodyside**	45	50
43R	**Power Group**	623	700
173	**Rear Wiper/Washer & Heated Dual Electric Remote Control Mirrors**	156	175
21A	**Seat, Power Drivers**	258	290
215	**Seat Height Adjust, Manual Driver's**	31	35
416	**SE Option** — Base	677	760
13B	**Sliding Roof, Power**	547	615
—	**Audio**		
588	radio, electronic AM/FM cassette/premium sound.......................................	290	325
582	radio, electronic AM/FM stereo/CD player/premium sound - w/pkg 251A.....	712	800
	w/pkg 253A, 261A or 263A..	423	475
915	graphic equalizer	120	135
91H	power antenna...	71	80

FORD

TAURUS

TAURUS 6 CYL

Code	Description	Dealer	List
P52	GL 4-Dr Sedan	14519	16140
P53	LX 4-Dr Sedan	16874	18785
P54	SHO 4-Dr Sedan	22151	24715
P57	GL 4-Dr Wagon	15481	17220
P58	LX 4-Dr Wagon	18311	20400
	Destination Charge:	525	525

Standard Equipment

TAURUS - GL: Exterior accent group, bodycolor grille, single aerodynamic halogen headlamps, lower bodyside urethane protection on lower doors and rocker panels, dual electric remote-control mirrors, color-keyed bodyside protection, color-keyed rocker panel moldings, clearcoat paint, full wheel covers, driver and front passenger air bags, front center dual armrests (single with bucket/console), rear center folding armrest (Sedan), illuminated front ashtray, two rear ashtrays, 16 oz. color-keyed carpeting, cigarette lighter, electronic digital clock with dimming feature, cupholder/coin holder, illuminated locking glove box, day/night inside rearview mirror, electronic AM/FM stereo radio with dual-access remote controls on instrument panel, split bench seats with dual recliners and front seatback map pockets, tilt steering column, color coordinated four-spoke steering wheel, power front disc/rear drum brakes, side window demisters, child-proof rear door locks, 3.0 liter V6 SEFI engine, tinted glass, illuminated entry system, luggage compartment light, power rack and pinion steering, independent MacPherson strut suspension, P205/65R15 BW tires, mini-spare tire, 4-speed automatic overdrive transmission, interval windshield wipers.

LX (in addition to or instead of GL equipment): Color-keyed lower bodyside cladding, paint stripe, bright machined cast aluminum wheels, cargo tie-down net, console with floor shift, convenience kit (includes lantern, tire pressure gauge, gloves, towel, headlamp bulbs), front and rear grab handles, light group, dual illuminated visor vanity mirrors, bucket seats with dual recliners and two-way adjustable front head restraints (Sedan), 6-way power driver's seat (Sedan), 60/40 split/fold-down second seat (Wagon), driver/passenger secondary sun visors for front/side coverage, manual air conditioning, power door locks, 3.8 liter V6 SEFI engine (Wagon), fuel door and decklid/liftgate release remote, automatic

CODE	DESCRIPTION	DEALER	LIST

headlamp on/off/delay, tachometer, warning alerts, automatic parking brake release, speed-sensitive variable assist power rack and pinion steering, power side windows with express-down driver's window.

SHO: Deck lid spoiler, black-out exterior sport treatment, bodycolor grille, cornering lamps, valence panel with fog lamps, color-keyed lower bodyside molding, dual electric remote-control mirrors, color-keyed bodyside moldings, color-keyed rocker panel moldings, clearcoat paint, sparkle unidirectional spoke cast aluminum wheels, driver and front passenger air bags, front center dual armrests (single with bucket/console), rear center folding seat, front illuminated ashtray, two rear ashtrays, cargo tie-down net, 18 oz. color-keyed carpeting, cigarette lighter, electronic digital clock with dimming feature, console with floor shift, convenience kit (includes lantern, tire pressure gauge, gloves, towel and replacement headlamp bulbs), cupholder/coin holder, vinyl door trim panels, floor mats, illuminated locking glove box, front and rear grab handles, light group, day/night inside rearview mirror, dual illuminated visor mirrors, high level audio system with dual access remote controls on instrument panel, cloth and leather bucket seats with dual recliners, 4-way adjustable front head restraints and front seatback map pockets, leather bolster seat trim, tilt steering column, leather-wrapped steering wheel, driver/passenger secondary sun visors for front/side coverage, air conditioning with electric temperature control, 130 amp alternator, power 4-wheel disc brakes with anti-lock braking system, rear window defroster, side window demisters, child-proof rear door locks, power door locks, dual exhaust system, 3.0 liter DOHC SEFI 24-valve V6 engine, 5-speed manual transmission, fuel door and decklid remote release, extended range fuel tank (18.4 gallons), tinted glass, automatic headlamps with on/off/delay, illuminated entry, tachometer, luggage compartment light, power antenna, speed control, speed-sensitive variable assist power rack and pinion steering, independent MacPherson strut front suspension, handling suspension, P215/60ZR16 94V BW high performance tires (touring tires when automatic is ordered), power side windows with express-down driver's window, interval windshield wipers.

Accessories

—	**Preferred Equipment Pkgs** — prices include pkg discounts		
203A	**GL Pkg 203A**	579	650
204A	**GL Pkg 204A**	1842	2070
208A	**LX 4-Dr Pkg 208A**	458	515
208A	**LX Wgn Pkg 208A**	628	705
211A	**SHO Pkg 211A**	NC	NC
—	**Groups**		
77A	**Group 1** — GL	855	960
	LX	143	160
	incls air conditioning and rear defroster		
77B	**Group 2** — w/GL Pkg 204A	992	1115
	LX	338	380
	incls decklid/liftgate/fuel door release, power locks, power windows, light group, speed control, cassette		
54A	**Group 3**	329	370
	incls power driver's seat, deluxe wheel covers		
54B	**Group 4**	360	405
	incls leather wrapped steering wheel, power antenna, remote keyless entry		
96W	**Group 5**	174	195
	incls rear window wiper/washer, cargo area cover		
99U	**Engine** — 3.0L - GL, LX 4-Dr, GL Wgn	STD	STD
994	**Engine** — 3.8L - NA w/203A, SHO	472	530
99Y	**Engine** — 3.0L DOHC - SHO	STD	STD

FORD

CODE	DESCRIPTION	DEALER	LIST
99P	**Engine** — 3.2L DOHC (incl w/automatic overdrive) - SHO, incl in pkgs		
445	**Transaxle** — 5-speed manual - SHO	STD	STD
44L	**Transaxle** — auto overdrive (std on GL/LX, incls 3.2L eng on SHO) - SHO...	703	790
422	**California Emissions System**	85	95
428	**High Altitude Emissions System**	NC	NC
—	**Tires**		
T32	P205/65R15 BSW - GL	STD	STD
T22	P215/60ZR16 BSW high performance - SHO w/manual trans	STD	STD
T25	P215/60R16 94V BSW touring - SHO w/automatic trans	NC	NC
508	conventional spare - GL, LX	62	70
—	**Seats**		
P	cloth split bench - GL	STD	STD
Q	cloth bucket/console - GL	NC	NC
B	leather bucket/console - GL	530	595
C	cloth split bench - LX Wagon	STD	STD
M	cloth bucket/console - LX 4-Dr	STD	STD
B	leather bucket/console - LX	441	495
A	leather split bench - LX	441	495
9	cloth & leather bucket - SHO	STD	STD
H	leather bucket - SHO	441	495
573	**Air Conditioning, Electronic Climate Control** — NA on GL	156	175
552	**Anti-Lock Braking System** — incls 4-wheel disc brakes	503	565
516	**Cellular Telephone, Storage Armrests**	445	500
12Y	**Floor Mats, Front & Rear**	40	45
596	**Load Floor Extension/"Picnic Table"** — Wagons only	76	85
902	**Locks, Power Door** — GL	218	245
53L	**Luxury Convenience Group** — SHO	1383	1555
53K	**LX Convenience Group**	916	1030
21A	**Power Seat, Driver Only**	258	290
21J	**Power Seats, Driver & Passenger** — LX only	258	290
214	**Seat, Rear Facing Third** — Wagons only	134	150
525	**Speed Control**	191	215
642	**Wheel Covers, Deluxe**	71	80
64R	**Wheels, Cast Aluminum/P205 15 Tires** — w/Pkg 204A	205	230
43R	**Windows, Power Side**	302	340
—	**Audio**		
58H	radio, electronic AM/FM stereo cassette	147	165
586	audio system, high level - LX w/77B Group 2	280	315
	LX w/o 77B Group 2	427	480
917	CD player (NA on GL)	418	470
916	Ford JBL audio system (NA on GL or Wagon)	445	500
631	**Battery, Heavy Duty** — 72 amp (NA on SHO)	27	30
153	**Bracket, Front License Plate**	NC	NC
41H	**Engine Block Immersion Heater**	18	20
662	**Suspension, Heavy Duty** — load carrying (NA on SHO)	23	25
144	**Remote Keyless Entry System** — GL w/o 77B Group 2	276	310
	incls decklid/liftgate/fuel door release		
	GL w/77B Group 2, LX	191	215

CODE	DESCRIPTION	DEALER	LIST

TEMPO

TEMPO 4 CYL

P31	GL 2-Dr Sedan	8713	9465
	(models registered in Chicago, Cincinnati, Denver, Detroit, Kansas, Pittsburgh, Southwest, Kansas City, Twin Cities)		
P31	GL 2-Dr Sedan	9869	10735
P36	GL 4-Dr Sedan	9869	10735
P37	LX 4-Dr Sedan	11530	12560
	Destination Charge:	485	485

Standard Equipment

TEMPO - GL: Color-keyed bumpers and grille, headlamps-on alert chimes, black LH sail mounted manual mirror, dual "halo" full surround greenhouse molding system, color-keyed bodyside moldings, deluxe 14" wheel covers, front and rear ashtrays, automatic shoulder belt restraint system, deluxe carpeting, cigarette lighter, electronic digital clock, consolette with cupholder, lockable glove box, footwell illumination, luggage compartment light, day/night inside rearview mirror, dual visor mirrors with covers, cloth low-back front bucket seats, color-keyed steering wheel, package tray, maintenance-free battery, power front disc/rear drum brakes, coolant recovery system, side window demisters, 2.3 liter HSC 4 cylinder EFI engine, front wheel drive, tinted glass, headlamp-on warning chime, inside hood release, dual note horn, electronic AM/FM stereo radio, luxury sound insulation package, power rack and pinion steering, independent MacPherson strut front suspension, P185/70R14 BW all-season tires, mini-spare tire, interval windshield wipers.

LX (in addition to or instead of GL equipment): Black dual electric remote-control outside rearview mirrors, dual upper bodyside stripes, polycast 14" wheels, fold-down front center armrest, cargo tie-down net, front and rear floor mats, passenger assist handles (4 Dr), light group (ashtray, glove box, engine compartment, dome, map), upgraded cloth seat trim with seatback pockets, unique door trim, trip odometer, illuminated entry system, sport instrumentation cluster, power lock group (includes power door locks, remote fuel filler door and remote decklid release, tilt steering wheel, touring suspension, P185/70R14 BW performance all-season tires.

Accessories

	Preferred Equip Pkgs — prices include pkg discounts		
225A	GL 2/4-Dr Pkg 225A	277	310

CODE	DESCRIPTION	DEALER	LIST
226A	**GL 2-Dr Pkg 226A**	1118	1255
226A	**GL 4-Dr Pkg 226A**	1153	1295
227A	**SRS GL 2-Dr Pkg 227A**	1025	1150
227A	**SRS GL 4-Dr Pkg 227A**	1060	1190
233A	**LX 4-Dr Pkg 233A**	855	960
225S	**GL 4-Dr Pkg 225S**	766	860
227S	**GL 4-Dr Pkg 227S**	993	1115
99X	**Engine — 2.3L HSC SEFI - GL & LX**	STD	STD
99U	**Engine — 3.0L V6 SEFI**	583	655
445	**Transaxle — 5-spd manual**	STD	STD
440	**Transaxle — 3-spd FLC automatic**	476	535
422	**California Emissions**	85	95
428	**High Altitude Emissions**	NC	NC
—	**Tires**		
T72	P185/70Rx14 BSW - GL	STD	STD
T73	P185/70Rx14 BSW performance (std on LX) - GL, LX	NC	NC
T7J	P185/70Rx14 WSW performance	71	80
—	**Seats**		
P	cloth low back buckets - GL	STD	STD
R	upgraded cloth low back buckets - LX	STD	STD
572	**Air Conditioning, Manual**	694	780
594	**Armrest, Front Center**	49	55
163	**Bracket, Front License Plate**	NC	NC
57Q	**Defroster, Rear Window**	143	160
41H	**Heater, Engine Block Immersion**	18	20
12H	**Floor Mats, Front**	23	25
12Q	**Floor Mats, Rear**	18	20
156	**Instrument Cluster, Sport**	76	85
943	**Light Group**	31	35
903	**Light Group, Power — 2-Dr**	263	295
	4-Dr	298	335
548	**Luggage Rack, Decklid**	98	110
54J	**Mirrors, Dual Electric Remote Control**	102	115
—	**Paint, Clearcoat**	76	85
21A	**Seat, Power Driver's**	258	290
525	**Speed Control**	191	215
52Q	**Steering Wheel, Tilt**	124	140
59H	**Supplemental Air Bag Restraint System (Driver Only) - SRS — GL**	414	465
	LX	290	325
64J	**Wheels, Polycast**	165	185
43R	**Windows, Power Side — 4-Dr only**	280	315
—	**Audio**		
589	radio, electronic AM/FM stereo/clock/cassette	134	150
58Y	radio credit option	209	235
913	radio sound system, premium	116	130

FORD

THUNDERBIRD

THUNDERBIRD 6 CYL
P62   LX 2-Dr.. 15124   16830

THUNDERBIRD 8 CYL
P64   Super Coupe 2-Dr.. 19938   22240

Destination Charge: 495   495

Standard Equipment

THUNDERBIRD - LX: Color-keyed front and rear 5 mph bumpers, halogen headlamps, dual elec remote control color-keyed mirrors, bodyside molding, styled road wheel covers, driver/front passenger air bags, full length console w/floor-mounted shift, dual console mounted cupholders, luxury level door trim with courtesy lights/illum door switches, driver's side footwell lights, illum entry system, leather shift knob, lights (map/dome, luggage compartment, front ashtray and glove box, rear seat courtesy lights), dual visor mirrors, luxury cloth bucket seats w/driver's six-way power, rear seat center armrest, side window defoggers, speed control, luxury leather-wrapped steering wheel, tilt steering wheel, manual air cond, 130 amp alternator, maintenance-free battery, power front disc/rear drum brakes, digital clock, 3.8 liter V6 EFI engine, tinted glass, dual note horn, performance analog instrument cluster (includes trip odometer, fuel gauge, temperature gauge, oil pressure gauge, voltmeter), power lock group, elec AM/FM stereo radio w/cassette, front and rear stabilizer bars, P205/70R15 BW all-season tires, mini-spare tire, electronic controlled automatic overdrive transmission, power side windows, interval windshield wipers.

SUPER COUPE (in addition to or instead of LX equipment): Lower bodyside cladding, fog lamps, 16" x 7" Directional cast aluminum wheels with locking lug nuts, driver's footrest, light group, articulated bucket seats in cloth/leather/vinyl trim with power adjusters, lumbar support and power adjustable seat back side bolsters, electronic semi-automatic temp control air conditioning, 110 amp alternator, traction-lok axle, power four-wheel disc brakes with anti-lock braking system, 3.8 liter V6 EFI supercharged/intercooled engine with dual exhaust, automatic ride, control adjustable suspension, P225/60ZR16 BW performance tires, 5-speed manual overdrive transmission.

Accessories

—	Preferred Equipment Pkgs — prices include pkg discounts		
155A	**LX Pkg 155A**..	NC	NC
157A	**Super Coupe Pkg 157A**..	NC	NC

CODE	DESCRIPTION	DEALER	LIST
994	**Engine** — 3.8L EFI - LX	STD	STD
99R	**Engine** — 3.8L EFI super charged - Super Coupe	STD	STD
99W	**Engine** — 4.6L EFI V8	459	515
445	**Transaxle** — 5-spd manual (std on Super Coupe) - Super Coupe	STD	STD
44L	**Transaxle** — 4-spd automatic overdrive (std on LX)	703	790
422	**California Emissions**	85	95
428	**High Altitude Emissions**	NC	NC
—	**Tires**		
T33	P205/70R15 BSW (std on LX) - LX	STD	STD
T37	P215/70R15 BSW - included in pkg - LX		
T24	P225/60ZR16 97V BSW performance - Super Coupe	STD	STD
T29	P225/60ZR16 97V BSW all season performance - Super Coupe	62	70
—	**Seats**		
X	luxury cloth buckets - LX	STD	STD
Y	leather seating surfaces buckets - LX	438	490
Z	cloth/leather/vinyl articulated buckets - Super Coupe........	STD	STD
1	leather seating surfaces articulated buckets - Super Coupe	547	615
552	**Anti-Lock Braking System**	503	565
18A	**Anti-Theft System**	209	235
153	**Bracket, Front License Plate**	NC	NC
632	**Cold Weather Group** — LX.....................................	267	300
	LX w/155A..	124	140
	LX w/4.6L engine...	245	275
	LX w/155A & w/4.6L engine	102	115
	SC w/auto, LX w/traction assist w/4.6L	160	180
	SC w/auto w/157A, LX w/traction assist w/155A w/4.6L	18	20
	SC w/manual, LX w/traction assist	182	205
	SC w/manual w/157A, LX w/traction assist w/155A	40	45
12H	**Floor Mats, Front**..	27	30
144	**Keyless Entry, Remote** — LX, SC w/luxury group...........	191	215
	Super Coupe..	263	295
13B	**Moonroof, Power**	658	740
516	**Telephone, Cellular "Hands Free"**...........................	472	530
553	**Traction Assist** (LX only) - LX	187	210
—	**Tri Coat Paint**	201	225
—	**Audio**		
586	elec AM/FM cassette radio w/premium sound (incl power antenna)	329	370
916	Ford JBL audio system...	445	500
919	compact disc changer, trunk mounted	699	785
411	**Group 1** — Super Coupe.......................................	712	800
	incls power lock group, speed control, 6-way power driver's seat		
432	**Group 2** — LX...	280	315
	Super Coupe..	143	160
	incls elec semi auto temp control (std on Super Cpe), rear window defroster		
463	**Group 3** — LX...	271	305
	Super Coupe..	85	95
	incls cast alum whls/P215/70Rx15 BSW (LX only), dual illum vanity mirrors		
545	**Luxury Group** — LX	516	580
	Super Coupe..	494	555
	incls autolamp group, illuminated entry (Super Coupe), Light Group (LX), 6-way power passenger seat, integrated warning lamp module (LX)		

METRO

METRO 3 CYL

CODE	DESCRIPTION	DEALER	LIST
1MS08	XFi 3-Dr Hatchback Coupe	6706	7195
1MR08	3-Dr Hatchback Coupe	6706	7195
1MR68	5-Dr Hatchback Sedan	7172	7695
	Destination Charge:	295	295

Standard Equipment

METRO: Radio antenna, power front disc/rear drum brakes, black front and rear bumpers (XFi), 1.0 liter single overhead camshaft 3-cylinder electronic fuel injection engine, stainless steel muffler and tailpipe exhaust, outside LH remote black mirror (XFi), rack and pinion steering, independent 4-wheel MacPherson strut front suspension, P145/80R12 all-season SBR BW tires, 5-speed manual transmission with 4th and 5th gear overdrive, styled steel wheels with center caps (XFi), cargo area trim, full carpeting (including cargo area), center console with cupholders and storage tray, front automatic door locks, rear child security door locks (1MR68), temperature gauge, 3-position dome light, lighter/power socket, inside day/night rearview mirror, front automatic lap/shoulder belts, Scotchgard fabric protector on seats, full-folding rear seat, high-back reclining front bucket seats with integral head restraints, cloth covered seating surface with vinyl backs and sides, self-aligning steering wheel, driver's door storage bin, headlights on reminder tone, rear-quarter swing-out window, body-color upper front/rear bumpers (NA - XFi), dual outside LH remote/RH manual black mirrors (NA - XFi), black bodyside moldings (NA - XFi), full wheel covers (NA - XFi), fixed intermittent wipers (NA - XFi).

Accessories

CODE	DESCRIPTION	DEALER	LIST
—	**Metro XFi Base Equipment Group 1** — 1MS08	NC	NC
	incld w/model		
—	**Metro XFi Preferred Equipment Group 2** — 1MS08	268	301
UL0	w/UL0 radio, add	174	195
	incls standard equipment, electronically tuned AM/FM stereo radio with seek, digital clock and four speakers		
—	**Metro Base Equipment Group 1** — 1MR08 & 1MR68	NC	NC
UL1	w/UL1 radio, add	268	301
UL0	w/UL0 radio, add	441	496
	incld w/model		

GEO

CODE	DESCRIPTION	DEALER	LIST
—	**Metro Preferred Equipment Group 2** — 1MR08 & 1MR68	909	1021
UL0	w/UL0 radio, add	174	195
	incls standard equipment, air conditioning, electronically tuned AM/FM		
	stereo radio with seek, digital clock and four speakers		
—	**Radio Equipment** — see pkgs		
UL1	radio - see pkgs		
	incls elec tuned AM/FM stereo radio w/seek, digital clock and four spKrs		
UL0	radio - see pkgs		
	incls electronically tuned AM/FM stereo radio with seek and scan, tone		
	select, stereo cassette tape, digital clock, theft deterrent and four speakers		
H2	**Cloth & Vinyl Bucket Seats**..	NC	NC
—	**Exterior Color** — paint, solid	NC	NC
LP2	**Engine** — 1.0 liter SOHC L3 EFI	NC	NC
C60	**Air Conditioning** — CFC free	641	720
D42	**Cover, Cargo Security**	45	50
C49	**Defogger** — rear window	134	150
R9W	**Defogger** — rear window, delete	NC	NC
YF5	**California Emission Requirements**..	62	70
FE9	**Federal Emission Requirements**	NC	NC
NG1	**New York State Emission Requirements**	62	70
B37	**Floor Mats** — front & rear	22	25
D35	**Mirrors, Dual Outside** — LH remote & RH manual, black	18	20
B84	**Moldings** — bodyside, black	45	50
U16	**Tachometer**	45	50
—	**Transmissions**		
MM5	5-speed manual w/4th & 5th gear overdrive	NC	NC
MX1	3-speed automatic...	441	495
C25	**Wiper/Washer** — rear window	111	125

PRIZM

PRIZM 4 CYL

1SK19	4-Dr Sedan (except Calif.)..	10215	10730
1SK19	4-Dr Sedan (Calif.)	9958	10460
1SK19/B4M	LSi 4-Dr Sedan (except Calif.)	10603	11500
1SK19/B4M	LSi 4-Dr Sedan (Calif.)	10354	11230
Destination Charge:	....	365	365

Special Order Please Rush Delivery!

BUSINESS REPLY MAIL
FIRST-CLASS MAIL   PREMIT NO. 11   SHRUB OAK, NY

POSTAGE WILL BE PAID BY ADRESSEE

Edmund's Publications Corp.

P. O. Box 338
Shrub Oak, NY 10588-9903

|ııı|||ıııı|ı|ı|ı|ıı|ı|ı|ı|ıı|ı|ıııııı|ı|ııı||

Special Order Please Rush Delivery!

NO POSTAGE
NECESSARY
IF MAILED
IN THE
UNITED STATES

BUSINESS REPLY MAIL
FIRST-CLASS MAIL   PREMIT NO. 11   SHRUB OAK, NY

POSTAGE WILL BE PAID BY ADRESSEE

Edmund's Publications Corp.

P. O. Box 338
Shrub Oak, NY 10588-9903

SAVE MONEY compared to single copies...

Standard Equipment

PRIZM: Radio antenna, power front disc/rear drum brakes, front and rear body-color bumpers, 1.6 liter dual overhead camshaft 16-valve 4-cylinder multi-port fuel injection engine, stainless steel exhaust, tinted glass, composite halogen headlights, dual outside LH remote/RH manual black mirrors, black bodyside moldings, rack and pinion steering, independent 4-wheel MacPherson strut front suspension, P175/65R14 all-season SBR BW tires, styled steel wheels with center cap, cargo area trim, full carpeting, center console includes cupholder and storage tray, rear child security door locks, cloth door trim, remote fuel door, molded cloth headliners, rear console heating ducts, 3-position dome light, lighter/power socket, inside day/night rearview mirror, headlights on reminder tone, restraint system (driver and passenger air bags, front lap/shoulder belts, rear center lap belt, rear outboard lap/shoulder belts), Scotchgard fabric protection on seats and door trim, reclining front bucket seats w/adjustable head restraints, vinyl headrests/seatback w/cloth bolsters, driver's door storage bin, door ajar warning light.

LSi (in addition to or instead of Prizm equipment): Black center pillar, full wheel covers, front and rear passenger assist grips, trunk lid/cargo area trim, console with armrest, cargo area light, covered dual visor mirrors, split folding 60/40 rear seat, full-cloth facing seat trim/side bolsters with cloth/vinyl seatbacks, tilt steering wheel, driver and passenger door storage bins.

Accessories

CODE	DESCRIPTION	DEALER	LIST
—	**Prizm Base Equipment Group 1** — 1SK19	NC	NC
UL1	w/UL1 radio, add	284	330
UL0	w/UL0 radio, add	452	525
—	**Prizm Preferred Group 2** — 1SK19	507	590
UL0	w/UL0 radio, add	168	195
	incls standard equipment, electronically tuned AM/FM stereo radio with seek, digital clock and four speakers, power steering		
—	**Prizm LSi Preferred Equipment Group 1** — 1SK19/B4M	NC	NC
UL1	w/UL1 radio, add	284	330
UL0	w/UL0 radio, add	452	525
	incls LSi equipment		
—	**Prizm LSi Preferred Equipment Group 2** — 1SK19/B4M	1329	1545
UL0	w/UL0 radio, add	168	195
UP0	w/UP0 radio, add	488	568
	incls LSi equipment, air conditioning, elec tuned AM/FM stereo radio with seek, digital clock and four speakers, black dual outside electric mirrors, power steering, trunk release remote, variable intermittent wipers		
—	**Prizm LSi Preferred Equipment Group 3** — 1SK19/B4M	1926	2240
UL0	w/UL0 radio, add	168	195
UP0	w/UP0 radio, add	488	568
	incls LSi equipment, air conditioning, electronically tuned AM/FM stereo radio with seek, digital clock and four speakers, black dual outside electric remote mirrors, power steering, trunk release remote, variable intermittent wipers, cruise control w/resume speed, power door locks, power windows		
—	**Radio Equipment** — see pkgs		
UL1	radio - see pkgs		
	incls electronically tuned AM/FM stereo radio with seek, digital clock and four speakers		
UL0	radio - see pkgs		
	incls electronically tuned AM/FM stereo radio with seek and scan, tone select, stereo cassette tape, digital clock, theft deterrent and four speakers		
UP0	radio - see pkgs		
	incls electronically tuned AM/FM stereo radio with seek and scan, tone		

GEO

CODE	DESCRIPTION	DEALER	LIST
	select, stereo cassette tape, compact disc player, digital clock, theft deterrent and six extended range speakers		
—	**Interior Trim**		
A2	cloth & vinyl bucket seats	NC	NC
B2	custom cloth bucket seats (std on Prizm LSi model)...................................	NC	NC
—	**Exterior Color** — paint, solid	NC	NC
C60	**Air Conditioning** — CFC free..	684	795
JM4	**Brakes** — 4-wheel anti-lock brake system	512	595
K34	**Cruise Control w/Resume Speed**	151	175
C49	**Defogger** — rear window...	146	170
R9W	**Defogger** — rear window, delete...	NC	NC
AU3	**Door Locks** — power	189	220
YF5	**California Emission Requirements**...	60	70
FE9	**Federal Emission Requirements**	NC	NC
NG1	**New York State Emission Requirements**	60	70
B37	**Floor Mats** — front & rear, carpeted, color-keyed..............................	34	40
CA1	**Sun Roof** — electric w/map light & tilt-up feature................................	568	660
U16	**Tachometer**	52	60
—	**Transmissions**		
MM5	5-speed manual w/4th & 5th gear overdrive	NC	NC
MX1	3-speed automatic...	426	495
MS7	4-speed electronically controlled automatic w/overdrive	667	775
—	**Engines**		
L01	1.6 liter DOHC 16-valve L4 MFI..	NC	NC
LV6	1.8 liter DOHC 16-valve L4 MFI..	303	352
	incls P185/65R14 all-season steel belted radial BW tires/rear stabilizer bar		
PG4	**Wheels** — 14" alloy...	288	335
CD4	**Wipers** — intermittent variable	34	40

CODE	DESCRIPTION	DEALER	LIST

TRACKER

TRACKER 2WD 4 CYL
CE10367 2-Dr Convertible 10343   10865

TRACKER 4WD 4 CYL
CJ10316 2-Dr.. 11705   12295
CJ10367 2-Dr Convertible 11553   12135
CJ10316/B2Z LSi 2-Dr 13104   13765
CJ10367/B2Z LSi 2-Dr Convertible.. 12852   13500

Destination Charge: 300   300

Standard Equipment

TRACKER: Radio antenna, power front disc/rear drum brakes, rear-wheel anti-lock brakes, front and rear bumpers with integral black rub strip, 1.6 liter single overhead camshaft 4-cylinder electronic fuel injection engine (available with FE9 Federal Emission only), 1.6 liter single overhead camshaft 16-valve 4-cylinder multi-port fuel injection engine (available with YF5 California or NG1 New York Emission only), stainless steel muffler and tailpipe exhaust, composite halogen headlights, front manual locking hubs, dual outside black mirrors, spare tire cover, full-size outside rear-mounted lockable spare tire and wheel, front MacPherson strut suspension, rear solid axle coil spring suspension, swing-open right-hand hinged door tailgate with lock, P195/75R15 all-season SBR BW tires (2WD), P205/75R15 all-season SBR BW tires (4x4), front and rear tow hooks, transfer case, 5-speed manual transmission with 5th gear overdrive, styled steel wheels with center caps, fixed intermittent wipers, front and rear passenger assist grips, cargo area trim, full carpeting including cargo area, center console with cupholders and storage tray, rear window defogger (NA - Convertible), tachometer (4x4), trip odometer, 3-position dome light, lighter/power socket, inside day/night rearview mirror, restraint system (front lap/shoulder belts, rear outboard lap/shoulder belts), Scotchgard fabric protection on seats, fold-and-stow rear bench seat (4x4), driver/passenger easy-entry seats, high-back reclining front bucket seats with integral head restraints, cloth bolsters and vinyl seatbacks, self-aligning steering wheel, driver and passenger door storage bins.

Accessories

—   **Tracker 2WD Convertible Base Equipment Group 1**

GEO

CODE	DESCRIPTION	DEALER	LIST
	CE10367	NC	NC
UL1	w/UL1 radio, add	272	306
UL0	w/UL0 radio, add	446	501
UP0	w/UP0 radio, add	798	897
	incls standard equipment		
—	**Tracker 2WD Convertible Preferred Equipment Group 2** — CE10367	517	581
UL0	w/UL0 radio, add	174	195
UP0	w/UP0 radio, add	526	591
	incls standard equipment, electronically tuned AM/FM stereo radio with seek, digital clock and four speakers, power steering		
—	**Tracker 4WD & Tracker 4WD Convertible Base Equipment Group 1** —		
	CJ10316 & CJ10367	NC	NC
UL1	w/UL1 radio, add	272	306
UL0	w/UL0 radio, add	446	501
UP0	w/UP0 radio, add	798	897
	incld w/model		
—	**Tracker 4WD/Tracker 4WD Convertible Preferred Equipment Group 2** —		
	CJ10316 & CJ10367	517	581
UL0	w/UL0 radio, add	174	195
UP0	w/UP0 radio, add	526	591
	incls standard equipment, electronically tuned AM/FM stereo radio with seek, digital clock and four speakers		
—	**Tracker 4WD LSi & Tracker 4WD LSi Convertible**		
	Base Equipment Group 1 — CJ10316/B2Z & CJ10367/B2Z	NC	NC
UL0	w/UL0 radio, add	174	195
UP0	w/UP0 radio, add	526	591
	incld w/model		
—	**Radio Equipment** — see pkgs		
UL1	radio - see pkgs		
	incls electronically tuned AM/FM stereo radio with seek, digital clock and four speakers		
UL0	radio - see pkgs		
	incls electronically tuned AM/FM stereo radio with seek and scan, tone select, stereo cassette tape, digital clock, theft deterrent and four speakers		
UP0	radio - see pkgs		
	incls electronically tuned AM/FM stereo radio with seek and scan, tone select, stereo cassette tape, compact disc player, digital clock, theft deterrent and four speakers		
—	**Interior Trim**		
L2	linear cloth bucket seats	NC	NC
E2	expressive cloth bucket seats	NC	NC
C2	custom cloth bucket seats - LSi & Tracker 4x4 LSi Convertible	NC	NC
—	**Exterior Color** — paint, solid	NC	NC
—	**Engines**		
LS5	1.6 liter SOHC L4 EFI (w/FE9 Emissions only)	NC	NC
L01	1.6 liter SOHC 16-valve L4 MFI (w/YF5 or NG1 Emissions only)	NC	NC
C60	**Air Conditioning** — CFC free	663	745
YF5	**California Emission Requirements**	62	70
FE9	**Federal Emission Requirements**	NC	NC
NG1	**New York State Emission Requirements**	62	70
B37	**Floor Mats** — front & rear - std on LSi models	25	28

CODE	DESCRIPTION	DEALER	LIST
B84	**Moldings** — bodyside - CJ10316 model (std on Tracker LSi)	53	59
	Convertible models (std on LSi Convertible)	76	85
—	**Seating**		
AP6	rear not desired - CE10367 model only	NC	NC
AM7	rear folding bench - CE10367 model only (std on 4x4 models)	396	445
NY7	**Skid Plates** — front differential & transfer case	67	75
N33	**Steering Wheel** — tilt	102	115
—	**Transmissions**		
MM5	5-speed manual w/5th gear overdrive	NC	NC
MX1	3-speed automatic	530	595
QA4	**Wheels** — 15" alloy w/steel spare	298	335

CONTINENTAL

CONTINENTAL 6 CYL

Code	Description	Dealer	List
M97	Executive 4-Dr Sedan	29296	33750
M98	Signature 4-Dr Sedan	30886	35600
	Destination Charge:	625	625

Standard Equipment

CONTINENTAL - EXECUTIVE: Bodycolor front and rear bumpers with bright insert, argent grille with bright surround, cornering lights, bodycolor dual power remote control heated outside mirrors with blue glass for reduced glare, bright belt and rocker panel moldings, bodycolor vinyl bodyside moldings with bright insert, geometric spoke aluminum wheels, rear quarter windows, driver side and front passenger air bags, dual front seat fold-down armrests, luggage compartment carpeting, electronic digital clock, coat hooks, overhead console with courtesy/reading lamps, front floor mats, illuminated glove compartment, roof rail assist handles, 4-way articulated front seat head restraints, rear compartment heat ducts, electronic instrumentation (includes speedometer, temperature, oil, battery charge, fuel gauges and tripminder computer), rear seat courtesy lights, front seat back and front door map pockets,

LINCOLN

day/night rearview mirror, electronic AM/FM stereo radio with search, cassette tape player and premium sound system, leather seating surfaces, 50/50 twin comfort seats with power driver's side, leather-wrapped steering wheel, dual color-keyed sun visors with flip-up stowage, air conditioning with automatic climate control, automatic power antenna, 72 amp maintenance-free battery, power 4-wheel disc brakes with anti-lock brake system, coolant recovery system, remote decklid release, decklid tie-down, defroster group (heated rear window and outside rearview mirrors), power door locks, 3.8 liter V6 SEFI engine, dual exhaust system, front wheel drive, remote fuel filler door, tinted glass, dual note horn, engine compartment light, automatic, parking brake release, speed control, front and rear stabilizer bars, speed-sensitive variable-assist power rack and pinion steering, tilt steering column, vehicle level control suspension, power side windows, interval windshield wipers, P205/70R15 BSW tires, mini spare tire, electronic 4-speed automatic overdrive transmission.

SIGNATURE (in addition to or instead of Executive equipment): Bodyside accent stripes, front and rear floor mats, dual illuminated visor mirrors, JBL sound system, 6-way/6-way twin comfort seats with dual power recliners and memory with remote feature, power decklid pulldown, automatic headlamps with on/off/delay system, keyless illuminated entry system.

Accessories

CODE	DESCRIPTION	DEALER	LIST
952A	**Preferred Equipment Pkg 952A** — Executive	NC	NC
	incls comfort/convenience group and remote keyless/illuminated entry		
953A	**Preferred Equipment Pkg 953A** — Executive	1140	1325
994	**Engine** — 3.8L EFI V6	STD	STD
44L	**Transaxle** — electronic automatic overdrive	STD	STD
422	**California Emissions System**	86	100
428	**High Altitude Emissions System**	NC	NC
T33	**Tires** — P205/70R15 BSW	STD	STD
—	**Seats**		
I/J	leather seating surface, twin comfort lounge	STD	STD
N	leather seating surfaces, individual seats - Executive	767	890
18A	**Alarm System, Anti-Theft**	250	290
94H	**Comfort/Convenience Group**	602	700
	incls 6-way power passenger seat, dual illuminated visor mirrors, headlamps with automatic on/off delay system, power decklid pulldown, rear floor mats, power passenger recliner		
945	**Console Group, Overhead**	302	350
	incls electronic digital compass and electrochromic automatically dimming rearview mirror, and electrochromic outside driver's mirror		
13B	**Moonroof, Power**	1302	1515
—	**Paint, White Opalescent Clearcoat Metallic**	202	235
144	**Remote Keyless/Illuminated Entry System**	258	300
516	**Telephone, Voice Activated Cellular**	594	690
64C	**Wheels, Double Window** — Executive	NC	NC
916	**Audio System, Ford JBL**	486	565
917	**Compact Disc Player**	515	600
41H	**Engine Block Immersion Heater**	52	60
153	**Front License Plate Bracket**	NC	NC

MARK VIII

MARK VIII 8 CYL

M91	2-Dr Coupe	33034	38050
Destination Charge:		625	625

Standard Equipment

MARK VIII: Body color front and rear bumpers with bright insert, bright grille, low profile halogen headlamps, cornering lamps, limousine doors, body color heated remote control outside mirrors with 3-position memory, body color bodyside molding with bright insert, aluminum alloy wheels, driver and front passenger air bags, front and rear seat cigarette lighters, full-length console, leather-wrapped gearshift knob, vinyl door trim panels with door map pockets and courtesy light, front and rear floor mats, illuminated lockable glove compartment, rear seat heat registers, four-way adjustable front head restraints, mechanical analog instrumentation with message center and programmable trip functions, service interval reminder, side window defoggers, individual all-leather seats, 6-way driver and passenger power seats with Autoglide seating system, dual power recliners and dual power lumbar control, 3-position driver memory with remote recall, speed control, leather-wrapped steering wheel, tilt steering column, dual illuminated vanity mirrors with secondary visors, air conditioning, power antenna, anti-theft alarm system, 72 amp maintenance free battery, 4-wheel disc anti-lock brakes, trunk cargo net, decklid and fuel filler door release, rear window defroster, power door locks, 4.6 liter four-cam V8 engine, dual exhaust, solar tinted glass, automatic headlamps with on/off delay, illuminated entry system, remote keyless entry system, underhood and luggage compartment lights, low oil warning light, electronic AM/FM stereo radio with cassette tape player and premium sound system, automatic dual dampening rear shock absorbers, front and rear stabilizer bars, speed-sensitive variable assist power rack/pinion steering, vehicle level control suspension, P225/60R16 speed-rated BW tires, electronically controlled 4-speed auto overdrive transmission, power windows, interval windshield wipers.

Accessories

99V	**Engine** — 4.6L four cam V8		STD	STD
44L	**Transmission** — automatic electronic overdrive		STD	STD
422	**California Emissions**		86	100
428	**High Altitude Emissions**		NC	NC
T23	**Tires** — P225/60R/16 BSW		STD	STD

LINCOLN

CODE	DESCRIPTION	DEALER	LIST
A	**Individual All-Leather Seating Surfaces**	STD	STD
61A	**Mirror** — electrochromic auto dimming inside/out	184	215
13B	**Moonroof, Power**	1302	1515
516	**Telephone, Cellular** — voice activated	594	690
553	**Traction Assist, Electronic**	184	215
64U	**Wheels, Chrome Directional**	726	845
916	**Ford/JBL Audio System**	486	565
919	**Compact Disc Changer** — trunk mounted	700	815
585	**Radio** — electronic AM/FM stereo w/compact disc player	250	290
41H	**Engine Block Immersion Heater**	52	60
153	**License Plate Bracket, Front**	NC	NC

TOWN CAR

TOWN CAR 8 CYL

M81	Executive 4-Dr Sedan	30166	34750
M82	Signature 4-Dr Sedan	31284	36050
M83	Cartier 4-Dr Sedan	33046	38100
	Destination Charge:	625	625

Standard Equipment

TOWN CAR - EXECUTIVE: Color-keyed bumpers with bodyside moldings, bright vertical grille, halogen headlamps, heated dual power remote control outside mirrors, color-keyed bodyside moldings, geometric driver and passenger air bags, dual front seat fold-down armrests, rear seat center fold-down, electronic alert chimes, electronic digital clock, coat hooks, cupholders, front and rear floor mats, illuminated lockable glove compartment, roof rail assist handles, electronic instrument cluster with message center, door courtesy lights, rear compartment reading light, dual beam dome/map light, luggage compartment light, day/night inside rearview mirror, dual illuminated visor mirrors, electronic AM/FM stereo radio with cassette tape player and premium sound system, cloth seat trim, twin comfort lounge seats with 6-way/6-way power and 2-way front seat head restraints, four-spoke leather-wrapped steering wheel, door pull straps, dual coverage sunvisors, air conditioning, automatic power antenna, 72 amp heavy duty battery, power 4-wheel disc brakes with anti-lock brake system, coolant recovery system, remote decklid release, power decklid pull-down, rear window defroster, 4.6 liter SOHC V8 SEFI engine, engine temperature gauge, remote fuel filler door release, dual exhaust, tinted glass, automatic on/off headlamps with delay, dual note horn, remote keyless entry system, illuminated entry system, cornering lamps, engine compartment lamp, low engine oil alert light, power door locks, automatic parking brake release, speed control, tilt steering wheel, P215/70R15 WSW SBR tires, electronic automatic overdrive transmission, power side windows with driver express-down feature, interval windshield wipers.

SIGNATURE (in addition to or instead of Executive equipment): Upper bodyside accent paint stripe, dual storage armrests with cupholders, front seat back map pockets.

CARTIER (in addition to or instead of Signature equipment): Vinyl door trim inserts with cloth or leather trim, Ford JBL audio system, cloth and leather seating surfaces, twin comfort lounge seats with 6-way/6-way power with dual power recliners, memory seat, power lumbar support and 2-way front seat head restraints.

Accessories

CODE	DESCRIPTION	DEALER	LIST
99W	**Engine** — 4.6L EFI 8-cylinder	STD	STD
44P	**Transmission** — 4-spd electronic automatic overdrive	STD	STD
422	**California Emissions**	86	100
428	**High Altitude Emissions**	NC	NC
T3P	**Tires** — P215/70R15 WSW	STD	STD
508	**Conventional Spare Tire**	190	220
A/P	**Twin Comfort Lounge** — cloth - Executive & Signature	STD	STD
H	**Twin Comfort Lounge** — cloth & leather seating surfaces - Cartier	STD	STD
B/D	**Twin Comfort Lounge** — leather - Executive & Signature	478	555
F	**Twin Comfort Lounge** — leather - Cartier	NC	NC
18A	**Alarm System, Anti-Theft**	250	290
663	**Ride Control Pkg**	246	285
	incls P225/70R15 WW tires, dual exhaust, auxiliary power steering oil cooler, higher rate front & rear springs w/revised shock tuning, larger front & rear stabilizer bars		
61A	**Mirror** — electric automatic dimming rearview	94	110
13B	**Moonroof, Power**	1302	1515
958	**Paint Treatment** — monotone	NC	NC
—	**Paint** — white opalescent clearcoat metallic	202	235
46E	**Seat, Programmable Memory** — std on Cartier	460	535
516	**Telephone, Cellular** — voice activated	594	690
553	**Traction Assist, Electronic**	184	215
916	**JBL Audio System** — std on Cartier	486	565
919	**Compact Disc Changer** — trunk mounted	700	815
64K	**Y Spoke Aluminum Wheel**	NC	NC
41H	**Engine Block Immersion Heater**	52	60
535	**Heavy Duty Trailer Tow**	400	465
	incls HD cooling, auxiliary transmission fluid cooler, auxiliary power steering fluid cooler, 1330 U-joint w/steel driveshaft, 3.55 ratio axle, additional wiring harness, HD turn signals & flashers, conventional size spare tire w/matching steel wheel, upgraded front stabilizer bar, HD 30mm shock absorbers w/revised tuning		

CODE	DESCRIPTION	DEALER	LIST
418	**Heavy Duty Pkg**	692	805
	incls HD cooling pkg, auxiliary transmission fluid cooler, auxiliary power steering fluid cooler, unique front stabilizer bar, HD shock absorbers, HD front suspension lower control arms, steel driveshaft w/1330 U-joint, 3.55 ratio traction-lok HD axle w/11" x 2 1/4" rear brake drums, P225/75R15 WSW tires, Y-spoke aluminum wheels, full-size matching spare tire, 84 amp battery, 130 amp alternator, HD frame, unique ABS brakes (front disc, rear drum), HD jack		
531	**Livery Pkg**	280	325
	incls auxiliary transmission fluid cooler, auxiliary power steering fluid cooler, 1300 U-joint w/steel driveshaft, HD 30mm shock absorbers, upgraded front stabilizer bar, 84 amp HD battery, 130 amp alternator, standard engine cooling system, P215/70R15 tires		
153	**License Plate Bracket, Front**	NC	NC

CAPRI

CAPRI 4 CYL

T01	Base 2-Dr Convertible	12118	13190
T03	XR2 2-Dr Convertible	13674	14900
	Destination Charge:	375	375

Standard Equipment

CAPRI - BASE: Bodycolor front and rear bumpers with rub strips, bodycolor grille, pop-up retractable halogen headlamps, bodycolor dual power outside mirrors, bodycolor side moldings, black front mud guards, styled steel wheels with center cap, driver and passenger air bags, cut-pile carpeting, digital clock, full console with armrest, cloth door trim, illuminated locking glove box, rear compartment heat ducts, flash-to-pass headlamps, side window demisters, footwell courtesy lights, dual map lights, luggage compartment light, day/night inside rearview mirrors, electronic AM/FM stereo radio, driver side seat tilt and height adjustment, driver side adjustable lumbar support, lockable fold-down rear seatback, four-spoke leather-wrapped steering wheel, cloth sunvisors with covered vanity mirrors, 70 amp alternator, 48 amp maintenance-free battery, power four-wheel disc brakes, 1.6 liter DOHC 16-valve MPI 4 cylinder engine, front wheel drive, tinted glass, front and rear stabilizer bars (except with automatic transmission), power rack and pinion steering, independent MacPherson strut front suspension, mini spare tire, P185/60R14 82V BW tires, 5-speed manual transmission with overdrive, lower bodyside urethane protection, power side windows, variable intermittent 2-speed windshield wipers.

XR2 (in addition to or instead of Base equipment): Fog lamps, bodycolor lower rocker panel moldings, rear decklid spoiler, 15" 7-spoke alloy wheels, unique door trim, electronic AM/FM stereo radio with cassette tape player, leather seat trim, air conditioning, 1.6 liter DOHC 16-valve turbocharged/intercooled MPI 4 cylinder engine, power door locks, speed control, sport tuned suspension, P195/50R15 82V BW tires, 5-speed manual transmission with 4th and 5th gear overdrive.

Accessories

CODE	DESCRIPTION	DEALER	LIST
—	**Preferred Equipment Pkgs**		
651A	**Base Pkg 651A** — Base	NC	NC
	incls manual air conditioning, power door locks, AM/FM ET radio		
	w/cassette, fingertip speed control, 5-spoke alloy wheels		
660A	**XR2 Pkg 660A** — XR2	NC	NC
	incls vehicle plus standard equipment		
—	**Engines**		
99Z	1.6L - Base	STD	STD
996	1.6L EFI turbo - XR2	STD	STD
—	**Transaxles**		
445	5-speed manual	STD	STD
44T	automatic (NA on XR2)	703	790
422	**California Emissions**	85	95
428	**High Altitude Emissions**	NC	NC
—	**Tires**		
T76	P185/60R14 82H BSW - Base	STD	STD
T31	P195/50R15 82V BSW - XR2	STD	STD
—	**Seats**		
J	cloth functional sport	STD	STD
L	leather functional sport	445	500
572	**Air Conditioning, Manual** — std on XR2	694	780
476	**Cover, Black Tonneau**	165	185
477	**Cover, White Tonneau**	165	185
902	**Door Locks, Power** — std on XR2	178	200
525	**Speed Control, Fingertip** — std on XR2	191	215
64B	**Alloy Wheels** — 5-spoke	298	335
—	**Audio Systems**		
58H	electronic AM/FM radio w/cassette (std on XR2)	147	165
586	premium electronic AM/FM radio w/cassette - Base w/o 651A	383	430
	Base w/651A or 660A	236	265
153	**License Plate Bracket, Front**	NC	NC

COUGAR XR7

COUGAR XR7 6 CYL

M62	XR7 2-Dr	14617	16260
	Destination Charge:	495	495

Standard Equipment

COUGAR XR7: Color-keyed front and rear bumpers, bright grille, low-profile aero halogen headlamps, dual bodycolor power remote-control mirrors, color-keyed bodyside molding with bright insert, luxury wheel covers, luxury 24 oz. color-keyed cut-pile carpeting, headlamps-on chimes, full-length floor console with storage and cupholders, map pockets, courtesy lamps, locking glove box, rear compartment heat ducts, instrument cluster (includes analog performance cluster with tachometer, fuel gauge, coolant temperature, 120 mph speedometer, oil pressure and voltmeter gauges), carpeted luggage compartment with cargo net, day/night inside rearview mirror, concealed driver and unconcealed passenger visor mirrors, electronic AM/FM stereo radio with cassette and four speakers, reclining bucket seats (includes luxury cloth and leather, power lumbar and two-way adjustable head restraints), rear seat center fold-down armrest, four-spoke luxury steering wheel with tilt feature, driver and front passenger air bag, manual air conditioning, 130 amp alternator, maintenance-free battery, power front disc/rear drum brakes, electric drive fan, 3.8 liter SEFI V6 engine, tinted glass, power rack and pinion steering, P205/70R15 BW all-season tires, mini spare tire, electric 4-speed automatic transmission, power side windows, 2-speed interval windshield washers.

Accessories

CODE	DESCRIPTION	DEALER	LIST
260A	**Preferred Equipment Pkg 260A**	881	990
	incls groups 1, 2 & 3 (see group content)		
—	**Groups**		
412	**Group 1**	365	410
	incls electric rear window defroster, light group w/dual illuminated visors, illuminated entry, front floor mats		
433	**Group 2**	458	515
	incls fingertip speed control, leather-wrapped steering wheel, cast aluminum wheels, P215/70R15 BSW tires		
466	**Group 3**	521	585

MERCURY

CODE	DESCRIPTION	DEALER	LIST
	incls power lock group, 6-way power driver's seat		
144	**Keyless Entry System**	191	215
13B	**Moonroof, Power**	658	740
553	**Traction Assist, Electronic**	187	210
	req's 552 anti-lock brakes		
21J	**6-Way Dual Power Seats** — w/Pkg 260A	258	290
—	**Tri-Coat Paint**	201	225
—	**Audio Systems**		
919	compact disc changer, trunk mounted	699	785
	req's 586 radio and 916 Ford/JBL audio system		
916	Ford/JBL audio system	445	500
	req's 586 radio and 919 CD changer		
586	electronic AM/FM stereo radio w/cassette & power antenna	329	370
632	**Cold Weather Group**	124	140
	w/4.6L engine	102	115
	w/traction assist	40	45
	w/4.6L engine & w/traction assist	18	20
	incls electric rear window defroster, traction-lok axle, engine block		
	immersion heater, 72-amp heavy-duty battery		
153	**License Plate Bracket, Front**	NC	NC
516	**Telephone, Cellular**	472	530
	req's 586 radio		
994	**Engine** — 3.8L SEFI V6	STD	STD
99W	**Engine** — 4.6L SOHC EFI V8	548	615
44L	**Transmission** — electronic automatic overdrive	STD	STD
422	**California Emission System**	85	95
428	**High Altitude Emission System**	NC	NC
—	**Tires**		
T33	P205/70R15 BSW	STD	STD
T37	P215/70R15 BSW		
	incl and only available w/group 2		
—	**Seats**		
5	individual w/cloth & leather seating surfaces	STD	STD
6	individual w/leather seating surfaces	436	490
573	**Air Conditioning** — electronic auto temp control	138	155
474	**Autolamp**	62	70
552	**Anti-Lock Braking System**	503	585

MERCURY

GRAND MARQUIS

GRAND MARQUIS 8 CYL

		DEALER	LIST
M74	GS 4-Dr Sedan	18690	20330
M75	LS 4-Dr Sedan	19852	21500
Destination Charge:		575	575

Standard Equipment

GRAND MARQUIS - GS Concealed front and rear bumpers with full wrap color-keyed covers and integrated rubstrip with bright insert, bright vertical grille, dual aerodynamic halogen headlamps, color-keyed dual remote-control power mirrors, wide bodyside moldings with bright insert, black rocker panel moldings, lower bodyside urethane protection, driver and right front passenger air bag supplemental restraint system, color-keyed floor carpeting, luggage compartment carpeting, cigarette lighter, electronic digital clock, door trim includes: full-length armrests/woodtone applique/courtesy lights (front door only)/pull straps/upper vinyl and lower carpeting/flocked map pockets; driver footrest, lockable illuminated bin-type glove box, inside day/night mirror, right-hand non-illuminated visor mirror, electronic AM/FM stereo cassette radio with four speakers, fold-down front seat center armrests, map pockets in front seatbacks, fold-down rear seat center armrest, spare tire cover, tilt steering column, color-keyed luxury 4-spoke steering wheel with twin horn buttons, trip odometer, luxury trunk carpet trim and cargo net, manual air conditioning, 95 amp alternator, autolamp on/off delay system, 58 amp/hr. maintenance-free battery, four-wheel disc power brakes, rear door child safety latches, reminder chimes, coolant recovery system, electronic voltage regulator, 4.6 liter EFI OHC V8 engine with sequential multi-port fuel injection, remote fuel door release, tethered screw-in gas cap, complete tinted glass, blend-air type heater/defroster with 3-speed blower, gas strut hood assist, inside hood release, dual-note horn, distributorless ignition, automatic parking brake release, nitrogen gas-pressurized shock absorbers, luxury sound insulation package, T125/80R16 BSW mini spare tire, speed sensitive variable-assist power steering, short and long arm coil spring front suspension with stabilizer bar, coil spring four-bar link rear suspension with stabilizer bar, P215/70R15 WSW Michelin XW4 all-season steel belted radial tires, electronic automatic overdrive transmission with overdrive lockout feature, power side windows with express down driver's side, concealed 2-speed electric windshield wipers with fluidic washer system, interval windshield wipers, cloth twin-comfort lounge seats with dual recliners/two-way cloth covered head restraints/6-way power driver's seat.

CODE	DESCRIPTION	DEALER	LIST

LS (in addition to or instead of GS equip): Luxury cloth on upper door trim panel instead of vinyl (vinyl w/leather seat trim), luxury cloth twin-comfort lounge seats w/dual recliners/two-way cloth covered front head restraints/fixed rear seat head restraints/6-way power seat w/power recliner and power lumbar.

Accessories

CODE	DESCRIPTION	DEALER	LIST
—	**Preferred Equipment Pkgs**		
157A	**GS Pkg 157A** — GS	204	225
	incls groups 1 & 2		
172A	**LS Pkg 172A** — LS	966	1055
	incls groups 1, 2 & 3		
—	**Groups**		
68G	**Group 1**	182	205
	incls electric rear window defroster, front and rear carpet floor mats		
65R	**Group 2**	454	510
	incls power lock group and fingertip speed control		
67M	**Group 3** — LS	886	995
	incls power radio antenna, illuminated entry system, front cornering lamps, rear license plate frame, luxury light group (incls dual illuminated visor mirrors, dual beam dome/map lights, engine compartment light, rear seat reading lamps, dual secondary sun visors for front/side coverage), bodyside paint stripe, leather-wrapped steering wheel, aluminum wheels		
99W	**Engine** — 4.6L SEFI V8	STD	STD
44P	**Transmission** — electronic automatic overdrive	STD	STD
422	**California Emissions System**	85	95
428	**High Altitude Emissions System**	NC	NC
T33	**Tires** — P215/70R15 WSW	STD	STD
508	**Conventional Spare Tire** — LS	165	185
—	**Seats**		
F	cloth twin comfort - GS	STD	STD
G	cloth twin comfort - LS	STD	STD
H	leather twin comfort - LS	472	530
553	**Anti-Lock Braking System w/Traction Assist**	592	665
155	**Electronic Group** — LS	458	515
	incls electronic cluster, tripminder computer, electronic automatic temperature control, 72-amp battery		
41G	**Handling Pkg** — LS w/Pkg 172A	948	1065
	all other	1322	1485
	incls 3.27 axle, anti-lock braking system w/traction assist, upsized front and rear stabilizer bar, P225/70R15 WSW tires, rear air suspension w/unique springs, unique tuned suspension (shocks, spring rates), unique steering gear, aluminum wheels, dual exhaust		
47J	**Illuminated Entry System**	71	80
144	**Keyless Entry System**	191	215
51Q	**Front Cornering Lamps**	58	65
152	**License Plate Frame, Rear**	9	10
943	**Luxury Light Group**	169	190
	incls dual illum visor mirrors, dual beam dome/map lights, engine compartment light, rear seat reading lamps, dual secondary sun visors for front/side coverage		
972	**Bodyside Paint Stripe**	54	60
21J	**6-Way Power Passenger Seat** — LS	343	385
	incls power lumbar and power recliner		

MERCURY

CODE	DESCRIPTION	DEALER	LIST
524	**Leather-Wrapped Steering Wheel**	80	90
664	**Rear Air Suspension — LS**	240	270
535	**Trailer Tow III — LS**	699	785
	incls 5000 lb. capacity, rear air spring suspension 72-amp heavy-duty battery, dual exhaust, trailer wiring harness, power steering oil cooler, transmission oil cooler, heavy-duty flashers, conventional spare tire (5th aluminum wheel), heavy-duty U-joint, 3.27 traction-lok axle (replaced w/3.27 conventional axle when trailer tow is ordered with ABS/traction assist [NA w/41G handling pkg])		
643	**Wheel Covers** — locking radial spoked - GS	263	295
64S	**Wheels, Aluminum — LS**	374	420
—	**Audio Systems**		
586	premium electronic AM/FM stereo radio w/cassette - LS	280	315
91H	power antenna	71	80
153	**License Plate Frame, Front**	NC	NC
41H	**Heater, Engine Block Immersion**	23	25

SABLE

SABLE 6 CYL

M50	GS 4-Dr Sedan	15948	17740
M53	LS 4-Dr Sedan	17960	20000
M55	GS 4-Dr Wagon	16981	18900
M58	LS 4-Dr Wagon	18948	21110
Destination Charge:		525	525

Standard Equipment

SABLE - ALL MODELS: Color-keyed front and rear bumpers, aero halogen headlamps, front cornering lamps, bodycolor dual power mirrors with tinted mirror, lower door and rocker panel urethane coating, rear ashtray, color-keyed 13.5 oz. carpeting, cloth door trim inserts, driver's left foot footrest, locking illuminated glove box, passenger assist grab handles, color-keyed cloth-covered headliner, rear compartment heat ducts, instrument cluster (backlighted mechanical with tachometer, temperature and fuel gauges, trip odometer, flash-to-pass, low fuel alert light), side window defoggers, courtesy light

MERCURY

switches on all doors, front seat back map pockets, day/night inside rearview mirror, four-spoke steering wheel, driver and front passenger air bags, manual air conditioning, 130 amp alternator, 58 amp maintenance-free battery, brake wear sensors, electronic alert chimes, electronic digital clock, coolant recovery system, electric rear window defroster, 3.0 liter SEFI V6 engine, stainless steel exhaust system with painted muffler, front wheel drive, tinted glass, inside hood release, dual note horn, child-proof rear door locks, front and rear stabilizer bars, variable-assist power rack and pinion steering, tilt steering column, MacPherson strut front suspension, P205/65R15 BW all-season radial tires, electronic 4-speed automatic overdrive transmission, two-speed interval windshield wipers.

SEDANS (in addition to or instead of All Model equipment): Color-keyed rocker panel molding (GS), color-keyed bodyside molding, deluxe wheel covers (GS), individual front center fold-down armrest (included in console on LS), rear seat center fold-down armrest, 2-way adjustable front head restraints (4-way adjustable on LS), integrated rear head restraints, alert lights for low washer fluid, lamp outage, door ajar and low oil level (LS), slide-out coin and cupholder trays, console-mounted cupholder (LS), luggage compartment light, driver covered and passenger non-covered visor mirrors with secondary driver's visor (GS), dual illuminated visors w/dual secondary visors for front/side coverage (LS), cargo tie-down net (LS), electronic AM/FM stereo radio w/four speakers (GS), electronic AM/FM stereo radio w/cass w/four speakers (LS), cloth 50/50 twin-comfort lounge seats and dual manual recliners, cloth individual bucket seats and dual manual recliners (LS), power driver's seat (LS), center console (LS), front seat power lumbar supports (LS), power front disc/rear drum brakes (GS), power 4-wheel anti-lock disc brakes (LS), remote decklid release (LS), remote release fuel filler door (LS), light group (LS), auto parking brake release (LS), alum wheels (LS), power side windows w/express down driver's window feature (LS).

WAGONS (in addition to or instead of All Model equipment): Black bumper step pad, luggage rack with adjustable rear crossbar, bright accent moldings on doors at beltline, color-keyed rocker panel molding (GS), color-keyed bodyside molding, deluxe wheel covers (GS), individual front center fold-down armrest, 2-way adjustable front head restraints (4-way adjustable on LS), load floor tie-down hooks, alert lights for low washer fluid, lamp outage, door ajar and low oil level (LS), slide-out coin and cupholder trays, driver covered and passenger non-covered visor with secondary driver's visor (GS), dual illuminated visors with dual secondary visors for front/side coverage (LS), cargo tie-down net (LS), electronic AM/FM stereo radio with four speakers (GS), electronic AM/FM stereo radio with cassette with four speakers (LS), cloth 50/50 twin-comfort lounge seats and dual manual recliners, power driver's seat (LS), front seat power lumbar supports (LS), 60/40 split folding second seat, power front disc/rear drum brakes (GS), power 4-wheel anti-lock disc brakes (LS), remote liftgate release (LS), remote-release fuel filler door (LS), light group (LS), automatic parking brake release (LS), aluminum wheels (LS), flip-up tailgate, power side windows with express down driver window feature (LS), rear window wiper.

Accessories

—	**Preferred Equipment Pkgs**		
450A	**GS Pkg 450A** — GS	711	800
	incls groups 1 & 2 (see group content)		
451A	**GS Pkg 451A** — GS	978	1100
	incls groups 1, 2 & 3 (see group content)		
461A	**LS Pkg 461A** — LS	868	975
	incls groups 1, 2 & 4 (see group content)		
462A	**LS Pkg 462A** — LS	1166	1310
	incls groups 1, 2, 4 & 5 (see group content)		
—	**Groups**		
46A	**Group 1** — GS	143	160
	LS	94	105
	incls light group, floor mats, accent stripe		

CODE	DESCRIPTION	DEALER	LIST
46B	**Group 2** — GS	795	895
	LS	409	460
	incls power windows, power door locks, speed control		
54A	**Group 3**	632	710
	incls power driver's seat, aluminum wheels, cassette		
54B	**Group 4**	1184	1330
	incls leather steering wheel, 3.8 liter V6 engine, high level cassette, power antenna, keyless entry		
77A	**Group 5**	476	535
	incls electronic instrument cluster, electronic air conditioning, autolamp		
—	**Engines**		
99U	3.0L EFI V6	STD	STD
99U	3.0L EFI V6 w/PEP 461, 462 & 548 Group 4	(472)	(530)
994	3.8L EFI V6	472	530
44L	**Transaxle** — electronic automatic overdrive	STD	STD
422	**California Emissions System**	85	95
428	**High Altitude Emissions**	NC	NC
—	**Tires**		
T32	P205/65R15 BSW	STD	STD
506	conventional spare tire...	62	70
—	**Seats**		
7	cloth individual - GS	NC	NC
6	cloth twin comfort - GS	STD	STD
K	cloth twin comfort - LS Wagon	STD	STD
L	cloth individual - LS Sedan	STD	STD
3	leather individual - LS	441	495
2	leather twin comfort - LS	441	495
573	**Air Conditioning, Electronic/Automatic** — NA on GS...................	158	175
552	**Anti-Lock Braking System** — incls 4-wheel disc brakes..............	503	585
631	**Battery, Heavy-Duty**	27	30
475	**Cargo Area Cover** — Wagon only	58	65
516	**Cellular Telephone**	445	500
20F	**Commercial Fleet Credit** — req's FIN; w/450A only	(414)	(465)
65Z	**Fuel Tank, Extended Range**	40	45
144	**Keyless Entry System** — req's 46B Group 2	263	295
138	**Moonroof, Power** — NA on GS..	658	740
—	**Audio Systems**		
58H	radio, electronic AM/FM stereo cassette.......................................	147	185
917	compact disc, digital...	418	470
214	**Seat, Rear Facing Third** — Wagons only	134	150
21A	**Seat, 6-Way Power Driver's**	258	290
21J	**Seats, 6-Way Dual Power**		
	w/PEP 450, 451 w/o 54A Group 3...	516	580
	w/PEP 451 w/54A Group 3, 461, 462..	258	290
524	**Steering Wheel, Leather-Wrapped** — req's 46B Group 2	80	90
662	**Suspension, Heavy-Duty**	23	25
64Z	**Wheels, Aluminum**	227	255
153	**Bracket, Front License Plate**	NC	NC
41H	**Engine Block Immersion Heater**	18	20
904	**Locks, Power Door** — driver switch only; GS Fleet only	302	340

TOPAZ GS

TOPAZ GS 4 CYL

Code	Description	Dealer	List
M31	GS 2-Dr Sedan	9497	10320
M36	GS 4-Dr Sedan	10361	11270
	Destination Charge:	485	485

MERCURY

Standard Equipment

TOPAZ GS: Bodycolor front and rear bumpers with rub strip, halogen headlamps, black dual power remote-control outside mirrors, bodycolor bodyside moldings, single-color dual bodyside paint stripes, lower bodyside urethane protection, turbine style wheel covers, front and rear ashtrays, color-keyed cut-pile carpeting, coat hooks, full console with cupholder and cassette tape storage, diagnostic alert module, front and rear floor mats, lockable glove box, passenger assist grab handles, sport instrumentation (includes tachometer, fuel gauge, temperature gauge, low fuel warning light and trip odometer), header-mounted map light, illuminated footwell lights, luggage compartment light, inside day/night rearview mirror, electronic AM/FM stereo radio with integral clock, low-back individual reclining seats with adjustable cloth-covered head restraints, cloth seat trim, flash-to-pass feature, 4-spoke color keyed steering wheel, color-keyed sunvisors with non-lighted covered mirrors, maintenance-free battery, power front disc/rear drum brakes, 2.3 liter SEFI HSC 4 cylinder engine, front wheel drive, tinted glass, inside hood release, dual note horn, childproof rear door locks, power rack and pinion steering, independent MacPherson strut front suspension with stabilizer bar, P185/70R14 BW all-season SBR tires, temporary spare tire, 5-speed manual transmission, 2-speed interval windshield wipers.

Accessories

Code	Description	Dealer	List
—	**Preferred Equipment Pkgs**		
352A	**GS Pkg 352A** — GS 2-Dr	739	830
	GS 4-Dr	774	870
	incls manual air conditioning, comfort/convenience group (incls front center armrest, electric decklid and fuel filler door release, light group), electric rear window defroster, power lock group (incls power door locks, electric decklid and fuel filler door release), automatic transmission		
354A	**GS 2-Dr Pkg 354A** — GS 2-Dr	739	830

CODE	DESCRIPTION	DEALER	LIST
	incls manual air conditioning, comfort/convenience group (incls front center armrest, electric decklid and fuel filler door release, light group), electric rear window defroster, AM/FM stereo radio w/cassette, deluxe luggage rack, 7-spoke aluminum wheels		
353A	**GS 4-Dr Pkg 353A** — GS 4-Dr	1108	1245
	incls GS Pkg 352A plus fingertip speed control, tilt steering wheel, power side windows, AM/FM stereo radio w/cassette		
99X	**Engine** — 2.3L HSC SEFI 4 cyl	STD	STD
99U	**Engine** — 3.0L V6 SEFI	583	655
445	**Transaxle** — 5-speed manual	STD	STD
440	**Transaxle** — 3-speed automatic	476	535
422	**California Emissions System**	85	95
428	**High Altitude Emissions**	NC	NC
—	**Tires**		
T72	P185/70R14 BSW	STD	STD
T73	P185/70R14 performance BSW - w/Pkg 354A	STD	STD
T7J	P185/70R14 performance WSW	71	80
U	**Seats** — cloth reclining low-back individual	STD	STD
59H	**Air Bag Supplemental Restraint System, Driver**	414	465
572	**Air Conditioning, Manual**	694	780
414	**Comfort/Convenience Group**	169	190
	incls front center armrest, electric decklid and fuel filler door release, light group		
57Q	**Defroster, Electric Rear Window**	143	160
903	**Power Lock Group** — 2-Dr	263	295
	4-Dr	298	335
	2-Dr w/Comfort/Convenience group	178	200
	4-Dr w/Comfort/Convenience group	213	240
	incls power door locks, electric decklid and fuel filler door release		
548	**Luggage Rack, Deluxe**	98	110
65M	**Max Edition Option Group**	258	290
589	**Radio** — electronic AM/FM stereo w/cassette	134	150
—	**Paint** — clearcoat	76	85
954	**Paint** — two-tone	134	150
21A	**Seat** — 6-way power driver's	258	290
525	**Speed Control, Fingertip**	191	215
52Q	**Tilt Steering Wheel**	124	140
64J	**Wheels, Polycast**	165	185
64D	**Wheels, 14" Cast Aluminum**	236	265
43R	**Windows, Power Side** — 4-Dr only	280	315
41H	**Heater, Engine Block Immersion**	18	20
153	**License Plate Bracket, Front**	NC	NC

TRACER

TRACER 4 CYL

Code	Description	Dealer	List
M10	Base 4-Dr Sedan	9428	10250
M15	Base 4-Dr Wagon	9674	10520
M14	LTS 4-Dr Sedan	11530	12560
	Destination Charge:	375	375

Standard Equipment

TRACER - ALL MODELS: Lower bodyside urethane protection coating, driver side air bag, luxury color-keyed cut-pile carpeting, color-keyed load floor carpeting, console (includes bin, lift-out tray/cupholder), passenger grab handles, coat hooks, molded cloth covered headliners, rear compartment heat ducts, analog (backlit) instrumentation includes speedometer, tachometer, fuel and temperature gauges, trip odometer, low fuel warning light; day/night inside rearview mirror, 60/40 split fold rear seat, cloth covered sun visors, heavy duty alternator, maintenance-free battery, distributorless electronic ignition, engine low coolant warning light, engine malfunction indicator light, tinted glass, single note horn, child safety rear door locks, temporary spare tire, front and rear stabilizer bars, four-wheel independent suspension, 5-speed manual transmission, 2-speed windshield wipers with variable interval feature.

SEDAN (in addition to or instead of All Model equipment): Bodycolor bumpers with bright insert, remote-control manual driver's side mirror, wide bodyside molding with bright insert, full width taillamps, 13" x 5" semi-styled steel wheels with plastic center cap, shift indicator light (manual transmission models), integral rear seat head restraints, dual non-illuminated visor mirrors, 2-way seat adjustment, 4-spoke sport steering wheel, power front disc/rear drum brakes, 1.9 liter SEFI 4 cylinder engine, electronic AM/FM stereo radio with clock, manual rack and pinion steering, P175/70R13 82S BW tires.

WAGON (in addition to or instead of Sedan equipment): Dual electric remote-control mirrors, vertical taillamps, 14" x 5" semi-styled wheels with full wheel cover, cargo cover, rear window defroster, remote fuel door release, speed sensitive power rack and pinion steering, P175/65R14 81S BW tires, rear window wiper/washer, integral rear seat head restraints deleted.

LTS (in addition to or instead of All Model equipment): Front air dam, bodycolor bumpers with red insert, dual electric remote-control mirrors, wide bodyside moldings with red insert, rear decklid spoiler, full width taillamps, 14" x 5.5" 7-spoke aluminum wheels, light group (includes cargo and engine compartment light, dual map lights, dual illuminated visor mirrors and rear door courtesy light switch), headlamp-on warning chime, dual illuminated visor mirrors, 4-way seat adjustment (driver seat tilts), integral rear seat head restraints, 4-spoke leather-wrapped sport steering wheel, power four-wheel disc

CODE	DESCRIPTION	DEALER	LIST

brakes, remote decklid release, rear window defroster, 1.8 liter DOHC 16-valve EFI 4 cylinder engine, remote fuel door release, electronic AM/FM stereo radio with cassette, speed control, speed-sensitive rack and pinion steering, tilt steering column, sport handling suspension, P185/60R14 82H BW tires:

Accessories

CODE	DESCRIPTION	DEALER	LIST
—	**Engines**		
99J	1.9L SEFI - Base	STD	STD
998	1.8L DOHC - LTS	STD	STD
—	**Transaxles**		
445	5-speed manual	STD	STD
44T	4-speed overdrive automatic	703	790
422	**California Emissions System**	62	70
428	**High Altitude Emissions System**	NC	NC
—	**Tires**		
T75	P175/65R14 BSW w/full wheel covers - Base	STD	STD
T83	P185/60R14 82H BSW performance - LTS	STD	STD
—	**Seats**		
A	cloth low-back individual - Base	STD	STD
B	cloth sport bucket - LTS	STD	STD
572	**Air Conditioning, Manual**	645	725
552	**Anti-Lock Braking System**	503	566
608	**Convenience Group**	316	355
	incls tilt steering and speed control		
548	**Luggage Rack, Deluxe — Wagon**	98	110
138	**Moonroof, Power — LTS**	468	525
538	**Power Group**	463	520
	incls power locks and power windows		
—	**Audio Systems**		
589	AM/FM stereo/cassette - std on LTS	147	165
585	AM/FM stereo w/CD player & premium sound - Base 4-Dr, Wagon	396	445
	LTS	249	280
913	premium sound system	116	130
41H	**Engine Block Immersion Heater**	18	20
153	**Front License Plate Bracket**	NC	NC

1993 VILLAGER
NOTE:*Information for the 1994 Villager was unavailable at time of publication.*

1993 VILLAGER 6 CYL

Code	Description	Dealer	List
V11	GS 3-Dr Wagon	15138	17015
V11	LS 3-Dr Wagon	19605	22090
Destination Charge:		540	540

Standard Equipment

VILLAGER GS: "Light bar" grille, halogen aero headlamps, front cornering lamps, black sail-mounted breakaway mirrors, clearcoat metallic paint (except black and white body colors), lower bodyside urethane protection, interval windshield wipers with washer, rear window wiper/washer, color-keyed aero wheel covers, color-keyed cut-pile carpets with full coverage floor mats, front and rear dome lamps with courtesy switches at all doors (with time delay on front lamp), color-keyed door trim panels with lower carpeting/cloth inserts/map pockets/courtesy lamps; three entry assist handles with integral coat hooks, front and rear full coverage floor mats, remote fuel filler door release, warning lamps for low fuel/low washer fluid/low oil/door ajar/temperature gauge/reminder chime for headlamp on, fasten seat belt, and key-in-ignition; backlighted mechanical instrument cluster with tachometer and trip odometer, side window defoggers, locking glove box with lamp, two stowage bins with removable rubber mat, slide out coinholder tray, interior hood release, day/night rearview mirror, electronic AM/FM radio with four speakers and clock, cupholders at each seating position (except at sliding door), flat load floor, cloth reclining bucket front seats with adjustable headrests/inboard armrests/two cupholders mounted (unique cloth trim on LS), cloth 3-passenger rear bench seat, 110 amp alternator, 60 amp/hr. maintenance-free battery, power front disc/rear drum brakes with four-wheel anti-lock, child safety seat provision, 3.0 liter V6 OHC engine with multi-port electronic fuel injection, electric fan drive, front wheel drive, fuel cap tether, 20 gallon fuel tank, interior hood release, dual-note horn, childproof side sliding door, nitrogen gas-filled shocks/struts, temporary spare tire mounted underbody, front stabilizer bar, power rack and pinion steering, MacPherson strut front suspension, Hotchkiss rear suspension, P205/75R15 BSW all-season radial tires, 4-speed electronic automatic overdrive transaxle with electronic power/economy switch, flip-out 2nd and 3rd row bodyside windows, color-keyed front and rear 5-mph impact bumpers with black bumper rub strips, tinted glass, black bodyside molding, 4-spoke steering wheel, cloth visors with dual covered mirrors.

LS (in addition to or instead of GS equipment): Color-keyed bumper rub strips, privacy glass, luggage rack, color-keyed bodyside moldings, color-keyed bodyside accent tape stripe, front air conditioning, rear window defroster, light group includes overhead map lights/front door step lamps/under I/P lamps with time delay; electronic AM/FM stereo cassette radio, cargo net, rear seat adjustable recliner which folds forward flat with tray surface, additional quick release 2-passenger bench seat with fold flat back (with tray surface and seat back recliner), map pockets on front seat backs, lockable storage under passenger seat, leather-wrapped steering wheel with tilt column, cloth visors with dual illuminated mirrors, power locks with side sliding door "memory," automatic fingertip speed control, power front door windows, remote power flip-out 3rd row bodyside windows.

Accessories

CODE	DESCRIPTION	DEALER	LIST
—	**Preferred Equipment Pkgs**		
691A	**Villager GS Pkg 691A**	1281	1507
	incls front air conditioning, electric rear window defroster, dual power mirrors, tilt wheel/speed control, power windows, power locks		
692A	**Villager LS Pkg 692A**	2166	2549
	incls equipment in Preferred Equipment Pkg 691A plus luggage rack, electronic AM/FM stereo cassette radio, underseat storage, 8-way power driver's seat, aluminum wheels with locking lug nuts		
695A	**Villager LS Pkg 695A**	293	345
	incls 8-way power driver's seat, aluminum wheels with locking lug nuts, flip open liftgate window, high level AM/FM cassette radio, two-tone paint		
696A	**Villager LS Pkg 696A**	1485	1748
	incls equipment in Preferred Equipment Pkg 695A plus rear air conditioning/auxiliary heater, electronic instrument cluster, keyless entry and autolamp on/off delay system, 4-way power passenger seat, quad bucket seats		
99W	**Engine — 3.0L EFI 6 cyl**	STD	STD
44P	**Automatic Overdrive Transaxle**	STD	STD
422	**California Emissions System**	87	102
428	**High Altitude Emissions System**	NC	NC
T70	**Tires — P205/75R15 BSW**	STD	STD
64V	**Wheels — aluminum w/locking lug nuts**	322	379
—	**Optional Seating**		
21A	7-passenger seating - std on LS	282	332
21H	quad bucket seats - LS	508	598
R	leather trim - LS	735	865
90F	seat, 4-way power pass - LS	165	194
90P	seat, 8-way power driver	335	394
572	**Air Conditioning** — std on LS	729	857
574	**Rear Air Conditioning & Auxiliary Heater** — GS	1125	1323
	w/PEP's 692A, 695A	396	466
57Q	**Electric Rear Window Defroster** — std on LS	143	168
17F	**Flip Open Liftgate Window**	77	90
153	**Front License Plate Bracket**	NC	NC
924	**Glass, Privacy** — std on LS	351	413
15A	**Instrument Cluster, Electronic** — LS	207	244
60A	**Keyless Entry & Autolamp On/Off Delay System** — LS	256	301

CODE	DESCRIPTION	DEALER	LIST
593	**Light Group & Power Rear Vent Windows** — std on LS	132	155
615	**Luggage Rack** — std on LS	121	143
543	**Mirrors, Dual Power** — std on LS	83	98
951	**Paint, Monotone** — LS	NC	NC
943	**Power Windows/Locks** — std on LS	451	530
434	**Storage, Underseat** — std on LS	31	37
85C	**Stripes, Bodyside Tape** — std on LS	36	43
439	**Sunroof, Power** — LS	659	776
684	**Suspension, Handling** — LS	74	87
52N	**Tilt Wheel/Speed Control** — GS	316	372
534	**Trailer Tow Package**	211	249
—	**Radio Systems**		
58T	electronic AM/FM stereo cassette - std on LS	203	239
588	high level AM/FM cassette - LS	282	332
91Q	supersound AM/FM cassette & CD player - LS	764	899
58Y	standard radio credit - GS	(78)	(91)

ACHIEVA S COUPE/SEDAN

ACHIEVA S 4 CYL

L37NR	S 2-Dr Coupe	12738	14075
L69NR	S 4-Dr Sedan	12828	14175
	Destination Charge:	485	485

Standard Equipment

ACHIEVA S: Freedom battery with automatic rundown protection, power front disc/rear drum anti-lock brakes, child safety seat anchors, warning chimes for seat belts/headlamps on/key-in-ignition/turn signal on; front and rear cupholders, side window defoggers, power automatic door locks, rear child-security

OLDSMOBILE

door locks (Sedan), 2.3 liter L4 Quad OHC engine with MFI (transverse-mounted with front-wheel drive); front/rear accent color fascias, cut-pile wall-to-wall floor carpeting w/carpeted lower doors and console, full luggage compartment carpeting, floor console w/shifter/storage armrest/ashtray/cigar lighter/coin holder/ele shift position display; composite halogen headlamps w/integral turn signal indicators, rear seat heat ducts, inside hood release, gas charged hood struts, instrument panel includes digital gauges; lamps include: header panel courtesy/map/glove box/ashtray/lower courtesy instrument panel/trunk/rear roof rail courtesy/reading; black outside driver side remote mirror, passenger-side manual mirror, side window frame and pillar applique moldings, deluxe bodyside accent color moldings, black rocker panel molding, Delco ETR AM/FM stereo radio w/seek-scan/digital clock/fixed-mast fender antenna; remote deck-lid release, remote fuel-filler door release, contour front bucket seats w/Opti-Ride suspension system/two-way adjusters/driver-side lumbar adjustment/passenger-side easy-entry feature (Coupe)/ recliners (Coupe & Sedan); rear bench seat, power rack-and-pinion steering, storage compartments include: map pockets in front doors and front seat backs/center instrument panel bin/overhead compartment; MacPherson front strut/rear coil spring suspension, P185/75R14 steel-belted radial-ply blackwall all-season tires, 5-speed manual trans w/floor shifter, driver/passenger side visors w/covered vanity mirrors and map straps, 14" x 6" wheels, deluxe bright wheel discs, Soft-Ray tinted windows (full roll-down rear on Sedan), wet-arm wiper system, driver side air bag, deluxe tilt steering wheel.

Accessories

CODE	DESCRIPTION	DEALER	LIST
1SA	**Option Pkg 1SA**	NC	NC
	incls vehicle plus standard equipment		
1SB	**Option Pkg 1SB — S Coupe**	1262	1468
	S Sedan...	1262	1468
	incls air cond, 4-way man driver side seat adjuster, gauge cluster (analog speedometer, tachometer, voltmeter, gauges for coolant temperature, oil pressure; trip odometer, warning lights for parking brake/low brake fluid, low coolant level, hazard flashers, low washer fluid & check oil level, plus warning lights for low fuel, generator, oil pressure & hot coolant activated by "check gauges" switch), Delco ETR AM/FM stereo radio (incls seek-scan, auto reverse cass, digital display clock & 4-spkr ext range snd sys), dual outside pwr mirrors, auxiliary F & R carpet floor mats, cruise control		
1SC	**Option Pkg 1SC — S Coupe**	1692	1968
	S Sedan...	1748	2033
	incls pkg 1SB equip plus 6-spkr dimensional sound system, pwr side windows w/driver side auto-down feature, remote lock control pkg (incls illuminated entry feature & keychain transmitter), rear window grid antenna		
AC3	**Seat Adjuster, 6-Way Power, Driver**..	232	270
AM9	**Rear Seat, Split Folding**	129	150
AP9	**Convenience Net, Trunk**	26	30
A31	**Windows, Power Side w/Driver Auto Down— Coupe**...............................	237	275
	Sedan...	292	340
	incl'd w/pkg 1SC		
BF9	**Floor Mats, Delete (Fleet Only)**..	(39)	(45)
B37	**Floor Mats, Front & Rear**	39	45
	incl'd w/pkgs 1SB, 1SC		
CF5	**Astroroof, Electric Sliding Glass**	512	595
C60	**Air Conditioner, Four-Season**...	714	830
	incl'd w/pkgs 1SB, 1SC		
K05	**Heater, Engine Block**	15	18
L40	**Engine, 2.3L Quad OHC MFI**	STD	STD
LD2	**Engine, 2.3L Quad 4 MFI**	353	410

CODE	DESCRIPTION	DEALER	LIST
L82	**Engine, 3100 V6 SFI**	353	410
MX1	**Transmission, 3-Spd Automatic**	477	555
MX0	**Transmission, 4-Spd Automatic w/Overdrive**	649	755
PF7	**Wheels, Aluminum 15" w/BW Touring Tires**	336	391
UM6	**Radio, AM/FM Stereo w/Cassette**	120	140
	incl'd w/pkgs 1SB, 1SC		
U1C	**Radio, AM/FM Stereo w/Compact Disc**	220	256
	NA w/pkg 1SA		
V56	**Luggage Carrier, Deck Lid**	99	115
NG1	**New York Emissions — w/L40/LD2**	86	100
	w/L82	NC	NC
YF5	**California Emissions — w/L40/LD2**	86	100
	w/L82	NC	NC

ACHIEVA SC COUPE/SL SEDAN

ACHIEVA SC/SL 4 CYL

F37NR	SC 2-Dr Coupe	15815	17475
F69NR	SL 4-Dr Sedan	15815	17475
Destination Charge:		485	485

Standard Equipment

ACHIEVA SC COUPE & SL SEDAN: Freedom battery with automatic rundown protection, power front disc/rear drum anti-lock power brakes, trunk cargo net, child safety seat anchors, warning chimes for: seat belts/headlamps on/key-in-ignition/turn signal on; front and rear cupholders, power automatic door locks, rear child-security door locks (Sedans), 2.3 liter L4 Quad 4 engine with MFI (transverse-mounted with front-wheel drive), front and rear body-color fascias, cut-pile wall-to-wall floor carpeting with carpeted lower doors and console, full luggage compartment carpeting, floor console includes: shifter/storage armrest/cassette storage tray/ashtray/cigar lighter/coin holder/electronic shift position display; composite halogen headlamps with integral turn signal indicators, rear seat heat ducts, inside hood release, gas-charged hood struts, instrument panel includes: analog speedometer/ tachometer/voltmeter/coolant temperature gauge/oil pressure gauge/trip odometer/parking brake warning light/low brake fluid warning light/low coolant level warning light/hazard flashers/low washer fluid warning light/check oil level warning light/low fuel warning light; warning lights for: generator/oil pressure/hot coolant (activated by "check gauges" switch); lamps include: header panel courtesy/map/glove box/ashtray/lower courtesy instrument panel/trunk/rear roof rail courtesy/reading; belt reveal moldings, Delco ETR AM/FM stereo radio with seek-scan/auto-reverse cassette/6 speaker Dimensional Sound system/digital clock/fixed-mast rear-mounted antenna; remote deck-lid release, remote fuel-filler door release, contour front bucket driver-side seat with Opti-Ride suspension system (4-way adjuster and lumbar adjustment); passenger-side seat with 2-way adjuster/easy-entry feature (Coupe)/recliners (Coupe & Sedan); split rear seat with luggage compartment pass-through, power rack-and-pinion steering, storage compartments include: map pockets in front doors and seat backs/center instrument panel bin/overhead compartment; driver and passenger-side visors with covered vanity mirrors and map straps, Soft-Ray tinted windows (full roll-down rear on Sedan), wet-arm wiper system, electronic cruise control with resume and acceleration features, side window defoggers and electric rear window defogger, dual exhaust system, special lower body side cladding and rocker moldings, auxiliary front and rear carpet floor mats, foglamps, black outside dual power mirrors, lighted visor vanity mirrors, rear aero wing, driver side air bag, leather-wrapped deluxe tilt steering wheel, MacPherson front strut suspension and rear coil springs, touring suspension components, P205/55R16 steel-belted radial ply BW touring tires, 5-speed manual transmission with floor shifter, 16" aluminum wheels, air conditioning.

Accessories

CODE	DESCRIPTION	DEALER	LIST
1SA	**Option Pkg 1SA**	NC	NC
	incls vehicle plus standard equipment		
1SB	**Option Pkg 1SB — SC Coupe**	344	400
	SL Sedan	400	465
	incls pwr windows w/driver side auto-down feature, remote door lock control pkg (incls illuminated entry feature & key-chain transmitter)		
AC3	**Seat Adjuster, 6-Way Power, Driver**	232	270
A31	**Windows, Power Side w/Driver Auto Down — Coupe**	237	275
	Sedan	292	340
	incl'd w/pkg 1SB		
CF5	**Astroroof, Electric Sliding Glass**	512	595
K05	**Heater, Engine Block**	15	18
LG0	**Engine, 2.3L High Output Quad 4 MFI**	STD	STD
LD2	**Engine, 2.3L Quad 4 MFI**	(120)	(140)
L82	**Engine, 3100 V6 SFI**	(120)	(140)
MX0	**Transmission, 4-Spd Automatic w/Overdrive**	649	755
U1C	**Radio, AM/FM Stereo w/Compact Disc**	220	256
WJ7	**Custom Leather Trim**	366	425
NG1	**New York Emissions — w/LG0/LD2**	86	100
	w/L82	NC	NC
YF5	**California Emissions — w/LG0/LD2**	86	100
	w/L82	NC	NC

BRAVADA

BRAVADA 6 CYL

CODE	DESCRIPTION	DEALER	LIST
V06TR	4-Dr Sport Utility	23525	25995
	Destination Charge:	475	475

CODE	DESCRIPTION	DEALER	LIST

Standard Equipment

BRAVADA: Gold metallic bodyside accent stripe, all-weather air conditioner, full-time all-wheel drive with viscous clutch, front and rear armrests, all-passenger seating position assist handles, Freedom high-capacity heavy-duty battery, power front disc/rear drum anti-lock brakes, front bumpers with integrated air dam and rear body color, cut-pile wall-to-wall carpeting with carpeted lower door panels, overhead console with digital compass/outside temperature readout/dual reading lamps; floor console with cupholders and dual auxiliary electrical outlets and power seat controls, rear convenience net, resume and acceleration feature cruise control, side window defoggers, electric rear window defogger, door locks with remote lock control package (includes two key-chain transmitters), 4.3 liter Vortec V6 engine with central port fuel injection, auxiliary front and rear carpeted floor mats, protective rear cargo mat, halogen headlamps, interior operated hood release, analog instrument panel gauge cluster includes: gauges for oil pressure/coolant temperature/voltmeter/fuel level/trip odometer/anti-lock brake monitor light; lamps include: interior dome/instrument panel convenience/under-hood/glove box/ashtray; front license plate bracket, power rear tailgate lock release, rooftop aero design luggage carrier with adjustable crossbar, inside day-night mirror with door-activated map lights, driver and passenger side electrically operated outside mirrors, moldings include: color-coordinated bodyside/rocker panel/wheel opening; locking rear differential posi-traction, Delco ETR AM stereo/FM stereo radio with seek-scan/auto-reverse cassette/music search/graphic equalizer/digital display clock/mast antenna; front reclining bucket seats with driver's side 6-way power adjustment, power lumbar adjustment for driver and passenger seats, folding rear bench seats with center armrest, power steering, leather-wrapped Tilt-Wheel steering wheel, independent front suspension system with torsion bars and stabilizer bar, rear semi-elliptic leaf spring suspension, high-pressure gas-assisted front and rear shock absorbers, P235/75R15 radial-ply all-season blackwall tires, full size spare tire, 4-speed automatic shift transmission, flo-thru ventilation w/console vent for rear seat passengers, auxiliary sunshade/extender visors, lighted vanity mirrors and convenience straps, cast aluminum 15" wheels (including spare), power side windows, Solar-Ray windshield/front door glass, deep-tint rear door/rear quarter/tailgate windows; pulse wiper system, rear-lift glass wiper and washer, foglamps.

Accessories

CODE	DESCRIPTION	DEALER	LIST
B94	**Gold Pkg**	52	60
K05	**Heater, Engine Block**	28	33
P16	**Tire Carrier, Exterior Spare**	137	159
QFN	**Tires, P235/75R15 WOL All-Season**	114	133
U1C	**Radio, AM/FM Stereo w/Compact Disc**	115	134
U52	**Electronic Instrument Panel Cluster**	168	195
WJ7	**Custom Leather Trim**	559	650
Z82	**Towing Pkg, 5,000 Lb Capacity**	219	255
NG1	**New York Emissions**	NC	NC
YF5	**California Emissions**	NC	NC

OLDSMOBILE

CUTLASS CIERA S SEDAN

CUTLASS CIERA S 4 CYL

G69AR	S 4-Dr Sedan	14029	15675
Destination Charge:		525	525

Standard Equipment

CUTLASS CIERA S SEDAN: Four-season air conditioner, Freedom battery, power front disc/rear drum anti-lock brakes, front and rear bumper moldings, automatic power door locks, front and rear door-pull handles, 2.2 liter L4 engine with MFI (transverse-mounted with front-wheel drive), cut-pile wall-to-wall floor carpeting with carpeted lower door panels, composite halogen headlamps, headlamp-on-reminder, interior-operated hood release, illuminated entry package, lamps include: dome/instrument panel ashtray/glove box/trunk/underhood; integrated map pockets into front door trim, black outside driver-side remote control mirror, passenger-side manual mirror, bright roof drip bodyside belt-reveal moldings, Delco ETR AM/FM stereo radio with seek-scan/digital display clock/dual rear speakers/fixed-mast fender antenna; 55/45 divided bench front seat with dual controls/center armrest/power reclining seat backs; full foam front and rear seat cushions, power rack-and-pinion steering, MacPherson front strut/rear variable-rate coil spring suspension, P185/75R14 steel-belted radial-ply white-stripe all-season tires, 3-speed automatic transmission with column shift, turn-on signal reminder chime, flo-thru ventilation, 14" x 5.5" wheels, bolt-on wheel discs, Soft-Ray tinted windows, side window and electric rear window defoggers, inside day/night rearview mirror with dual reading lamps, driver and passenger side covered visor vanity mirrors, deluxe tilt steering wheel with vinyl trim, pulse wiper system.

Accessories

1SA	**Option Pkg 1SA**	NC	NC
	incls vehicle plus standard equipment		
1SB	**Option Pkg 1SB**	483	562
	ncls frt seat storage armrest w/dual cupholders, auxiliary F & R carpet floor mats, cruise control w/resume & acceleration features, electrically operated o/s driver & pass side mirrors, Delco ETR AM/FM stereo radio w/seek/scan, auto reverse cass, digital display clock & dual rear spkrs w/extended range		
1SC	**Option Pkg 1SC**	1060	1232

CODE	DESCRIPTION	DEALER	LIST
	incls pkg 1SB equip plus 6-spkr dimensional sound audio system, pwr frt fender antenna, pwr windows w/driver-side auto-down feature, remote control lock pkg incls door & trunk-lid lock release controls, illuminated entry feature & pwr trunk release		
AG1	**Seat Adjuster, 6-Way Power, Driver**	262	305
AP9	**Convenience Net, Trunk**	26	30
AU0	**Remote Lock Control Pkg**	159	185
	incl'd w/pkg 1SC		
A31	**Windows, Power Side w/Driver Auto Down**	292	340
	incl'd w/pkg 1SC		
BF9	**Floor Mats, Delete (Fleet Only)**	(39)	(45)
BX2	**Molding Pkg**	130	151
B34/B35	**Floor Mats, Front & Rear**	39	45
	Incl'd w/pkgs 1SB, 1SC		
D90	**Accent Stripe, Body**	39	45
G66	**Load-Carrying Pkg (Fleet Only)**	91	106
K05	**Heater, Engine Block**	15	18
LN2	**Engine, 2.2L 4 Cyl MFI**	STD	STD
L82	**Engine, 3100 V6 SFI w/4-Spd Auto Trans**	697	810
NV7	**Variable Effort Steering**	53	62
N91	**Wheel Discs, Simulated Wire w/Locks**	206	240
PH5	**Wheels, Aluminum 14" w/BW Touring Tires**	254	295
QFE	**Tires, P185/75R14 SBR BW All-Season (Fleet Only)**	(41)	(48)
QMW	**Tires, P195/75R14 SBR BW All-Season (Fleet Only)**	(50)	(58)
QMX	**Tires, P195/75R14 SBR WW All-Season**	34	40
UX1	**Radio, AM/FM Stereo w/Cassette, Equalizer**	129	150
	NA w/pkgs 1SA, 1SB		
V08	**Cooling System, High Capacity**	34	40
V52	**Luggage Carrier, Deck Lid**	99	115
WJ7	**Custom Leather Trim**	366	425
NG1	**New York Emissions — w/LN2**	NC	NC
	w/L82	86	100
YF5	**California Emissions — w/LN2**	NC	NC
	w/L82	86	100

CUTLASS CRUISER S WAGON

CUTLASS CRUISER S 6 CYL

J35AR	S 4-Dr Wagon	15372	17175
	Destination Charge:	525	525

Standard Equipment

CUTLASS CRUISER S WAGON: Four-season air conditioner, Freedom battery, power front disc/rear drum anti-lock brakes, front and rear bumper moldings, side window defogger, automatic power door locks (including tailgate lock release), front and rear door-pull handles, cut-pile wall-to-wall floor carpeting with carpeted lower door panels and cargo area, composite halogen headlamps, headlamp-on reminder, interior-operated hood release, illuminated entry package, lamps include: dome/instrument panel ashtray/glove box/cargo area/underhood, integrated map pockets into front door trim, black outside driver-side remote-control mirror, passenger-side manual mirror, bodyside moldings, bright roof drip and belt reveal moldings, Delco ETR AM/FM stereo radio with seek-scan/digital display clock/dual rear speakers/fixed-mast fender antenna; 55/45 divided bench front seat with dual controls/center armrest/power reclining seat backs; split-folding rear seat backs, full-foam front and rear seat cushions, power rack-and-pinion steering, deluxe steering wheel with vinyl rim, MacPherson front strut/rear variable-rate coil spring suspension; P185/75R14 steel-belted radial-ply white-stripe all-season tires, 3-speed automatic transmission with column shift, turn-signal-on reminder chime, flo-thru ventilation, 14" x 5.5" wheels, bolt-on wheel discs, Soft-Ray tinted windows, 3100 SFI V6 engine with sequential port fuel injection, transverse-mounted with front-wheel drive, inside day/night mirror with dual reading lamps, driver and passenger covered visor vanity mirrors.

Accessories

1SA	**Option Pkg 1SA**		NC	NC
	incls vehicle plus standard equipment			
1SB	**Option Pkg 1SB**		617	717
	incls frt seat storage armrest w/dual cupholders, auxiliary F & R carpet			
	floor mats, cruise control w/resume & acceleration features, elec operated			
	o/s driver & pass side mirrors, Delco ETR AM/FM stereo radio w/seek-scan,			
	auto reverse cass, digital display clock, dual rear spkrs w/extended range;			
	rear window air deflector, chrome rooftop luggage carrier			

OLDSMOBILE

CODE	DESCRIPTION	DEALER	LIST
1SC	**Option Pkg 1SC**	1141	1327
	incls pkg 1SB equip plus 6-spkr dimensional sound audio system, pwr frt fender antenna, pwr windows w/driver side auto-down feature, remote lock control pkg (incls door & tailgate lock release controls, illuminated entry feature & key-chain transmitter)		
AG1	**Seat Adjuster, 6-Way Power, Driver**............................	262	305
AU0	**Remote Lock Control Pkg**..	108	125
	incl'd w/pkg 1SC		
A31	**Windows, Power Side w/Driver Auto Down**..................	292	340
	incl'd w/pkg 1SC		
BF9	**Floor Mats, Delete (Fleet Only)**	(39)	(45)
BX2	**Molding Package**	130	151
BX3	**Paneling, Body Side & Tailgate**	280	325
B34/B35	**Floor Mats, Front & Rear**	39	45
	incl'd w/pkgs 1SB, 1SC		
D90	**Accent Stripe, Body**	39	45
G66	**Load-Carrying Pkg (Fleet Only)**	91	106
K05	**Heater, Engine Block**	15	18
N91	**Wheel Discs, Simulated Wire w/Locks**	206	240
PH5	**Wheels, Aluminum 14" w/BW Touring Tires**	254	295
QFE	**Tires, P185/75R14 SBR BW All-Season (Fleet Only)**..	(41)	(48)
QMW	**Tires, P195/75R14 SBR BW All-Season (Fleet Only)** ..	(15)	(18)
QMX	**Tires, P195/75R14 SBR WW All-Season**......................	34	40
UX1	**Radio, AM/FM Stereo w/Cassette, Equalizer**	129	150
	NA w/pkgs 1SA, 1SB		
V08	**Cooling System, High Capacity**	34	40
Z05	**Third Seat, Rear-Facing**..	282	328
NG1	**New York Emissions**	86	100
YF5	**California Emissions**..	86	100

CUTLASS SUPREME CONVERTIBLE

CUTLASS SUPREME 6 CYL

T67WR	2-Dr Convertible	22116	25275
Destination Charge:		525	525

CODE	DESCRIPTION	DEALER	LIST

Standard Equipment

CUTLASS SUPREME CONVERTIBLE: Touch-control electronic air conditioner, Freedom battery, power 4-wheel anti-lock disc brakes, body color front and rear bumper fascias, full-length shifting console with armrest and storage (plus cupholder), pillar-mounted door handles with illuminated driver-side lock, automatic power door locks, interior door-pull handles, dual engine cooling fans, deluxe cut-pile wall-to-wall floor carpeting with carpeted lower door panels, front-end panel rocket emblem, mini-quad headlamps with flash-to-pass provision on turn signal, headlamp-on reminder, headlamp switch location lamp, interior operated hood release, instrument panel and glove box courtesy lamps, black outside driver and passenger remote-control mirrors, driver and passenger side covered visor vanity mirrors, color-coordinated wheel opening moldings, Delco ETR AM/FM stereo radio w/seek-scan/auto-reverse cassette/digital display clock/dual rear speakers/rear quarter fixed-mast antenna; full foam front and rear seat cushions, power rack-and-pinion steering, four-wheel independent suspension system with touring car ride and handling components, MacPherson front struts, P225/60R16 steel-belted radial-ply blackwall tires, power folding vinyl top, automatic overdrive transmission with floor shifter, power trunk-lid lock release, deluxe trunk trim, turn-signal-on reminder chime, flo-thru ventilation, aluminum-styled 16" wheels, power side windows with auto-down feature, Soft-Ray tinted windows, wet arm wiper system, electronic cruise control with resume and acceleration features, side window and electric rear window defoggers, front and rear carpet floor mats, foglamps, illuminated entry feature, leather trimmed seating areas, inside day/night rearview mirror with dual reading lamps, driver's-side air bag, front bucket seats with reclining seat back (6-way driver side power adjuster, 4-way passenger side manual seat adjuster), individual rear bucket seats with deluxe folding console, leather-wrapped tilt steering wheel, instrument panel rallye cluster (includes full analog electro-mechanical gauge cluster, speedometer, tachometer and gauges for fuel level, engine temperature and voltmeter, plus engine oil level monitor), 3100 SFI V6 engine with sequential port fuel injection, transverse-mounted front wheel drive.

Accessories

CODE	DESCRIPTION	DEALER	LIST
1SA	**Option Pkg 1SA**	NC	NC
	incls vehicle plus standard equipment		
1SB	**Option Pkg 1SB**	255	296
	incls remote lock control pkg (incls illumination pkg, unlocked door reminder light, key-chain transmitter), lighted visor vanity mirrors, blk rear qtr pwr antenna		
1SC	**Option Pkg 1SC**	594	691
	incls pkg 1SB equip plus auto elec comfort control air conditioner, leather-wrapped steering wheel w/steering wheel touch controls		
AP9	**Convenience Net, Trunk**	26	30
B84	**Moldings, Body Side**	52	60
K05	**Heater, Engine Block**	15	18
L82	**Engine, 3100 SFI V6**	STD	STD
LQ1	**Twin Dual Cam V6 Engine Pkg**	933	1085
UT6	**Radio, AM/FM Stereo w/Cassette, Equalizer** — w/o pkg 1SC	112	130
	w/pkg 1SC	86	100
UV6	**Head-Up Instrument Display**	215	250
UC1	**Radio, AM/FM Stereo w/Compact Disc** — w/o pkg 1SC	220	256
	w/pkg 1SC	194	226
NG1	**New York Emissions** — w/L82	NC	NC
	w/LQ1	86	100
YF5	**California Emissions** — w/L82	NC	NC
	w/LQ1	86	100

CUTLASS SUPREME S COUPE/SEDAN

CUTLASS SUPREME S 6 CYL

Code	Description	Dealer	List
H47WR	S 2-Dr Coupe	15203	17375
H69WR	S 4-Dr Sedan	15291	17475
	Destination Charge:	525	525

Standard Equipment

CUTLASS SUPREME S COUPE/SEDAN: Electronic air conditioner with touch controls, Freedom battery, power 4-wheel disc anti-lock brakes, body-color front and rear bumper fascias, black front and rear bumper moldings with bright trim, automatic power door locks, interior door-pull handles, dual engine cooling fans, cut-pile wall-to-wall floor carpeting with carpeted lower door panels, floor console with shifter and storage armrest with cupholder, front-end panel rocket emblem, composite halogen headlamps, headlamp-on reminder, headlamp switch locator lamp, interior operated hood release, black outside driver-side remote-control mirror, passenger-side manual mirror, bright window frame and belt reveal moldings, Delco ETR AM/FM stereo radio with seek-scan/digital display clock/dual rear speakers/rear quarter fixed-mast antenna; contour front bucket seats with reclining seat backs and 4-way manual adjustment, power rack and pinion steering, 4-wheel fully independent suspension system with MacPherson front struts and rear transverse fiberglass leaf spring plus shock struts, P205/70R15 steel-belted radial-ply blackwall all-season tires, deluxe trunk trim, turn-signal-on reminder chime, flo-thru ventilation, 15" x 6" wheels, bolt-on turbine style wheel discs, Soft-Ray tinted windows, wet arm wiper system, side window and electric rear window defoggers, 3100 SFI V6 engine with sequential port fuel injection, transverse-mounted front-wheel drive, illuminated entry feature, lamps (instrument panel, glove box, roof rail courtesy and trunk), inside day/night rearview mirror with dual reading lamps, driver and passenger side covered visor vanity mirrors, driver's side air bag, deluxe tilt steering wheel, instrument panel rallye cluster (includes full analog electro-mechanical gauge cluster for speedometer, tachometer and gauges for fuel level, engine temperature and voltmeter plus engine oil level monitor), electronic-shift automatic overdrive transmission with floor shifter.

OLDSMOBILE

CODE	DESCRIPTION	DEALER	LIST

Accessories

CODE	DESCRIPTION	DEALER	LIST
1SA	**Option Pkg 1SA**	NC	NC
	incls vehicle plus standard equipment		
1SB	**Option Pkg 1SB — S Coupe**	419	487
	S Sedan	419	487
	incls cruise control w/resume & acceleration features, auxiliary F & R carpet floor mats, blk electrically operated o/s driver & pass side mirrors, Delco ETR AM/FM stereo radio (incls seek-scan, auto-reverse cass, extended range spkr system & digital display clock)		
1SC	**Option Pkg 1SC — S Coupe**	1035	1203
	S Sedan	1090	1268
	incls pkg 1SB equip plus remote lock control pkg (incls illumination pkg, pwr trunk-lid lock release, driver side unlocked door reminder light, key-chain transmitter), pwr windows w/auto-down feature, blk pwr rear qtr antenna, lighted visor vanity mirrors		
1SD	**Option Pkg 1SD — S Coupe**	1766	2053
	S Sedan	1821	2118
	incls 1SC equip + seat adjuster, custom trim, auto elec comfort control air cond, leather-wrapped steering wheel w/steering wheel touch controls		
AC3/AG1	**Seat Adjuster, 6-Way Power, Driver**................................	262	305
	incl'd w/pkg 1SD		
AM6	**Seat, 55/45 Div Bench w/Driver & Pass Recliners**	NC	NC
	incls storage armrest, & column shift		
AP9	**Convenience Net, Trunk**	26	30
A31	**Windows, Power Side w/Driver Auto Down — Coupe**............	237	275
	Sedan	292	340
	incl'd w/pkgs 1SC, 1SD		
BF9	**Floor Mats, Delete (Fleet Only)**	(39)	(45)
BYP	**Sport Luxury Pkg — w/o WJ7, pkg 1SD**	785	913
	w/WJ7, pkg 1SD	708	823
B20	**Custom Trim, Split Folding Rear Seat Back**........................	129	150
	incl'd w/WJ7, pkg 1SD		
B34/B35	**Floor Mats, Front & Rear**	39	45
	incl'd w/pkgs 1SB, 1SC, 1SD		
B84	**Moldings, Body Side**...	52	60
CF5	**Astroroof, Electric Sliding Glass**	598	695
K05	**Heater, Engine Block**	15	18
L82	**Engine, 3100 SFI V6**	STD	STD
LQ1	**Twin Dual Cam V6 Engine Pkg — w/o BYP**	1307	1520
	w/BYP	966	1123
PH3	**Wheels, Aluminum 15"**...	245	285
UT6	**Radio, AM/FM Stereo w/Cassette, Equalizer — w/pkg 1SC**....	112	130
	w/pkg 1SD	86	100
	pkg 1SC or 1SD req'd		
UV6	**Head-Up Instrument Display**	215	250
U1C	**Radio, AM/FM Stereo w/Compact Disc — w/pkg 1SC**	220	256
	w/pkg 1SD —*pkg 1SC or 1SD req'd*	194	226
V56	**Luggage Carrier, Deck Lid**..	99	115
WJ7	**Custom Leather Trim**	572	665
NG1	**New York Emissions — w/L82**	NC	NC
	w/LQ1..	86	100
YF5	**California Emissions — w/L82**	NC	NC
	w/LQ1..	86	100

EIGHTY-EIGHT ROYALE SEDAN

EIGHTY-EIGHT ROYALE 6 CYL

		DEALER	LIST
N69HR	4-Dr Sedan	18266	20875
	Destination Charge:	575	575

Standard Equipment

EIGHTY-EIGHT ROYALE: Air conditioner, Freedom battery, power front disc/rear drum anti-lock brakes, cigar lighter, convenience group includes: underhood and trunk lamps/covered visor vanity mirrors/chime tones; high capacity cooling equipment, side window defoggers, deluxe luggage compartment trim, jack-in-the-box tool kit, rear child-security door locks, 3800 V6 engine with tuned port fuel injection (transverse-mounted with front-wheel drive), cut-pile wall-to-wall floor carpeting with carpeted lower door panels, composite halogen headlamps, headlamp-on reminder, interior operated hood release, instrument panel analog gauge cluster includes: fuel and temperature gauges, front license plate bracket, outside remote-control driver side mirror, passenger-side manual mirror, gray protective bodyside moldings, body-color wheel opening moldings, belt reveal and drip-bright moldings, Delco ETR AM/FM stereo radio with seek-scan/digital clock/dual rear speakers with extended range/fixed-mast rear quarter antenna, 55/45 divided front seat with individual controls and reclining seat back (plus center armrest), front and rear full-foam seat cushions, power rack-and-pinion steering, deluxe Tilt-Wheel steering wheel with vinyl rim, four-wheel fully independent suspension system with MacPherson front struts/coil springs at rear/rear stabilizer bar; P205/70R15 steel-belted radial-ply all-season blackwall tires, elec shift auto overdrive transmission with column shift, trip odometer, turn-signal-on reminder chime, pass-key vehicle security system, flo-thru ventilation, auxiliary sunshade visors, 15" x 6" wheels, deluxe disc wheel trim, power side windows, Soft-Ray tinted glass windows (EZ Kool solar control rear), pulse wiper system, elec rear window defroster, power door locks, driver and passenger side air bags.

Accessories

			DEALER	LIST
1SA	**Option Pkg 1SA**		NC	NC
	incls vehicle plus standard equipment			
1SB	**Option Pkg 1SB**		886	1030
	incls 15" aluminum wheels, frt seat storage armrest w/dual cupholders, cruise control w/resume & acceleration features, auxiliary F & R carpet			

OLDSMOBILE

CODE	DESCRIPTION	DEALER	LIST
	floor mats, trunk cargo net, Delco ETR AM/FM stereo radio (incls seek-scan, auto-reverse cass, digital display clock, 6-spkr dimensional sound system, pwr rear qtr antenna)		
1SC	**Option Pkg 1SC**	1434	1667
	incls pkg 1SB equip plus seat adjuster (6-way pwr w/pwr recliner, divided bench seat - driver side), pwr trunk-lid lock release, reading lamps (dual F & R, lighted visor vanity mirrors)		
AG1	**Seat Adjuster, 6-Way Power w/Power Recliner, Driver**	301	350
	incl'd w/pkg 1SC		
BF9	**Floor Mats, Delete (Fleet Only)**	(39)	(45)
D90	**Accent Stripe, Body**	39	45
K05	**Heater, Engine Block**	15	18
NW9	**Traction Control System**	151	175
N91	**Wheel Discs, Simulated Wire w/QGZ WW Tires**	NC	NC
	NA w/pkg 1SA		
QGZ	**Tires, P205/70R15 SBR WW All-Season**	65	76
T2T	**Remote Accessory Control Pkg**	194	225
ULO	**Radio, AM/FM Stereo w/Cass, 6-Spkr Dimensional Sound System**	228	265
	incl'd w/pkgs 1SB, 1SC		
UP0	**Radio, AM/FM Stereo w/Cass, Compact Disc**	341	396
	NA w/pkg 1SA		
US7	**Antenna, Power Rear Quarter**	73	85
	incl'd w/pkgs 1SB, 1SC		
WJ7	**Custom Leather Trim**	525	610
	NA w/pkg 1SA		
NG1	**New York Emissions**	NC	NC
YF5	**California Emissions**	NC	NC

EIGHTY-EIGHT ROYALE LS SEDAN

EIGHTY-EIGHT ROYALE LS 6 CYL

Y69HR	LS 4-Dr Sedan	20016	22875
Destination Charge:		575	575

OLDSMOBILE

CODE	DESCRIPTION	DEALER	LIST

Standard Equipment

EIGHTY-EIGHT ROYALE LS: Air cond, Freedom battery, power front disc/rear drum anti-lock brakes, convenience group includes: trunk lamps, covered visor vanity mirrors/chime tones; high-capacity engine cooling, electronic cruise control with resume and acceleration features, side window defoggers, deluxe luggage compartment trim, "jack-in-the-box" tool kit, power door locks, rear child-security door locks, 3800 V6 engine with tuned port fuel injection (transverse-mounted with front-wheel drive), cut-pile wall-to-wall floor carpeting with carpeted lower door panels, auxiliary front and rear floor mats, composite halogen headlamps, headlamp-on reminder, interior operated hood release, instrument panel analog gauge cluster includes: fuel and coolant temperature gauges, lamps include: instrument panel ashtray/glove box door/courtesy/warning; front and rear reading lamps, front license plate bracket, driver and passenger side color-coordinated elec outside remote-control mirrors, wide accent-color lower bodyside moldings, body-color wheel opening moldings, belt reveal and drip-bright moldings, Delco ETR AM/FM stereo radio with seek-scan/auto-reverse cass/digital display clock/6-speaker Dimensional Sound system/power rear quarter antenna; 55/45 divided front seat w/individual controls and reclining seat backs (includes storage armrest with dual cupholders), front/rear full-foam seat cushions, power rack-and-pinion steering, deluxe Tilt-Wheel steering wheel w/vinyl rim, four-wheel fully independent suspension system w/MacPherson front struts/coil springs at rear/rear stabilizer bar; P205/70R15 steel-belted radial-ply blackwall all-season tires, elec shift auto overdrive trans w/column shift, trip odometer, power trunk-lid lock release, turn-signal-on reminder chime, pass-key vehicle security system, flo-thru ventilation, auxiliary sunshade visors, 15" x 6" wheels, deluxe wheel discs, power side windows, Soft-Ray tinted windows (EZ Kool solar control rear), pulse wiper system, cigar lighter and auxiliary 12-volt outlet, elec rear window defogger, front seat map pockets, driver and passenger side air bags.

Accessories

CODE	DESCRIPTION	DEALER	LIST
1SA	**Option Pkg 1SA**	NC	NC
	incls vehicle plus standard equipment		
1SB	**Option Pkg 1SB — w/o WE6, WJ7**	1330	1547
	w/WE6, w/o WJ7	1047	1217
	w/WJ7, w/o WE6	1287	1497
	w/WE6 & WJ7	1004	1167
	incls air conditioner (dual-zone auto elec comfort control, inside/outside temperature indicator), 15" alum wheels, overhead console w/storage compartment & dual reading lamps, steering wheel touch controls, luxury/ convenience pkg (incls remote accessory control pkg, dual lighted visor vanity mirrors, F & R reading lamps, driver-side 6-way pwr seat adjuster w/pwr recliner), reminder pkg (incls indicators for low fuel, low coolant, low oil pressure, high engine temp & low washer fluid level), trunk cargo net, rear seat armrest w/storage & cupholders		
D90	**Accent Stripe, Body**	39	45
K05	**Heater, Engine Block**	15	18
NW9	**Traction Control System**	151	175
N91	**Wheel Discs, Simulated Wire w/QGZ WW Tires — w/o pkg 1SB**	272	316
	w/pkg 1SB	NC	NC
PA3	**Wheels, Aluminum 15"**	284	330
	incl'd w/pkg 1SB		
QGZ	**Tires, P205/70R15 SBR WW All-Season**	65	76
	incl'd w/N91		
R8S	**Comfort Pkg**	477	555
R9H	**Luxury/Convenience Pkg**	624	725
	incl'd w/pkg 1SB		

OLDSMOBILE

CODE	DESCRIPTION	DEALER	LIST
UP0	Radio, AM/FM Stereo w/Cass, Compact Disc	341	396
U2A	Elect Cluster w/Driver Information Center	297	345
WE6	LSS Pkg	727	845
WJ7	Custom Leather Trim — w/o WE6	486	565
	w/WE6	409	475
NG1	New York Emissions	NC	NC
YF5	California Emissions	NC	NC

NINETY-EIGHT REGENCY SEDAN

NINETY-EIGHT REGENCY 6 CYL

X69CR	4-Dr Sedan	22641	25875
Destination Charge:		625	625

Standard Equipment

NINETY-EIGHT REGENCY SEDAN: Electronic comfort control air conditioner with rear seat duct and outside temperature display, front seat storage armrest, rear seat center armrest, instrument panel and dual rear ashtrays, Freedom battery, power front disc/rear drum anti-lock brakes, cut-pile wall-to-wall carpeting with carpeted lower door panels, instrument panel cigar lighter with 12-volt auxiliary outlet, convenience group includes: trunk lamps/covered visor vanity mirrors/chime tones; high-capacity cooling equipment, electronic cruise control with resume and acceleration features, dual front cupholders, side window defoggers, electric rear window defogger, deluxe luggage compartment trim, power door locks, rear child-security door locks, front and rear door-pull handles, 3800 V6 tuned port fuel injection engine (transverse-mounted with front-wheel drive), front and rear auxiliary floor mats, headlamp-on reminder, composite halogen headlamps, interior operated hood release, instrument panel gauge cluster, courtesy warning door lamps, lamps include: instrument panel ashtray/courtesy/glove box; front and rear reading lamps, front license plate bracket, driver and passenger side exterior electric mirrors, color-coordinated bodyside moldings, Delco ETR AM/FM stereo radio with seek-scan/digital display clock/dual rear speakers with extended range; power rear quarter antenna, power remote fuel-filler door, 55/45 divided front bench seat with dual controls/6-way power; passenger side manual seat

OLDSMOBILE

CODE	DESCRIPTION	DEALER	LIST

with seat back recliners and storage armrest, front and rear full-foam seat cushions, power rack-and-pinion steering, deluxe Tilt-Wheel steering wheel with vinyl rim, four-wheel fully independent suspension system with MacPherson front struts/automatic load-leveling/rear coil springs, front and rear stabilizer bars, P205/70R15 steel-belted radial-ply white-stripe ride tires, electronic shift automatic overdrive transmission with column shift, power trunk-lid lock release, turn-signal-on reminder chime, pass-key vehicle security system, flo-thru ventilation, 15" x 6" wheels, simulated wire 15" wheel discs with locks, power side windows, EZ Kool solar control windows, pulse wiper system, map pockets in front seatbacks, color-coordinated wheel opening moldings, driver and passenger side air bags, rear bench seat with center armrest, sunvisors with auxiliary shades.

Accessories

CODE	DESCRIPTION	DEALER	LIST
1SA	**Option Pkg 1SA**	NC	NC
	incls vehicle plus standard equipment		
1SB	**Option Pkg 1SB**	1245	1448
	incls reminder pkg (incls indicators for low fuel, low oil pressure, low coolant level, high eng temp & low washer fluid level), lighted visor vanity mirrors, seat adjuster (6-way pwr, divided bench seat w/pwr recliner - pass side), steering wheel touch controls, trunk cargo net, remote accessory control pkg (incls illumination pkg, retained accessory pwr, remote lock control for doors & trunk, two key-chain transmitters & programmable auto door locks), auto air conditioning (incls dual-zone heat, ventilation), audio system (8-spkr w/woofers), driver & pass seat pwr lumbar adjusters		
CF5	**Astroroof, Electric Sliding Glass**	856	995
D90	**Accent Stripe, Body**	39	45
FW1	**Computer Command Ride System — w/o WJ7**	404	470
	w/WJ7	327	380
K05	**Heater, Engine Block**	15	18
NW9	**Traction Control System**	151	175
PH6	**Wheels, Aluminum 15"**	113	131
UL0	**Radio, AM/FM Stereo w/Cass** — incl'd w/pkg 1SB	168	195
UP0	**Radio, AM/FM stereo w/cass, Compact Disc**	341	396
	NA w/pkg 1SA		
U2A	**Electric Cluster w/Driver Information Center**	297	345
WJ7	**Custom Leather Trim**	443	515
NG1	**New York Emission Equipment**	NC	NC
YF5	**California Emission Equipment**	NC	NC

NINETY-EIGHT REGENCY ELITE SEDAN

NINETY-EIGHT REGENCY ELITE 6 CYL

	DEALER	LIST
W69CR Elite 4-Dr Sedan	24478	27975
Destination Charge:	625	625

Standard Equipment

NINETY-EIGHT REGENCY ELITE SEDAN: Dual-zone automatic electronic comfort control air conditioner with rear seat duct and outside temperature display, front seat storage armrests, rear seat center armrests, instrument panel ashtray, dual rear ashtrays, Freedom battery, power front disc/rear drum anti-lock brakes, cut-pile wall-to-wall carpeting with carpeted lower door panels, instrument panel cigar lighter with auxiliary 12-volt outlet, overhead storage console, convenience group includes: trunk lamps/covered visor vanity mirrors/chime tones; high-capacity cooling equipment, electronic cruise control with resume and acceleration features, dual front cupholders, side window defoggers/electric rear window defoggers, deluxe luggage compartment trim, automatic power door locks, rear child-security door locks, front and rear door-pull handles, 3800 V6 tuned port fuel injection engine (transverse-mounted with front-wheel drive), auxiliary front and rear floor mats, headlamp-on reminder, composite halogen headlamps, interior operated hood release, instrument panel gauge cluster includes: indicators for low fuel/low oil pressure/low oil level/high engine temperature/low washer fluid; lamps include: instrument panel ashtray/courtesy/glove box/front and rear reading; front license plate bracket, exterior driver and passenger electric mirrors, driver and passenger side lighted visor vanity mirrors, color-coordinated bodyside moldings, Delco ETR AM/FM stereo radio w/seek-scan/music search/auto-reverse cassette/digital display clock/8-speaker sound system; power rear quarter antenna, remote accessory control package includes: retained accessory power illumination package/remote lock control for doors and trunk/two key-chain transmitters, power remote fuel-filler door release, driver-side front seat inflatable restraint system, 55/45 divided front bench seat w/6-way driver and passenger side power adjusters/storage armrest, front/rear full-foam seat cushions, power rack-and-pinion steering, deluxe Tilt-Wheel steering wheel w/vinyl rim/touch controls for HVAC and radio; four-wheel fully independent suspension steering with MacPherson front struts/automatic load-leveling/rear coil springs; P205/70R15 steel-belted radial-ply white-stripe ride tires, electronic shift automatic overdrive transmission w/column shift, power trunk-lid lock release, turn-signal-on reminder chime, pass-key vehicle security system, flo-thru ventilation, cast alum 15" wheels, power side windows w/driver-side auto-down feature, EZ Kool solar control windows, pulse wiper system, sunvisors with auxiliary shades.

OLDSMOBILE

CODE	DESCRIPTION	DEALER	LIST

Accessories

1SA	**Option Pkg 1SA** .... *incls vehicle plus standard equipment*	NC	NC
1SB	**Option Pkg 1SB** .... *incls pwr trunk pull-down, twilight sentinel auto headlight control, o/s driver-side electrochromic auto mirror w/defog feature, inside day/night electrochromic auto mirror w/compass, memory controls (automatically adjusts driver-side seat & o/s mirrors to preset positions for two drivers), frt fender cornering lamps*	546	635
CF5	**Astroroof, Electric Sliding Glass**	856	995
D90	**Accent Stripe, Body**	39	45
FW1	**Computer Command Ride System** — w/o WJ7	404	470
	w/WJ7	327	380
K05	**Heater, Engine Block**	15	18
L67	**Supercharged 3800 V6 Engine Pkg** — w/WJ7	1403	1631
	w/WJ7	1325	1541
NW9	**Traction Control System** — incl'd w/L67	151	175
N91	**Wheel Discs, Simulated Wire w/Locks**	NC	NC
UP0	**Radio, AM/FM Stereo w/Cass, Compact Disc**	341	396
U2A	**Elect Cluster w/Driver Information Center**	297	345
WJ7	**Custom Leather Trim**	443	515
NG1	**New York Emissions**	NC	NC
YF5	**California Emissions**	NC	NC

SILHOUETTE

SILHOUETTE 6 CYL

M06UR	3-Dr Minivan	18186	20095
Destination Charge:		530	530

Standard Equipment

SILHOUETTE: Front touch-control air conditioner, front and rear air distribution system, ashtrays include:

front/center row/third row; Freedom battery, power front disc/rear drum anti-lock brakes, front and rear body color bumper fascias, front and third-row cigar lighters, lower center console with locking storage/HVAC and radio controls/dual cupholders; defoggers include: side window/front/rear; 3.1 liter V6 engine with throttle-body fuel injection (transverse-mounted with front-wheel drive), deluxe cut-pile wall-to-wall floor carpeting with carpeted lower door panels, carpeted front and rear floor mats, foglamps, composite halogen headlamps, headlamp-on reminder, interior operated hood release, carpeted instrument panel cover, instrument panel Rallye Cluster includes: electrically driven needle speedometer/tachometer/trip and total odometer/voltmeter/temperature gauge/oil pressure gauge; driver and passenger side outside fold-away electrically operated mirrors, bodyside body color moldings, rear cargo area 12-volt concealed auxiliary power outlet, Delco ETR AM/FM stereo radio with seek-scan/digital display clock/dual front and rear speakers/integrated roof radio antenna; seven-passenger seating includes: front buckets with folding armrests/3 center seats/2 rear modular seats; driver-side 4-way manual seat adjuster; front, center and rear row full-foam seat cushions, power rack-and-pinion steering, MacPherson front strut suspension system, rear variable-rate coil spring suspension, P205/70R15 steel-belted radial-ply blackwall all-season tires, automatic transmission with column shifter, flo-thru ventilation, 15" x 6" aluminum-styled wheels, pulse wiper system, rear window wiper, deluxe tilt steering wheel, tinted glass, solar treated windshield, driver's side air bag, instrument panel lamp, glove box courtesy lamp, driver and passenger side covered visor vanity mirrors.

Accessories

CODE	DESCRIPTION	DEALER	LIST
1SA	**Option Pkg 1SA**	NC	NC
	incls vehicle plus standard equipment		
1SB	**Option Pkg 1SB**	1428	1660
	incls convenience pkg (incls pwr side windows w/auto-down feature, programmable auto pwr door locks w/sliding door delay feature, cruise control w/resume & acceleration features, convenience net, deep tint glass (all glass behind frt doors), overhead console, rooftop luggage carrier, remote lock control pkg (incls door lock release, illuminated entry feature, & key-chain transmitter), Delco ETR AM/FM stereo radio (incls seek-scan, auto reverse cass & digital display clock)		
1SC	**Option Pkg 1SC** — w/o C54	2812	3270
	w/C54	2662	3095
	incls pkg 1SB equip plus pwr sliding door, 3800 V6 eng, seat adjuster (6-way pwr bucket seat - driver side), leather-wrapped steering wheel w/steering wheel touch controls		
AD9	**Integrated Child Seats, Dual**	194	225
AG9	**Seat Adjuster, 6-Way Power, Driver** — incl'd w/pkg 1SC	232	270
AJ1	**Deep Tint Glass** — incl'd w/pkgs 1SB, 1SC	211	245
AP9	**Convenience Net, Cargo Area** — incl'd w/pkgs 1SB, 1SC	26	30
B4A	**Black Roof Delete**	NC	NC
C34	**Air Conditioner, Auxiliary Rear**	387	450
C54	**Sunroof, Pop-Up** — NA w/pkg 1SA/1SB	301	350
E58	**Power Sliding Door** — incl'd w/pkg 1SC	254	295
FE3	**Touring Suspension System** — incl'd w/V92	176	205
K05	**Heater, Engine Block**	15	18
L27	**Engine, 3800 V6 w/4-Spd Auto Trans**	688	800
	incl'd w/pkg 1SC		
NW9	**Traction Control System**	301	350
R9T	**Convenience Pkg** — incl'd w/pkgs 1SB, 1SC	688	800
UM6	**Radio, AM/FM Stereo w/Cassette**	120	140
	avail w/pkg 1SA, incl w/pkg 1SB		
UN6	**Radio, AM/FM Stereo w/Cassette**	26	30
	available w/pkg 1SB, incl'd w/pkg 1SC		

OLDSMOBILE

CODE	DESCRIPTION	DEALER	LIST
U1C	**Radio, AM/FM Stereo w/Compact Disc** — w/pkg 1SB	220	256
	w/pkg 1SC	194	226
	NA w/pkg 1SA		
V54	**Luggage Carrier, Rooftop** — incl'd w/pkgs 1SB, 1SC	125	145
V92	**Towing Pkg, 3,000 Lb Capacity**	305	355
WJ7	**Custom Leather Trim** — w/o pkg 1SC	748	870
	w/pkg 1SC	671	780
	NA w/pkg 1SA		
NG1	**New York Emissions**	NC	NC
YF5	**California Emissions**	NC	NC

OLDSMOBILE *SPECIAL EDITION*

Listed below are the "special edition" models that Oldsmobile will be selling in 1994. These "special edition" cars are value priced with no-haggle window stickers. Oldsmobile's goal is to give customers bottom-line prices up front. The special edition models are each equipped with a designated package of popular accessories and carry a lower manufacturer's suggested retail price than the traditional models from which they are derived.

ACHIEVA SPECIAL EDITION

L37NR & R7B	**S Special Edition 2-Dr Coupe**	12767	13510

incls Achieva S Coupe standard equipment plus air conditioning, 3-speed automatic transmission, carpeted front and rear floor mats

L69NR & R7B	**S Special Edition 4-Dr Sedan**	12767	13510

incls Achieva S Sedan standard equipment plus air conditioning, 3-speed automatic transmission, carpeted front and rear floor mats

L37NR & R7C	**S Special Edition 2-Dr Coupe**	13712	14510

incls Achieva S Coupe standard equipment plus 2.3L quad 4 engine, 4-speed automatic transmission, power windows, air conditioning, dual power mirrors, speed control, carpeted front and rear floor mats, AM/FM ETR stereo radio with cassette, analog gauges (trip odometer, tachometer, voltmeter, temp and oil pressure)

L69NR & R7C	**S Special Edition 4-Dr Sedan**	13712	14510

incls Achieva S Sedan standard equipment plus 2.3L quad 4 engine, 4-speed automatic transmission, power windows, air conditioning, dual power mirrors, speed control, carpeted front and rear floor mats, AM/FM ETR stereo radio with cassette, analog gauges (trip odometer, tachometer, voltmeter, temp and oil pressure)

F37NR & R7D	**SC Special Edition 2-Dr Coupe**	15602	16510

incls Achieva SC Coupe standard equipment plus 3.1L V6 engine, 4-speed automatic transmission and power windows

F69NR & R7D	**SL Special Edition 4-Dr Sedan**	15602	16510

incls Achieva SL Sedan standard equipment plus 3.1L V6 engine, 4-speed automatic transmission and power windows

Destination Charge:		485	485

Accessories *for Achieva Special Edition*

AX3	**Remote Lock Control Pkg** — F37NR & R7D model, F69NR & R7D model	108	125

OLDSMOBILE *SPECIAL EDITION*

CODE	DESCRIPTION	DEALER	LIST
K05	**Engine Block Heater**	15	18
LD2	**Engine, 2.3L Quad 4 MFI** — L37NR & R7C model, L69NR & R7C model	353	410
	F37NR & R7D model, F69NR & R7D model	NC	NC
L82	**Engine, 3100 V6 SFI** — L37NR & R7C model, L69NR & R7C model	353	410
MM5	**Transmission, 5-Speed Manual** —		
	L37NR & R7B model, L69NR & R7B model..	(477)	(555)
MXO	**Transmission, 4-Speed Auto w/Overdrive** —		
	L37NR & R7B model, L69NR & R7B model *available only in CA, HI, NY*	172	200
NG1	**New York Emission Equipment**	NC	NC
YF5	**California Emission Equipment**	NC	NC

BRAVADA SPECIAL EDITION

VO6TR & R7B	**Special ion 4-Dr Sport Utility**	23417	24520
	incls Bravada standard equipment plus leather seats, heavy duty towing pkg, outside spare tire carrier, electronic instrument cluster		
Destination Charge:	....	475	475

Accessories for Bravada Special Edition

B94	**Gold Pkg**	NC	NC
K05	**Engine Block Heater**	28	33
QFN	**Tires, P235/75R15 WOL All-Season**	NC	NC
NG1	**New York Emission Equipment**	NC	NC
YF5	**California Emission Equipment**	NC	NC

CUTLASS CIERA S SPECIAL EDITION

G69AR & R7B	**S Speciadition 4-Dr Sedan**..	12864	13470
	incls Cutlass Ciera S Sedan standard equipment plus carpeted front and rear floor mats		
G69AR & R7C	**S Special Edition 4-Dr Sedan**.......................................	14619	15470
	incls Cutlass Ciera S Sedan standard equipment plus 3.1L V6 engine, 4-speed automatic transmission, power windows, armrest with storage compartment, carpeted front and rear floor mats, speed control, dual power mirrors, AM/FM ETR stereo radio with cassette		
Destination Charge:	....	525	525

Accessories for Cutlass Ciera S Special Edition

AU0	**Remote Lock Control Pkg** — G69AR & R7C model	159	185
K05	**Engine Block Heater**	15	18
L82	**Engine** — 3100 V6 SFI w/4-spd auto trans - G69AR & R7B model	697	810
UM6	**Radio, AM/FM Stereo w/Cassette** — G69AR & R7B model	120	140
NG1	**New York Emission Equipment**	NC	NC
YF5	**California Emission Equipment**	NC	NC

CODE	DESCRIPTION	DEALER	LIST

CUTLASS CRUISER S SPECIAL EDITION

J35AR & R7DS **Special Edition 4-Dr Wagon** 15564 16470
     *incls Cutlass Cruiser S Wagon standard equipment plus power windows,
     third rear seat, rear quarter vent windows, cargo cover, luggage rack, air
     deflector, AM/FM ETR stereo radio w/cass, speed control, dual power
     mirrors, armrest w/storage compartment, carpeted front/rear floor mats*

Destination Charge: 525 525

Accessories for Cutlass Cruiser S Special Edition

AU0	**Remote Lock Control Pkg**	108	125
K05	**Engine Block Heater**	15	18
NG1	**New York Emission Equipment**	NC	NC
YF5	**California Emission Equipment**	NC	NC

CUTLASS SUPREME S SPECIAL EDITION

H47WR & R7B **S Special Edition 2-Dr Coupe** 15564 16470
     *incls Cutlass Supreme S Coupe standard equipment plus sport luxury pkg
     (incls cast aluminum wheels, P215/60R16 performance tires, fog lights,
     wheel lip moldings, rocker panel moldings, leather-wrapped steering
     wheel), power windows, speed control, dual power mirrors, carpeted front
     and rear mats, AM/FM ETR stereo radio with cassette*

H69WR & R7B **S Special Edition 4-Dr Sedan** 15564 16470
     *incls Cutlass Supreme S Sedan standard equipment plus sport luxury pkg
     (incls cast aluminum wheels, P215/60R16 performance tires, fog lights,
     wheel lip moldings, rocker panel moldings, leather-wrapped steering
     wheel), power windows, speed control, dual power mirrors, carpeted front
     and rear mats, AM/FM ETR stereo radio with cassette*

H47WR & R7C **S Special Edition 2-Dr Coupe** 16509 17470
     *incls Cutlass Supreme S Coupe standard equipment plus sport luxury pkg
     (incls cast aluminum wheels, P215/60R16 performance tires, fog lights,
     wheel lip moldings, rocker panel moldings, leather-wrapped steering
     wheel), leather seat trim, power driver's seat with 6-way adjuster, custom
     trim, AM/FM ETR stereo radio with cass, 6-speakers, power antenna,
     speed control, dual illuminated visor vanity mirrors, dual outside power
     mirrors, power windows, carpeted front and rear floor mats, remote control
     lock pkg (incls illum pkg, key chain transmitter and power trunk-lid release)*

H69WR & R7B **S Special Edition 4-Dr Sedan** 16509 17470
     *incls Cutlass Supreme S Sedan standard equipment plus sport luxury pkg
     (incls cast aluminum wheels, P215/60R16 performance tires, fog lights,
     wheel lip moldings, rocker panel moldings, leather-wrapped steering
     wheel), leather seat trim, power driver's seat with 6-way adjuster, custom
     trim, AM/FM ETR stereo radio with cassette, 6-speakers, power antenna,
     speed control, dual illuminated visor vanity mirrors, dual outside power
     mirrors, power windows, carpeted front and rear floor mats, remote control
     lock pkg (incls illumination pkg, key chain transmitter and power trunk-lid
     release)*

Destination Charge: 525 525

OLDSMOBILE *SPECIAL EDITION*

CODE	DESCRIPTION	DEALER	LIST

Accessories for Cutlass Supreme S Special Edition

CODE	DESCRIPTION	DEALER	LIST
AU0	**Remote Lock Pkg** — H47WR & R7B model, H69WR & R7B model............	159	185
K05	**Engine Block Heater**	15	18
LQ1	**Twin Dual Cam V6 Engine Pkg**	966	1123
NG1	**New York Emission Equipment**	NC	NC
YF5	**California Emission Equipment**	NC	NC

EIGHTY-EIGHT SPECIAL EDITION

N69HR & R7B Royale Special Edition 4-Dr Sedan.............................. **18546** **19420**

incls Eighty-Eight Royale standard equipment plus speed control, styled aluminum wheels with locks, AM/FM ETR stereo radio with cassette, power antenna, 6 speakers, carpeted front and rear floor mats, armrest with storage compartment, cargo net, dual illuminated visor vanity mirrors, power driver's seat with 6-way adjuster, dual power mirrors, dual front and rear reading lights, power trunk release.

Y69HR & R7C Royale LS Special Edition 4-Dr Sedan.............................. **21411** **22420**

incls Eighty-Eight Royale LS standard equipment plus LSS pkg, leather seat trim, speed control, styled aluminum wheels with locks, AM/FM ETR stereo radio with cassette, power antenna, 6 speakers, carpeted front and rear floor mats, armrest with storage compartment, cargo net, auto air cond, steering wheel touch controls, rear armrest with storage compartment, overhead console, luxury/convenience pkg, reminder pkg (indicators for fuel, coolant, oil pressure and washer fluid), dual reading lamps, cornering lights, auto day/night mirror, power passenger seat with 6-way adjuster

Destination Charge:..		575	575

Accessories for Eighty-Eight Special Edition

CODE	DESCRIPTION	DEALER	LIST
K05	**Engine Block Heater**	15	18
N91	**Wheel Discs** — simulated wire w/QGZ WW tires - N69HR & R7B model	NC	NC
NW9	**Traction Control System** — Y69HR & R7C model	151	175
T2T	**Remote Accessory Control Pkg** — N69HR & R7B model......................	194	225
WJ7	**Custom Leather Trim** — N69HR & R7B model	525	610
NG1	**New York Emission Equipment**	NC	NC
YF5	**California Emission Equipment**	NC	NC

NINETY-EIGHT SPECIAL EDITION

X69CR & R7B Regency Special Edition 4-Dr Sedan.............................. **23273** **24370**

incls Ninety-Eight Regency Sedan standard equipment plus leather seat trim, aluminum wheels, dual zone air conditioning, power passenger seat with 6-way adjuster, steering wheel touch controls, remote accessory control pkg (incls illumination pkg, two key chain transmitters, remote lock group, retained accessory power), dual illuminated visor vanity mirrors, cargo net, AM/FM ETR stereo radio with cassette, 8-speaker audio system with two woofers, reminder pkg (incls indicators for fuel, oil pressure, temperature, brakes, oil level and washer fluid level)

Destination Charge:..		625	625

CODE	DESCRIPTION	DEALER	LIST

Accessories for Ninety-Eight Special Edition

CODE	DESCRIPTION	DEALER	LIST
K05	**Engine Block Heater**	15	18
NW9	**Traction Control System**	150	175
N91	**Wheel Discs, Simulated Wire w/Locks**	NC	NC
—	**Cloth Trim**	(443)	(515)
NG1	**New York Emission Equipment**	NC	NC
YF5	**California Emission Equipment**	NC	NC

SILHOUETTE SPECIAL EDITION

		DEALER	LIST
M06UR & R7B	**Special Edition 3-Dr Minivan**	18589	19465

incls Silhouette standard equipment plus 3.8L V6 engine, 4-speed
automatic transmission, AM/FM ETR stereo radio with cassette, luggage
rack, deep tinted glass, remote control lock pkg, power windows, power
door locks, speed control, convenience net, overhead console

		DEALER	LIST
Destination Charge:		530	530

Accessories for Silhouette Special Edition

CODE	DESCRIPTION	DEALER	LIST
AG9	**Seat Adjuster, 6-Way Power, Driver**	232	270
B4A	**Black Roof Delete**	NC	NC
C34	**Air Conditioning, Auxiliary Rear**	387	450
K05	**Engine Block Heater**	15	18
WJ7	**Custom Leather Trim**	748	870
NG1	**New York Emission Equipment**	NC	NC
YF5	**California Emission Equipment**	NC	NC

CODE	DESCRIPTION	DEALER	LIST

ACCLAIM

ACCLAIM

PH41/21A 4-Dr Sedan 11339   12470
    incls 2.5L 4 cyl eng & 5-spd man trans

PH41/22D 4-Dr Sedan 12376   13649
    incls 2.5L 4 cyl eng, 3-spd auto trans, air conditioning, rear window
    defroster, floor mats, speed control, tilt steering column

PH41/24D 4-Dr Sedan 12376   13649
    incls 2.5L flex fuel MPI eng, 3-spd auto trans, air conditioning, rear window
    defroster, floor mats, speed control, tilt steering column

PH41/26D 4-Dr Sedan 12992   14374
    incls 3.0L V6 MPI eng, 3-spd auto trans, air cond, rear window defroster,
    floor mats, speed control, tilt steering column, P195/70R14 BSW tires

PH41/24E 4-Dr Sedan 13127   14532
    incls 2.5L flex fuel MPI eng, 3-spd auto trans, air cond, rear window
    defroster, floor mats, speed control, tilt steering column, pwr door locks,
    heated dual pwr remote mirrors, rear split folding bench seat, remote trunk
    release, pwr windows

PH41/28E 4-Dr Sedan 13890   15430
    incls 3.0L V6 MPI eng, 4-spd auto trans, air conditioning, rear window
    defroster, floor mats, speed control, tilt steering column, pwr door locks,
    heated dual pwr remote mirrors, rear split folding bench seat, remote trunk
    release, pwr windows, P195/70R14 BSW tires

Standard Equipment

ACCLAIM: Air conditioning, soft fascia bumpers with integral nerf and 5-mph protection, warning chimes (headlamps on, seat belt, key in ignition), electric rear window defroster, full stainless steel exhaust system, front and rear floor mats, tinted glass, locking glove box, bright grille, single halogen aero-style headlights, counter balanced internal release hood, dual note electric horn, lamps (ash receiver, glove box, trunk, dome), black outside dual remote mirrors, dual visor mirrors, bodyside moldings with bright strip, AM/FM ETR stereo radio with digital clock, seek and four speakers; 50/50 split bench seat, "Austin" cloth seat trim, electronic speed control, tilt steering column, four "Commodore" wheel covers, deluxe intermittent wipers/washers, 2.5 liter EFI 4-cylinder engine, power rack and pinion steering, power front disc/rear drum brakes, 3-speed automatic transmission.

CODE	DESCRIPTION	DEALER	LIST

Accessories

CODE	DESCRIPTION	DEALER	LIST
BR1	**Brakes** — 4-wheel anti-lock disc (NA on 26D)	594	699
ADS	**Argent Special Edition Decor Group** — 22D, 24D, 26D, 24E, 28E *incls luggage rack, 14" cast alum "Bullet" wheels (NA w/TKJ or ASH)*	170	200
ASH	**Gold Special Equip Decor Group** — 22D, 24D, 26D, 24E, 28E *incls gold badging & molding inserts, luggage rack, 14" cast aluminum* *road wheels w/gold accents (NA w/TKJ or ADS)*	170	200
GFA	**Rear Window Defroster** — req'd in NY	147	173
JPS	**Power Driver Seat** — 24E, 28E	260	306
JPB	**Power Door Locks** — 22D, 24D, 26D	213	250
NAE	**California Emissions**	87	102
NBY	**New York Emissions**	87	102
LET	**Mini Trip Computer/Message Center** — 22D, 24D, 26D, 24E, 28E	79	93
RAS	**Radio** — 22D, 24D, 26D, 24E, 28E *incls AM/FM stereo w/cass, clock & 4 spkrs*	145	170
TBB	**Tire** — conventional spare	81	95
TKJ	**Tires** — 22D, 24E, 28E	88	104
	26D, 28E *incls P195/70R14 WSW SBR tires (NA w/ADS or ASH)*	62	73
—	**Seats** — cloth frt buckets, rear fixed - 21A	STD	STD
—	**Seats** — cloth frt 50/50 bench, rear fixed - 22D, 24D, 26D	STD	STD
—	**Seats** — cloth frt 50/50 bench rear split folding - 24E, 28E	NC	NC
—	**Paint** — special color or metallic	82	97

1993 COLT
NOTE: Information for the 1994 Colt models was unavailable at time of publication.

1993 COLT 4 CYL

PE21	Base 2-Dr Sedan	7705	8039
PL21	GL 2-Dr Sedan	8343	8741
PL41	Base 4-Dr Sedan	9140	9597
PH41	GL 4-Dr Sedan	9992	10580
Destination Charge:		430	430

Standard Equipment

COLT - 2 DR: 75 amp alternator, front armrests, power assisted front disc/rear drum brakes, 5-mph bumper system, passenger compartment carpeting, center floor console with armrest and storage, side window demisters, stainless steel exhaust system, gauges include: temperature / fuel / speedometer/odometer; flush aero-style halogen headlights, molded cloth headliner, inside hood release, single note horn, lights include: dome/variable intensity panel; warning lights include: oil pressure/brakes/seat belts/door ajar/parking brake/check engine/alternator/automatic transmission indicator; 1.5 liter 4-cylinder engine, 5-speed manual transmission, black side window opening moldings, manual rack and pinion type steering, 2-spoke steering wheel, strut-type independent front suspension with coil springs, multi-link rear suspension with coil springs, vinyl mat trunk trim, 2-speed windshield wipers, gray bumpers, black outside door handles, vinyl door/quarter trim, floor instrument cluster illumination, outside left manual mirror, high-back vinyl bucket reclining front seats, low-back vinyl rear bench seat, four argent styled steel wheels, four bright center cap wheel covers.

GL 2 DR (in addition to or instead of BASE 2 DR equipment): One assist grip, color-keyed bumpers, cigarette lighter, dual sliding instrument panel cupholder, color-keyed door handles, cloth and vinyl door/quarter trim with map pockets, trip odometer gauge with push button reset, back lighting instrument cluster illumination, remote dual manual outside mirrors, passenger side visor mirror (uncovered), bodyside color-keyed moldings, reclining cloth-face bucket front seats with adjustable head restraints, low-back cloth-face rear bench seat, split-folding rear seat, rear seat passenger side easy entry, full wheel covers.

COLT - 4 DR: 75 amp alternator, front and rear armrests, three assist grips, power-assisted front disc/rear drum brakes, 5-mph color-keyed bumper system, passenger compartment carpeting, center floor console with armrest storage, dual sliding instrument panel cupholder, side window demisters, child protection door locks, cloth and vinyl door/quarter trim with map pockets, stainless steel exhaust system, gauges include: temperature / fuel / speedometer/odometer/trip odometer with push-button reset; rear seat heater ducts, flush aero-style halogen headlights, molded cloth headliner, inside hood release, back lighting instrument cluster illumination, lights include: dome/variable intensity panel; warning for: oil pressure/brakes/seat belts/door ajar/parking brake/check engine/alternator/automatic transmission indicator; 5-speed manual transmission, black side window opening moldings, manual rack and pinion type steering, strut-type independent front suspension with coil springs, multi-link rear suspension with coil springs, carpeted mat trunk trim, 2-speed windshield wipers, black outside door handles, single note horn, outside left manual mirror, 1.5 liter 4-cylinder engine, reclining cloth-face front bucket seats with adjustable head restraints, low-back cloth-face rear bench seat, 2-spoke steering wheel, half wheel covers.

GL 4 DR (in addition to or instead of BASE 4 DR equipment): Lower sill and bumper accent, cigarette lighter, color-keyed door handles, remote fuel-filler door release, tachometer gauge (manual trans. only), dual note horn, low fuel/trunk warning light; remote outside dual manual mirrors, covered driver side visor mirror, uncovered passenger side visor mirror, 1.8 liter 4-cylinder engine, color-keyed bodyside moldings, reclining full-cloth front bucket seats with adjustable head restraints, split-folding full-cloth rear bench seat with center armrest, driver's seat tilt/height control, 3-spoke luxury soft-feel steering wheel, semi-sport suspension with front sway bar and gas-pressure shocks, remote trunk release with over-ride feature, side trunk trim, full wheel covers, fixed-time intermittent windshield wipers.

Accessories

—	**Value Pkgs** — Base 2-Dr		
B	**Pkg B** — Base 2-Dr	57	66
	incls rear window defroster		

PLYMOUTH

CODE	DESCRIPTION	DEALER	LIST
C	**Pkg C** — Base 2-Dr	344	400
	incls rear window defroster, tinted glass, AM/FM radio w/clock & 4 spkrs		
—	**Value Pkgs** — Base 4-Dr		
B	**Pkg B** — Base 4-Dr	57	66
	incls rear window defroster		
C	**Pkg C** — Base 4-Dr	738	858
	incls rear window defroster, 4-door convenience group 1, floor mats, tinted glass, bodyside moldings, AM/FM stereo radio w/clock & 4 speakers, power steering		
	Pkg D — Base 4-Dr	501	582
	incls rear window defroster, 4-door convenience group 1, floor mats, tinted glass, black bodyside moldings, AM/FM radio w/clock & 4 speakers, full wheel covers		
—	**Value Pkgs** — GL 2-Dr		
G	**Pkg G** — GL 2-Dr...	NC	NC
	incls rear window defroster, tinted glass, AM/FM radio w/clock & 4 spkrs		
H	**Pkg H** — GL 2-Dr...	1099	1278
	I>incls rear window defroster, tinted glass, 2-door convenience group, air cond, AM/FM radio w/cassette, clock & 4 speakers; power steering		
K	**Pkg K** — 2-Dr	1570	1826
	incls rear window defroster, tinted glass, 2-door convenience group, air conditioning, AM/FM radio w/cassette, clock & 4 speakers; power steering, sport appearance pkg		
—	**Value Pkgs** — GL 4-Dr		
G	**Pkg G** — GL 4-Dr...	1242	1444
	incls air cond, rear window defroster, 4-door convenience group 2, floor mats, tinted glass, AM/FM radio w/cass, clock & 4 spkrs; power steering		
H	**Pkg H** — GL 4-Dr...	1570	1826
	incls air conditioning, rear window defroster, 4-door convenience group 2, floor mats, tinted glass, AM/FM radio w/cassette, clock & 4 speakers; power steering, power locks, power windows		
K	**Pkg K** — GL 4-Dr...	1576	1832
	incls air conditioning, rear window defroster, 4-door convenience group 2, floor mats, tinted glass, AM/FM radio w/cassette, clock & 4 speakers; power steering, sport appearance group		
L	**Pkg L** — GL 4-Dr...	1990	2314
	incls air cond, rear window defroster, 4-door convenience group 2, floor mats, tinted glass, AM/FM radio w/cassette, clock & 4 speakers; power steering, power door locks, power windows, sport appearance group		
HAA	**Air Conditioning** — std on GL 4-Dr	679	790
MJC	**Moldings** — bodyside, gray - Base 2-Dr...................................	46	54
NAE	**California Emissions**	NC	NC
RAT	**Radio** — AM/FM w/clock & 4 speakers - Base..........................	233	271
RAW	**Radio** — AM/FM w/cassette, clock & 4 speakers - Base 4-Dr, GL 2-Dr.......	156	181
AJB	**Brakes** — 4-wheel anti-lock - GL 4-Dr	829	964
EJA	**Engine** — 1.8L 4-cylinder MPI - Base 4-Dr	324	377
DGA	**Transmission** — 3-speed automatic - GL 2-Dr...........................	445	518
DGB	**Transmission** — 4-speed automatic - Base 4-Dr	603	701
	GL 4-Dr...	551	641

1993 LASER

NOTE: Information for the 1994 Laser models was unavailable at time of publication.

1993 LASER 4 CYL

CODE	DESCRIPTION	DEALER	LIST
PM24	Base 2-Dr Hatchback	10687	11406
PH24	RS 2-Dr Hatchback	12739	13749
PH24	RS Turbo FWD 2-Dr Hatchback	14105	15267
MH24	RS Turbo AWD 2-Dr Hatchback	16039	17371
	Destination Charge: Alaska	550	550
	: Other States	430	430

Standard Equipment

LASER - BASE: Maintenance-free battery, power front and rear disc brakes, stainless steel exhaust system, front and rear body color fascias, driver's side "dead pedal" foot rest, instrument panel includes: speedometer/tamper resistant odometer/oil pressure/tachometer/temperature/fuel and trip odometer; lights include: cargo/cigarette lighter/glove box/ignition/illumination delay interior/overhead console; body color bodyside moldings, dual visor vanity mirrors with covers, 5-speed manual transmission, remote release fuel fill and liftgate, high-back bucket front seats with recliner, tilt steering column, variable intermittent windshield wipers, standard alternator, open floor console with coin holder, single horn, dual manual remote black exterior mirrors, AM/FM ETR radio with 4 speakers and digital clock, 1.8 liter MPI 4-cylinder engine, 2-passenger cloth and vinyl split folding rear seat, four 15" wheel covers.

RS (in addition to or instead of Base equipment): Floor console with armrest cover and cupholder, electric rear window defroster, sport-tuned chrome tip exhaust system, front carpeted color-keyed floor mats, full-tinted glass with windshield sun shade band, dual horn, exterior dual-power remote body color mirrors, AM/FM stereo cassette radio with 6 speakers and clock, 2.0 liter MPI 4-cylinder engine, driver's seat adjustable lumbar support, cloth front seats, rear liftgate body color spoiler, power assisted rack and pinion steering, removable Tonneau cover, four 16" Turbine wheel covers.

RS TURBO FWD (in addition to or instead of RS equipment): Heavy duty alternator, front lower fascia-mtd fog lamps, turbo-boost gauge, gray sill applique moldings with front stone guard, 2.0 liter MPI 4-cylinder turbo engine, driver's side front seat wing/thigh/headrest, leather-wrapped sport steering wheel.

CODE	DESCRIPTION	DEALER	LIST

RS TURBO AWD (in addition to or instead of RS FWD equipment): Four 16" "Seven Spoke" argent or gold wheels.

Accessories

CODE	DESCRIPTION	DEALER	LIST
DGB	**Transmission** — 4-speed automatic - Base, RS	608	716
	RS Turbo	728	857
B	**Pkg B** — Base	703	827
	incls console cupholder, rear window defroster, floor mats, power steering, lower bodyside and rear fascia stripe, decklid-mounted rear spoiler, tonneau cover, wheel covers		
C	**Pkg C** — Base	1406	1654
	incls Pkg B contents plus air conditioning		
D	**Pkg D** — Base	1760	2070
	incls Pkg C contents plus AM/FM stereo radio w/cassette, clock and 6 speakers; speed control		
F	**Pkg F** — RS	783	921
	incls air conditioning, console cupholder, floor mats, lower bodyside and rear fascia stripe		
23G/24G	**Pkg 23G/24G** — RS	1266	1489
	incls Pkg F contents plus AM/FM stereo radio w/cassette, graphic equalizer, clock and 6 speakers; speed control, liftgate wiper/washer		
23H/24H	**Pkg 23H/24H** — RS	1805	2124
	incls Pkg 23G/24G contents plus fog lamps, power door locks, two-tone sill moldings, power windows		
M	**Pkg M** — RS Turbo AWD	80	94
	incls console cupholder, floor mats, lower bodyside/rear fascia stripe		
Q	**Pkg Q** — RS Turbo AWD	1711	2013
	incls Pkg M contents plus air conditioning, power door locks, fog lamps, AM/FM stereo radio w/cassette, graphic equalizer, clock and 6 speakers; speed control, power windows, liftgate wiper/washer		
25G	**Pkg 25G** — RS Turbo FWD	1082	1273
	incls air conditioning, console cupholder, floor mats, speed control, lower bodyside/rear fascia stripe, liftgate wiper/washer		
25H/26H	**Pkg 25H/26H** — RS Turbo FWD	1711	2013
	incls Pkg 25G contents plus fog lamps, power door locks, AM/FM stereo radio w/cassette, graphic equalizer, clock and 6 speakers; power windows		
BRF	**Brakes** — anti-lock - all except Base	802	943
RDP	**Compact Disc Player** — all except Base	439	517
NAE	**California Emissions**	NC	NC
GFA	**Rear Window Defroster** — Base	111	130
GWB	**Sunroof** — removable glass	317	373
ASH	**Gold Decor Package** — all except Base	NC	NC
WNB	**Alloy Wheels** — RS, RS Turbo FWD	288	339
RAN	**Radio** — AM/FM stereo w/cassette, clock & 6 speakers - Base	168	198

SUNDANCE/DUSTER

SUNDANCE 4 CYL

CODE	DESCRIPTION	DEALER	LIST
PL24	Base 2-Dr Hatchback	8263	8806
PL44	Base 4-Dr Sedan Hatchback	8631	9206

DUSTER 6 CYL

CODE	DESCRIPTION	DEALER	LIST
PS24	Base 2-Dr Hatchback	10156	10946
PS44	Base 4-Dr Sedan Hatchback	10516	11346
	Destination Charge:	505	505

Standard Equipment

SUNDANCE: Black exterior door handles, black fascias, bright grille, black narrow bodyside moldings, 5-mph protection bumpers, warning buzzer (headlights on, seat belts, key in ignition chimes), child protection door locks (4-Door only), stainless steel quiet tuned exhaust system, clear windshield and door glass, tinted quarter (2-Door only) and rear window glass, single rectangular halogen aero-style headlights, counter balanced hood with inside release, color-keyed passenger compartment carpeting, mini console with front and rear storage trays, cloth covered headliner, black instrument panel bezel, removable shelf panel, "Classic" cloth upper/vinyl lower door trim panels, lamps (dome, ignition key/cigar lighter), black outside left remote manual mirror, cloth and vinyl reclining front bucket seats, cloth and vinyl rear bench seat with one-piece folding back, firm suspension, four "Mirage" styled steel wheels with black hub caps, 2.2 liter EFI 4-cylinder engine, 5-speed manual transmission, power rack and pinion steering, power front disc/rear drum brakes.

DUSTER: Color-keyed lower bodyside appliques, body color door handles, unique color-keyed fascias, body color grille, body color rear spoiler, 5-mph protection bumpers, warning buzzer (headlights on, seat belts, key in ignition chimes), child protection door locks (4-Door only), performance tuned exhaust system, clear windshield and door glass, tinted quarter (2-Door only) and rear window glass, single rectangular halogen aero-style headlights, counter balanced hood with inside release, color-keyed passenger compartment carpeting, mini console with front and rear storage trays, cloth covered headliner, woodgrain instrument panel bezel (with champagne interior), removable shelf panel, "Austin" cloth upper door trim panels with contrasting insert and lower carpeting, lamps (dome, ignition key, cigar lighter), black outside dual remote manual mirrors, AM/FM ETR stereo radio with seek, clock and two speakers; cloth and vinyl reclining front bucket seats, cloth and vinyl rear bench seats with one-piece folding back, sport suspension, four color-keyed "Triad" wheel covers, 2.5 liter EFI 4-cylinder engine, 5-speed manual transmission, power front disc/rear drum brakes, power rack and pinion steering.

CODE	DESCRIPTION	DEALER	LIST

Accessories

CODE	DESCRIPTION	DEALER	LIST
Y	**Pkg Y** — Sundance...	1313	1545
	incls air cond, rear window defroster, bodycolor fascias, F & R floor mats, color-keyed instrument panel bezels, light group, man remote dual o/s mirrors, dual visor vanity mirrors, color-keyed narrow bodyside moldings, radio (AM/FM stereo w/clock & 4 spkrs), bodyside & decklid stripe, tinted glass, 14" "Commodore" design wheel covers, deluxe windshield wipers		
H	**Pkg H** — Duster..	831	978
	incls air conditioning, console (floor mounted w/cupholders, storage & armrest), rear window defroster, F & R floor mats, fog lamps, dual note horn, remote liftgate release, light group, dual visor vanity mirrors, radio (AM/FM stereo w/cass, clock & 4 spkrs), tach, tinted glass, warning chimes (key-in-ignition, seatbelts, headlamps-on), deluxe windshield wipers		
HAA	**Air Conditioning** — incls tinted glass	765	900
BR1	**Brakes** — anti-lock	594	699
CUN	**Console** — overhead w/compass & temp - Duster w/pkg H	225	265
	reqs JPA, JPB & GTK; NA w/GWB		
GFA	**Rear Window Defroster** — req'd in New York	147	173
JPB	**Power Door Locks** — Sundance 2-Dr w/pkg Y...................................	169	199
	Sundance 4-Dr w/pkg Y..	204	240
	Duster 2-Dr..	169	199
	Duster 4-Dr..	204	240
JPS	**Power Driver Seat** — Duster w/pkg H—*reqs JPA, JPB & GTK*...............	260	306
NAE	**California Emissions**..	87	102
NBY	**New York Emissions**...	87	102
CLE	**Floor Mats** — front & rear	39	46
	incl'd in pkg Y & H		
NHK	**Engine Block Heater** — avail in Alaska only....................................	17	20
ADA	**Light Group**	65	77
	incl'd in pkg Y & H		
JKE	**Remote Liftgate Release** — Sundance w/pkg Y.................................	20	24
GTE	**Mirrors** — man remote dual o/s - Sundance....................................	59	69
GTK	**Mirrors** — pwr remote dual o/s - Duster w/pkg H	48	57
RAL	**Radio** — Sundance	241	284
	incls AM/FM stereo w/clock & 2 spkrs		
RAS	**Radio** — Sundance w/o pkg Y	428	504
	Sundance w/pkg Y..	145	170
	Duster...	187	220
	incls AM/FM stereo w/cass, clock & 4 spkrs		
RAY	**Radio** — Duster w/o pkg H	442	520
	Duster w/pkg H...	255	300
	incls AM/FM stereo w/cass, graphic equalizer, clock & 4 Infinity spkrs [reqs JPB & JHA]		
RBC	**Radio** — Duster w/o pkg H	587	690
	Duster w/pkg H...	400	470
	incls AM/FM stereo w/CD player, graphic equalizer, clock & 4 Infinity spkrs [reqs JPB & JHA]		
TBB	**Tire** — conventional spare - Sundance	72	85
	w/steel wheel (Duster)	72	85
	w/aluminum wheel (Duster)	181	213

PLYMOUTH

CODE	DESCRIPTION	DEALER	LIST
NHM	**Speed Control** — reqs SUA	190	224
GWB	**Sunroof**..	322	379
	Duster NA w/CUN		
SUA	**Tilt Steering Column** — reqs JHA	126	148
JPA	**Power Windows** — Duster 2-Dr w/pkg H	225	265
	Duster 4-Dr w/pkg H..	281	331
	reqs GTK & JPB		
JHA	**Deluxe Windshield Wipers**..	56	66
	incl'd in pkg Y & H		
WHM	**Wheels** — Sundance w/o pkg Y...	320	376
	Sundance w/pkg Y...	279	328
	incls 14" cast aluminum "Bullet" design		
WJF	**Wheels** — Duster	279	328
	incls 15" cast aluminum "Cathedral" design		
—	**Paint** — extra cost	82	97
EDF	**Engine** — 2.2L EFI 4 cyl - Sundance..................................	STD	STD
EDM	**Engine** — 2.5 L EFI 4 cyl - Sundance.................................	243	286
	Duster..	(590)	(694)
EFA	**Engine** — 3.0L MPI V6 - Duster	STD	STD
DDM	**Transmission** — 5-spd man - Sundance..............................	STD	STD
DDN	**Transmission** — 5-spd man - Duster...................................	STD	STD
DGA	**Transmission** — 3-spd auto -Sundance...............................	473	557
	Duster w/2.5L 4 cyl eng...	473	557
DGB	**Transmission** — 4-spd auto - Duster...................................	621	730

VOYAGER FWD

VOYAGER FWD 4 CYL

HL52	Base	13541	14819

PLYMOUTH

PLYMOUTH

CODE	DESCRIPTION	DEALER	LIST

VOYAGER FWD 6 CYL

HH52	SE	16374	18039
HP52	LE	19739	21863
HP52	LX	20187	22372

Destination Charge:	560	560

Standard Equipment

VOYAGER FWD - BASE: Chimes (headlights on, seat belt, key in ignition), cupholders, child protection side door locks, stainless steel exhaust system, front and rear body color fascias with accent nerf, tinted glass, inside hood release, single horn, body sound insulation, front/rear dome lamps, fold away exterior aero manual mirrors, non-illuminated visor mirrors, AM/FM stereo ETR radio with digital clock, seek and four speakers; five-passenger seating (three-passenger fixed rear bench seat), quick release intermediate and rear seats, driver and passenger highback reclining bucket seats, molded deluxe cloth seat trim, underbody spare tire carrier with cable winch, storage compartments, compact spare tire, four "Commodore" wheel covers, vented side/quarter/sliding door windows, liftgate window wipers/washers with fixed intermittent wipe, 2-speed windshield wipers with variable intermittent wipe.

SE (in addition to or instead of BASE equipment): Dual horn, power liftgate release, power fold away exterior aero blk mirrors, non-illum visor mirrors, bodyside accent color (2 colors) moldings, AM/FM stereo ETR radio w/cass, digital clock, seek, Dolby/four spKrs, seven-passenger seating (two-passenger fixed bench and three-passenger), elec speed control, tilt steering column, four "Conclave" wheel covers.

LE (in addition to or instead of SE equipment): Front air conditioning, lower bodyside and sill accent appliques, front storage console with coin holder, overhead console (compass, outside temperature, 4-function trip computer, front and rear reading lights), electric rear window defroster, front and rear body color fascias with bright nerf, floor mats, automatic time delay headlights, deluxe body sound insulation, remote keyless entry, map and liftgate lamps, light package (ash receiver, front), roof luggage rack, heated power foldaway exterior aero black mirrors, illuminated visor mirrors, accent color bodyside molding deleted, power front and side door locks, front dome lamp deleted, driver/ passenger reclining bucket seats w/adjustable headrests, molded luxury cloth seat trim, power quarter vent windows.

Accessories

T	**Base Family Value Pkg T**	181	213
	incls air conditioning, dual horns, accent color bodyside molding, under front passenger seat storage drawer, power liftgate release, map and cargo lighting enhancements		
B	**SE Family Value Pkg B**	181	213
	incls air cond, map, cargo lighting enhancements, rear window defroster		
D	**SE Family Value Pkg D**	985	1159
	incls air conditioning, map and cargo lighting enhancements, rear window defroster, forward and overhead consoles, power door locks, floor mats, gauges (oil pressure, voltage and tachometer), deluxe insulation, light group, power rear quarter vent windows		
K	**Two Tone Pkg K — LE**	260	306
	incls power driver seat, power windows, radio (AM/FM with cassette, equalizer and six Infinity speakers), sunscreen glass		
M	**"LX" Pkg M — LX**	366	431
	incls power driver's seat, power windows, radio (AM/FM with cassette, equalizer and six Infinity speakers), sunscreen glass, sport handling group, "LX" decor group		
HAA	**Climate Group I — Base**	728	857
	incls air conditioning		

PLYMOUTH

CODE	DESCRIPTION	DEALER	LIST
AAA	**Climate Group II** — w/family value pkg..	352	414
	incls air conditioning and sunscreen glass [NA w/ASK]		
AJK	**Convenience Group I** — Base w/Pkg T	316	372
	incls speed control and tilt		
AAC	**Convenience Group II** — Base w/Pkg T	590	694
	SE w/Pkg B	225	265
	incls speed control and tilt, power mirrors and power door locks		
AAD	**Convenience Group III** — SE w/Pkg B...	572	673
	SE w/Pkg D	347	408
	incls speed control and tilt, power mirrors, power door locks, power *windows and keyless remote entry*		
CYE	**Seating Group I** — 7-passenger seating - Base	294	346
CYK	**Seating Group II** — 7-passenger seating w/integrated child seat - Base	485	570
	SE, LE, LX	191	225
CYS	**Seating Group III** — 7-passenger quad command - SE, LE, LX	507	597
CYT	**Seating Group IV** — 7-passenger convert-a-bed - SE, LE, LX	470	553
TBB	**Loading & Towing Group I**...	93	109
	incls conventional spare		
AAE	**Loading & Towing Group II** — Base w/Pkg T	151	178
	SE, LE	151	178
	w/AAG (SE w/Pkg B or D, LE w/Pkg K, LX)	124	146
	incls conventional spare tire and firm ride heavy load suspension		
AAF	**Loading & Towing Group III** — SE w/Pkg B or D	473	556
	w/ASH (SE w/Pkg B or D)	376	442
	LE w/Pkg K	376	442
	w/AAG or ASK (SE w/Pkg B or D, LE w/Pkg K, LX)	349	410
	incls conven spare tire, firm ride heavy load suspension, trailer tow group		
WJF	**Wheels I** — 15" aluminum wheels - LE w/Pkg K....................................	309	363
AAG	**Sport Handling Group** — SE w/Pkg B or D (NA w/ASK)	203	239
	LE w/Pkg K (incls WJF)	415	488
—	**Radio Equipment**		
RAS	,radio - Base	145	170
	incls AM/FM stereo with cassette, clock & four speakers		
RCE	Infinity speaker system - SE...	172	202
RBC	radio - SE w/Pkg D	426	501
	LE w/Pkg K or L	145	170
	incls AM/FM stereo with CD player, equalizer, clock, six Infinity spkrs		
BRL	**Brakes** — anti-lock - SE w/Pkg B or D...	584	687
	w/AAF, AAG, ASH, ASK or WJF (SE w/Pkg B or D).......................................	509	599
	LE, LX	509	599
ASH	**Gold Special Edition Decor Group** — SE w/Pkg B or D.............................	213	250
	incls gold badging, 15" front disc/rear drum brakes, gold day light opening *accent stripe, bodyside body color molding, P205/70R15 BSW SBR tires,* *15" cast aluminum "Lace" wheels with gold accents*		
ASK	**Sport Wagon Decor Group** — SE w/Pkg B or D..	638	750
	incls accent color fascias with black rub strips, fog lights, leather-wrapped *steering wheel, sunscreen glass, sport handling group, 15" cast aluminum* *5-spoke wheels*		
GFA	**Rear Window Defroster** — SE	143	168

CODE	DESCRIPTION	DEALER	LIST
JPB	**Power Door Locks** — Base w/Pkg T	225	265
NAE	**California Emissions**	87	102
NBY	**New York Emissions**	87	102
NHK	**Engine Block Heater** — available in Alaska only	29	34
MWG	**Luggage Rack**	122	143
TLB	**Tires** — Base w/Pkg T, SE w/Pkg B or D	122	143
	incls P205/70R14 WSW SBR tires (NA w/AAF, AAG, BRL, ASH or ASK)		
TPC	**Tires** — SE w/Pkg B or D, LE w/Pkg K..	59	69
	incls P205/70R15 WSW SBR tires (req's BRL or AAF on SE models; NA w/AAG, ASH or ASK)		
EDM	**Engine** — 2.5L EFI 4 cylinder - Base	STD	STD
EFA	**Engine** — 3.0L MPI V6 - SE, LE, LX	STD	STD
EGA	**Engine** — 3.3L MPI V6 - SE, LE, LX	87	102
DDM	**Transmission** — 5-speed manual - Base	STD	STD
DGA	**Transmission** — 3-speed automatic - Base	511	601
	SE, LE	STD	STD
DGB	**Transmission** — 4-speed automatic - Base	679	799
	SE, LE	168	198
	LX	STD	STD
—	**Seats** — cloth highback buckets - Base, SE.......................................	STD	STD
—	**Seats** — cloth lowback buckets - LE, LX	STD	STD
—	**Seats** — leather lowback buckets - LE, LX..	735	865
—	**Paint** — special color or metallic	82	97

GRAND VOYAGER FWD

GRAND VOYAGER FWD 6 CYL

HL53	Base :..	16434	18078
HH53	SE...	17425	19204
HP53	LE...	20574	22783
	Destination Charge:..	560	560

CODE	DESCRIPTION	DEALER	LIST

Standard Equipment

GRAND VOYAGER FWD - BASE: Chimes (headlights on, seat belt, key in ignition), cupholders, child protection side door locks, stainless steel exhaust system, front and rear body color fascias with accent nerf, tinted glass, single horn, body sound insulation, front/rear dome lamps, fold away exterior aero manual mirrors, non-illuminated visor mirrors, AM/FM ETR stereo radio with digital clock, seek and four speakers; seven-passenger seating (two-passenger fixed bench and three-passenger), quick release intermediate and rear seats, driver and passenger highback reclining bucket seats, deluxe cloth molded seat trim, underbody spare tire carrier with cable winch, storage compartments, compact spare tire, four "Conclave" wheel covers, vented side/quarter/sliding door windows, liftgate window wipers/washers with fixed intermittent wipe, 2-speed windshield wipers with variable intermittent wipe.

SE (in addition to or instead of BASE equipment): Dual horn, power liftgate release, power fold away exterior aero black mirrors, accent color (2 colors) bodyside moldings, AM/FM ETR stereo radio with cassette, digital clock, seek, Dolby and four speakers; electronic speed control, tilt steering column, storage compartments.

LE (in addition to or instead of SE equipment): Front air conditioning, lower bodyside and sill accent appliques, front storage console with coin holder, overhead console (compass, outside temperature, 4-function trip computer, front and rear reading lights), electric rear window defroster, power front and side door locks, front and rear body color fascias with bright nerf, floor mats, auto time delay headlights, deluxe body sound insulation, remote keyless entry, map and liftgate lamps, light package (ash receiver, front), roof luggage rack, heated power fold away exterior aero black mirrors, illuminated visor mirrors, driver and passenger reclining bucket seats, molded luxury cloth seat trim, power quarter vent windows.

Accessories

CODE	DESCRIPTION	DEALER	LIST
T	**Base Family Value Pkg T**	181	213
	incls air conditioning, dual horns, bodyside accent color molding, under front passenger seat storage drawer, power liftgate release, map and cargo lighting enhancements		
B	**SE Family Value Pkg B**	181	213
	incls air cond, map/cargo lighting enhancements, rear window defroster		
D	**SE Family Value Pkg D**	985	1159
	incls air conditioning, map and cargo lighting enhancements, rear window defroster, forward and overhead consoles, power door locks, floor mats, gauges (oil pressure, voltage, tachometer), deluxe insulation, light group, illuminated visor vanity mirror, power rear quarter vent windows		
K	**Two-Tone Pkg K** — LE	260	306
	incls power driver seat, power windows, radio (AM/FM w/cassette, equalizer and six Infinity speakers), sunscreen glass		
L	**Woodgrain Pkg L** — LE	818	962
	incls power driver seat, power windows, radio (AM/FM w/cassette, equalizer and six Infinity speakers), sunscreen glass, woodgrain group		
HAA	**Climate Group I** — Base	728	857
	incls air conditioning		
AAA	**Climate Group II** — w/family value pkg	352	414
	incls air conditioning and sunscreen glass [NA w/ASK]		
AAB	**Climate Group III** — Base w/Pkg T	840	988
	SE w/Pkg B	840	988
	SE w/Pkg D	748	880
	w/ASK (SE w/Pkg B)	488	574
	w/ASK (SE w/Pkg D)	396	466

CODE	DESCRIPTION	DEALER	LIST
	w/AAF (SE w/Pkg B)	786	925
	w/AAF (SE w/Pkg D)	695	818
	w/ASK & AAF (SE w/Pkg B)	434	511
	w/ASK & AAF (SE w/Pkg D)	343	404
	LE w/Pkg K or L	396	466
	w/AAF (LE w/Pkg K or L)	343	404
	incls air conditioning, sunscreen glass, rear heat/air cond		
AJK	**Convenience Group I** — Base w/Pkg T	316	372
	incls speed control and tilt		
AAC	**Convenience Group II** — Base w/Pkg T	590	694
	SE w/Pkg B	225	265
	incls speed control and tilt, power mirrors/power door locks		
AAD	**Convenience Group III** — SE w/Pkg B	572	673
	SE w/Pkg D	347	408
	incls speed control and tilt, power mirrors, power locks, power windows and keyless entry		
CYK	**Seating Group I** — 7-passenger seating w/integrated child seat - Base	191	225
CYS	**Seating Group II** — 7-passenger quad command - SE, LE	507	597
CYT	**Seating Group IV** — 7-passenger convert-a-bed - SE, LE	470	553
TBB	**Loading & Towing Group I**	93	109
	incls conventional spare		
AAE	**Loading & Towing Group II** — Base w/Pkg T	151	178
	SE, LE	151	178
	w/AAG (SE w/Pkg B or D, LE w/Pkg K or L)	124	146
	incls conventional spare tire and firm ride heavy load suspension		
AAF	**Load & Towing Group III** — SE w/Pkg B or D	376	442
	LE w/Pkg K or L	376	442
	w/AAG or ASK (SE w/Pkg B or D, LE w/Pkg K or L)	349	410
	incls conventional spare tire, firm ride heavy load suspension and trailer tow group		
WJF	**Wheels I** — 15" aluminum wheels - LE w/Pkg K	309	363
AAG	**Sport Handling Group** — SE w/Pkg B or D (NA w/ASK) 106	125	
	LE w/Pkg L (NA w/ASK)	106	125
	LE w/Pkg K (incls WJF)	415	488
—	**Radio Equipment**		
RAS	radio - Base	145	170
	incls AM/FM stereo w/cassette, clock & 4 speakers		
RCE	Infinity speaker system - SE w/Pkg B or D	172	202
RBC	radio - SE w/Pkg D	426	501
	LE w/Pkg K or L	145	170
	incls AM/FM stereo w/CD player, equalizer, clock and 6 Infinity spkrs		
BRL	**Brakes** — anti-lock - SE w/Pkg B or D	509	599
	LE	509	599
ASH	**Gold Special Edition Decor Group** — SE w/Pkg B or D	213	250
	incls gold badging, gold day light opening accent stripe, bodyside body color molding, 15" cast aluminum "Lace" wheel with gold accents		
ASK	**Sport Wagon Decor Group** — SE w/Pkg B or D	638	750
	incls accent color fascias with black rub strips, fog lights, leather-wrapped steering wheel, sunscreen glass, sport handling group, 15" cast aluminum 5-spoke wheels		

PLYMOUTH

CODE	DESCRIPTION	DEALER	LIST
GFA	**Rear Window Defroster** — Base, SE	143	168
JPB	**Power Door Locks** — Base w/Pkg T	225	265
NAE	**California Emissions**	87	102
NBY	**New York Emissions**	87	102
NHK	**Engine Block Heater** — available in Alaska only	29	34
MWG	**Luggage Rack**	122	143
TPC	**Tires** — Base w/Pkg T	59	69
	SE w/Pkg B or D	59	69
	LE w/Pkg K or L	59	69
	incls P205/70R15 WSW SBR tires (NA w/AAG, ASH or ASK)		
—	**Paint** — special color or metallic	82	97
—	**Seats** — cloth highback buckets - Base, SE	STD	STD
—	**Seats** — cloth lowback buckets - LE	STD	STD
—	**Seats** — leather lowback buckets (NA w/CYK) - LE	735	865
EFA	**Engine** — 3.0L MPI V6 - Base	STD	STD
EGA	**Engine** — 3.3L MPI V6 - SE, LE	STD	STD
EGH	**Engine** — 3.8L MPI V6 - LE	257	302
DGA	**Transmission** — 3-speed automatic - Base	STD	STD
DGB	**Transmission** — 4-speed automatic - Base	168	198
	SE, LE	STD	STD

GRAND VOYAGER AWD

GRAND VOYAGER AWD 6 CYL

PH53	SE	19781	21882
PP53	LE	22930	25460
Destination Charge:		560	560

CODE	DESCRIPTION	DEALER	LIST

Standard Equipment

GRAND VOYAGER AWD - SE: Chimes (headlights on, seat belt, key in ignition), cupholders, child protection side door locks, stainless steel exhaust system, front and rear body color fascias with accent nerf, tinted glass, dual horn, body sound insulation, power liftgate release, front/rear dome lamps, power fold away exterior aero black mirrors, non-illuminated visor mirrors, accent color (2 colors) bodyside moldings, AM/FM ETR stereo radio with cassette, digital clock, seek, Dolby and four speakers; seven-passenger seating, quick release intermediate and rear seats, driver and passenger highback reclining bucket seats, deluxe cloth molded seat trim, underbody spare tire carrier with cable winch, electronic speed control, tilt steering column, storage compartments, compact spare tire, four "Conclave" wheel covers, vented side/quarter/sliding door windows, liftgate window wipers and washers with fixed intermittent wipe, 2-speed windshield wipers with variable intermittent wipe.

LE (in addition to or instead of SE equipment): Front air conditioning, lower bodyside and sill accent appliques, front storage console with coin holder, overhead console (compass, outside temperature, 4-function trip computer, front and rear reading lights), electric rear window defroster, power front and side door locks, front and rear body color fascias with bright nerf, floor mats, automatic time delay headlights, deluxe body sound insulation, remote keyless entry, front dome lamp deleted, map and liftgate lamps, light package (ash receiver, front) roof luggage rack, heated power fold away exterior aero black mirrors, illuminated visor mirrors, accent color bodyside moldings deleted, driver and passenger reclining bucket seats, molded luxury cloth seat trim, power quarter vent windows.

Accessories

CODE	DESCRIPTION	DEALER	LIST
B	**SE Family Value Pkg B**...	181	213
	incls air cond, map/cargo lighting enhancements, rear window defroster		
D	**SE Family Value Pkg D**...	985	1159
	incls air conditioning, map and cargo lighting enhancements, rear window defroster, forward and overhead consoles, deluxe insulation, floor mats, gauges (oil pressure, voltage and tachometer), illuminated visor vanity mirrors, light group, power door locks, power rear quarter vent windows		
K	**Two-Tone Pkg K** — LE...	260	306
	incls power driver's seat, power windows, radio (AM/FM stereo w/cassette, equalizer, clock and 6 speakers), sunscreen glass		
L	**Woodgrain Pkg L** — LE..	818	962
	incls power windows, power driver's seat, radio (AM/FM stereo w/cassette, equalizer, clock and 6 speakers), sunscreen glass, woodgrain group		
AAC	**Convenience Group I** — SE w/Pkg B..	225	265
	incls power mirrors and power locks		
AAD	**Convenience Group II** — SE w/Pkg B...	572	673
	SE w/Pkg D...	347	408
	incls power mirrors, power locks, power windows/keyless remote entry		
AAA	**Climate Group I** — SE w/Pkg B or D..	352	414
	incls sunscreen glass		
AAB	**Climate Group II** — SE w/Pkg B..	840	988
	SE w/Pkg D...	748	880
	w/ASK (SE w/Pkg B)...	488	574
	w/ASK (SE w/Pkg D)...	396	466
	w/AAF (SE w/Pkg B)...	786	925
	w/AAF (SE w/Pkg D)...	695	818
	w/ASK & AAF (SE w/Pkg B)	434	511
	incls sunscreen glass and rear heater/air conditioning		
CYK	**Seating Group II** — 7-passenger seating w/integrated child seat..............	191	225

PLYMOUTH

PLYMOUTH

GRAND VOYAGER AWD

CODE	DESCRIPTION	DEALER	LIST
CYS	**Seating Group III** — 7-passenger quad command	507	597
CYT	**Seating Group IV** — 7-passenger convert-a-bed	470	553
TBB	**Loading & Towing Group I**	93	109
	incls conventional spare tire		
AAF	**Loading & Towing Group II** — SE w/Pkg B or D	317	373
	LE w/Pkg K or L	317	373
	incls conventional spare tire and heavy duty trailer tow group		
—	**Radio Equipment**		
RCE	Infinity speaker system - SE w/Pkg B or D	172	202
RBC	radio - SE w/Pkg D	426	501
	LE w/Pkg K or L	145	170
	incls AM/FM stereo w/CD player, graphic equalizer, clock/6 Infinity spkrs		
ASH	**Gold Special Edition Decor Group** — SE w/Pkg B or D	213	250
	incls gold badging, gold day light opening accent stripe, bodyside body color moldings, 15" cast alum "Lace" wheels w/gold accents [NA w/ASK]		
ASK	**Sport Wagon Decor Group** — SE w/Pkg B or D	638	750
	incls accent color fascias with black rub strip, fog lights, leather-wrapped steering wheel, sunscreen glass, P205/70R15 all-season touring LBL SBR tires, 15" cast aluminum 5-spoke wheels		
GFA	**Rear Window Defroster** — SE	143	168
NAE	**California Emissions**	87	102
NBY	**New York Emissions**	87	102
NHK	**Engine Block Heater** — available in Alaska only	29	34
MWG	**Luggage Rack**	122	143
TPC	**Tires** — SE w/Pkg B or D	59	69
	LE w/Pkg K or L	59	69
	incls P205/70R15 WSW SBR (NA w/ASH or ASK)		
WJV	**Wheels** — 15" cast aluminum - LE w/Pkg K	309	363
EGA	**Engine** — 3.3L MPI V6	STD	STD
EGH	**Engine** — 3.8L MPI V6 - LE w/Pkg K or L	257	302
—	**Seats** — cloth highback buckets - SE	STD	STD
—	**Seats** — cloth lowback buckets - LE	STD	STD
—	**Seats** — leather lowback buckets - LE	735	865
	NA w/CYK		
—	**Paint** — special color or metallic	82	97

PLYMOUTH

178

EDMUND'S NEW CAR PRICES

BONNEVILLE SE

BONNEVILLE SE 6 CYL

X69R	4-Dr Sedan	17871	20424
	Destination Charge:	575	575

Standard Equipment

BONNEVILLE SE: Fixed mast antenna, fog lamps, tinted glass, halogen headlamps, LH remote and RH manual sport mirrors, P215/65R15 touring SBR tires, compact spare, 15" bolt-on wheel covers, driver and passenger side air bags, manual air conditioning, power door locks, analog instrumentation (speedometer, fuel, coolant temperature), front overhead console, reading lamps, rear rail courtesy lamps, warning lights cluster, front and rear floor mats, RH and LH covered visor vanity mirrors, ETR AM/FM stereo radio with clock and four-speaker sound system, rear seat pass-through, 45/55 split bench seats with manual recliners, four-spoke steering wheel, tilt wheel adjustable steering column, Pass-Key II theft deterrent system, power windows with driver-side "express-down" feature, Freedom II battery, power disc/drum brakes, 4-wheel anti-lock brake system, stainless steel exhaust system, front wheel drive, V6 SFI OHV engine, 4-speed automatic transmission, power rack and pinion steering.

Accessories

1SA	**SE Pkg 1SA**		NC	NC
	incls vehicle w/std equip			
1SB	**SE Pkg 1SB**		540	628
	incls lamp group, cruise control, rally gauges & tachometer, illuminated entry system, AM/FM stereo radio w/clock, seek/scan & auto reverse			
1SC	**SE Pkg 1SC**		1102	1281
	incls SE pkg 1SB equip plus remote control decklid release, pwr spt mirrors, driver 6-way pwr seat, elec rr window defogger, variable effort strng			
1SD	**SE Pkg 1SD**		1670	1942
	incls SE Pkg 1SC equip plus pwr antenna, LH & RH illuminated visor vanity mirrors, leather wrapped steering wheel, twilight sentinel, custom interior, remote keyless entry			
1SC/H4U	**SE Value Equip Group 1SC/H4U**		2603	3009
	incls SE pkg 1SC equip plus H4U sport luxury edition			

CODE	DESCRIPTION	DEALER	LIST
1SD/H4U	**SE Value Equip Group 1SD/H4U**..	2770	3204
	incls SE pkg 1SD equip plus H4U sport luxury edition		
—	**Radio Equipment**		
UN6	ETR AM/FM stereo cass w/auto reverse	146	170
U1C	ETR AM/FM stereo - w/o 1SB, 1SC, 1SD	341	396
	w/1SB, 1SC,1SD...	194	226
	incls compact disc player		
UT6	ETR AM/FM stereo - w/o H4U, AS7, T2Z or 1SD	396	460
	w/H4U or AS7 or T2Z & w/o 1SD..	353	410
	w/1SD...	280	325
	incls cass w/auto reverse & 7-band graphic equalizer		
UP3	ETR AM/FM stereo - w/o H4U, AS7, T2Z or 1SD	590	686
	w/H4U or AS7 or T2Z & w/o 1SD..	547	636
	w/1SD...	474	551
	incls compact disc & 7-band graphic equalizer		
L27	**Engine** — 3.8 liter TPI 3800 V6	STD	STD
FE9	**Federal Emissions**...	NC	NC
YF5	**California Emissions**	NC	NC
NG1	**New York Emissions**	NC	NC
—	**Tires**		
QPH	P215/65R15 BSW STL touring	STD	STD
QNX	P225/60R16 BSW STL touring - w/o H4U & Y52	72	84
	w/H4U and/or Y52..	NC	NC
—	**Interiors**		
—	45/45 split bench w/metrix cloth...	STD	STD
B20	custom interior with 45/55 split bench - w/doral cloth w/o 1SD	202	235
	w/1SD...	NC	NC
B20	custom interior w/bucket seats - w/doral cloth w/o 1SD	434	505
	w/1SD...	150	174
B20	custom interior w/bucket seats w/leather seating areas - w/o 1SD or H4U...	1212	1409
	w/1SD & w/o H4U..	884	1028
	w/H4U	NC	NC
B57	**Monotone Appearance Pkg** — w/o H4U	172	200
	w/H4U	NC	NC
Y52	**Performance & Handling Pkg** — w/o H4U..	558	649
	w/H4U	194	225
C49	**Defogger, Electric Rear Window**	146	170
K05	**Engine Block Heater**	15	18
T2Z	**Enhancement Group** — w/o AS7, H4U or 1SD	177	206
	w/AS7 (cloth) & w/o 1SD...	95	110
	w/AS7 (leather) or H4U & w/o 1SD...	52	60
	w/1SD...	NC	NC
US7	**Power Antenna** — w/o H4U, UT6 & UP3..	73	85
	w/H4U and/or w/UT6 or UP3	NC	NC
AG1/AC3	**Power Seat, Driver 6-Way**	262	305
AG2/AC1	**Power Seat, Passenger 6-Way**	262	305
AU0	**Remote Keyless Entry**..	116	135
D58	**Spoiler, Rear Deck Delete**...	(95)	(110)

CODE	DESCRIPTION	DEALER	LIST
T43	**Spoiler, Rear Deck** — w/o H4U..	95	110
	w/H4U	NC	NC
CF5	**Sunroof, Power Glass** — w/o 1SD, AS7, H4U or T2Z (reqs D64)	856	995
	w/1SD, AS7, H4U or T2Z..	856	995
NW9	**Traction Control** — w/o Y52	151	175
	w/Y52	NC	NC
PF5	**Wheel, 16" 5-Blade Aluminum** — w/o Y52	292	340
	w/Y52	NC	NC
N73	**Wheel, 16" Aluminum Gold Crosslace**	NC	NC
N60	**Wheel, 16" Aluminum Silver Crosslace**	NC	NC
D64	**Mirrors** — lighted LH & RH visor..	83	96

BONNEVILLE SSE

BONNEVILLE SSE 6 CYL

Z69R	4-Dr Sedan	22649	25884
Destination Charge:		575	575

Standard Equipment

BONNEVILLE SSE: Fixed mast antenna, fog lamps, tinted glass, halogen headlamps, LH remote and RH manual sport mirrors, P215/65R15 touring SBR tires, compact spare, 15" bolt-on wheel covers, driver and passenger side air bags, manual air conditioning, power door locks, analog instrumentation (speedometer, fuel, coolant temperature), front overhead console, reading lamps, rear rail courtesy lamps, warning lights cluster, front and rear floor mats, RH and LH covered visor vanity mirrors, ETR AM/FM stereo radio with clock and four-speaker sound system, rear seat pass-through, 45/55 split bench seats with manual recliners, four-spoke steering wheel, tilt wheel adjustable steering column, Pass-Key II theft deterrent system, power windows with driver-side "express-down" feature, Freedom II battery, power disc/drum brakes, 4-wheel anti-lock brake system, stainless steel exhaust system, front wheel drive, V6 SFI OHV engine, 4-speed automatic transmission, power rack and pinion steering, power mast antenna, heated power mirrors with blue tint, monotone bodyside moldings, monotone ground

PONTIAC

CODE	DESCRIPTION	DEALER	LIST

effects package, rear deck lid spoiler, P225/60R16 BW Eagle GA touring SBR tires, 16" cast aluminum Torque Star wheels, emergency road kit, front floor console with storage, cruise control, custom trim (includes illuminated visor vanity mirrors, console with rear air conditioning vents, overhead console with power outlet, convenience net, deluxe floor mats), deck lid release, electric rear window defogger, illuminated entry system and retained accessory power, electronic compass/driver information center, headlamps-on warning, rear rail reading lamps, twilight sentinel, luggage compartment cargo net, ETR AM/FM stereo radio with auto-reverse cassette and seven-band graphic equalizer (includes clock, touch control seek up/down, search and replay, leather-wrapped steering wheel with radio controls, Delco theft lock and six-speaker system), 45/45 bucket seats with center console storage, six-way bucket power driver's seat, rear center armrest with dual cup holders, electronic load leveling, stainless steel split dual rectangular exhaust system, variable effort power steering.

Accessories

Code	Description	Dealer	List
1SA	**SSE Pkg 1SA**	NC	NC
	incls vehicle w/std equip		
1SB	**SSE Pkg 1SB**	1238	1440
	incls remote keyless entry, head-up display, elec rear-view mirror, elec auto air conditioning, 8 spkr sound system, pass 6-way pwr seat, anti-theft system (incls key activated door locks & fuel filler door), traction control		
—	**Engines**		
L27	3.8 liter TPI 3800 V6	STD	STD
L67	3.8 liter TPI 3800 V6 supercharged (reqs WA6)	NC	NC
FE9	**Federal Emissions**	NC	NC
YF5	**California Emissions**	NC	NC
NG1	**New York Emissions**	NC	NC
—	**Tires**		
QNX	P225/60R16 BSW STL touring	STD	STD
QVF	P225/60ZR16 BSW STL (reqs WA6)	NC	NC
—	**Interiors**		
—	45/45 buckets w/doral cloth	STD	STD
AS7	45/45 buckets w/leather seating areas	734	854
AL7	45/45 articulating buckets w/leather seating areas - w/o 1SB	1207	1404
	w/1SB	945	1099
WA6	**SSEI Supercharger Pkg — w/o AS7 (leather) or AL7**	1068	1242
	w/AS7 (leather) or AL7	1004	1167
FW1	**Computer Command Ride**	327	380
K05	**Engine Block Heater**	15	18
AC1	**Power Seat, Passenger 6-Way**	262	305
UP3	**Radio — ETR AM/FM stereo w/compact disc**	194	226
	incls 7-band graphic equalizer		
AU0	**Remote Keyless Entry**	116	135
D58	**Spoiler, Rear Deck Delete**	(95)	(110)
CF5	**Sunroof, Power Glass**	844	981
NW9	**Traction Control**	151	175
N73	**Wheels —** 16" aluminum gold crosslace	NC	NC
N60	**Wheels —** 16" aluminum silver crosslace	NC	NC
PA6	**Wheels —** 16" aluminum sparkle silver torque star	NC	NC

CODE	DESCRIPTION	DEALER	LIST

FIREBIRD

FIREBIRD 6 CYL

S87R	2-Dr Firebird Coupe	12805	13995

FIREBIRD 8 CYL

V87R	2-Dr Formula Coupe	16465	17995
V87R	2-Dr Trans Am Coupe	18204	19895
V87R	2-Dr Trans Am GT Coupe	19576	21395
Destination Charge:		490	490

Standard Equipment

FIREBIRD - BASE: Front air dam, fixed mast antenna, bodycolor bumpers, tinted glass, concealed quartz halogen headlamps, rear license plate with lamp, LH remote and RH manual sport mirrors, clearcoat paint finish, rear deck lid spoiler, P215/60R16 BW touring SBR tires, compact spare tire, 16" x 7" cast aluminum machine faced wheels with gray ports, controlled-cycle windshield wipers, driver and passenger air bags, full-length console, side window defogger, cloth seats, locking glove box, analog instrumentation (includes tachometer, coolant temperature, oil pressure indicator, voltmeter, trip odometer, low coolant warning lamps, low oil warning lamp, 115 mph speedometer), carpeted front mats, day/night rearview mirror with reading lamps, RH and LH covered visor vanity mirrors, ETR AM/FM stereo radio with auto-reverse cassette, clock and Delco theft lock, rear deck lid release, reclining front bucket seats, folding rear seat, two-way manual front seat adjuster, four-spoke steering wheel, tilt-wheel adjustable steering column, built-in door storage areas, chime warning system for safety belts and headlamps-on, covered visor vanity mirrors, 105 amp alternator, Freedom II battery, power front disc/rear drum brakes, four-wheel anti-lock braking system, stainless steel exhaust system, low oil level monitor and warning, 3.4 liter V6 engine, 5-speed manual transmission, rear wheel drive, power rack and pinion steering, front and rear stabilizer bars, ride and handling suspension, Pass-Key II theft deterrent system.

FORMULA (in addition to or instead of Base equipment): P235/55R16 touring SBR tires, bright silver 16" x 8" Sport cast aluminum wheels, air conditioning, 125 amp alternator, power four-wheel disc brakes, limited slip differential posi-traction, 5.7 liter V8 engine, 6-speed manual transmission performance suspension.

CODE	DESCRIPTION	DEALER	LIST

TRANS AM (in addition to or instead of Formula equipment): Fog lamps, LH and RH power remote sport mirrors with blue glass, rocker panel extension, moldings, cruise control, power automatic door locks, analog instrumentation (includes tachometer, coolant temperature, oil pressure indicator, voltmeter, trip odometer, low coolant warning light, low oil warning lamp and 155 mph speedometer), power windows with driver side "express-down" feature.

TRANS AM GT (in addition to or instead of Trans Am equipment): Bodycolor bodyside molding, P245/50ZR16 high performance Goodyear Eagle GS-C BW SBR tires, elec rear window defogger, rear floor mats, ETR AM/FM stereo radio w/auto-reverse cassette and seven-band graphic equalizer (includes clock, touch control, seek up/down, search/replay, leather-wrapped steering wheel with radio controls, leather appointment group, Delco theft lock, high performance 10-speaker system), four-way manual driver seat adjuster/two-way manual front passenger seat adjuster, remote keyless entry system.

Accessories

CODE	DESCRIPTION	DEALER	LIST
1SA	**Firebird Pkg 1SA**	NC	NC
	incls vehicle w/std equip		
1SB	**Firebird Pkg 1SB**	864	1005
	incls air cond, rear floor mats, body side moldings, man drivers side 4-way seat adjuster		
1SC	**Firebird Pkg 1SC**	2082	2421
	incls Firebird pkg 1SB equip plus pwr door locks, pwr windows, cruise control, pwr sport mirrors, remote keyless entry, ETR AM/FM stereo radio w/auto reverse cass & graphic equalizer, clock, seek up/down, steering wheel controls, 10 spkr sound system & leather appointment group [reqs pwr door locks & pwr windows]		
1SA	**Formula Pkg 1SA**	NC	NC
	incls vehicle w/std equip		
1SB	**Formula Pkg 1SB**	779	906
	incls air conditioning, rear floor mats, body side moldings, pwr door locks, pwr windows, cruise control, pwr sport mirrors		
1SC	**Formula Pkg 1SC**		
	incls Formula Pkg 1SB equip plus remote keyless entry, ETR AM/FM stereo radio w/auto reverse cass & graphic equalizer, clock, seek up/down, steering wheel controls, 10 spkr sound system & leather appointment group [reqs pwr door locks & pwr windows]		
1SA	**Trans Am Pkg 1SA**	NC	NC
	incls vehicle w/std equip		
1SA	**Trans Am GT Pkg 1SA**	NC	NC
	incls vehicle w/std equip		
—	**Radio Equipment**		
UN6	ETR AM/FM stereo w/auto reverse cass	STD	STD
U1C	ETR AM/FM stereo - Firebird, Formula, Trans Am.............................	194	226
	incls compact disc player..	387	450
UP3	ETR AM/FM stereo - w/o 1SC (Firebird, Formula)	581	676
	w/1SC (Firebird, Formula)	194	226
	Trans Am	581	676
	Trans Am GT	194	226
—	**Engines**		
L32	3.4 liter SFI V6 - Firebird..	STD	STD
LT1	5.7 liter SFI V8 - Formula, Trans Am, Trans Am GT	STD	STD
FE9	**Federal Emissions**...	NC	NC

CODE	DESCRIPTION	DEALER	LIST
YF5	**California Emissions**	86	100
NG1	**New York Emissions**	86	100
—	**Tires**		
QPE	P215/60R16 BSW STL touring - Firebird	STD	STD
QMT	P235/55R16 BSW touring (std Formula) - Firebird	114	132
QLC	P245/50ZR16 BSW STL (std Trans Am GT) - Formula	124	144
—	**Interiors**		
—	bucket seats w/metrix cloth - Firebird, Formula, Trans Am	STD	STD
AR9	articulating bucket seats w/leather - Firebird, Formula, Trans Am	671	780
—	articulating bucket seats w/metrix cloth - Trans Am GT	STD	STD
AQ9	articulating bucket seats w/leather - Trans Am GT	409	475
Y82	**Trans Am Option**	STD	STD
Y83	**Trans Am GT Option**	STD	STD
C60	**Air Conditioning** — std Formula, Trans Am, Trans Am GT	770	895
C41	**Non-Air Conditioning** — Formula	770	895
B84	**Body Color Side Moldings** — std Trans Am GT	52	60
K34	**Cruise Control, Resume Speed** — std Trans Am, Trans Am GT	194	225
C49	**Defogger, Rear Window** — std Trans Am GT	146	170
CC1	**Hatch Roof, Removable w/Locks & Stowage**	770	895
DE4	**Hatch Roof Sunshades**	22	25
VK3	**License Plate Bracket, Front**	NC	NC
B35	**Mats, Rear Floor** — std Trans Am GT	13	15
DG7	**Mirrors** — LH/RH pwr, blue glass - Firebird, Formula	83	96
AU3	**Power Door Locks** — std Trans Am, Trans Am GT	189	220
A31	**Power Windows** — std Trans Am, Trans Am GT	249	290
GU5	**Rear Performance Axle** — Formula	95	110
AU0	**Remote Keyless Entry** — std Trans Am GT	116	135
AH3	**Seat Adjuster, Manual Driver Side 4-Way** — Firebird	30	35
AC3	**Seat, Driver Power 6-Way** — w/o 1SB & 1SC (Firebird)	262	305
	w/1SB & 1SC (Firebird)	232	270
	Formula, Trans Am	262	305
—	**Transmissions**		
MM5	5-speed manual - Firebird	STD	STD
MN	66-speed manual - Formula, Trans Am, Trans Am GT	STD	STD
MX0	4-speed automatic	533	620
40P	**White Wheels** — NA on Firebird	NC	NC

GRAND AM

GRAND AM 4 CYL

CODE	DESCRIPTION	DEALER	LIST
E37R	SE 2-Dr Coupe	11450	12514
E69R	SE 4-Dr Sedan	11542	12614
W37R	GT 2-Dr Coupe	13738	15014
W69R	GT 4-Dr Sedan	13829	15114
	Destination Charge	485	485

Standard Equipment

GRAND AM - SE: Fixed mast antenna, soft fascia bumpers with integral rub strips, tinted glass, composite wraparound headlamps, fog lamps, LH remote and RH manual sport mirrors, wide bodyside moldings, wraparound taillamps, P185/75R14 BW SBR tires, compact spare tire, trunk valet lockout feature, 14" custom bolt-on wheel covers, "wet-arm" windshield wipers, driver-side air bag, front seat armrest with storage bin, front floor console with storage and coin holder, deck lid release, automatic power door locks, analog gauges, trip odometer, headlamp-on warning lights, interior lamp group including trunk lighting, illuminated entry system, carpeted front and rear floor mats, day/night rearview mirror, RH and LH visor vanity mirrors, ETR AM/FM stereo radio with seek up/down and clock, grid cloth interior seat fabric, 45/45 reclining bucket seats, easy-entry front passenger feature (Coupes), rear seat headrests, four-spoke sport steering wheel, front door map pockets, upper and lower glove compartments with cup holders, overhead compartment, Freedom battery with rundown protection, power disc/drum brakes, four-wheel anti-lock braking system, stainless steel exhaust system, front wheel drive, 2.3 liter quad OHC 4 cylinder engine, 5-speed manual transmission, power rack and pinion steering, MacPherson strut front suspension.

GT (in addition to or instead of SE equipment): Front, side and rear skirt aero extensions, rear decklid spoiler, neutral density wraparound taillamps, P205/55R16 BW Eagle GT+4 SBR tires, 16" bright-faced aluminum or white wheel covers, controlled-cycle windshield wipers, air conditioning, analog gauges (speedometer, odometer, tachometer, coolant temperature, oil pressure indicator, voltmeter, trip odometer), tilt wheel adjustable steering column, dual exhaust systems with chrome tipped exhaust outlets, 2.3 liter quad 4 DOHC H.O. 16-valve 4 cylinder engine.

CODE	DESCRIPTION	DEALER	LIST

Accessories

CODE	DESCRIPTION	DEALER	LIST
1SA	**SE Pkg 1SA**...	NC	NC
	incls vehicle w/std equip		
1SB	**SE Pkg 1SB**...	1355	1575
	incls custom air conditioning, tilt steering wheel, controlled cycle windshield wipers, cruise control, elec rear window defogger, ETR AM/FM stereo radio w/auto reverse cass		
1SC	**SE Pkg 1SC** — SE Coupe	1794	2086
	SE Sedan..	1850	2151
	incls SE pkg 1SB equip plus split folding rear seat, pwr windows w/driver side express down, LH & RH pwr mirrors		
1SA	**GT Pkg 1SA**...	NC	NC
	incls vehicle w/std equip		
1SB	**GT Pkg 1SB**...	460	535
	incls cruise control, elec rear window defogger, ETR AM/FM stereo w/auto reverse cass		
1SC	**GT Pkg 1SC** — GT Coupe	900	1046
	GT Sedan..	955	1111
	incls GT pkg 1SB equip plus split folding rear seat, pwr windows w/drivers express down, LH & RH pwr mirrors		
—	**Radio Equipment**		
UM6	ETR AM/FM stereo cass w/auto reverse	120	140
UX1	ETR AM/FM stereo cass w/auto reverse - w/o 1SB & 1SC	323	375
	w/1SB or 1SC	202	235
	incls 5 band equalizer & 6 spkr sound system		
UP3	ETR AM/FM stereo w/compact disc - w/o 1SB & 1SC	499	580
	w/1SB or 1SC	378	440
	incls 5 band equalizer & 6 spkr sound system		
—	**Engines**		
L40	2.3 liter Quad OHC (NA GT)	STD	STD
LD2	2.3 liter DOHC FI 4 cyl (NA SE) - GT	(120)	(140)
LG0	2.3 liter DOHC FI H.O. 4 cyl (std GT, NA SE)	NC	NC
L82	3.1 liter 3100 FI V6 - SE	353	410
	GT	(120)	(140)
FE9	**Federal Emissions**...	NC	NC
YF5	**California Emissions** — NC w/L82 eng	86	100
NG1	**New York Emissions** — NC w/L82 eng	86	100
—	**Tires**		
QFE	P185/75R14 BSW STL (NA GT)................................	STD	STD
QPD	P195/65R15 BSW STL touring (NA GT).....................	113	131
QMS	P205/55R16 BSW STL touring (NA GT).....................	192	223
QLG	P205/55R16 BSW STL (NA SE, std GT).....................	STD	STD
—	**Interiors - Coupes**		
B9	buckets w/grid cloth	STD	STD
C9	buckets w/spectra cloth		
	pricing impact of C9:		
B20	sport interior group - w/o 1SC................................	372	432
	w/1SC	243	282
—	buckets w/prado leather seating areas		
B20	sport interior group - w/o 1SC................................	780	907

PONTIAC

CODE	DESCRIPTION	DEALER	LIST
	w/1SC..	651	757
—	**Interiors - Sedans**		
D9	buckets w/grid cloth	STD	STD
E9	buckets w/spectra cloth		
	pricing impact of E9:		
B20	sport interior group - w/o 1SC..	372	432
	w/1SC..	243	282
—	buckets w/prado leather seating area		
B20	sport interior group - w/o 1SC..	780	907
	w/1SC..	651	757
C60	**Air Conditioning, Custom** — (std GT)	714	830
C41	**Non Air Conditioning**..	NC	NC
K34	**Cruise Control, Resume Speed**..	194	225
C49	**Defogger, Electric Rear Window**	146	170
K05	**Engine Block Heater**	15	18
UB3	**Gages, Rally & I.P Tach** — (std GT)..	95	111
VK3	**License Plate Bracket, Front**	NC	NC
DG7	**Mirrors** — sport LH/RH pwr	74	86
AC3	**Power Seat, Driver 6-Way** — w/o B20	292	340
	w/B20..	262	305
A31	**Power Windows** — (express down driver's side)		
	Coupe w/o 1SC	237	275
	Sedan w/o 1SC	292	340
	Coupe & Sedan w/1SC	NC	NC
AX3	**Remote Keyless Entry**	116	135
AM9	**Seat, Split Folding Rear** — w/o B20 & 1SC	129	150
	w/B20 and/or 1SC	NC	NC
T43	**Rear Deck Spoiler** — std GT..	95	110
N33	**Steering Wheel, Tilt** — std GT	125	145
MM5	**Transmission** - 5-spd manual	STD	STD
MX1	**Transmission** — 3-spd automatic..	477	555
MX0	**Transmission** — 4-spd automatic..	649	755
PG1	**Wheel Covers** - bolt on 15" crosslaced (NA GT)..............................	47	55
PH7	**Wheels** — 16" sport aluminum (NA GT)	258	300
QB4	**Wheels** — aluminum 16" SE specific (NA GT)	258	300
V2C	**Wheels** — aluminum 16" bright faced (NA SE)..................................	NC	NC
CD4	**Windshield Wipers** — controlled cycle (std GT)................................	56	65

GRAND PRIX SE COUPE

GRAND PRIX SE COUPE 6 CYL

J37R	2-Dr Coupe	15345	16770
Destination Charge:		525	525

Standard Equipment

GRAND PRIX SE COUPE: Fixed mast antenna, soft fascia type bumpers with integral rub strips, tinted glass, mini-quad halogen headlamps, fog lamps, lower aero ground effects, LH and RH power remote body color sport mirrors, compact spare tire, controlled cycle "wet-arm" windshield wipers, driver and passenger side air bags, electronic air conditioning, front floor console, cruise control, deck lid release, electric rear window defogger, power automatic door locks with unlock and relock feature, mechanical analog instrumentation (includes speedometer, tachometer, coolant temperature, fuel and trip odometer), entry lighting, luggage compartment trim, front and rear floor mats, day/night rearview mirror, RH and LH covered visor vanity mirrors, steering wheel radio controls, tilt wheel adjustable steering column, front door map pockets, pocketed visor storage, power windows with LH "express-down" feature, Freedom II battery, 4-wheel disc brakes, stainless steel exhaust system, front wheel drive, 3.1 liter V6 SFI engine, 4-speed automatic transmission, power rack and pinion steering, MacPherson strut front suspension, 16" x 6.5" cast aluminum five blade wheels with wheel locks, ETR AM/FM stereo radio with seek up/down, auto reverse cassette and clock; sport bucket seats with reclining backs, rear seat headrests, sport four-spoke leather steering wheel.

Accessories

1SA	**Grand Prix Coupe Pkg 1SA**	NC	NC
	incls vehicle with standard equipment		
1SB	**Grand Prix Coupe Pkg 1SB**	1194	1388
	incls electronic front air conditioning, tilt steering wheel, cruise control, power sport LH & RH mirrors, ETR AM/FM radio w/auto reverse cassette		
1SC	**Grand Prix Coupe Pkg 1SC**	2070	2383

PONTIAC

CODE	DESCRIPTION	DEALER	LIST
	incls Grand Prix Coupe Pkg 1SB plus power locks, power windows, rear window electric defogger, deep tinted glass, 7-passenger seating		
1SD	**Grand Prix Coupe Pkg 1SD**	2543	2933
	incls Grand Prix Coupe Pkg 1SC plus power seat, remote keyless entry, luggage rack		
1SE	**Grand Prix Coupe Pkg 1SE**	3382	3908
	incls Grand Prix Coupe Pkg 1SD plus AM/FM radio w/cass & 5-band equalizer, auto level control, 15" self sealing touring tires, 15" alum wheels		
—	**Engines**		
L82	3.1 liter 3100 SFI V6	STD	STD
LQ1	3.4 liter DOHC V6 - w/o B4S	968	1125
	w/B4S	NC	NC
	incls split dual exhaust and sport suspension		
FE9	**Federal Emissions**	NC	NC
YF5	**California Emissions** — NC w/L82 engine	86	100
NG1	**New York Emissions** — NC w/L82 engine	86	100
—	**Tires**		
QPE	P215/60R16 BSW STL touring	STD	STD
QXJ	P225/60R16 BSW STL performance - w/o B4U & B4S	41	48
	w/B4U or B4S	NC	NC
—	**Seats**		
AR9	buckets w/Cordae cloth	STD	STD
B20	sport buckets w/Doral cloth	336	391
B20	sport buckets w/Prado leather seating areas	744	866
U1C	**Radio**	194	226
	incls AM/FM stereo w/compact disc player		
UT6	**Radio**	194	225
	incls ETR AM/FM stereo w/auto reverse cassette, 7-band equalizer and 8-speaker performance sound system		
UP3	**Radio**	388	451
	incls ETR AM/FM stereo/CD player, 7-band equalizer and 8-speaker performance sound system		
C67	**Air Conditioning, Electronic Front**		
	w/1SB, 1SC, 1SD or 1SE	NC	NC
	w/o 1SB, 1SC, 1SD or 1SE	714	830
C34	**Air Conditioning & Heater, Rear** — incls front		
	w/o 1SC, 1SD and 1SE	1101	1280
	w/1SC, 1SD or 1SE	387	450
C40	**Air Conditioning Delete**	NC	NC
G67	**Automatic Level Control**	172	200
B2Q	**Black Roof Delete**	NC	NC
C49	**Defogger, Electric Rear Window**	146	170
K05	**Engine Block Heater**	15	18
VK3	**Front License Plate Bracket**	NC	NC
AJ1	**Glass, Deep Tint**	211	245
B4U	**Special Edition** — w/o B4S	516	600
	w/B4S	NC	NC
B4S	**GTP Performance Package**	1380	1605
UV8	**Cellular Phone Provisions**	30	35
NC5	**Exhaust, Split Dual**	77	90

CODE	DESCRIPTION	DEALER	LIST
UV6	**Head-Up Display**	215	250
U40	**Trip Computer**	171	199
US7	**Power Antenna**	73	85
JL9	**Power Brakes, Anti-Lock**	387	450
AC3	**Power Seat, Driver 6-Way**	262	305
AU0	**Remote Keyless Entry**	116	135
D81	**Spoiler, Rear Deck**	150	175
CF5	**Sunroof, Power Glass — w/B20**	556	646
16P	**Wheels, Aluminum White Painted 16"**	NC	NC

GRAND PRIX SE SEDAN

GRAND PRIX SE SEDAN 6 CYL

JI9R	4-Dr Sedan	14476	16174
Destination Charge:		525	525

Standard Equipment

GRAND PRIX SE SEDAN: Fixed mast antenna, soft fascia type bumpers with integral rub strips, tinted glass, halogen headlamps, fog lamps, lower aero ground effects, mirrors, compact spare tire, controlled cycle "wet-arm" windshield wipers, driver and passenger side air bags, electronic air conditioning, front floor console, cruise control, deck lid release, electric rear window defogger, power automatic door locks with unlock and relock feature, mechanical analog instrumentation (includes speedometer, tachometer, coolant temperature, fuel and trip odometer), entry lighting, luggage compartment trim, front and rear floor mats, day/night rearview mirror, RH and LH covered visor vanity mirrors, steering wheel radio controls, tilt wheel adjustable steering column, front door map pockets, pocketed visor storage, power windows with LH "express-down" feature, Freedom II battery, 4-wheel disc brakes, stainless steel exhaust system, front wheel drive, 3.1 liter V6 SFI engine, 4-speed automatic transmission, power rack and pinion steering, MacPherson strut front suspension, LH remote and RH manual sport mirrors, P205/70R15 BW touring SBR tires, 15" Sport wheel covers with "bolt-on" feature, ETR AM/FM stereo radio with clock (includes seek up/down feature), front 45/55 split seats with folding armrest and reclining seatbacks, rear seat headrests, 4-spoke sport steering wheel.

PONTIAC

CODE	DESCRIPTION	DEALER	LIST
Accessories			
1SA	**Grand Prix Sedan Pkg 1SA**	NC	NC
	incls vehicle w/std equip		
1SB	**Grand Prix Sedan Pkg 1SB**	617	717
	incls cruise control, dual visor covered mirrors, pwr sport mirrors, elec rear window defogger, AM/FM stereo radio w/auto reverse cass, remote control decklid release		
1SC	**Grand Prix Sedan Pkg 1SC**	1644	1912
	incls Grand Prix Sedan pkg 1SB equip plus F & R floor mats, steering wheel radio controls, driver 6-way pwr seat, anti-lock pwr brakes, remote keyless entry, pwr antenna		
—	**Engines**		
L82	3.1 liter SFI V6	STD	STD
LQ1	3.4 liter DOHC V6 w/split dual exhaust & sport suspension - w/o B4Q..........	968	1125
	w/B4Q..	NC	NC
FE9	**Federal Emissions**..	NC	NC
YF5	**California Emissions** — NC w/L82 eng..	86	100
NG1	**New York Emissions** — NC w/L82 eng..	86	100
—	**Tires**		
QIN	P205/70R15BSW STL touring	STD	STD
QPE	P215/60R16 BSW STL touring	96	112
QXJ	P225/60R16 BSW STL performance - w/o B4Q	129	150
	w/B4Q..	NC	NC
—	**Interiors**		
—	45/55 split bench w/Cordae cloth	STD	STD
B20	45/55 split bench w/Doral cloth - w/1SB..	420	488
	w/1SC..	338	393
B20	sport buckets w/Doral cloth - w/1SB..	540	628
	w/1SC..	458	533
	w/B4Q..	NC	NC
B20	sport buckets w/Prado leather seating areas - w/1SB	949	1103
	w/1SC..	867	1008
	w/B4Q..	409	475
B4Q	**GT Performance Pkg** — w/1SB	1890	2198
	w/1SC..	1809	2103
UV8	**Cellular Phone Provisions**..	30	35
K34	**Cruise Control, Resume Speed**	194	225
A90	**Deck Lid Release**	52	60
C49	**Defogger, Electric Rear Window**	146	170
B37	**Front & Rear Floor Mats** — w/o B20	39	45
	w/B20..	NC	NC
K05	**Engine Block Heater**	15	18
NC5	**Exhaust, Split Dual**	77	90
UV6	**Head-Up Display**	215	250
U40	**Trip Computer**	171	199
VK3	**License Plate Bracket, Front**	NC	NC
DD2	**Mirrors, Dual Covered Visor Vanity** — w/o B20, 1SB & 1SC............	12	14
	w/B20 and/or w/1SB or 1SC..	NC	NC
US7	**Power Antenna**	73	85

PONTIAC

PONTIAC

CODE	DESCRIPTION	DEALER	LIST
JL9	**Power Brakes, Anti-Lock**..	387	450
AC3	**Power Seat, Driver 6-Way**	262	305
—	**Radio Equipment**		
UK3	radio controls, steering wheel - w/o B20, UT6, UP3 & 1SC...........................	151	175
	w/B20 and w/o UT6, UP3 & 1SC	108	125
	w/UT6, UP3, U1C or 1SC...	NC	NC
	incls leather-wrapped steering wheel		
UN6	ETR AM/FM stereo radio w/auto reverse cass	146	170
U1C	ETR AM/FM stereo w/compact disc - w/o 1SB & 1SC................................	341	396
	w/1SB or 1SC..	194	226
UT6	ETR AM stereo/FM stereo w/auto reverse cass - w/1SC........................	194	225
	w/1SB w/o B20...	344	400
	w/1SB w/B20..	301	350
	incls 7-band equalizer & steering wheel controls		
UP3	ETR AM stereo/FM stereo - w/1SC...	388	451
	w/1SB w/o B20...	538	626
	w/1SB w/B20..	495	576
AU0	**Remote Keyless Entry**	116	135
CF5	**Sunroof, Power Glass** — w/o B20	598	695
	w/B20..	556	646
NW0	**Wheels, Aluminum Sport Bright Faced** — w/o B4Q...............................	237	275
	w/B4Q	NC	NC
PH3	**Wheels, Aluminum Sport Bright Faced 15"**	237	275
16P	**Wheels - Color White** — replaces silver on NW0...................................	NC	NC

SUNBIRD

SUNBIRD 4 CYL

B37R	LE 2-Dr Coupe	9129	9764
B69R	LE 4-Dr Sedan	9129	9764
B67R	LE 2-Dr Convertible	14515	15524

SUNBIRD 6 CYL

| L37R | SE 2-Dr Coupe | 11244 | 12424 |
| | Destination Charge: | 475 | 475 |

Standard Equipment

SUNBIRD - LE COUPE/SEDAN: Air dam, fixed mast antenna, tinted glass, halogen headlamps, LH remote and RH manual sport mirrors, wide bodycolor bodyside moldings, P185/75R14 BW all-season SBR tires, compact spare, custom 14" bolt-on wheel covers, fluidic windshield wipers, cut-pile carpeting, front floor console, side window defogger, automatic power door locks with automatic unlock/relock feature, grid cloth interior, mechanical analog instrumentation (includes speedometer, coolant temperature, fuel and trip odometer), dome lights, illuminated entry, rear quarter courtesy lights, fuel carpeted luggage compartment, day/night rearview mirror, ETR AM/FM stereo radio with seek/scan and clock, deluxe urethane four-spoke steering wheel with self-aligning feature, front center console, front door map pockets, Freedom II battery, power disc/drum brakes, four-wheel anti-lock braking system, stainless steel single side dual exhaust system, front wheel drive, oil level indicator, 2.0 liter OHC 4 cylinder MPI engine, 5-speed manual transmission, power rack and pinion steering, MacPherson strut front suspension, 22 mm front stabilizer bar.

SE COUPE (in addition to or instead of LE Coupe/Sedan equipment): Aero extensions, specific front and rear fascia with semi-hidden headlamps, fog lamps, narrow bodycolor bodyside moldings with aero extensions, rear deck lid spoiler, P195/65R15 BW touring SBR tires, 15" Crosslace wheel covers, mechanical analog instrumentation (includes speedometer, tachometer, coolant temperature, oil pressure, indicator), trip odometer (V6 models), RH and LH covered visor vanity mirrors, 3.1 liter V6 MPI engine, ride and handling suspension, 28 mm front stabilizer bar, 19 mm rear stabilizer bar.

LE CONVERTIBLE (in addition to or instead of LE Coupe/Sedan equipment): Rear deck lid spoiler, P195/65R15 BW touring SBR tires, 15" Crosslace wheel covers, controlled cycle windshield wipers, front seat armrest including storage bin, power convertible top, RH and LH covered visor vanity mirror, power windows with driver side "express-down" feature.

PONTIAC

CODE	DESCRIPTION	DEALER	LIST

Accessories

CODE	DESCRIPTION	DEALER	LIST
1SA	**LE Coupe/Sedan Pkg 1SA**..	NC	NC
	incls vehicle w/std equip		
1SB	**LE Coupe/Sedan Pkg 1SB**..	1061	1234
	incls custom air conditioning, front seat armrest, remote control decklid release, AM/FM stereo radio w/auto reverse cass, tilt steering wheel, controlled cycle windshield wipers		
1SC	**LE Coupe/Sedan Pkg 1SC** — LE Coupe	1698	1974
	LE Sedan	1694	1969
	incls LE Coupe/Sedan pkg 1SB equip plus convenience net, cruise control, pwr windows w/drivers express down, split folding rear seat, rear deck spoiler (Coupe)		
1SA	**SE Coupe Pkg 1SA**...	NC	NC
	incls vehicle w/std equip		
1SB	**SE Coupe Pkg 1SB**...	1061	1234
	incls custom air conditioning, front seat armrest, remote control decklid, AM/FM stereo radio w/auto reverse cass, tilt steering wheel, controlled cycle windshield wipers		
1SC	**SE Coupe Pkg 1SC**	1637	1904
	incls SE Coupe pkg 1SB equip plus convenience net, cruise control, pwr windows w/drivers express down, split folding rear seat		
1SA	**LE Convertible Pkg 1SA**	NC	NC
	incls vehicle w/std equip		
1SB	**LE Convertible Pkg 1SB**	1175	1366
	incls custom air conditioning, convenience net, cruise control, remote control decklid release, AM/FM stereo w/auto reverse cass, tilt steering wheel, controlled cycle windshield wipers		
—	**Engines**		
LE4	2.0 liter overhead Cam FI 4 cyl..	STD	STD
LH0	3.1 liter FI V6 (std SE)	612	712
	incls rally gauges		
FE9	**Federal Emissions**...	NC	NC
YF5	**California Emissions** — (NC when LE4 w/MX1)	86	100
NG1	**New York Emissions** — (NC when LE4 w/MX1)	86	100
—	**Tires**		
QFE	P185/75R14 BSW STL - LE	STD	STD
QME	P195/70R14 BSW STL touring - LE Coupe & Sedan	121	141
	LE Convertible..	(15)	(17)
QPD	P195/65R15 BSW STL touring - LE Coupe & Sedan	136	158
—	**Interiors**		
—	buckets w/grid cloth - all except LE Convertible	STD	STD
—	buckets w/grid cloth - LE Convertible	STD	STD
B20	buckets w/white vinyl interior trim - LE Convertible w/o W25 ...	65	75
	LE Convertible w/W25...	NC	NC
W25	**Special Appearance Pkg** — LE Convertible (NA w/1SA).....	272	316
C60	**Air Conditioning, Custom**	675	785
C41	**Non-Air Conditioning**	NC	NC
K34	**Cruise Control, Resume Speed**...	194	225
C49	**Defogger, Electric Rear Window**	146	170
K05	**Engine Block Heater**	15	18
VK3	**License Plate Bracket, Front**	NC	NC
B37	**Mats, Carpet Front & Rear** — std SE	28	33
A31	**Power Windows, Drivers Side Express Down** — Coupe....	228	265

PONTIAC

CODE	DESCRIPTION	DEALER	LIST
	Sedan..	284	330
—	**Radio Equipment**		
UN6	ETR AM/FM stereo w/auto reverse cass..	146	170
UC1	ETR AM/FM stereo w/compact disc player -		
	LE Coupe & Sedan w/o 1SB & 1SC..	341	396
	w/1SB or 1SC..	194	226
	LE Convertible w/o 1SB..	341	396
	w/1SB..	194	226
	SE Coupe w/o 1SB & 1SC	341	396
	w/1SB & 1SC	194	226
AM9	**Seat, Split Folding Rear** — NA Convertible	129	150
T43	**Spoiler, Rear Deck** — LE Coupe	60	70
N33	**Steering Wheel, Tilt**	125	145
AD3	**Sunroof, Removable** — NA Sedan, Convertible	301	350
MM5	**Transmission** — 5-spd manual..	NC	NC
MX1	**Transmission** — 3-spd auto	426	495
PG1	**Wheel Covers** — 15" crosslace - LE Coupe & Sedan........................	47	55
N78	**Wheels** — 14" aluminum hi-tech turbo w/locking pkg - LE Coupe & Sedan	237	275
PF7	**Wheels** — 15" aluminum star w/locking pkg - LE Coupe & Sedan	237	275
	w/o W25 (LE Convertible)...	189	220
	w/W25 (LE Convertible)...	NC	NC
	SE Coupe..	189	220
16P	**Wheels** — white 15" aluminum star	NC	NC

TRANS SPORT SE

TRANS SPORT SE 6 CYL

M06R	Minivan..	15719	17369
	Destination Charge:	530	530

Standard Equipment

TRANS SPORT SE: Integrated roof antenna, polymer composite bumpers with integral rub strips,

CODE	DESCRIPTION	DEALER	LIST

composite body panels that resist dents and rust, fog lamps, heat-repelling solar-coated glass windshield, rear flip-out side glass windows, tinted glass, composite halogen headlamps, one-piece liftgate, LH remote and RH manual with fold-and-stow feature sport mirrors, black roof treatment moldings, lower aero molding, monotone paint theme, rear liftgate two-speed wiper/washer, P205/70R15 BW all-season tires, compact spare with hoist cable, 15" styled bolt-on wheel covers, controlled-cycle "wet-arm" windshield wipers, "quiet package" acoustical insulation, driver-side air bag, front side windows defoggers, child safety door locks, fabric seats, instrumentation (mechanical analog speedometer, odometer, tachometer, coolant temperature, oil pressure indicator, voltmeter and trip odometer), lamp group (overhead map lights, rear dome reading lamps, cargo area lamps, underhood light), front and rear floor mats, day/night rearview mirror, RH and LH covered visor vanity mirrors, rear auxiliary power socket, ETR AM/FM stereo radio with clock, reclining front bucket seats with headrests, four-way manual driver-side seat adjuster, four-spoke sport steering wheel, front and side door map pockets, cup and mug holder tray with center instrument panel lower console, lockable under-dash storage, glove box, mesh net front seatback pockets, rear quarter storage compartments, Freedom II battery, power disc/drum brakes, 4-wheel anti-lock braking system, engine coolant recovery system, stainless steel exhaust system, front wheel drive, 3.1 liter V6 engine, 3-speed automatic transmission, power rack and pinion steering, fully independent MacPherson strut suspension.

Accessories

CODE	DESCRIPTION	DEALER	LIST
1SA	**SE Pkg 1SA**..	NC	NC
	incls vehicle w/std equip		
1SB	**SE Pkg 1SB**..	1073	1248
	incls front air conditioning, tilt steering wheel, cruise control, pwr sport mirrors, ETR AM/FM stereo radio w/auto reverse cass		
1SC	**SE Pkg 1SC**..	2070	2383
	incls SE pkg 1SB equip plus single key pwr door locks, pwr windows w/drivers side express down, elec rear window defogger, deep tinted glass, 7-pass seating, convenience net		
1SD	**SE Pkg 1SD**..	2543	2933
	incls SE pkg 1SC equip plus drivers 6-way pwr seat, remote keyless entry, luggage rack		
1SE	**SE Pkg 1SE**..	3382	3908
	incls SE pkg 1SD equip plus auto level control, 15" self sealing touring tires, 15" aluminum sport wheels, ETR AM stereo FM stereo w/auto reverse cass & 5-band equalizer, clock, seek up/down, search & replay, leather wrapped steering wheel w/radio controls		
—	**Engines**		
LG6	3.1 liter FI V6	STD	STD
	incls 3-spd auto trans		
L27	3800 V6	704	819
	incls 4-spd auto trans		
FE9	**Federal Emissions**..	NC	NC
YF5	**California Emissions**	NC	NC
NG1	**New York Emissions**..	NC	NC
—	**Tires**		
XGY	P205/70R15 BSW STL	STD	STD
XIN	P205/70R15 BSW STL touring - w/o P42 & 1SE..............	30	35
	w/P42 or 1SE	NC	NC
—	**Interiors**		
—	5-passenger seating w/Milliweave cloth	STD	STD

PONTIAC

CODE	DESCRIPTION	DEALER	LIST
ZP7	7-passenger seating w/Milliweave cloth - w/o 1SC, 1SD & 1SE	606	705
	w/1SC, 1SD or 1SE	NC	NC
ZP7	7-passenger seating w/Prado leather - w/1SD or 1SE	748	870
C67	**Air Conditioning, Electronic Front** — w/1SB, 1SC, 1SD, 1SE	NC	NC
	w/o 1SB, 1SC, 1SD, 1SE	714	830
C34	**Air Conditioning & Heater Rear** (Incls Front) — w/o 1SB, 1SC, 1SD & 1SE	1101	1280
	w/1SB, 1SC, 1SD or 1SE	387	450
C40	**Air Conditioning Delete**	NC	NC
G67	**Automatic Level Control**	172	200
B2Q	**Black Roof Delete**	NC	NC
C49	**Defogger, Electric Rear Window**	146	170
K05	**Engine Block Heater**	15	18
VK3	**Front License Plate Bracket**	NC	NC
AJ1	**Glass, Deep Tint**	211	245
AD8	**Integral Child Seat** — one	108	125
AD9	**Integral Child Seat** — two	194	225
V54	**Luggage Rack**	151	175
DD9	**Mirrors, Sport LH Power, RH Power Breakaway**	41	48
AB5	**Power Door Locks, Single Key**	258	300
AG9	**Power Seat, Driver 6-Way**	232	270
E58	**Power Sliding Door**	254	295
A31	**Power Windows, Drivers Side Express Down**	237	275
—	**Radios**		
UM6	ETR AM/FM stereo w/auto reverse cass - w/o 1SB, 1SC, 1SD	120	140
	w/1SB, 1SC, 1SD	NC	NC
UX1	ETR AM/FM cass & 5-band equalizer - w/1SD	271	315
	w/1SE	NC	NC
U1A	ETR AM/FM compact disc & 5-band equalizer - w/1SD	465	541
	w/1SE	177	206
AU0	**Remote Keyless Entry**	116	135
C54	**Sunroof, Pop-Up**	258	300
NW9	**Traction Control**	301	350
V92	**Trailer Provisions**	129	150
P42	**15" Touring Tires** — self sealing	159	185
PH3	**15" Aluminum Wheels**	237	275
15P	**15" Aluminum Wheels, Bright Faced**	237	275

| CODE | DESCRIPTION | DEALER | LIST |

SATURN

SATURN 4 CYL

CODE	DESCRIPTION	DEALER	LIST
ZZF69	SL 4-Dr Sedan (5-spd)	8996	9995
ZZG69	SL1 4-Dr Sedan (5-spd)	9716	10795
ZZH69	SL1 4-Dr Sedan (auto)	10436	11595
ZZJ69	SL2 4-Dr Sedan (5-spd)	10616	11795
ZZK69	SL2 4-Dr Sedan (auto)	11336	12595
ZZE27	SC1 2-Dr Coupe (5-spd)	10526	11695
ZZF27	SC1 2-Dr Coupe (auto)	11246	12495
ZZG27	SC2 2-Dr Coupe (5-spd)	11606	12895
ZZH27	SC2 2-Dr Coupe (auto)	12326	13695
ZZG35	SW1 4-Dr Wagon (5-spd)	10526	11695
ZZH35	SW1 4-Dr Wagon (auto)	11246	12495
ZZJ35	SW2 4-Dr Wagon (5-spd)	11336	12595
ZZK35	SW2 4-Dr Wagon (auto)	12056	13395
Destination Charge:		330	330

Standard Equipment

SATURN - ALL MODELS: Front wheel drive, 5-speed manual transmission, 5-mph front and rear bumpers, dent-resistant exterior panels on fenders, doors, quarters and fascias, integral bodyside moldings, high gloss polyurethane clearcoat paint finish, flush tinted glass, adjustable driver and front passenger head restraints, cloth door trim panels, 60/40 fold-down rear seatbacks, fabric seats, rear seat heater ducts, reclining front seatbacks, fully trimmed trunk/cargo area, AM/FM stereo radio with seek/scan tuning and four 6" speakers, digital quartz clock, rear window defogger, 3-speed intermittent windshield wipers, headlamps-on chime, high mounted audio controls, interior storage features, passenger vanity mirror, adjustable steering column, remote fuel filler door release, independent 4-wheel suspension, power front disc/rear drum brakes, rack and pinion steering, driver-side air bag, automatic shoulder/manual lap belt system for driver and front passenger, manual lap/shoulder safety belts for rear seats, flash to pass headlamps, halogen headlamps, child security rear door locks, combined low engine oil pressure and coolant level telltale, tachometer, coolant temperature gauge, centralized electrical fuse centers, long-life engine coolant, maintenance-free suspension, maintenance-free battery, scissors jack, self-adjusting accessory drive belt, stainless steel exhaust system, steel spaceframe construction, 1.9

SATURN

CODE	DESCRIPTION	DEALER	LIST

liter SOHC 4 cylinder TBI engine (SL, SL1, SC1, SW1), 1.9 liter DOHC 4 cylinder PFI engine (SL2, SC2, SW2), P175/70R14 84S radial tires (SL, SL1, SC1, SW1), P195/60R15 87T radial tires (SL2, SW2), P195/60R15 87H radial tires (SC2).

Accessories

CODE	DESCRIPTION	DEALER	LIST
—	**Pkg 1** — SL1	1620	1800
	SC1	1476	1640
	SW1	1589	1765
	SW2	1589	1765
	incls air conditioning, pwr windows, pwr locks, pwr passenger side mirror, speed control		
—	**Pkg 2** — SL2	1859	2065
	SC2	1656	1840
	incls air conditioning, pwr windows, pwr locks, pwr passenger side mirrors, "sawtooth" alloy wheels, speed control		
—	**California Emissions** — SL2, SC2, SW2	59	65
—	**New York Emissions** — SL2, SC2, SW2	59	65
C60	**Air Conditioning**	797	885
C66	**Air Conditioning Prep** — SL, SL1, SC1, SW1	235	NC
K34	**Speed Control** — NA on SL	216	240
—	**Anti-Lock Brakes** — w/5-spd trans	608	675
	w/auto trans (incls traction control)	653	725
CF5	**Power Sunroof** — SL1, SL2, SC1, SC2	585	650
D80	**Rear Spoiler** — SL2, SC1, SC2	158	175
T96	**Fog Lights** — SL2, SW2	135	150
PG5	**Alloy Wheels** — "teardrop" - SC2	180	200
PH6	**Alloy Wheels** — "sawtooth" - SL2, SW2	270	300
	SC1	360	400
AB5	**Power Door Locks** — SL1, SW1	221	245
—	**Leather Trim** — SL2, SC2, SW2	594	660
—	**Mirror** — passenger side, outside - SL1	32	35
	incl in pkg 1 & 2		
UM6	**Radio** — AM/FM stereo w/cassette	176	195
UU6	**Radio** — AM/FM stereo w/cassette & equalizer	320	355
U1C	**Radio** — AM/FM stereo w/CD player & equalizer	540	600
U79	**Coaxial Speakers** — extended range	63	70

Specifications and EPA Mileage Ratings

contents

202 **buick**

203 **cadillac**

204 **chevrolet**

206 **chrysler**

207 **dodge**

209 **eagle**

210 **ford**

212 **geo**

213 **lincoln**

213 **mercury**

214 **oldsmobile**

215 **plymouth**

217 **pontiac**

218 **saturn**

BUICK

Specifications and EPA Mileage Ratings

	CENTURY CUSTOM SDN	CENTURY SPECIAL SDN	CENTURY SPECIAL WGN	LE SABRE CUSTOM SDN	LE SABRE LIMITED SDN	PARK AVENUE SDN	PARK AVENUE ULTRA SDN	ROADMASTER SDN	ROADMASTER LIMITED SDN	ROADMASTER ESTATE WGN	REGAL CUSTOM CPE	REGAL CUSTOM SDN
Length (in.)	189.1	189.1	190.9	200.0	200.0	205.2	205.2	215.8	215.8	217.5	193.6	194.8
Width (in.)	69.4	69.4	69.4	73.6	73.6	73.6	73.6	78.1	78.1	79.9	72.5	72.5
Height (in.)	54.2	54.2	54.2	55.7	55.7	55.1	55.1	55.9	55.9	60.3	53.0	54.5
Curb Weight (lbs.)	2976	2974	3134	3449	3449	3533	3637	4191	4279	4572	3240	3338
Wheelbase (in.)	104.9	104.9	104.9	110.8	110.8	110.8	110.8	115.9	115.9	115.9	107.5	107.5
Track, front (in.)	58.7	58.7	58.7	60.4	60.4	60.4	60.4	61.7	61.7	62.1	59.5	59.5
Track, rear (in.)	56.7	56.7	56.7	60.4	60.4	60.6	60.6	60.7	60.7	64.1	58.0	58.0
Head Room, front (in.)	38.6	38.6	38.6	38.8	38.8	38.9	38.9	39.2	39.2	39.6	37.6	38.6
Head Room, rear (in.)	38.3	38.3	38.9	37.8	37.8	37.9	37.9	38.6	38.6	39.4	37.0	37.7
Shoulder Room, front (in.)	55.9	55.9	55.9	59.1	59.1	58.7	58.7	63.3	63.3	63.4	57.6	57.8
Shoulder Room, rear (in.)	56.0	56.0	56.0	58.9	58.9	58.9	58.9	63.3	63.3	63.5	56.8	57.8
Hip Room, front (in.)	50.0	50.0	50.0	54.6	54.6	55.0	55.0	56.9	56.9	56.9	52.0	52.7
Hip Room, rear (in.)	54.3	54.3	54.3	54.4	54.4	54.3	54.3	56.9	56.9	57.1	53.1	53.2
Leg Room, front (in.)	42.1	42.1	42.1	42.5	42.5	42.7	42.7	42.1	42.1	42.3	42.3	42.4
Leg Room, rear (in.)	35.9	35.9	34.8	40.4	40.4	40.7	40.7	38.9	38.9	37.3	34.8	36.2
Luggage Capacity (cu. ft.)	16.2	16.2	41.6	17.1	17.1	20.3	20.3	21.0	21.0	54.7	15.6	15.9
Engine Type	L4	L4	L4	V6	V6	V6	V6	V8	V8	V8	V6	V6
Displacement (cu. in.)	133.0	133.0	133.0	231.0	231.0	231.0	231.0	350.0	350.0	350.0	191.0	191.0
Fuel System	MPFI	MPFI	MPFI	SFI	SFI	SFI	SFI	SFI	SFI	SFI	SFI	SFI
Compression Ratio	9.0:1	9.0:1	9.0:1	9.0:1	9.0:1	9.0:1	8.5:1	10.5:1	10.5:1	10.5:1	9.5:1	9.5:1
BHP @ RPM (net)	120 @ 5200	120 @ 5200	120 @ 5200	170 @ 4800	170 @ 4800	225 @ 3200	225 @ 5000	260 @ 5000	260 @ 5000	260 @ 5000	160 @ 5200	160 @ 5200
Torque @ RPM (net)	130 @ 4000	130 @ 4000	130 @ 4000	225 @ 3200	225 @ 3200	225 @ 3200	275 @ 3200	330 @ 3200	330 @ 3200	330 @ 3200	185 @ 4000	185 @ 4000
Fuel Capacity (gals.)	16.5	16.5	16.5	18.0	18.0	18.0	18.0	23.0	23.0	22.0	16.5	16.5
EPA City/Hwy (mpg) —manual	NA	NA	NA	NA	NA	NA	NA	NA	NA	NA	NA	NA
EPA City/Hwy (mpg) —auto	24/34	24/34	24/34	19/29	19/29	19/28	17/26	17/25	17/25	17/25	19/30	19/30

Specifications and EPA Mileage Ratings	REGAL LIMITED SDN	REGAL GRAN SPORT CPE	REGAL GRAN SPORT SDN	SKYLARK CUSTOM CPE	SKYLARK CUSTOM SDN	SKYLARK LIMITED SDN	SKYLARK GRAND SPORT CPE	SKYLARK GRAN SPORT SDN	DE VILLE CONCOURS	DE VILLE SDN	ELDORADO CPE	ELDORADO TOURING CPE
Length (in.)	194.8	193.6	194.8	189.1	189.1	189.1	189.1	189.1	209.7	209.7	202.2	202.2
Width (in.)	72.5	72.5	72.5	67.5	67.5	67.5	67.5	67.5	76.6	76.6	75.5	75.5
Height (in.)	54.5	53.0	54.5	53.2	53.2	53.2	53.2	53.2	56.0	56.3	53.9	53.9
Curb Weight (lbs.)	3362	3335	3429	2791	2855	2939	2985	3038	3985	3758	3774	3818
Wheelbase (in.)	107.5	107.5	107.5	103.4	103.4	103.4	103.4	103.4	113.8	113.8	108.0	108.0
Track, front (in.)	59.5	59.5	59.5	55.8	55.8	55.8	55.8	55.8	60.9	60.9	60.9	60.9
Track, rear (in.)	58.0	58.0	58.0	56.6	56.6	56.6	56.6	56.6	60.9	60.9	60.9	60.9
Head Room, front (in.)	38.6	37.6	38.6	37.8	37.8	37.8	37.8	37.8	38.5	38.5	37.4	37.4
Head Room, rear (in.)	37.7	37.0	37.7	36.5	37.0	37.0	36.5	37.0	38.4	38.4	38.3	38.3
Shoulder Room, front (in.)	57.8	57.6	57.8	53.6	54.1	54.1	53.6	54.1	61.1	61.1	58.2	58.2
Shoulder Room, rear (in.)	57.8	56.8	57.8	55.0	53.4	53.4	55.0	53.4	61.3	61.3	57.6	57.6
Hip Room, front (in.)	52.7	52.0	52.7	49.1	49.1	49.1	49.1	49.1	56.1	56.1	57.6	57.6
Hip Room, rear (in.)	53.2	53.1	53.2	50.3	50.3	50.3	50.3	50.3	55.9	55.9	55.7	55.7
Leg Room, front (in.)	42.4	42.3	42.4	43.3	43.3	43.3	43.3	43.3	42.6	42.6	42.6	42.6
Leg Room, rear (in.)	36.2	34.8	36.2	32.5	33.5	33.5	32.5	33.5	43.3	43.3	36.1	36.1
Luggage Capacity (cu. ft.)	15.9	15.6	15.9	13.3	13.3	13.3	13.3	13.3	20.0	20.0	15.3	15.3
Engine Type	V6	V6	V6	L4	L4	L4	V6	V6	V8	V8	V8	V8
Displacement (cu. in.)	231.0	231.0	231.0	138.0	138.0	138.0	191.0	191.0	279.0	299.0	279.0	279.0
Fuel System	SFI	SFI	SFI	MPFI	MPFI	MPFI	SFI	SFI	TPI	SPFI	TPI	TPI
Compression Ratio	9.0:1	9.0:1	9.0:1	9.5:1	9.5:1	9.5:1	9.5:1	9.5:1	10.3:1	9.5:1	10.3:1	10.3:1
BHP @ RPM (net)	170 @ 4800	170 @ 4800	170 @ 4800	115 @ 5200	115 @ 5200	115 @ 5200	155 @ 5200	155 @ 5200	270 @ 5600	200 @ 4100	270 @ 5600	295 @ 6000
Torque @ RPM (net)	225 @ 3200	225 @ 3200	225 @ 3200	140 @ 3200	140 @ 3200	140 @ 3200	185 @ 4000	185 @ 4000	300 @ 4000	275 @ 3000	300 @ 4000	290 @ 4400
Fuel Capacity (gals.)	16.5	16.5	16.5	15.2	15.2	15.2	15.2	15.2	20.0	20.0	20.0	20.0
EPA City/Hwy (mpg) —manual	NA	NA	NA	NA	NA	NA	NA	NA	NA	NA	NA	NA
EPA City/Hwy (mpg) —auto	19/29	19/29	19/29	22/32	22/32	22/32	22/32	22/32	16/25	16/25	16/25	16/25

CADILLAC

Specifications and EPA Mileage Ratings

Specifications and EPA Mileage Ratings	FLEETWOOD SDN	SEVILLE LUXURY SDN	SEVILLE TOURING SDN	ASTRO REG 2WD	ASTRO EXT 2WD	ASTRO REG AWD	ASTRO EXT AWD	BERETTA CPE	BERETTA Z26 CPE	CAMARO CPE	CAMARO Z28 CPE	CAMARO CVT
Length (in.)	225.1	204.1	204.1	176.8	186.8	176.8	186.8	183.4	183.4	193.2	193.2	193.2
Width (in.)	78.0	74.2	74.2	77.5	77.5	77.5	77.5	68.2	68.2	74.1	74.1	74.1
Height (in.)	57.1	54.5	54.5	76.2	76.2	76.2	76.2	56.2	56.2	51.3	51.3	52.0
Curb Weight (lbs.)	4478	3830	3892	3897	3987	4160	4241	2649	2795	3247	3424	3324
Wheelbase (in.)	121.5	111.0	111.0	111.0	111.0	111.0	111.0	103.4	103.4	101.1	101.1	101.1
Track, front (in.)	61.7	60.9	60.9	65.1	65.1	65.1	65.1	55.6	55.6	60.7	60.7	60.7
Track, rear (in.)	60.7	60.9	60.9	65.1	65.1	65.1	65.1	55.1	55.1	60.6	60.6	60.6
Head Room, front (in.)	38.7	38.0	38.0	39.2	39.2	39.2	39.2	38.1	38.1	37.2	37.2	38.0
Head Room, rear (in.)	39.1	38.3	38.3	38.7	38.7	38.7	38.7	37.4	37.4	35.3	35.3	39.0
Shoulder Room, front (in.)	64.3	58.9	58.9	64.0	64.0	64.0	64.0	55.4	55.4	57.4	57.4	57.4
Shoulder Room, rear (in.)	64.0	57.5	57.5	67.1	67.1	67.1	67.1	55.6	55.6	55.8	55.8	43.5
Hip Room, front (in.)	59.2	55.0	55.0	64.9	64.9	64.9	64.9	50.9	50.9	52.8	52.8	52.8
Hip Room, rear (in.)	59.8	57.6	57.6	50.9	50.9	50.9	50.9	51.2	51.2	44.4	44.4	43.7
Leg Room, front (in.)	42.5	43.0	43.0	41.6	41.6	41.6	41.6	43.4	43.4	43.0	43.0	43.0
Leg Room, rear (in.)	43.9	39.1	39.1	38.5	38.5	38.5	38.5	35.0	35.0	26.8	26.8	26.8
Luggage Capacity (cu. ft.)	21.1	14.4	14.4	151.8	170.4	151.8	170.4	13.41	13.41	12.9	7.6	7.6
Engine Type	V8	V8	V8	V6	V6	V6	V6	L4	L4	V6	V8	V8
Displacement (cu. in.)	350.0	279.0	279.0	262.0	262.0	262.0	262.0	133.0	138.0	207.0	350.0	350.0
Fuel System	SPFI	TPI	TPI	EFI	EFI	CPI	CPI	MFI	MFI	SFI	SFI	SFI
Compression Ratio	9.68:1	10.3:1	10.3:1	9.3:1	9.3:1	9.1:1	9.1:1	9.0:1	10.0:1	9.0:1	10.5:1	10.5:1
BHP @ RPM (net)	260 @ 5000	270 @ 5600	295 @ 6000	165 @ 4000	165 @ 4000	200 @ 4400	200 @ 4400	120 @ 5200	170 @ 6200	160 @ 4600	275 @ 5000	275 @ 5000
Torque @ RPM (net)	335 @ 2400	300 @ 4000	290 @ 4400	235 @ 2000	235 @ 2000	260 @ 3600	260 @ 3600	130 @ 4000	150 @ 5200	200 @ 3600	325 @ 2400	325 @ 2000
Fuel Capacity (gals.)	23.0	20.0	20.0	27.0	27.0	27.0	27.0	15.6	15.6	15.0	15.5	15.5
EPA City/Hwy (mpg) —manual	NA	NA	NA	NA	NA	NA	NA	NA	NA	NA	NA	NA
EPA City/Hwy (mpg) —auto	16/25	16/25	16/25	NA	NA	NA	NA	NA	NA	NA	NA	NA

CHEVROLET

Specifications and EPA Mileage Ratings

	CAMARO Z28 CVT	CAPRICE SDN	CAPRICE LS SDN	CAPRICE WGN	CAVALIER RS CPE	CAVALIER RS SDN	CAVALIER VL CPE	CAVALIER VL SDN	CAVALIER Z24 CVT	CAVALIER Z24 CPE	CORSICA SDN	CORVETTE CVT	CORVETTE CPE
Length (in.)	193.2	214.1	214.1	217.3	182.3	182.3	182.3	182.3	182.3	182.3	183.4	178.5	178.5
Width (in.)	74.1	77.0	77.0	79.6	66.3	66.3	66.3	66.3	66.3	66.3	68.2	70.7	70.7
Height (in.)	52.0	55.7	55.7	60.9	52.0	53.6	52.0	53.6	52.0	52.0	56.2	47.3	46.3
Curb Weight (lbs.)	3500	4036	4054	4449	2526	2515	2509	2520	2678	2695	2665	3361	3309
Wheelbase (in.)	101.1	115.9	115.9	115.9	101.3	101.3	101.3	101.3	101.3	101.3	103.4	96.2	96.2
Track, front (in.)	60.7	61.8	61.8	62.1	55.6	55.6	55.6	55.6	55.6	55.6	55.6	57.7	57.7
Track, rear (in.)	60.6	62.3	62.3	64.1	55.4	55.4	55.4	55.4	55.2	55.2	55.1	59.0	59.0
Head Room, front (in.)	38.0	39.2	39.2	39.6	37.8	39.1	37.8	39.1	38.7	37.8	38.1	36.5	36.5
Head Room, rear (in.)	39.0	37.9	37.9	36.6	36.1	37.4	36.1	37.4	37.3	36.1	37.4	NA	NA
Shoulder Room, front (in.)	57.4	63.4	62.6	63.4	52.9	52.7	52.9	52.7	52.5	52.8	55.4	53.9	53.9
Shoulder Room, rear (in.)	43.5	63.4	62.9	48.6	52.9	52.7	52.9	52.7	38.2	52.9	55.6	NA	NA
Hip Room, front (in.)	52.8	57.0	57.0	56.9	49.8	48.1	49.8	48.1	47.8	47.6	50.9	50.8	50.8
Hip Room, rear (in.)	43.7	56.9	56.9	43.7	49.4	48.8	49.4	48.8	38.2	49.4	51.2	NA	NA
Leg Room, front (in.)	43.0	42.2	42.2	42.2	42.6	42.1	42.6	42.1	42.2	42.6	43.4	42.0	42.0
Leg Room, rear (in.)	26.8	39.5	39.5	30.5	31.2	33.3	31.2	33.3	32.0	31.2	35.0	NA	NA
Luggage Capacity (cu. ft.)	7.6	20.4	20.4	54.7/92.7	13.2	13.0	13.2	13.0	10.7	13.2	13.51	6.6	12.6
Engine Type	V8	V8	V8	V8	L4	L4	L4	L4	V6	V6	L4	V8	V8
Displacement (cu. in.)	350.0	265.0	265.0	265.0	133.0	133.0	133.0	133.0	191.0	191.0	133.0	350.0	350.0
Fuel System	SFI	SFI	SFI	SFI	MFI	MFI	MFI	MFI	MFI	MFI	MFI	SFI	SFI
Compression Ratio	10.5:1	9.9:1	9.9:1	9.9:1	9.0:1	9.0:1	9.0:1	9.0:1	8.89:1	8.89:1	9.0:1	10.5:1	10.5:1
BHP @ RPM (net)	275 @ 5000	200 @ 5200	200 @ 5200	200 @ 5200	120 @ 5200	120 @ 5200	120 @ 5200	120 @ 5200	140 @ 4200	140 @ 4200	120 @ 5200	300 @ 5000	300 @ 5000
Torque @ RPM (net)	325 @ 2000	245 @ 2400	245 @ 2400	245 @ 2400	130 @ 4000	130 @ 4000	130 @ 4000	130 @ 4000	185 @ 3200	185 @ 3200	130 @ 4000	340 @ 3600	340 @ 3600
Fuel Capacity (gals.)	15.5	23.0	23.0	22.0	15.2	15.2	15.2	15.2	15.2	15.2	15.6	20.0	20.0
EPA City/Hwy (mpg) —manual	NA	NA	NA	NA	NA	NA	NA	NA	NA	NA	NA	NA	NA
EPA City/Hwy (mpg) —auto	NA	NA	NA	NA	NA	NA	NA	NA	NA	NA	NA	NA	NA

Specifications and EPA Mileage Ratings	CORVETTE ZR-1 CPE	IMPALA SS SDN	LUMINA SDN	LUMINA EURO CPE	LUMINA EURO SDN	LUMINA EURO 3.4 SDN	LUMINA Z34 CPE	LUMINA MINIVAN	CHRYSLER	CONCORDE SDN	LE BARON CVT	LE BARON LE SDN	LE BARON LANDAU SDN
Length (in.)	178.5	214.1	198.3	198.3	198.3	198.3	199.3	191.5		202.8	184.8	182.7	182.7
Width (in.)	73.1	77.0	71.0	71.7	71.0	71.0	71.7	73.9		74.4	69.2	68.1	68.1
Height (in.)	46.3	55.7	53.6	53.3	53.6	53.6	53.3	65.7		56.3	52.4	53.7	53.7
Curb Weight (lbs.)	3512	4218	3333	3269	3369	3550	3440	3554		3379	3122	2971	2971
Wheelbase (in.)	96.2	115.9	107.5	107.5	107.5	107.5	107.5	109.8		113.0	100.6	103.5	103.5
Track, front (in.)	57.7	61.8	59.5	59.5	59.5	59.5	59.5	59.2		62.0	57.6	57.6	57.6
Track, rear (in.)	60.6	62.3	58.0	58.0	58.0	58.0	58.0	61.4		62.0	57.6	57.2	57.2
Head Room, front (in.)	36.5	39.2	38.7	37.5	38.7	38.7	37.5	39.2		38.4	38.3	41.9	41.9
Head Room, rear (in.))	NA	37.9	38.0	37.1	38.0	38.0	37.1	37.8		37.2	37.0	37.9	37.9
Shoulder Room, front (in.)	53.9	63.4	58.2	57.5	58.2	58.2	57.5	60.6		58.9	55.9	53.9	53.9
Shoulder Room, rear (in.)	NA	63.4	56.2	56.9	56.2	56.2	56.9	62.2		58.9	45.7	54.2	54.2
Hip Room, front (in.)	50.8	57.0	52.3	51.4	52.3	52.3	51.4	55.5		56.1	52.4	51.7	51.7
Hip Room, rear (in.)	NA	56.9	52.3	52.0	52.3	52.3	52.0	41.7		58.8	37.6	52.0	52.0
Leg Room, front (in.)	42.0	42.2	42.4	42.4	42.4	42.4	42.4	40.0		42.3	42.4	41.9	41.9
Leg Room, rear (in.)	NA	39.5	36.9	34.8	36.9	36.9	34.8	36.8		38.7	33.0	38.3	38.3
Luggage Capacity (cu. ft.)	12.6	20.4	15.7	15.6	15.7	15.7	15.6	19.0		16.6	9.2	14.4	14.4
Engine Type	V8	V8	V6	V6	V6	V6	V6	V6		V6	V6	V6	V6
Displacement (cu. in.)	350.0	350.0	191.0	191.0	191.0	207.0	207.0	191.0		201.5	181.4	181.4	181.4
Fuel System	MFI	SFI	MFI	MFI	MFI	SFI	SFI	EFI		SMPI	SMPI	SMPI	SMPI
Compression Ratio	11.0:1	10.5:1	8.89:1	8.89:1	8.89:1	9.25:1	9.25:1	8.5:1		8.9:1	8.9:1	8.9:1	8.9:1
BHP @ RPM (net)	405 @ 5800	260 @ 5000	140 @ 4400	140 @ 4400	140 @ 4400	210 @ 5200	200 @ 5000	120 @ 4200		161 @ 5300	141 @ 5000	142 @ 5000	142 @ 5000
Torque @ RPM (net)	385 @ 5200	330 @ 3200	185 @ 3200	185 @ 3200	185 @ 3200	215 @ 4000	215 @ 4000	175 @ 2200		181 @ 3200	171 @ 2400	171 @ 2400	171 @ 2400
Fuel Capacity (gals.)	20.0	23.0	16.5	16.5	16.5	16.5	16.5	20.0		18.0	14.0	16.0	16.0
EPA City/Hwy (mpg) —manual	NA	NA	NA	NA	NA	NA	NA	NA		NA	NA	NA	NA
EPA City/Hwy (mpg) —auto	NA	NA	NA	NA	NA	NA	NA	NA		18/26	NA	20/27	21/29

DODGE

Specifications and EPA Mileage Ratings	LHS SDN	NEW YORKER SDN	T&C FWD WGN	T&C AWD WGN	CARAVAN 2WD	CARAVAN SE 2WD	CARAVAN LE 2WD	CARAVAN GRAND 2WD	CARAVAN GRAND SE 2WD	CARAVAN GRAND SE 4WD	CARAVAN GRAND LE 2WD	CARAVAN GRAND LE 4WD
Length (in.)	207.4	207.4	192.8	192.8	178.1	178.1	178.1	192.8	192.8	192.8	192.8	192.8
Width (in.)	74.4	74.4	72.0	72.0	72.0	72.0	72.0	72.0	72.0	72.0	72.0	72.0
Height (in.)	55.7	55.7	66.7	67.8	66.0	66.0	66.0	66.7	66.7	67.8	66.7	67.8
Curb Weight (lbs.)	3483	3457	3977	4267	3306	3306	3306	3574	3574	4008	3574	4008
Wheelbase (in.)	113.0	113.0	119.3	119.3	112.3	112.3	112.3	119.3	119.3	119.3	119.3	119.3
Track, front (in.)	62.0	62.0	59.9	59.9	59.9	59.9	59.9	59.9	59.9	59.9	59.9	59.9
Track, rear (in.)	62.0	62.0	62.1	62.1	62.1	62.1	62.1	62.1	62.1	62.1	62.1	62.1
Head Room, front (in.)	39.3	39.3	39.1	39.1	39.1	39.1	39.1	39.1	39.1	39.1	39.1	39.1
Head Room, rear (in.)	37.8	37.8	38.4	37.6	38.6	38.6	38.6	38.4	38.4	38.4	38.4	38.4
Shoulder Room, front (in.)	58.7	58.7	57.5	57.5	57.5	57.5	57.5	57.5	57.5	57.5	57.5	57.5
Shoulder Room, rear (in.)	58.2	58.2	60.5	59.8	60.5	60.5	60.5	60.5	60.5	60.5	60.5	60.5
Hip Room, front (in.)	56.8	56.8	53.7	53.7	53.7	53.7	53.7	53.7	53.7	53.7	53.7	53.7
Hip Room, rear (in.)	51.2	51.2	57.1	48.3	57.1	57.1	57.1	57.1	57.1	57.1	57.1	57.1
Leg Room, front (in.)	42.3	42.3	38.3	38.3	38.3	38.3	38.3	38.3	38.3	38.3	38.3	38.3
Leg Room, rear (in.)	40.6	40.6	37.6	38.5	43.4	43.4	43.4	37.7	37.7	37.7	37.7	37.7
Luggage Capacity (cu. ft.)	17.9	17.9	17.7/141.3	17.7/141.3	NA	NA	NA	NA	NA	NA	NA	NA
Engine Type	V6	V6	V6	V6	L4	V6	V6	V6	V6	V6	V6	V6
Displacement (cu. in.)	214.7	214.7	203.5	203.5	153.0	181.4	181.4	181.4	201.5	201.5	201.5	201.5
Fuel System	SMPI	SMPI	SMPI	SMPI	EFI	SMPI	SMPI	SMPI	SMPI	SMPI	SMPI	SMPI
Compression Ratio	10.5:1	10.5:1	9.0:1	9.0:1	8.9:1	8.9:1	8.9:1	8.9:1	8.9:1	8.9:1	8.9:1	8.9:1
BHP @ RPM (net)	214 @ 5800	214 @ 5800	162 @ 4400	162 @ 4400	100 @ 4800	142 @ 5000	142 @ 5000	142 @ 5000	162 @ 4800	162 @ 4800	162 @ 4800	162 @ 4800
Torque @ RPM (net)	221 @ 2800	221 @ 2800	213 @ 3600	213 @ 3600	135 @ 2800	173 @ 2400	173 @ 2400	173 @ 2400	194 @ 3600	194 @ 3600	194 @ 3600	194 @ 3600
Fuel Capacity (gals.)	18.0	18.0	20.0	18.0	20.0	20.0	20.0	20.0	20.0	18.0	20.0	18.0
EPA City/Hwy (mpg) —manual	NA	NA	NA	NA	20/30	NA	NA	NA	NA	NA	NA	NA
EPA City/Hwy (mpg) —auto	18/26	18/26	17/22	16/21	20/26	19/24	19/24	19/24	18/23	17/22	18/23	17/22

Specifications and EPA Mileage Ratings

	COLT 2DR	COLT ES 2DR	COLT 4DR	COLT ES 4DR	INTREPID SDN	INTREPID ES SDN	SHADOW 2DR HBK	SHADOW ES 2DR HBK	SHADOW 4DR HBK	SHADOW ES 4DR HBK	SPIRIT SDN	STEALTH CPE	STEALTH R/T CPE
Length (in.)	171.1	171.1	174.0	174.0	201.7	201.7	171.9	171.9	171.9	171.9	181.2	178.9	180.3
Width (in.)	66.1	66.1	66.1	66.1	74.4	74.4	67.3	67.3	67.3	67.3	68.1	72.4	72.4
Height (in.)	51.4	51.4	51.4	51.4	56.3	56.3	53.1	53.1	53.1	53.1	53.5	49.1	49.1
Curb Weight (lbs.)	2085	2085	2195	2195	3271	3370	2608	2608	2643	2643	2824	3064	3164
Wheelbase (in.)	96.1	96.1	98.4	98.4	113.0	113.0	97.2	97.2	97.2	97.2	103.5	97.2	97.2
Track, front (in.)	57.1	57.1	57.1	57.1	62.0	62.0	57.6	57.6	57.6	57.6	57.6	61.4	61.4
Track, rear (in.)	57.5	57.5	57.5	57.5	62.0	62.0	57.2	57.2	57.2	57.2	57.2	62.2	62.2
Head Room, front (in.)	38.6	38.6	38.6	38.6	38.4	38.4	38.3	38.3	38.3	38.3	38.4	37.1	37.1
Head Room, rear (in.)	36.4	36.4	36.2	36.2	37.2	37.2	37.4	37.4	37.0	37.0	37.9	34.1	34.1
Shoulder Room, front (in.)	53.9	53.9	53.9	53.9	59.0	59.0	54.5	54.5	54.5	54.5	54.3	55.9	55.9
Shoulder Room, rear (in.)	54.1	54.1	53.5	53.5	58.9	58.9	52.5	52.5	54.4	54.4	55.0	52.0	52.0
Hip Room, front (in.)	54.9	54.9	54.9	54.9	56.2	56.2	52.8	52.8	52.9	52.9	51.7	56.7	56.7
Hip Room, rear (in.)	53.7	53.7	52.0	52.0	58.1	58.1	44.3	44.3	44.3	44.3	52.0	46.9	46.9
Leg Room, front (in.)	42.9	42.9	42.9	42.9	42.3	42.3	41.5	41.5	41.5	41.5	41.9	44.2	44.2
Leg Room, rear (in.)	31.1	31.1	33.5	33.5	38.7	38.7	34.0	34.0	34.0	34.0	38.3	28.5	28.5
Luggage Capacity (cu. ft.)	10.5	10.5	10.5	10.5	16.7	16.7	13.2	13.2	13.1	13.1	14.4	11.1	11.1
Engine Type	L4	L4	L4	L4	V6	V6	L4	V6	L4	V6	L4	V6	V6
Displacement (cu. in.)	89.6	89.6	111.9	111.9	201.5	201.5	153.0	181.4	153.0	181.4	153.0	181.4	181.4
Fuel System	SMPI	SMPI	SMPI	SMPI	SMPI	SMPI	EFI	SMPI	EFI	SMPI	EFI	SMPI	SMPI
Compression Ratio	9.2:1	9.2:1	9.5:1	9.5:1	8.9:1	8.9:1	8.9:1	8.9:1	8.9:1	8.9:1	8.9:1	8.9:1	10.0:1
BHP @ RPM (net)	92 @ 6000	92 @ 6000	113 @ 6000	113 @ 6000	161 @ 5300	161 @ 5300	100 @ 4800	141 @ 5000	100 @ 4800	141 @ 5000	100 @ 4800	164 @ 5500	222 @ 6000
Torque @ RPM (net)	93 @ 3000	93 @ 3000	116 @ 4500	116 @ 4500	181 @ 3200	181 @ 3200	135 @ 2800	171 @ 2400	135 @ 2800	171 @ 2400	135 @ 2800	185 @ 4000	201 @ 4500
Fuel Capacity (gals.)	13.2	13.2	13.2	13.2	18.0	18.0	14.0	14.0	14.0	14.0	16.0	19.8	19.8
EPA City/Hwy (mpg) —manual	32/40	32/40	27/34	27/34	NA	NA	25/32	19/28	25/32	19/28	NA	18/24	19/25
EPA City/Hwy (mpg) —auto	29/33	29/33	27/34	27/34	20/28	20/28	23/28	21/29	23/28	21/29	23/28	18/24	18/23

Specifications and EPA Mileage Ratings

	STEALTH R/T TURBO CPE	VIPER ROADSTER	SUMMIT DL CPE	SUMMIT ES CPE	SUMMIT ESi CPE	SUMMIT ES SDN	SUMMIT ESi SDN	SUMMIT LX SDN	SUMMIT DL WGN	SUMMIT LX WGN	SUMMIT AWD WGN	TALON DL CPE
Length (in.)	180.3	175.1	171.1	171.1	171.1	174.0	174.0	174.0	168.5	168.5	168.5	172.4
Width (in.)	72.4	75.7	66.1	66.1	66.1	66.1	66.1	66.1	66.7	66.7	66.7	66.7
Height (in.)	49.3	43.95	51.4	51.4	51.4	51.4	51.4	51.4	62.1	62.1	62.6	51.4
Curb Weight (lbs.)	3797	3476	2085	2085	2085	2195	2195	2195	2734	2734	3064	2549
Wheelbase (in.)	97.2	96.2	96.1	96.1	96.1	98.4	98.4	98.4	99.2	99.2	99.2	97.2
Track, front (in.)	61.4	59.6	57.1	57.1	57.1	57.1	57.1	57.1	57.5	57.5	57.3	57.7
Track, rear (in.)	62.2	60.6	57.5	57.5	57.5	57.5	57.5	57.5	57.5	57.5	57.5	57.1
Head Room, front (in.)	37.1	NA	38.6	38.6	38.6	38.6	38.6	38.6	40.0	40.0	40.0	37.9
Head Room, rear (in.)	34.1	NA	36.4	36.4	36.4	36.2	36.2	36.2	38.6	38.6	38.6	34.1
Shoulder Room, front (in.)	55.9	53.8	53.9	53.9	53.9	53.9	53.9	53.9	55.1	55.1	55.1	53.9
Shoulder Room, rear (in.)	52.0	NA	54.1	54.1	54.1	53.5	53.5	53.5	55.1	55.1	55.1	52.4
Hip Room, front (in.)	56.7	NA	54.9	54.9	54.9	54.9	54.9	54.9	50.2	50.2	50.2	55.1
Hip Room, rear (in.)	46.9	NA	53.7	53.7	53.7	52.0	52.0	52.0	52.6	52.6	52.6	45.7
Leg Room, front (in.)	44.2	42.6	42.9	42.9	42.9	42.9	42.9	42.9	40.8	40.8	40.8	43.9
Leg Room, rear (in.)	28.5	NA	31.1	31.1	31.1	33.5	33.5	33.5	36.1	36.1	36.1	28.5
Luggage Capacity (cu. ft.)	11.1	11.8	10.5	10.5	10.5	10.5	10.5	10.5	34.6	34.6	34.6	10.2
Engine Type	V6	V10	L4	L4	L4	L4	L4	L4	L4	L4	L4	L4
Displacement (cu. in.)	181.4	488.0	89.6	89.6	89.6	111.9	111.9	111.9	111.9	143.0	143.0	107.0
Fuel System	SMPI	SMPI	SMPI	SMPI	SMPI	SMPI	SMPI	SMPI	SMPI	SMPI	SMPI	SMPI
Compression Ratio	8.0:1	9.1:1	9.2:1	9.2:1	9.2:1	9.5:1	9.5:1	9.5:1	9.5:1	9.5:1	9.5:1	9.0:1
BHP @ RPM (net)	320 @ 6000	400 @ 4600	92 @ 6000	92 @ 6000	92 @ 6000	113 @ 6000	113 @ 6000	113 @ 6000	113 @ 6000	136 @ 5500	136 @ 5500	92 @ 5000
Torque @ RPM (net)	315 @ 2500	480 @ 3600	93 @ 3000	93 @ 3000	93 @ 3000	116 @ 4500	116 @ 4500	116 @ 4500	116 @ 4500	145 @ 4250	145 @ 4250	105 @ 3500
Fuel Capacity (gals.)	19.8	22.0	13.2	13.2	13.2	13.2	13.2	13.2	14.5	14.5	14.5	15.8
EPA City/Hwy (mpg) —manual	18/24	13/21	32/40	32/40	32/40	27/34	27/34	27/34	23/29	21/28	19/24	23/32
EPA City/Hwy (mpg) —auto	NA	NA	23/33	23/33	23/33	27/34	27/34	27/34	23/28	20/26	19/23	23/30

EAGLE

Specifications and EPA Mileage Ratings	TALON ES CPE	TALON TSi FWD CPE	TALON TSi AWD CPE	VISION ESi SDN	VISION TSi SDN	AEROSTAR REG 2WD WGN	AEROSTAR REG 4WD WGN	AEROSTAR EXT 2WD WGN	AEROSTAR EXT 4WD WGN	CROWN VICTORIA SDN	ESCORT 3DR	ESCORT LX 3DR
Length (in.)	172.4	172.4	172.4	201.6	201.6	174.9	174.9	190.3	190.3	212.4	170.0	170.0
Width (in.)	66.9	66.9	66.9	74.4	74.4	71.7	71.7	72.0	72.0	77.8	66.7	66.7
Height (in.)	51.4	51.4	52.0	55.8	55.8	72.2	73.2	72.3	73.2	56.8	52.5	52.5
Curb Weight (lbs.)	2712	2789	3109	3344	3486	NA	NA	NA	NA	3786	2304	2325
Wheelbase (in.)	97.2	97.2	97.2	113.0	113.0	118.9	118.9	118.9	118.9	114.4	98.4	98.4
Track, front (in.)	57.7	57.7	57.7	62.0	62.0	61.5	61.5	61.5	61.5	62.8	56.5	56.5
Track, rear (in.)	57.1	57.1	57.3	62.0	62.0	60.0	60.0	60.0	60.0	63.3	56.5	56.5
Head Room, front (in.)	37.9	37.9	37.9	38.4	38.4	39.5	39.5	39.5	39.5	39.4	38.4	38.4
Head Room, rear (in.)	34.1	34.1	34.1	37.2	37.2	37.3	37.3	37.5	37.5	38.0	37.6	37.6
Shoulder Room, front (in.)	53.9	53.9	53.9	59.0	59.0	NA	NA	NA	NA	60.6	53.0	53.0
Shoulder Room, rear (in.)	52.4	52.4	52.4	58.4	58.4	NA	NA	NA	NA	60.2	52.6	52.6
Hip Room, front (in.)	55.1	55.1	55.1	56.2	56.2	NA	NA	NA	NA	59.1	51.3	51.3
Hip Room, rear (in.)	45.7	45.7	45.7	58.7	58.7	NA	NA	NA	NA	58.7	46.6	46.6
Leg Room, front (in.)	43.9	43.9	43.9	42.3	42.3	41.4	41.4	41.4	41.4	42.5	41.7	41.7
Leg Room, rear (in.)	28.5	28.5	28.5	38.7	38.7	37.4	37.4	39.7	39.7	39.7	34.6	34.6
Luggage Capacity (cu. ft.)	10.2	10.2	6.2	16.6	16.6	139.3	139.3	167.7	167.7	20.6	17.3/35.2	17.3/35.2
Engine Type	L4	L4	L4	V6	V6	V6	V6	V6	V6	V8	L4	L4
Displacement (cu. in.)	122.0	122.0	122.0	201.5	214.7	182.0	245.0	182.0	245.0	281.0	114.0	114.0
Fuel System	SMPI	SMPI	SMPI	SMPI	SMPI	EFI	DFI	EFI	DFI	SEFI	SEFI	SEFI
Compression Ratio	9.0:1	7.8:1	7.8:1	8.9:1	10.5:1	9.2:1	9.0:1	9.2:1	9.0:1	9.0:1	9.0:1	9.0:1
BHP @ RPM (net)	135 @ 6000	195 @ 6000	195 @ 6000	161 @ 5300	214 @ 5800	135 @ 4600	155 @ 4000	135 @ 4600	155 @ 4000	190 @ 4200	88 @ 4400	88 @ 4400
Torque @ RPM (net)	125 @ 5000	203 @ 3000	203 @ 3000	181 @ 3200	221 @ 2800	160 @ 2800	230 @ 2400	160 @ 2800	230 @ 2400	260 @ 3200	108 @ 3800	108 @ 3800
Fuel Capacity (gals.)	15.8	15.8	15.8	18.0	18.0	21.0	21.0	21.0	21.0	20.0	11.9	11.9
EPA City/Hwy (mpg) —manual	21/28	21/28	21/28	NA	18/26	NA	NA	NA	NA	NA	NA	NA
EPA City/Hwy (mpg) —auto	19/23	19/23	19/23	20/28	NA	NA	NA	NA	NA	NA	NA	NA

FORD

Specifications and EPA Mileage Ratings

Specifications and EPA Mileage Ratings	ESCORT GT 3DR	ESCORT LX 4DR	ESCORT 5DR	ESCORT LX WGN	PROBE 3DR	PROBE GT 3DR	TAURUS GL SDN	TAURUS LX SDN	TAURUS SHO SDN	TAURUS GL WGN	TAURUS LX WGN	TEMPO GL 2DR	TEMPO GL 4DR
Length (in.)	170.0	170.9	170.0	171.3	178.7	179.5	192.0	192.0	192.0	193.1	193.1	176.7	177.0
Width (in.)	66.7	66.7	66.7	66.7	69.8	69.8	70.7	70.7	70.7	70.7	70.7	68.3	68.3
Height (in.)	52.5	52.7	52.5	53.6	51.6	51.6	54.1	54.1	54.1	55.5	55.5	52.8	52.9
Curb Weight (lbs.)	2447	2371	2419	2419	2690	2921	3104	3104	3104	3272	3272	2511	2569
Wheelbase (in.)	98.4	98.4	98.4	98.4	102.8	102.8	106.0	106.0	106.0	106.0	106.0	99.9	99.9
Track, front (in.)	56.5	56.5	56.5	56.5	59.8	59.4	61.6	61.6	61.6	61.6	61.6	54.9	54.9
Track, rear (in.)	56.5	56.5	56.5	56.5	59.8	59.4	60.5	60.5	60.5	59.9	59.9	57.6	57.6
Head Room, front (in.)	38.4	38.4	38.4	38.4	37.8	37.8	38.3	38.3	38.3	38.6	38.6	37.5	37.5
Head Room, rear (in.)	37.6	37.4	37.6	38.5	34.8	34.8	37.6	37.6	37.6	38.1	38.1	36.8	36.8
Shoulder Room, front (in.)	53.0	53.0	53.0	53.0	52.0	52.0	57.5	57.5	57.5	57.5	57.5	53.9	53.9
Shoulder Room, rear (in.)	52.6	53.7	53.7	53.7	53.9	53.9	57.6	57.6	57.6	57.5	57.5	54.0	53.3
Hip Room, front (in.)	51.3	50.4	50.4	50.4	53.9	53.9	55.2	55.2	55.2	55.2	55.2	48.8	48.8
Hip Room, rear (in.)	46.6	48.0	48.0	48.0	48.6	48.6	54.8	54.8	54.8	57.0	57.0	51.8	51.0
Leg Room, front (in.)	41.7	41.7	41.7	41.7	43.1	43.1	41.7	41.7	41.7	41.7	41.7	41.5	41.5
Leg Room, rear (in.)	34.6	34.6	34.6	34.6	28.5	28.5	37.7	37.7	37.7	36.9	36.9	36.0	36.0
Luggage Capacity (cu. ft.)	17.3/35.2	12.1	17.6/36.0	30.6/66.9	18.0	18.0	18.0	18.0	18.0	38.3/83.1	38.3/83.1	13.2	12.9
Engine Type	L4	L4	L4	L4	L4	V6	V6	V6	V6	V6	V6	L4	L4
Displacement (cu. in.)	109.0	114.0	114.0	114.0	122.0	153.0	182.0	182.0	182.0	182.0	232.0	141.0	141.0
Fuel System	EFI	SEFI	SEFI	SEFI	SEFI	SEFI	SEFI	SEFI	SEFI	SEFI	SEFI	SEFI	SEFI
Compression Ratio	9.0:1	9.0:1	9.0:1	9.0:1	9.0:1	9.2:1	9.3:1	9.3:1	8.8:1	9.3:1	9.0:1	9.0:1	9.0:1
BHP @ RPM (net)	127 @ 6500	88 @ 4400	88 @ 4400	88 @ 4400	118 @ 5500	164 @ 5600	140 @ 4800	140 @ 4800	220 @ 6200	140 @ 4800	140 @ 3800	96 @ 4200	96 @ 4200
Torque @ RPM (net)	114 @ 4500	108 @ 3800	108 @ 3800	108 @ 3800	127 @ 4500	160 @ 4800	165 @ 3250	165 @ 3250	200 @ 4800	165 @ 3250	215 @ 2200	126 @ 2600	126 @ 2600
Fuel Capacity (gals.)	13.2	11.9	11.9	11.9	15.5	15.5	16.0	16.0	18.4	16.0	16.0	15.9	15.9
EPA City/Hwy (mpg) —manual	NA	NA	NA	NA	NA	NA	NA	NA	NA	NA	NA	NA	NA
EPA City/Hwy (mpg) —auto	NA	NA	NA	NA	NA	NA	NA	NA	NA	NA	NA	NA	NA

Specifications and EPA Mileage Ratings

	TEMPO LX 4DR	THUNDERBIRD LX SDN	THUNDERBIRD SC SDN	GEO	METRO XFI CPE	METRO CPE	METRO SDN	PRIZM SDN	PRIZM LSI SDN	TRACKER 2WD CVT	TRACKER 4WD CVT	TRACKER 4WD HT
Length (in.)	177.0	200.3	200.3		147.4	147.4	151.4	172.64	172.64	142.5	142.5	142.5
Width (in.)	68.3	72.7	72.7		62.7	62.7	62.7	66.34	66.34	64.2	64.2	64.2
Height (in.)	52.9	52.5	53.0		52.4	52.4	53.5	52.76	52.76	65.6	65.6	65.6
Curb Weight (lbs.)	2569	3570	3570		1621	1650	1694	2348	2359	2125	2301	2323
Wheelbase (in.)	99.9	113.0	113.0		89.2	89.2	93.1	97.05	97.05	86.6	86.6	86.6
Track, front (in.)	54.9	61.6	61.6		53.7	53.7	53.7	57.48	57.48	54.9	54.9	54.9
Track, rear (in.)	57.6	60.2	60.2		52.8	52.8	52.8	56.50	56.50	55.1	55.1	55.1
Head Room, front (in.)	37.5	38.1	38.1		37.8	37.8	38.8	38.82	38.82	39.5	39.5	40.0
Head Room, rear (in.))	36.8	37.5	37.5		36.5	36.5	38.0	37.09	37.09	38.3	38.3	38.1
Shoulder Room, front (in.)	53.9	59.0	59.0		51.6	51.6	51.6	53.78	53.78	52.2	52.2	52.2
Shoulder Room, rear (in.)	53.3	58.9	58.9		50.5	50.5	50.6	53.27	53.27	50.2	50.2	50.2
Hip Room, front (in.)	48.8	55.6	55.6		51.1	51.1	51.1	51.3	51.3	51.8	51.8	51.8
Hip Room, rear (in.)	51.0	56.6	56.6		42.5	42.5	42.7	54.3	54.3	41.9	41.9	41.9
Leg Room, front (in.)	41.5	42.5	42.5		42.5	42.5	42.5	42.44	42.44	42.1	42.1	42.1
Leg Room, rear (in.)	36.0	35.8	35.8		29.8	29.8	32.6	32.99	32.99	31.6	31.6	31.6
Luggage Capacity (cu. ft.)	12.9	15.1	15.1		10.3	10.3	10.5	12.66	12.66	8.9	8.9	8.7
Engine Type	L4	V6	V6		L3	L3	L3	L4	L4	L4	L4	L4
Displacement (cu. in.)	141.0	232.0	232.0		61.0	61.0	61.0	97.0	97.0	97.0	97.0	97.0
Fuel System	SEFI	SEFI	SEFI		EFI	EFI	EFI	MFI	MFI	EFI	EFI	EFI
Compression Ratio	9.0:1	9.0:1	8.2:1		9.5:1	9.5:1	9.5:1	9.5:1	9.5:1	8.9:1	8.9:1	8.9:1
BHP @ RPM (net)	96 @ 4200	140 @ 3800	210 @ 4000		49 @ 4700	52 @ 5700	52 @ 5700	105 @ 5800	105 @ 5800	80 @ 5400	80 @ 5400	80 @ 5400
Torque @ RPM (net)	126 @ 2600	215 @ 2400	315 @ 2600		58 @ 3300	58 @ 3300	58 @ 3300	100 @ 4800	100 @ 4800	94 @ 3000	94 @ 3000	94 @ 3000
Fuel Capacity (gals.)	15.9	18.0	18.0		10.6	10.6	10.6	13.2	13.2	11.1	11.1	11.1
EPA City/Hwy (mpg) —manual	NA	NA	NA		NA	NA	NA	NA	NA	NA	NA	NA
EPA City/Hwy (mpg) —auto	NA	NA	NA		NA	NA	NA	NA	NA	NA	NA	NA

Specifications and EPA Mileage Ratings

	LINCOLN CONTINENTAL SDN	LINCOLN MARK VIII CPE	LINCOLN TOWN CAR SDN	MERCURY CAPRI CVT	MERCURY CAPRI XR2 CVT	MERCURY COUGAR XR7 SDN	MERCURY GRAND MARQUIS SDN	MERCURY SABLE SDN	MERCURY SABLE WGN	MERCURY TOPAZ GS 2DR	MERCURY TOPAZ GS 4DR
Length (in.)	205.1	206.9	218.9	167.1	167.1	199.9	212.4	192.2	193.3	176.7	177.0
Width (in.)	72.3	74.6	76.9	64.6	64.6	72.7	77.8	70.9	70.9	68.3	68.3
Height (in.)	55.4	53.6	56.9	50.4	49.9	52.5	56.8	54.1	55.5	52.8	52.9
Curb Weight (lbs.)	3576	3768	4039	2423	NA	3564	3787	3126	3275	2531	2588
Wheelbase (in.)	109.0	113.0	117.4	94.7	94.7	113.0	114.4	106.0	106.0	99.9	99.9
Track, front (in.)	62.3	61.6	62.8	54.9	54.9	61.6	62.8	61.6	61.6	54.9	54.9
Track, rear (in.)	61.1	60.2	63.3	56.0	56.0	60.2	63.3	60.5	59.9	57.6	57.6
Head Room, front (in.)	38.7	38.1	39.0	37.8	37.8	38.1	39.4	38.3	38.6	37.5	37.5
Head Room, rear (in.)	38.4	37.5	38.0	34.4	34.4	37.6	38.1	37.7	38.1	48.8	48.8
Shoulder Room, front (in.)	57.5	58.9	62.0	50.9	50.9	59.0	60.5	57.5	57.5	53.9	53.9
Shoulder Room, rear (in.)	57.4	59.5	62.0	36.2	36.2	58.9	60.3	57.5	57.5	54.0	53.3
Hip Room, front (in.)	56.5	56.7	57.2	52.4	52.4	56.6	59.7	54.8	54.8	48.8	48.8
Hip Room, rear (in.)	56.5	56.7	59.7	40.6	40.6	56.6	59.0	55.6	57.0	51.8	51.0
Leg Room, front (in.)	41.7	42.6	42.6	41.2	41.2	42.5	42.5	41.7	41.7	41.5	41.5
Leg Room, rear (in.)	39.2	32.5	41.6	25.8	25.8	36.5	38.8	37.1	36.9	36.0	36.0
Luggage Capacity (cu. ft.)	19.1	14.4	22.3	6.2	6.2	15.1	20.6	18.0	38.3/83.1	13.2	12.9
Engine Type	V6	V8	V8	L4	L4	V6	V8	V6	V6	L4	L4
Displacement (cu. in.)	232.0	281.0	281.0	97.5	97.5	NA	281.0	182.0	182.0	141.0	141.0
Fuel System	SEFI	SEFI	SEFI	9.4:1	EFI	SEFI	SEFI	SEFI	SEFI	SEFI	SEFI
Compression Ratio	9.0:1	9.8:1	9.0:1	9.4:1	7.9:1	9.0:1	9.0:1	9.3:1	9.3:1	9.0:1	9.0:1
BHP @ RPM (net)	160 @ 4400	280 @ 5500	210 @ 4600	100 @ 5750	132 @ 5000	140 @ 3800	260 @ 3200	140 @ 4800	140 @ 4800	96 @ 4200	96 @ 4200
Torque @ RPM (net)	225 @ 3000	285 @ 4500	270 @ 3400	95 @ 5500	136 @ 3000	215 @ 2400	270 @ 3400	165 @ 3250	165 @ 3250	126 @ 2600	126 @ 2600
Fuel Capacity (gals.)	18.4	18.0	20.0	11.1	11.1	18.0	20.0	16.0	16.0	15.9	15.9
EPA City/Hwy (mpg) —manual	NA	NA	NA	NA	NA	NA	NA	NA	NA	NA	NA
EPA City/Hwy (mpg) —auto	NA	NA	NA	NA	NA	NA	NA	NA	NA	NA	NA

Specifications and EPA Mileage Ratings

	TRACER SDN	TRACER LTS SDN	TRACER WGN	VILLAGER WGN	OLDSMOBILE ACHIEVA S CPE	ACHIEVA S SDN	ACHIEVA SC CPE	ACHIEVA SL SDN	BRAVADA	CUTLASS CIERA S SDN	CUTLASS CIERA SL SDN	CUTLASS CIERA CRUISER S WGN
Length (in.)	170.9	170.9	171.3	189.9	187.9	187.9	187.9	187.9	178.9	190.3	190.3	194.4
Width (in.)	66.7	66.7	66.7	73.7	67.2	67.2	67.2	67.2	65.2	69.5	69.5	69.5
Height (in.)	52.7	52.7	53.6	67.6	53.1	53.1	53.1	53.1	65.5	54.1	54.1	54.5
Curb Weight (lbs.)	2393	2458	2476	NA	2717	2779	2717	2779	4031	2833	2833	3086
Wheelbase (in.)	98.4	98.4	98.4	112.2	103.4	103.4	103.4	103.4	107.0	104.9	104.9	104.9
Track, front (in.)	56.5	56.5	56.5	63.4	55.6	55.6	55.6	55.6	55.6	58.7	58.7	58.7
Track, rear (in.)	56.5	56.5	56.5	63.4	55.3	55.3	55.3	55.3	54.1	57.0	57.0	57.0
Head Room, front (in.)	38.4	38.4	38.4	39.4	37.8	37.8	37.8	37.8	39.1	38.6	38.6	38.6
Head Room, rear (in.))	37.4	37.4	38.5	37.3	36.5	37.0	36.5	37.0	38.8	38.3	38.3	38.9
Shoulder Room, front (in.)	53.0	53.0	53.0	62.1	53.6	54.1	53.6	54.1	53.9	55.8	55.8	55.8
Shoulder Room, rear (in.)	53.7	53.7	53.7	NA	55.0	53.4	55.0	53.4	55.6	56.0	56.0	56.0
Hip Room, front (in.)	50.4	50.4	50.4	56.8	49.1	49.2	49.1	49.2	50.5	50.3	50.3	50.3
Hip Room, rear (in.)	48.0	48.0	48.0	NA	50.3	50.2	50.3	50.2	52.6	54.3	54.3	54.3
Leg Room, front (in.)	41.7	41.7	41.7	39.9	43.3	43.3	43.3	43.3	42.5	42.1	42.1	42.1
Leg Room, rear (in.)	34.6	34.6	34.6	36.1	32.5	33.5	32.5	33.5	36.5	35.8	35.8	34.7
Luggage Capacity (cu. ft.)	12.1	12.1	66.9	126.4	14.0	14.0	14.0	14.0	74.3	15.8	15.8	74.4
Engine Type	L4	L4	L4	V6	L4	L4	L4	L4	V6	L4	V6	V6
Displacement (cu. in.)	114.0	109.0	114.0	182.0	138.0	138.0	138.0	138.0	262.0	133.0	191.0	191.0
Fuel System	SEFI	EFI	SEFI	EFI	MPFI	MPFI	MPFI	MPFI	CPI	MPFI	MPFI	MPFI
Compression Ratio	9.0:1	9.0:1	9.0:1	9.0:1	9.5:1	9.5:1	10.0:1	10.0:1	9.1:1	9.0:1	9.5:1	9.5:1
BHP @ RPM (net)	88 @ 4400	127 @ 6500	88 @ 4400	151 @ 4800	115 @ 5200	115 @ 5200	170 @ 6200	170 @ 6200	200 @ 4500	120 @ 5200	160 @ 5200	160 @ 5200
Torque @ RPM (net)	108 @ 3800	114 @ 4500	108 @ 3800	174 @ 4400	140 @ 3200	140 @ 3200	150 @ 5200	150 @ 5200	260 @ 3600	130 @ 4000	185 @ 4000	185 @ 4000
Fuel Capacity (gals.)	11.9	13.2	11.9	20.0	15.2	15.2	15.2	15.2	20.0	16.5	16.5	16.5
EPA City/Hwy (mpg) —manual	NA	NA	NA	NA	NA	NA	NA	NA	NA	NA	NA	NA
EPA City/Hwy (mpg) —auto	NA	NA	NA	NA	NA	NA	NA	NA	NA	NA	NA	NA

PLYMOUTH

Specifications and EPA Mileage Ratings	COLT 4DR	COLT 2DR	ACCLAIM SDN	SILHOUETTE SPORT UTILITY	98 REGENCY ELITE SDN	98 REGENCY SDN	EIGHTY-EIGHT ROYALE LS SDN	EIGHTY-EIGHT ROYALE SDN	CUTLASS SUPRM CVT	CUTLASS SUPRM S SDN	CUTLASS SUPRM S CPE	CUTLASS CIERA CRUISER SL WGN
Length (in.)	174.0	171.1	181.2	194.2	205.5	205.5	200.4	200.4	193.9	193.7	193.9	194.4
Width (in.)	66.1	66.1	68.1	73.9	74.6	74.6	74.1	74.1	71.0	71.0	71.0	69.5
Height (in.)	51.4	51.4	53.5	65.7	54.8	54.8	55.7	55.7	54.3	54.8	53.3	54.5
Curb Weight (lbs.)	2195	2085	2831	3676	3527	3512	3469	3439	3638	3405	3307	3086
Wheelbase (in.)	98.4	96.1	103.5	109.8	110.7	110.7	110.8	110.8	107.0	107.0	107.0	104.9
Track, front (in.)	57.1	57.1	57.6	59.2	61.5	61.5	60.4	60.4	59.5	59.5	59.5	58.7
Track, rear (in.)	57.5	57.5	57.2	61.4	60.3	60.3	60.4	60.4	58.0	58.0	58.0	57.0
Head Room, front (in.)	38.6	38.6	38.4	39.2	60.3	60.3	38.7	38.7	38.5	38.7	37.6	38.6
Head Room, rear (in.)	36.2	36.4	37.9	37.5	37.7	37.7	38.3	38.3	38.9	38.3	37.0	38.9
Shoulder Room, front (in.)	53.9	53.9	54.3	60.6	59.0	59.0	59.0	59.0	57.6	57.4	57.6	55.8
Shoulder Room, rear (in.)	53.5	54.1	55.0	62.2	58.1	58.1	58.3	58.3	57.2	56.6	57.2	56.0
Hip Room, front (in.)	54.9	54.9	51.7	55.5	56.5	56.5	55.4	55.4	51.9	52.6	51.9	50.3
Hip Room, rear (in.)	52.0	53.7	52.0	41.7	54.8	54.8	54.1	54.1	51.5	55.0	53.3	54.3
Leg Room, front (in.)	42.9	42.9	41.9	40.7	42.7	42.7	42.5	42.5	42.3	42.4	42.3	42.1
Leg Room, rear (in.)	33.5	31.1	38.3	34.0	40.7	40.7	38.7	38.7	34.8	36.2	34.8	34.7
Luggage Capacity (cu. ft.)	10.5	10.5	14.4	112.6	20.2	20.2	17.5	17.5	12.1	15.5	15.5	74.4
Engine Type	L4	L4	L4	V6	V6	V6	V6	V6	V6	V6	V6	V6
Displacement (cu. in.)	111.9	89.6	153.0	191.0	231.0	231.0	231.0	231.0	191.0	191.0	191.0	191.0
Fuel System	SMPI	SMPI	EFI	TBI	TPI	TPI	TPI	TPI	MPFI	MPFI	MPFI	MPFI
Compression Ratio	9.5:1	9.2:1	8.9:1	8.5:1	9.0:1	9.0:1	9.0:1	9.0:1	9.5:1	9.5:1	9.5:1	9.5:1
BHP @ RPM (net)	113 @ 6000	93 @ 6000	100 @ 4800	120 @ 4400	170 @ 4800	170 @ 4800	170 @ 4800	170 @ 4800	185 @ 5200	160 @ 5200	160 @ 5200	160 @ 5200
Torque @ RPM (net)	116 @ 4500	92 @ 3000	135 @ 2800	175 @ 2200	225 @ 3200	225 @ 3200	225 @ 3200	225 @ 3200	185 @ 4000	185 @ 4000	185 @ 4000	185 @ 4000
Fuel Capacity (gals.)	13.2	13.2	16.0	20.0	18.0	18.0	18.0	18.0	16.5	16.5	16.5	16.5
EPA City/Hwy (mpg) —manual	27/34	32/40	NA	NA	NA	NA	NA	NA	NA	NA	NA	NA
EPA City/Hwy (mpg) —auto	27/34	29/33	23/28	NA	NA	NA	NA	NA	NA	NA	NA	NA

Specifications and EPA Mileage Ratings

	COLT VISTA FWD WGN	COLT VISTA FWD SE WGN	COLT VISTA AWD WGN	LASER CPE	LASER RS CPE	LASER RS TURBO CPE	LASER AWD RS TURBO CPE	SUNDANCE 2DR HBK	SUNDANCE 4DR HBK	SUNDANCE DUSTER 2DR HBK	SUNDANCE DUSTER 4DR HBK	VOYAGER 2WD	VOYAGER SE 2WD
Length (in.)	168.5	168.5	168.5	172.8	172.8	172.8	172.8	171.9	171.9	171.9	171.9	178.1	178.1
Width (in.)	66.7	66.7	66.7	66.7	66.7	66.7	66.7	67.3	67.3	67.3	67.3	72.0	72.0
Height (in.)	62.1	62.1	62.6	51.4	51.4	51.4	52.0	53.1	53.1	53.1	53.1	66.0	66.0
Curb Weight (lbs.)	2734	2734	3064	2531	2690	2756	3073	2608	2643	2608	2643	3306	3306
Wheelbase (in.)	99.2	99.2	99.2	97.2	97.2	97.2	97.2	97.2	97.2	97.2	97.2	112.3	112.3
Track, front (in.)	57.5	57.5	57.3	57.7	57.7	57.7	57.7	57.6	57.6	57.6	57.6	59.9	59.9
Track, rear (in.)	57.5	57.5	57.5	57.1	57.1	57.1	57.3	57.2	57.2	57.2	57.2	62.1	62.1
Head Room, front (in.)	40.0	40.0	40.0	37.9	37.9	37.9	37.9	38.3	38.3	38.3	38.3	39.1	39.1
Head Room, rear (in.)	38.6	38.6	38.6	34.1	34.1	34.1	34.1	37.4	37.0	37.4	37.0	38.6	38.6
Shoulder Room, front (in.)	55.1	55.1	55.1	53.9	53.9	53.9	53.9	54.5	54.5	54.5	54.5	57.5	57.5
Shoulder Room, rear (in.)	55.1	55.1	55.1	52.4	52.4	52.4	52.4	52.5	54.4	52.5	54.4	60.5	60.5
Hip Room, front (in.)	50.2	50.2	50.2	55.1	55.1	55.1	55.1	52.8	52.9	52.8	52.9	53.7	53.7
Hip Room, rear (in.)	52.6	52.6	52.6	45.7	45.7	45.7	45.7	44.3	44.3	44.3	44.3	57.1	57.1
Leg Room, front (in.)	40.8	40.8	40.8	43.9	43.9	43.9	43.9	41.5	41.5	41.5	41.5	38.3	38.3
Leg Room, rear (in.)	36.1	36.1	36.1	28.5	28.5	28.5	28.5	34.0	34.0	34.0	34.0	43.4	43.4
Luggage Capacity (cu. ft.)	34.6/79.0	34.6/79.0	34.6/79.0	25.7	25.7	25.7	21.7	13.2	13.1	13.2	13.1	NA	NA
Engine Type	L4	L4	L4	L4	L4	L4	L4	L4	L4	L4	L4	L4	V6
Displacement (cu. in.)	111.9	143.0	143.0	107.0	122.0	122.0	122.0	135.0	135.0	153.0	153.0	153.0	181.4
Fuel System	SMPI	SMPI	SMPI	SMPI	SMPI	SMPI	SMPI	EFI	EFI	SMPI	SMPI	EFI	SMPI
Compression Ratio	9.5:1	9.5:1	9.5:1	9.0:1	9.0:1	7.8:1	7.8:1	9.5:1	9.5:1	8.9:1	8.9:1	8.9:1	8.9:1
BHP @ RPM (net)	113 @ 6000	136 @ 5500	136 @ 5500	92 @ 5000	135 @ 6000	195 @ 6000	195 @ 6000	93 @ 4800	93 @ 4800	100 @ 4800	100 @ 4800	100 @ 4800	142 @ 5000
Torque @ RPM (net)	116 @ 4500	145 @ 4250	145 @ 4250	105 @ 3500	125 @ 5000	203 @ 3000	203 @ 3000	122 @ 3200	122 @ 3200	135 @ 2800	135 @ 2800	135 @ 2800	173 @ 2400
Fuel Capacity (gals.)	14.5	14.5	14.5	15.8	15.8	15.8	15.8	14.0	14.0	14.0	14.0	20.0	20.0
EPA City/Hwy (mpg) —manual	21/28	19/24	19/24	23/32	22/29	21/28	20/25	27/32	27/32	25/32	25/32	20/30	NA
EPA City/Hwy (mpg) —auto	20/26	19/23	19/23	23/30	19/23	19/23	18/21	23/29	23/29	23/28	23/28	20/26	19/24

Specifications and EPA Mileage Ratings	VOYAGER LE 2WD	VOYAGER GRAND 2WD	VOYAGER GRAND SE 2WD	VOYAGER GRAND SE 4WD	VOYAGER GRAND LE 2WD	VOYAGER GRAND LE 4WD	BONNEVILLE SE SDN	BONNEVILLE SSE SDN	FIREBIRD CPE	FIREBIRD FORMULA CPE	FIREBIRD TRANS AM CPE	FIREBIRD TRANS AM GT CPE
Length (in.)	178.1	192.8	192.8	192.8	192.8	192.8	199.5	201.1	195.6	195.6	197.0	197.0
Width (in.)	72.0	72.0	72.0	72.0	72.0	72.0	74.5	74.5	74.5	74.5	74.5	74.5
Height (in.)	66.0	66.7	66.7	67.8	66.7	67.8	55.7	55.7	52.0	52.0	51.7	51.7
Curb Weight (lbs.)	3306	3574	3574	4008	3574	4008	3446	3587	3232	3425	3447	3494
Wheelbase (in.)	112.3	119.3	119.3	119.3	119.3	119.3	110.8	110.8	101.1	101.1	101.1	101.1
Track, front (in.)	59.9	59.9	59.9	59.9	59.9	59.9	60.4	60.8	60.7	60.7	60.7	60.7
Track, rear (in.)	62.1	62.1	62.1	62.1	62.1	62.1	60.3	60.6	60.6	60.6	60.6	60.6
Head Room, front (in.)	39.1	39.1	39.1	39.1	39.1	39.1	39.0	39.0	37.2	37.2	37.2	37.2
Head Room, rear (in.))	38.6	38.4	38.4	38.4	38.4	38.4	38.3	38.3	35.3	35.3	35.3	35.3
Shoulder Room, front (in.)	57.5	57.5	57.5	57.5	57.5	57.5	59.8	59.8	57.4	57.4	57.4	57.4
Shoulder Room, rear (in.)	60.5	60.5	60.5	60.5	60.5	60.5	59.4	59.4	55.8	55.8	55.8	55.8
Hip Room, front (in.)	53.7	53.7	53.7	53.7	53.7	53.7	57.2	57.2	52.8	52.8	52.8	52.8
Hip Room, rear (in.)	57.1	57.1	57.1	57.1	57.1	57.1	57.1	57.1	44.4	44.4	44.4	44.4
Leg Room, front (in.)	38.3	38.3	38.3	38.3	38.3	38.3	43.0	43.0	43.0	43.0	43.0	43.0
Leg Room, rear (in.)	43.4	37.7	37.7	37.7	37.7	37.7	38.6	38.6	28.9	28.9	28.9	28.9
Luggage Capacity (cu. ft.)	NA	NA	NA	NA	NA	NA	18.0	18.0	12.9	12.9	12.9	12.9
Engine Type	V6	V6	V6	V6	V6	V6	V6	V6	V6	V8	V8	V8
Displacement (cu. in.)	181.4	181.4	201.5	201.5	201.5	201.5	231.0	231.0	207.0	350.0	350.0	350.0
Fuel System	SMPI	SMPI	SMPI	SMPI	SMPI	SMPI	SPFI	SPFI	SPFI	SPFI	SPFI	SPFI
Compression Ratio	8.9:1	8.9:1	8.9:1	8.9:1	8.9:1	8.9:1	9.0:1	9.0:1	9.0:1	10.5:1	10.5:1	10.5:1
BHP @ RPM (net)	142 @ 5000	142 @ 5000	162 @ 4800	162 @ 4800	162 @ 4800	162 @ 4800	170 @ 4800	170 @ 4800	160 @ 4600	275 @ 5000	275 @ 5000	275 @ 5000
Torque @ RPM (net)	173 @ 2400	173 @ 2400	194 @ 3600	194 @ 3600	194 @ 3600	194 @ 3600	225 @ 3200	225 @ 3200	200 @ 3600	325 @ 2400	325 @ 2400	325 @ 2400
Fuel Capacity (gals.)	20.0	20.0	20.0	18.0	20.0	18.0	18.0	18.0	15.5	15.5	15.5	15.5
EPA City/Hwy (mpg) —manual	NA	NA	NA	NA	NA	NA	NA	NA	NA	NA	NA	NA
EPA City/Hwy (mpg) —auto	19/24	19/24	18/23	17/22	18/23	17/22	NA	NA	NA	NA	NA	NA

PONTIAC

Specifications and EPA Mileage Ratings

Specification	SATURN SC1 CPE	TRANS SPORT SE VAN	SUNBIRD SE CPE	SUNBIRD LE CVT	SUNBIRD LE SDN	SUNBIRD LE CPE	GRAND PRIX SE SDN	GRAND PRIX SE CPE	GRAND AM GT SDN	GRAND AM GT CPE	GRAND AM SE SDN	GRAND AM SE CPE
Length (in.)	173.2	192.2	180.7	180.7	180.7	180.7	194.9	194.8	186.9	186.9	186.9	186.9
Width (in.)	67.5	74.6	66.2	66.2	66.2	66.2	71.9	71.9	67.5	67.5	67.5	67.5
Height (in.)	50.6	65.7	52.2	52.4	53.9	52.2	54.8	52.8	53.2	53.2	53.2	53.2
Curb Weight (lbs.)	2280	3540	2682	2661	2502	2484	3370	3275	2882	2822	2793	2736
Wheelbase (in.)	99.2	109.8	101.3	101.3	101.3	101.3	107.5	107.5	103.4	103.4	103.4	103.4
Track, front (in.)	56.8	59.2	55.6	55.6	55.6	55.4	59.5	59.5	55.9	55.9	55.9	55.9
Track, rear (in.)	56.0	61.4	55.4	55.4	55.4	55.4	58.0	58.0	55.4	55.4	55.4	55.4
Head Room, front (in.)	37.5	39.2	37.8	38.2	38.8	37.8	38.6	37.8	37.8	37.8	37.8	37.8
Head Room, rear (in.)	35.1	37.8	36.1	36.5	37.4	36.1	37.7	36.6	37.0	36.5	37.0	36.5
Shoulder Room, front (in.)	53.7	60.6	52.5	52.5	52.9	52.5	57.2	57.3	54.0	54.0	54.0	54.0
Shoulder Room, rear (in.)	51.3	62.2	52.8	36.9	53.2	52.8	57.4	57.3	54.2	55.4	54.2	55.4
Hip Room, front (in.)	51.3	NA	47.8	47.8	47.7	47.8	53.1	52.0	49.1	49.1	49.1	49.1
Hip Room, rear (in.)	49.2	NA	49.6	38.1	49.2	49.6	54.3	53.3	51.4	52.6	51.4	52.6
Leg Room, front (in.)	42.6	40.1	42.1	42.1	42.1	42.1	42.4	42.3	43.3	43.3	43.3	43.3
Leg Room, rear (in.)	26.5	36.8	32.0	32.0	33.7	32.0	36.2	34.8	34.9	33.9	34.9	33.9
Luggage Capacity (cu. ft.)	10.9	112.6	12.6	10.4	13.0	12.6	15.5	14.9	13.2	13.2	13.2	13.2
Engine Type	L4	V6	V6	L4	L4	L4	V6	V6	L4	L4	L4	L4
Displacement (cu. in.)	116.03	191.0	191.0	121.0	121.0	121.0	191.0	191.0	138.0	138.0	138.0	138.0
Fuel System	TBI	TBI	MPFI	MPFI	MPFI	MPFI	SPFI	SPFI	MPFI	MPFI	MPFI	MPFI
Compression Ratio	9.3:1	8.5:1	8.9:1	9.2:1	9.2:1	9.2:1	9.5:1	9.5:1	10.0:1	10.0:1	9.5:1	9.5:1
BHP @ RPM (net)	85 @ 5000	120 @ 4400	140 @ 4200	110 @ 5200	110 @ 5200	110 @ 5200	160 @ 5200	160 @ 5200	175 @ 6200	175 @ 6200	115 @ 5200	115 @ 5200
Torque @ RPM (net)	107 @ 2400	175 @ 2200	185 @ 3600	124 @ 3600	124 @ 3600	124 @ 3600	185 @ 4000	185 @ 4000	150 @ 5200	150 @ 5200	140 @ 3200	140 @ 3200
Fuel Capacity (gals.)	12.8	20.0	15.2	15.2	15.2	15.2	16.5	16.5	15.2	15.2	15.2	15.2
EPA City/Hwy (mpg) —manual	28/37	NA	NA	NA	NA	NA	NA	NA	NA	NA	NA	NA
EPA City/Hwy (mpg) —auto	26/35	NA	NA	NA	NA	NA	NA	NA	NA	NA	NA	NA

Specifications and EPA Mileage Ratings

Specifications and EPA Mileage Ratings	SATURN SC2 CPE	SATURN SL SDN	SATURN SL1 SDN	SATURN SL2 SDN	SATURN SW1 WGN	SATURN SW2 WGN
Length (in.)	173.2	176.3	176.3	176.3	176.3	176.3
Width (in.)	67.5	67.2	67.2	67.2	67.6	67.6
Height (in.)	50.6	52.5	52.5	52.5	53.7	53.7
Curb Weight (lbs.)	2376	2314	2314	2405	2362	2447
Wheelbase (in.)	99.2	102.4	102.4	102.4	102.4	102.4
Track, front (in.)	56.8	56.8	56.8	56.8	56.8	56.8
Track, rear (in.)	56.0	56.0	56.0	56.0	56.0	56.0
Head Room, front (in.)	37.5	38.5	38.5	38.5	38.8	38.8
Head Room, rear (in.)	35.1	36.3	36.3	36.3	37.4	37.4
Shoulder Room, front (in.)	53.7	54.3	54.3	54.3	54.3	54.3
Shoulder Room, rear (in.)	51.3	54.3	54.3	54.3	54.3	54.3
Hip Room, front (in.)	51.3	51.7	51.7	51.7	51.7	51.7
Hip Room, rear (in.)	49.2	50.7	50.7	50.7	50.7	50.7
Leg Room, front (in.)	42.6	42.5	42.5	42.5	42.5	42.5
Leg Room, rear (in.)	26.5	32.6	32.6	32.6	32.6	32.6
Luggage Capacity (cu. ft.)	10.9	11.9	11.9	11.9	30.9	30.9
Engine Type	L4	L4	L4	L4	L4	L4
Displacement (cu. in.)	116.03	116.03	116.03	116.03	116.03	116.03
Fuel System	MPFI	TBI	TBI	MPFI	TBI	MPFI
Compression Ratio	9.5:1	9.3:1	9.3:1	9.5:1	9.3:1	9.5:1
BHP @ RPM (net)	124 @ 5600	85 @ 5000	85 @ 5000	124 @ 5600	85 @ 5000	124 @ 5600
Torque @ RPM (net)	122 @ 4800	107 @ 2400	107 @ 2400	122 @ 4800	107 @ 2400	122 @ 4800
Fuel Capacity (gals.)	12.8	12.8	12.8	12.8	12.8	12.8
EPA City/Hwy (mpg) —manual	25/34	28/37	28/37	25/34	28/37	25/34
EPA City/Hwy (mpg) —auto	23/32	26/35	26/35	23/32	25/25	23/32

How the fuel economy estimates are obtained:

The estimates of the number of miles a vehicle can travel on a gallon of fuel are based on results of the U.S. Environmental Protection Agency (E.P.A.) "Emissions Standards Test Procedure."

This procedure is used to certify that cars, vans, and light trucks comply with the Clean Air Act, as amended. Each year, Manufacturers submit new vehicle codes to the E.P.A. The procedure for testing simulates every day driving conditions. Each vehicle is tested under controlled labratory conditions by a professional driver. By Using a dynometer to simulate driving conditions, the driver can test each vehicle under identical circumstances in exactly the same way each time. Therefore, the obtained results can be compared accurately. The test vehicles are broken in, properly maintained, and driven in test conditions which simulate warm weather and dry, level roads. The quality of the fuel used is also very closely controlled. The test conditions are those the E.P.A. must use to assure emissions measurements. However, no test can cover all possible combinations of actual road conditions, climate, driving and car-care habits of individual drivers.

Dealer Incentives Manufacturer Rebates

These are programs offered by the manufacturers to increase the sales of slow-selling models or to reduce excess inventories. While the manufacturer's rebates are passed directly on to the buyer, dealer incentives are passed on only to the dealer — who may or may not elect to pass the savings on to the customer.

The following incentives and rebates were in effect at time of publication. Please note, however, that these programs often change frequently.

For updated information regarding Dealer Incentives and Manufacturer's Rebates, call Nationwide Auto Brokers, Inc. at 313-559-6661.

	MFG'S REBATE ($)
BUICK	
Century	750
LeSabre	750
Park Avenue	1000
Regal	750
Roadmaster	750
Skylark	750
*Rebates not available on National Marketing cars.	
CHRYSLER	
LeBaron Convertible	1000
LeBaron Sedan	1500
DODGE	
Colt 2-Dr (1993)	500
Colt 4-Dr (1993)	1000
Minivans	500
Spirit	1500
Stealth	1000
EAGLE	
Summit Coupe	500
Summit Sedan	1000
Summit Wagon	500
Talon	700
FORD	
Aerostar	750
Escort	200-500
Taurus GL & LX	500
Taurus SHO	1000
Tempo	300
GEO	
Tracker	1000

	MFG'S REBATE ($)
LINCOLN	
Continental	1000
Town Car	1000
MERCURY	
Sable	500
Topaz	500
Tracer	200-500
OLDSMOBILE	
Achieva	750
Bravada	1000
Cutlass Ciera	750
Cutlass Supreme	750
Eighty-Eight	750
Ninety-Eight	750
Silhouette	1000
*Rebates not available on Special Edition models.	
PLYMOUTH	
Acclaim	1500
Colt 2-Dr (1993)	500
Colt 4-Dr (1993)	1000
Laser (1993)	700
Minivans	500
Sundance	1000
PONTIAC	
Bonneville	750
Grand Am	750
Grand Prix Sedan	750
Sunbird	500
Trans Sport	750

At the time of publication Dealer Incentive weren't being offered on any 1994 cars

READER QUESTIONNAIRE

To help us improve the information content of our books,
please complete this questionnaire and mail to:

Edmund Publications Corporation
300 N. Sepulveda Blvd., Suite 2050
El Segundo, Ca 90245

1. **Where did you purchase this Edmund's Book?**
   ❏ BOOKSTORE   ❏ NEWSSTAND   ❏ OTHER

2. **How many times have you purchased editions of Edmund's USED CAR PRICES books?**
   ❏ ONCE   ❏ TWICE   ❏ THREE TIMES   ❏ FOUR TIMES OR MORE

3. **What is your vehicle preference?**
   CHECK ONE: ❏ AMERICAN   ❏ IMPORT
   CHECK ONE OR MORE: ❏ CAR   ❏ VAN   ❏ TRUCK   ❏ SPORTS UTILITY

4. **What is your budget/price for buying a new vehicle?**
   ❏ UNDER $10,000   ❏ $10 - 15,000   ❏ $15 - 20,000   ❏ $20 - 30,000
   ❏ $30 -40,000   ❏ $40,00 AND UP

5. **Which Edmund's NEW VEHICLE PRICE GUIDES have you purchased in the past?**
   ❏ AMERICAN CARS   ❏ IMPORTS   ❏ VAN, PICKUP, SPORTS UTILITY   ❏ ECONOMY

6. **Would you like to use a computerized version of Edmund's Price Guides?**
   ❏ NO   YES FOR: ❏ IBM PC   ❏ WINDOWS   ❏ MACINTOSH

ANY COMMENTS: _____
_____
_____

To be advised directly of special offers from Edmund's, please complete the following. Thank you.

NAME _____
ADDRESS _____
CITY, STATE, ZIP _____
TELEPHONE _____

N2703

STEP-BY-STEP COSTING FORM

MAKE: _____

MODEL: _____

BODY STYLE: _____

EXTERIOR COLOR: _____

INTERIOR COLOR: _____

TOP COLOR (IF APPL.) _____

ITEMS	DEALER COST	LIST PRICE	BEST DEAL
Basic Model Price Only			
Optional Equipment			
1.			
2.			
3.			
4.			
5.			
6.			
7.			
8.			
9.			
10.			
11.			
12.			
13.			
14.			
15.			
16.			
17.			
18.			
19.			
20.			
Dealer Advertising Amount			
Dealer Preparation Amount			
Initial Gas & Oil			
Freight Amount (to your area)			
TOTAL COST —*Excluding Local Sales Tax, Registration & Inspection Fees*			

STEP-BY-STEP COSTING FORM

MAKE: _____

MODEL: _____

BODY STYLE: _____

EXTERIOR COLOR: _____

INTERIOR COLOR: _____

TOP COLOR (IF APPL.) _____

ITEMS	DEALER COST	LIST PRICE	BEST DEAL
Basic Model Price Only			
Optional Equipment			
1.			
2.			
3.			
4.			
5.			
6.			
7.			
8.			
9.			
10.			
11.			
12.			
13.			
14.			
15.			
16.			
17.			
18.			
19.			
20.			
Dealer Advertising Amount			
Dealer Preparation Amount			
Initial Gas & Oil			
Freight Amount (to your area)			
TOTAL COST —*Excluding Local Sales Tax, Registration & Inspection Fees*			

STEP-BY-STEP COSTING FORM

MAKE: _____

MODEL: _____

BODY STYLE: _____

EXTERIOR COLOR: _____

INTERIOR COLOR: _____

TOP COLOR (IF APPL.) _____

ITEMS	DEALER COST	LIST PRICE	BEST DEAL
Basic Model Price Only			
Optional Equipment			
1.			
2.			
3.			
4.			
5.			
6.			
7.			
8.			
9.			
10.			
11.			
12.			
13.			
14.			
15.			
16.			
17.			
18.			
19.			
20.			
Dealer Advertising Amount			
Dealer Preparation Amount			
Initial Gas & Oil			
Freight Amount (to your area)			
TOTAL COST —*Excluding Local Sales Tax, Registration & Inspection Fees*			

STEP-BY-STEP COSTING FORM

MAKE: _____   EXTERIOR COLOR: _____

MODEL: _____   INTERIOR COLOR: _____

BODY STYLE: _____   TOP COLOR (IF APPL.) _____

ITEMS	DEALER COST	LIST PRICE	BEST DEAL
Basic Model Price Only			
Optional Equipment			
1.			
2.			
3.			
4.			
5.			
6.			
7.			
8.			
9.			
10.			
11.			
12.			
13.			
14.			
15.			
16.			
17.			
18.			
19.			
20.			
Dealer Advertising Amount			
Dealer Preparation Amount			
Initial Gas & Oil			
Freight Amount (to your area)			
TOTAL COST —*Excluding Local Sales Tax, Registration & Inspection Fees*			

STEP-BY-STEP COSTING FORM

MAKE: _____

MODEL: _____

BODY STYLE: _____

EXTERIOR COLOR: _____

INTERIOR COLOR: _____

TOP COLOR (IF APPL.) _____

ITEMS	DEALER COST	LIST PRICE	BEST DEAL
Basic Model Price Only			
Optional Equipment			
1.			
2.			
3.			
4.			
5.			
6.			
7.			
8.			
9.			
10.			
11.			
12.			
13.			
14.			
15.			
16.			
17.			
18.			
19.			
20.			
Dealer Advertising Amount			
Dealer Preparation Amount			
Initial Gas & Oil			
Freight Amount (to your area)			
TOTAL COST —*Excluding Local Sales Tax, Registration & Inspection Fees*			

WHAT'S IT WORTH?

Are you selling your car? Find out what your used car is worth <u>before</u> you sell or trade it. Find out today's market value through the Edmund's Auto Hotline:

1-900-786-AUTO
(1-900-786-2886)

$2.50 per minute
4-6 minutes per call.
Must be 18 or older to use this service

Edmund Publications Corp., El Segundo, CA

Edmund's CLASSIFIED ADS

THE CAR AUCTION NEWS
GET THE FACTS, WHERE AND WHEN?
ORDER NOW! 1 YEAR SUBSCRIPTION
SEND $9.94 TO MILLS PUBLISHING. 810
W. LAGUNA RD., FULLERTON, CA 92635

To Place a Classified Ad

Standard Rate:
$5.00 per word.
20 word minimum.
Bold Face Type:
add $1.00 per word.
Borders:
$25.00 per column inch.
Classified Display:
$125 per column inch

Counting Words: Two initials,
abbreviations, numerals and
symbols are counted as one word.
Telephone number including area
code and zip codes are one word.
(Zip code must appear in every ad
with an address). Multiple name
cities are counted as one word.
Normal punctuation is no charge.

*Payment must be received with copy.
Check, Money Order, MasterCard or
Visa accepted.*

Payment:
❏ Check or Money Order
❏ Visa
❏ MasterCard
❏ P.O. No._____

Credit Card #   Expires
_____

Cardholder Name:
_____

Signature

**Call 407-767-0557 or fax 407-767-6583 or
mail to: P.O. Box 1139, Longwood, FL 32752**

Edmund's · SINGLE COPIES / ORDER FORM

Please send me:

❏ **USED CAR PRICES** *(includes S&H)* ....$ 8.25

❏ **NEW CAR PRICES** *(includes S&H)*...$ 7.25

❏ **VAN, PICKUP, SPORT UTILITY BUYER'S GUIDE** *(includes S&H)*....$ 7.25

❏ **IMPORT CAR PRICES** *((includes S&H)* ....$ 7.25

❏ **ECONOMY CAR BUYING GUIDE** *(includes S&H)*...........................$ 8.25

Name _____

Address _____

City, State, Zip _____

Phone _____

SN2703

PAYMENT: ❏ MASTERCARD ❏ VISA ❏ CHECK or MONEY ORDER $_____
Make check or money order payable to:
Edmund Publications Corporation, *P.O. Box 338, Shrub Oak, NY 10588*
For more information or to order by phone, call **(914) 962-6297**

Credit Card # _____ Exp. Date: _____

CardHolder Name _____ Signature _____

*Prices above are for shipping within the U.S. and Canada only. Other countries please add $5.00 to
the cover price per book (via air mail) and $2.00 to the cover price per book (surface mail). Please
pay through an American Bank or with American currency. Rates subject to change without notice.*

Edmund's **SUBSCRIPTIONS / ORDER FORM**

Please send me a one-year subscription for:

❏ **USED CAR PRICES** (*includes bulk rate shipping/handling*) ....$ **29.75**
CANADA $37.25/FOREIGN COUNTRIES $53.75 (*includes air mail shipping/handling*)
now 6 issues instead of 4

❏ **NEW CAR PRICES** (*includes bulk rate shipping/handling*) ....$ **15.00**
CANADA $18.75/FOREIGN COUNTRIES $27.00 (*includes air mail shipping/handling*)
3 issues per year

❏ **VAN, PICKUP, SPORTS UTILITY** (*includes bulk rate shipping/handling*) ....$ **15.00**
CANADA $18.75/FOREIGN COUNTRIES $27.00 (*includes air mail shipping/handling*)
3 issues per year

❏ **IMPORT CAR PRICES** (*includes bulk rate shipping/handling*) ....$ **15.00**
CANADA $18.75/FOREIGN COUNTRIES $27.00 (*includes air mail shipping/handling*)
3 issues per year

❏ **NEW VEHICLE PRICES** (*includes bulk rate shipping/handling*) ....$ **55.00**
CANADA $68.75/FOREIGN COUNTRIES $99.00 (*includes air mail shipping/handling*)
- includes the complete automotive market of new vehicles - 11books:

- • 3 NEW CAR PRICES (Domestic)
- • 3 IMPORT CAR PRICES
- • 3 VAN, PICKUP, SPORT UTILITY
- • 2 ECONOMY CAR BUYING GUIDE

❏ **NEW & USED CAR PRICES** (*includes bulk rate shipping/handling*) ....$ **59.75**
CANADA $74.75/FOREIGN COUNTRIES $107.75 (*includes air mail shipping/handling*)
12 books:

- • 6 USED CAR PRICES
- • 3 NEW CAR PRICES (Domestic)
- • 3 IMPORT CAR PRICES

❏ **PREMIUM SUBSCRIPTION** (*includes bulk rate shipping/handling*) ....$ **84.75**
CANADA $106.00/FOREIGN COUNTRIES $152.75 (*includes air mail shipping/handling*)
- includes all of the above - 17 books:

- • 6 USED CAR PRICES
- • 3 NEW CAR PRICES (Domestic)
- • 3 IMPORT CAR PRICES
- • 3 VAN, PICKUP, SPORT UTILITY
- • 2 ECONOMY CAR BUYING GUIDE

Name _____

Address _____ Phone _____

City, State, Zip _____

PAYMENT: ❏ MASTERCARD   ❏ VISA   ❏ CHECK or MONEY ORDER —AMOUNT $_____
Make check or money order payable to: **Edmund Publications Corporation,**
P. O. Box 338, Shrub Oak, NY 10588   *Rates subject to change without notice.*

Credit Card # _____ Exp. Date: _____

Cardholder Name: _____ Signature: _____

N2703

SCHEDULED RELEASE DATES FOR 1993/94*

VOL. 27/28		RELEASE DATE	COVER DATE
U2706	USED CAR PRICES	NOV 93	JAN 94
I2703	IMPORT CAR PRICES	DEC 93	APR 94
U2801	USED CAR PRICES	JAN 94	MAR 94
N2801	NEW CAR PRICES [Domestic]	FEB 94	JUN 94
S2801	VAN, PICKUP, SPORT UTILITY BUYER'S GUIDE	FEB 94	JUN 94
I2801	IMPORT CAR PRICES	MAR 94	JUL 94
E2801	ECONOMY CAR BUYER'S GUIDE	FEB 94	JUN 94
U2802	USED CAR PRICES	MAR 94	MAY 94
N2802	NEW CAR PRICES [Domestic]	MAY 94	NOV 94
S2802	VAN, PICKUP, SPORT UTILITY BUYER'S GUIDE	MAY 94	NOV 94
U2803	USED CAR PRICES	MAY 94	JUL 94
I2802	IMPORT CAR PRICES	JUN 94	DEC 94
E2802	ECONOMY CAR BUYER'S GUIDE	JUN 94	OCT 94
U2804	USED CAR PRICES	JUL 94	SEP 94
U2805	USED CAR PRICES	SEP 94	NOV 94
N2803	NEW CAR PRICES [Domestic]	NOV 94	FEB 95
S2803	VAN, PICKUP, SPORT UTILITY BUYER'S GUIDE	NOV 94	FEB 95

*Subject to Change